To:- Uncle Richard.
With all our love.
Sonia, Colin
Debbie & Philip.

18. IV. 1974.

Parish Church, Bury, Lancashire

As it appeared before rebuilding.

HISTORY

OF THE

BOROUGH OF BURY

AND

NEIGHBOURHOOD,

IN THE

COUNTY OF LANCASTER.

BY

B. T. BARTON,

REPORTER.

"Nothing extenuate, nor set down aught in malice."—*Shakespere.*

First Printed by
NORTH OF ENGLAND CO-OPERATIVE
PRINTING SOCIETY
Balloon-Street, Manchester

Republished 1973 by
E. J. MORTEN (Publishers) E. & L. ASS.
10 Warburton Street, Didsbury
Manchester, England

ISBN 0 901598 74 7

Printed in Great Britain by
The Scolar Press Limited, Menston, Yorkshire

TO

THE RIGHT HON. THE EARL OF DERBY,

LORD

OF THE

MANOR OF BURY,

THIS WORK

IS,

BY KIND PERMISSION,

RESPECTFULLY DEDICATED BY

THE AUTHOR.

PREFACE.

In these days of progress—progress in commerce and manufactures, as well as in science, art, literature, and indeed all those virtues, attributes, and excellencies which tend to the development of civilisation and the expelling of superstitious, foolish, and antiquated notions—it is pleasing and by no means uninteresting to recal, as it were, the "memories of the past," and to compare the "light of other days" with the light of the days in which we live.

In reviewing the history of any town, especially any of our manufacturing towns, a reflective mind is almost instinctively led to a comparison of what are often called "the good old days" with those of modern times. And this reflection of the past, and comparison with the present, cannot but be fraught with many a valuable lesson to the studiously inclined, and have a tendency to befit him more for the age in which he lives, to expand his ideas, and perhaps to look more hopefully into posterity. I quite agree with Stukeley, who, years ago, said, "'Tis the knowledge of antiquity that can give us a maturity in judgment, either in persons or things." The reader of history is led to reflect upon the lives of great men who have left behind them

Footprints on the sands of time;

Men who by their genius, their assiduity, and diligence in the task they undertook to perform, have left behind them a name which will ever be remembered in the annals of history, and, still more, have added to the wealth and greatness of the country which gave them birth. While many of our manufacturing towns which have risen to the positions they now occupy by the practical use of many valuable mechanical inventions and improvements, swarm with statues of naval and military heroes, we look in vain for monuments in honour of Watt, of George Stephenson, of Arkwright, of Crompton, and a host of others. England owes all her present greatness to her men of thought—it is her boast, and poets have in many ways apostrophised the fact.

In the perusal of this work the reader will find reference to the lives of a few men who either first saw the light of day in this district, or who, by their long residence in the locality and the imprints of the greatness which they left behind them, have made it impossible for any writer, desirous of doing justice to the history of this neighbourhood, to pass by their career unnoticed. The writer of the history of any town has a great many difficulties to contend with ; his task necessitates a diligent research into public and, perhaps, private documents ; and in order to accomplish his object he has to depend to a great extent upon the liberality of those who are possessed of any facts, written or unwritten, bearing upon the subject. It is therefore with pleasure that I have to acknowledge my thanks to many kind friends who have facilitated my investigations, and otherwise aided me in the practical execution of the work. Without the least inviduous distinction, I especially beg to acknowledge my obligations to Jesse Leach, Esq., of Heywood; the Rev. B. Withers, Mr. George Booth, and Mr. Saul, of Prestwich. I am also indebted to Mr. John Heap (proprietor of the *Bury Times* newspaper), who recently published in his journal a series of chapters upon the early history of Bury, from which I have made a few extracts.

It only now remains for me to thank those gentlemen who have already given in their names as subscribers, and to express a hope that the work will be found by them and others as useful and interesting as they had expected.

B. T. BARTON.

January, 1874.

CONTENTS.

CHAPTER I.

PAGE.

Early History of the Town—Bury Castle—The Flemings and the Trade of the Town, &c.—The Magistracy—Peel Monument—Printing—The Old Political Parties in Bury—Bury Bellmen—The Roman Road—The Savings Bank—Physic and Law—Union Square—The Distress in Russia in 1812— The Sports of the Early Inhabitants—Bury Lane—The Wreck of the "Rothsay Castle"—The Public Charities—Victories of the Army and Navy, and Rejoicings in Bury—An Over-anxious Butcher—A Husband's Legacy and a Wife's Opinion—The Public Amusements and "Assemblies"— Fall of Moss-lane Theatre—Simnel Sunday—Bury Armoury and Drill Hall   1

CHAPTER II.

Bury and Bolton Canal: the Upsetting of a Packet-boat—The "Old Hare and Hounds"—The name "Jane" and "Spinning Jennies"—Pedestrianism— The Second Theatre at Bury and Mr. Stanton—The Rev. John Wesley's Visit to Bury—"Jenny Roth'ell" and "Ivin Tree" Cottage—"Th' Paddle Wo'," or Paddle Wall—Bury and the Parliamentary Troops in 1648— Appearance of the Town in its Early Days—Mr. Frank Nuttall and Miss Yates—"Yorkshire Johnny"—Bury Bridge and the Ship Inn—The Wylde—Football Matches—"The Ginnel" and the "Crooked Billet"— The Dungeon—Drs. Bevin, Platt, Cunliffe, and Parks—The Pillory and the Old Cross—The Old Court House—Butcher-lane—The Old Boar's Head Inn—The Old Grey Mare Inn—Otter Hunting—Bury and Her Patriots 29

CHAPTER III.

The Discovery of Roman Relics at Walmersley—The Old Bury Constables—Ox Roasting at Bury Old Cross—The Yates and Peel Family—The Black Bull Inn, Blackburn—One Hundred and Three Years Ago—The Mistress of the Black Bull Inn—Dress of the Period—Mrs. Yates, the Maternal Great-grandmother of the late Sir Robert Peel—The Young Traveller's Visit to Darwen—Brinscall, Anglezark, Horwich, &c.—Cockey Moor—Pedlers and Pack Horses—Brooksmouth—The Hope and Anchor—The Claytons of Bamber Bridge—Home Weaving—Mr. Peel's Survey of the Site of his Future Printworks—Old Mill—The Miller's House—Doctor's-lane and Mansion—The "Ground"—Mr. William Yates—First Workshops—Fires— The Partnership—The Bleachworks—A Thief with Horns and Tail—Price of Calico—Apprentice Children 46

CHAPTER IV.

PAGE.

Conduct and Character of Mr. Peel—Beggars—Early Patterns and Prints—Pencillers—Female Designers—Pinners—Engraving—" Long Jack o' Booth's "—Mr. Yates—An Ounce of Tobacco—Sir Robert's Infancy—Mrs. Peel—Confidence between Parents and Children—Boyish Sports and Recreations—Handsome Present to the Government—The Exportation of Machinery, &c.—The Bury Loyal Association of Volunteers—Presentation of Colours to the Volunteers—Speeches of Lady Clerke and Lieutenant-Colonel Peel—Volunteer Field Days—Names from the old " Roll Call "—An Old Volunteer Song 63

CHAPTER V.

Captain Starkie's Troop—Mr. Yates and Horse Racing—The Profits on Bury Ground—Mr. Peel's Baronetcy and Mr. Halliwell—Mr. Edmund Yates's Marriage : his Illness : Death of Mrs. Cunliffe—Mr. William Yates and His Family—Irwell House and " The Tenters "—Messrs. Hardman, Norris, and Hamer—The Extension of the Firm—The Genealogy of the Peel Family—Burrs Mill : An Old Wages or Mill Book—Benevolence of Sir Robert Peel and the Firm—Sir Robert Peel and the Representation of Tamworth — Handsome Contribution to the Government — The Second Lady Peel—Death of Sir Robert Peel—Lady Peel and Preston Guild—" Syphax " and " Nero "—Mr. Smiles's Account of Sir Robert Peel—Testimonies as to the Character of Sir Robert Peel—William Yates Peel—Sir William Peel, K.C.B.—The Right Hon. F. Peel—A Cock Fight—Captain Yates and the Dinner Party—The Old Residence of the Wrigley Family 76

CHAPTER VI.

" Circumstances alter Cases "—Cockey Moor-lane—Witchcraft or " The Black Art "—The Plumber and Sir Robert Peel—Gas Making—Thomas Openshaw, Esq.—James Clerke, Esq., and Sir William Clerke—Hutchinson Family—Tharcake and Parkin—Mr. Ellis Cunliffe, surgeon—John Warburton, Esq. 99

CHAPTER VII.

" Cheshire Shore's Neezing Club : " its History and Doings—The Whitehead Family—The Walker Family—The Nuttall Family—John Partington—Mr. Samuel Smith—Bury Grammar School—The Coaching Days—Mr. Thomas Norris—The Athenæum—The Ragged School—The late Mr. John Hall 115

CHAPTER VIII.

The National School—The Cemetery—The Greenhalgh Family—The late Mr. Charles Openshaw—Richard and James Pilkington—The Dispensary—The Union Offices—The Shrievalty—Co-operation—The Grant Family .. 132

CHAPTER IX.

The Parish Church—Rectors of Bury from 1507—The Rector's Power to Grant Leases of Glebe Lands—St. John's Church—St. Paul's Church—St. Thomas's Church—Holy Trinity Church—St. Peter's Church—St. Mark's School 146

CHAPTER X.

PAGE.

The Chapels—Temperance Hall—The Market—The late Edmund Grundy—
John and Robert Kay—The Riot of 1826—The Parliamentary Elections
of 1832, 1835, 1837, 1847 158

CHAPTER XI.

The Parliamentary Elections of 1852, 1857, 1859, 1865, and 1868—The Census
Returns of Bury and District—Population of the Borough in 1861 and
1871—Population of the Townships in 1861 and 1871—Districts of Local
Boards—Population of Ecclesiastical Districts 179

CHAPTER XII.

Gentry of Bury and Neighbourhood in 1664—Hat Manufacture—The Monumental Tablets in the Old Parish Church—Early History of Elton—All
Saints' Church, Elton—A Prolific Family—St. Stephen's Schools, Elton—
Primitive Methodism in Elton—The Brandlesholme Bull—Ancient Disputes as to Tenants' Rights—Early History of Tottington—St. John's
Free Church, Tottington—The Wesleyans of Tottington—Early History
of Ramsbottom—The Grant Family—Chatterton Fight—Mr. Henry
Pendlebury—St. Andrew's Church, Ramsbottom—St. Andrew's Presbyterian Church, Ramsbottom—Nuttall Hall—The Grant's Arms, Ramsbottom 194

CHAPTER XIII.

Early History of Holcombe—Mr. Henry Pendlebury—Early History of Rad-
cliffe—Radcliffe Tower—Fair Helen of Radcliffe—Radcliffe "Shag"—
Rev. Samuel Compston—William Cockerill and Family—The Lancaster
Family—Radcliffe Parish Church—List of Rectors of Radcliffe since
1583—St. Thomas's Church, Radcliffe—St. John's Church, Radcliffe—
Primitive Methodist Chapel, Radcliffe—Richard Wroe, D.D.—Walmersley
and Summerseat—The late John Robinson Kay—The late Christopher
Roberts 222

CHAPTER XIV.

Early History of Prestwich—The Prestwich Poor-law Union—The Charities
of Prestwich—Prestwich Schools—The Parish Church of Prestwich—
Extracts from the Accounts of St. Mary's Church, Prestwich—The Tablets
in Prestwich Parish Church—Mrs. Julia Younge—Rectors of Prestwich—
Kirkhams—An Unwelcome Tithe—The Death of Mr. Huskisson—Handsome Presents—Rhodes—Great Heaton—Little Heaton—Prestwich Parish
in 1778—Whitefield and Stand, Unsworth—The Dragon of Unsworth 247

CHAPTER XV.

Early History of Heywood—Peter Heywood and the Gunpowder Plot—
Heywood Hall—The Progress of Manufactories in Heap—Railway and
Canal Traffic—The Mechanics' Institution—The Places of Worship in
Heywood—The Heywood Magistracy—The Rise and Progress of Congre-
gationalism in Heywood—Early History of Bamford—Peacock Hall—Bury
Improvement Commissioners since 1846............................. 274

CHAPTER XVI.

Chronological History of Bury and Neighbourhood—The House of Stanley.... 296

BURY.

◆

CHAPTER I.

Early History of the Town—Bury Castle—The Flemings and the Trade of the Town, &c.—The Magistracy—Peel Monument—Printing—The Old Political Parties in Bury—Bury Bellmen—The Roman Road—The Savings Bank— Physic and Law—Union Square—The Distress in Russia in 1812—The Sports of the Early Inhabitants—Bury Lane—The Wreck of the "Rothsay Castle"— The Public Charities—Victories of the Army and Navy, and Rejoicings in Bury—An Over-anxious Butcher—A Husband's Legacy and a Wife's Opinion— The Public Amusements and "Assemblies"—Fall of Moss-lane Theatre— Simnel Sunday—Bury Armoury and Drill Hall.

BURY is a parish, parliamentary borough, and market town. It is a polling place for the county, and is in the Bolton division of the hundred of Salford, in the archdeaconry and deanery of Manchester. The town stands on the left bank of the river Irwell, about two miles from the confluence of the Roch. The word Bury is Saxon, signifying either a castle or market town, and it is supposed to be the more applicable to Bury at a very early period. Formerly the town was governed by twenty-seven commissioners, nine of whom were elected annually, in the month of June, by the ratepayers, under an act of Parliament granted on the 27th July, 1846. This act was extended on the 25th July, 1872, and the public business of the town is now conducted by thirty commissioners, ten of whom are returned in June of each year. Previous to 1846 the town may be said to be almost wholly without local government, except a little which it derived from the court-leet of the lord of the manor, the Earl of Derby. Three constables were chosen annually at the court-leet, under whose authority a deputy-constable was the head of the police. Six commissioners are returned for each of the five wards into which the town is divided, the names of the wards being Church, Redvale, East, Moorside, and Elton. The town is distant 198 miles N.N.W. of London, 6 miles E.N.E. of Bolton, 35 E.N.E. of Liverpool, 7¾ from Manchester, and 15 from Wigan. The parish comprises the townships of Bury, Elton, Heap, Ainsworth, Ashworth, Birtle-cum-Bamford, Hopwood, Pilkington, Pilsworth, Radcliffe, Tottington-lower-End, and Walmersley-cum-Shuttleworth.   By the census returns of 1871, the township of Bury is stated to contain 41,517 inhabitants ; in 1861 the population was 30,399 ; and in 1851, 30,852 inhabitants.   In 1793 the town contained only 2,090 inhabitants.

Woollen manufacture is carried on in Bury to a considerable extent, and there are also extensive cotton mills, iron and brass foundries, paper mills, and bleach works.   At an early date Bury was one of the fees belonging to the Royal manor of Tottington, which was held by the Lacies, who enjoyed this possession soon after the Conquest, along with the lordship of Blackburnshire.

EARLY HISTORY.

According to the *Testa de Nevill*, in the reign of Henry III., Adam de Bury held a knight's fee in Bury of the fee of the Earl of Lincoln, who held it of the King's tenant-in-chief, Earl Ferrers, and Bury at the time was part of the Countess of Lincoln's dowry.   Adam de Montebegon, mesne lord of Tottington under the Lacies, and lord of Hornby, gave four bovates of land in Tottington to Edward de Buri, as the marriage portion of his daughter Aliz or Alicia, and William de Penieston then held that land with Cecilia, the daughter of Alicia.   In enumerating the fees of Roger de Montebegon, who died in the 9th John (1207-8), it is said that Adam de Buri holds one knight's fee by ancient tenure.   This was one of the eight fees which Roger held within the same jurisdiction. Robert Gredle, Baron of Manchester, gave to another of his family, Robert de Buri the elder, fourteen bovates of land of his demesne of Mamecestre, to be held by the service of half a knight, and his heirs held that land.   But the Bury family were not the sole proprietors at this period, for Henry de Emeleden was also found to hold two fees in Tottington and in Bury of ancient tenure.   In 35 Henry III. (1251), Edmund de Lacy obtained a charter for free warren in his manor of Tottington, and also in other manors ; and in 22 Edward I. (1294), Henry de Lacy had a similar grant.

On the death of Henry de Lacy, the manor of Bury passed to Thomas, Earl of Lancaster, in right of his wife Alicia, the heiress of the Earl of Lincoln.   At what period it passed from the local family is not clearly ascertained ; but after the death of Thomas, Earl of Lancaster, and on the erection of the duchy of Lancaster in 1351, Roger Pilkington is enumerated among the duchy tenants, as holding one knight's fee in Bury, which Adam de Bury formerly held of the Honor of Lancaster.

In an inquisition post mortem, taken 36 Edward III. (1362), Bure, in Salfordshire, is found along with Totinton among the vast possessions of Henry, the first Duke of Lancaster. The Bury family do not seem to have entirely ceased their connection with the parish for many reigns afterwards, for by an inquisition post mortem in the Duchy Records (1539), Ralph Bury was found possessed of lands in Bury, Myddleton, and Totyngton; and in the Harleian MSS. is preserved a monumental inscription on Thomas, son of John Bury, of Bury Hall, Co. Lanc., and Eliz. his wife, daughter of Thomas Stafford, of Bradfield, in Berks, Esq., dated 1613. The last mention in the Duchy Records of this family is Richard Bury, a proprietor of land in Middleton in 1621. In 1351, Roger de Pilkington held one knight's fee in Bury, formerly held by Sir Adam de Bury, and which appears to have passed in marriage from the Burys to the Pilkingtons. In the reign of Edward IV. a licence was granted by that monarch to Sir Thomas Pilkington, a devoted adherent to the House of York, to kernel and embattle his manor-house at Stand in Pilkington; and this continued the family residence till on the attainder of Sir Thomas Pilkington in 1 Henry VII. (1485), the manor of Bury and the other estates of the Pilkington family being forfeited, were granted by the crown, under the great seal, to Thomas, first Earl of Derby; and in 13 Henry VII. (1521), this manor is found among the possessions of the Stanleys, Earls of Derby, in which family it still remains. In the same reign, Leland thus speaks of this place:—" Byri on Irwell, 4. or V. miles from Manchestre, but a poore market. There is a Ruine of a Castel by the paroch Chirch yn the Towne. It longgid with the Towne sumtime to the Pilkentons, now to the Erles of Darby. Pilkenton had a place hard by Pilkenton parke, 3 mile from Manchestre." Camden, in the reign of Elizabeth, describes it as a market-town not less considerable than Rochdale; but Blome, who wrote in the time of Charles II., says, "Bury is a market-town, of no great account, on the Thursdays."

As before stated, the Earl of Derby is Lord of the Manor of Bury, and owner of nearly all the land in the borough, with the exception of the glebe and a little freehold land held by different owners. The court-leet and view of frank-pledge for the manor of Bury, with the court baron of the Earl of Derby, is held at Easter and Michaelmas in each year.

The town is lighted by gas supplied from the public gasworks, which were purchased from a private company in the year 1857, for the sum of £52,249. Since that time they have been considerably extended, at a large outlay.

The Acts of 1846 and 1872 grants power to the commissioners to levy a general rate and a sewer rate, the amount of both being limited, unless with the consent of the parishioners. The usual practice is to levy two ninepenny general rates in the year, and two sixpenny rates, or, in all, two shillings and sixpence yearly. The commissioners have also since 1864 been constituted into a Burial Board for the district, and have power to levy burial rates. Under the Public Works Loan Act the commissioners have borrowed altogether—For paving purposes, £23,000; for sewering, £10,000 ; and for the purposes of the Burial Board, £15,000.

In 1818 the old church wall was pulled down to widen the street, and on that occasion human skulls and bones were tossed up and down the street like bowls and jacks upon a bowling green. Recently the wall fronting Fleet-street has been still further set back, greatly to the improvement of that thoroughfare.

BURY CASTLE.

Bury was not the site of a Roman station, as is supposed by many persons, but that of a Saxon ; and upon the banks of the old course of the Irwell, in Castlecroft, formerly stood one of the ancient baronial castles of Lancashire. Nothing now remains visible of the ancient structure, but remains of the foundations have been dug up, and coins have been found on the site from the mints of the Edwards, Henry VIII., Elizabeth, and the Stuarts. During the erection of some of the houses in Clerke-street, which were formed out of what was called the Church Field, five cannon balls were dug out of the ground at a depth of nearly two yards. Three of these balls seemed to be about ten-pounders, and the others about half that weight. The most important discovery near this place was made on the 25th August, 1865, by a number of workmen employed by the Improvement Commissioners. They were engaged in making a sewer, and in the course of their labours they came upon the foundation wall of the ancient Castle of Bury, the sewer crossing the west wall at what appeared to have been the keep. As might be expected, the discovery created considerable interest, and the commissioners were induced to extend their excavations in a line with the wall southward. The main foundation-wall was scarcely two feet thick, and was buttressed every few feet. The masons' marks, chiefly an X, were found upon some of the stones. The outer foundation-walls, if entire, represent a quadrangle of about 110 by 113 feet. The inner walls were very strong, being more than six feet in thickness ; in form a parallelogram, measuring externally about 82 by

76 feet, and internally 69 by 63 feet. From the appearance of the ruins they appeared to have been a sort of peel or keep, with a space of about 20 feet between its outer face and the inside of the outer boundary wall.

It is not improbable that this Castle of Bury once formed an outlying fortress, garrisoned by troops from the greater body of Roman soldiers permanently occupying Manchester ; or, earlier still, a place of defence and outlook occupied by other invaders to whom this part of the realm had been subjected. Its position would imply this. The road between Bury and Manchester, at that time, from the nature of the ground, the most accessible route by which these marauders could reach their settlements, would be anciently, as in similar places, merely a rude track, winding, devious, uncertain ; sometimes ascending, to avoid the lower marshy land, permeated by springs; and often taking a circuitous course merely because the peculiarities of the surface, in the entire absence of artificial formation, rendered it more generally safe or accessible. Or, instead of being a station for armed men, the Tower or Castle of Bury, with its wide-reaching prospect over the valley and towards the beautiful hills beyond, may have been the chosen peaceful home of some official dignitary of rank and wealth, placed in Britain by duties pertaining to the army of imperial Rome, and here spending the time in pleasant ease and leisure.

THE FLEMINGS AND THE TRADE OF THE TOWN, ETC.

There can be but little doubt that a number of the emigrant Flemings established themselves in the parish of Bury in the reign of Edward the Third, and that they fabricated their webs from the fleeces grown in the Forest of Tottington. The first distinct notice that we have, however, of the manufactures of Bury is in the reign of Henry the Eighth, when Leland says, "Yerne sumtime made abowte Buri, a market towne on Irwel." An aulneger was appointed at Bury by Act of Parliament in the reign of Queen Elizabeth, to stamp woollen cloth, for the purpose of preventing it from being unduly stretched on the tenters. The advantages which Bury possesses as a manufacturing station have, doubtless, tended greatly to obtain for it that success which it has for so long enjoyed. Although the Roch and the Irwell are not navigable in the district, these streams are made use of in many ways, and add much to the beauty of the district, as they pursue their winding courses through the country. The abundant supply of coal in the neighbourhood is a great local advantage, particularly to manufacturers, many of whom can have their supplies carted directly from the pits, thus saving a considerable item every year in the shape of railway transit, as compared with many other manufacturing towns. The town is not situated upon a main line of railway, but the facilities offered by the East Lancashire and Lancashire and Yorkshire Railway Companies, both of which have stations in the centre of the town, are such that the main lines can be reached in a very short time. The direct communication with Manchester on the one hand, and the thriving and populous towns of East Lancashire on the other, is an important feature in a commercial sense, and has doubtless tended considerably to place Bury in the enviable position it now occupies among the other manufacturing towns in the county. The manufacturing and commercial prosperity of the town has also been influenced by the canal which connects Bury with Bolton and Manchester.

THE MAGISTRACY.

The petty sessional division comprises the townships of Bury, Elton, Ainsworth, Ashworth, Birtle-cum-Bamford, Walmersley-cum-Shuttleworth, Tottington-Lower-End, Tottington-Higher-End, Radcliffe, Pilkington, Pilsworth, and Hopwood. The sessions are held in the Court House, in the Town Hall, every Monday and Thursday, before one or more of the following magistrates :—

	Appointed.
John Grundy, Esq.	Jan. 11, 1841
H. Hardman, Esq.	Feb. 28, 1842
R. N. Philips, Esq., M.P., The Park	Jan. 11, 1847
Wm. Fenton, Esq., Meadowcroft	Feb. 28, 1848
Joseph Fenton, Esq., Bamford Hall	Jan. 3, 1853
Thomas Wrigley, Esq., Timberhurst	Jan. 9, 1854
Richard Bealey, Esq., Radcliffe	Feb. 25, 1856
John Hutchinson, Esq., Bury	Aug. 25, 1858
Jonathan Mellor, Esq.	July 4, 1859
O. O. Walker, Esq., Chesham	April 8, 1863
Joseph Fenton, jun., Esq.	Aug. 3, 1863
Charles Cheetham, Esq.	May 23, 1864
John Fenton, Esq., Plumpton Hall	Feb. 27, 1865
Richard Kay, Esq., Heywood	Feb. 27, 1865
T. L. Openshaw, Esq., Heaton Grove	April 18, 1866
J. S. Walker, Esq., Limefield	May 28, 1866
J. J. Mellor, Esq., The Ferns	April 10, 1867
James Fenton, Esq.	April 15, 1867
Jesse Leach, Esq., Heywood	Jan. 6, 1869
Edward Mucklow, Esq., Woodhill	Oct. 18, 1869
James Wrigley, Esq., Ash Meadow	Oct. 18, 1869
J. P. Ede, Esq.	Oct. 25, 1869
E. G. Wrigley, Esq., Broadoaks	Oct. 22, 1871
T. B. Willans, Esq., Harefield Hall	Aug. 19, 1871

The clerks to the magistrates are Mr. William Harper, Messrs. T., A., and J. Grundy and Co.; Mr. W. P. Woodcock, and Messrs. George Whitehead, Son, and Dodds.

PEEL MONUMENT.

A statue monument of the late Sir Robert Peel was erected by public subscription in 1852. The subscription amounted to about £3,000. The design selected from the models of the various sculptors who competed, and which were exhibited in the Bury Athenæum, was one prepared by Mr. E. H. Bailey, R.A. It consists of a bronze statue of the statesman, standing in a commanding position upon a pedestal of Scotch granite 112 feet 6 inches in height, and enclosed within a strong iron palisading. It stands on the Wylde, near to the entrance to the Parish Church, and not being blocked up by any buildings, is a very conspicuous object. The pecuniary liabilities and other obligations of the Monument Committee were transferred to the Bury Improvement Commissioners, who received the monument in charge and trust for the people of Bury, in whose keeping it still remains.

PRINTING.

In the year 1789, the first printing press was made by Mr. Robert Collinge, of Bury, for Mr. Robert Howorth, of Union-square, who kept a circulating library, and afterwards became the overseer of Bury. After the lapse of many years the press was bought by Mr. Benjamin Crompton, and worked by men who understood the business. As the population and machinery increased in Bury, printing presses and the demand for printing increased in like manner, and now there are several printing establishments in the town, the oldest firm being that of Mr. Crompton, in Fleet-street.

THE OLD POLITICAL PARTIES IN BURY.

In these days there are only two political parties in the town, the Liberals and the Conservatives, or, as they are commonly called, the Reds and the Blues. Formerly there were in Bury a variety of political names, such as Painites, Jacobins, Rumpers, Republicans, Carlislites, and Chartists. The Painites were the followers of Mr. Paine, and were very numerous in Bury about eighty years ago. Paine's "Age of Reason," and his "Rights of Man," were eagerly bought and read in this town, and the disputes ran so high among the people that one party burned Paine in effigy in the Market-place. The legislature at last passed an Act to the effect that if any of Paine's writings were found in the homes of the people they were punishable by law, and if this was put in force in its rigour it would be transportation. Paine's writings were, however, secretly circulated among the people, although the authorities of the town and others exercised considerable diligence in

suppressing them.   After the Painites had been discomfited in this town
and county, the name of Jacobin arose.   The name was first given to a
party in France, who were most zealous in giving the revolution a turn
towards Republicanism.   The word Jacobin ran through the first
revolutionists in France, and with great rapidity it overspread England.
Many corners in Bury were filled with Jacobins, who were headed by
certain individuals.   Gradually the Jacobins and their leaders dwindled
away in Bury, and upon their ruins there arose what at that time were
called Rumpers, or the Rump Party.   These Rumpers in Bury exerted
themselves to hinder the carrying on of the French war, after they had
beheaded their King, and the most influential among them went up and
down the town getting signatures against the lives and fortunes of men
who had signed an opposite petition to restore legitimacy on the throne
of France.   For a time the Rump Party commanded with great authority,
and though they opposed everything the Church and State imposed,
their opposition proved futile, for the war against the French proceeded
rapidly, until all Europe was moved against the French people for their
cruelties with the guillotine and the beheading of their King.

BURY BELLMEN.

So far as can be·ascertained, the first bellman in Bury was Mr.
William Crompton.   He officiated as bellman, parish clerk, and sexton
in the town in the year 1744.   He was succeeded by his cousin, Mr.
Richard Walker, and his son Ralph assisted him as sexton for the church
and bellman for the parish of Bury.   Mr. Walker at that time kept the
post-office, in an old house next to the Rectory gates.   As he accidently
broke his leg, and was unable to perform the duties of his office, he sent
for Mr. Samuel Buckley, father to Mr. James Buckley, hat manufacturer,
and requested him to take the bell.   To secure the bell in the Buckley
family, he took a journey to the Earl of Derby, at Knowsley Hall, where
the noble earl made him a present of the bell, and for some time afterwards he was the town's crier.   At that time there was one sedan chair
in Bury, in which Miss Judith Holker was carried by Mr. Samuel
Buckley, bellman, and Mr. Benjamin Taylor, on visits to ladies of Bury.
It may not, perhaps, be out of place to state here that the Buckley
family have been of some note in Bury.   They formerly had land that
lay contiguous to the town, and this land was remarkable for the wells
of pure water that were upon it.   These wells took their name from the
Buckley family, and that portion of Bury is now known by the name of
Buckley Wells.   Mr. Samuel Buckley officiated as bellman of Bury until
he enlisted in what at that time was called Lord Grey's regiment, in

which he died. His brother James succeeded him as town's crier and bailiff of the manor until his death. James's son Samuel then became bellman and bailiff. Samuel for some time kept the Commercial Inn and Commercial Buildings. The top storey of the buildings was used by the Court of Requests and Petty Sessions, and the bottom room was fitted up as a concert room. When Mr. Samuel Buckley ceased to officiate as bellman, he employed a man named Chadwick as his deputy. Like other men in business he was not allowed to enjoy the emoluments of town crier without competition, for a man named Edmund Riley purchased a speaking trumpet, through which he cried, "Oh, yes! Oh, yes! Oh, yes!" at the corner of every street prior to entering upon the subject of his announcement. James Parr, of Barlow-street, is now the bellman.

THE ROMAN ROAD.

Mr. J. Just, in giving an account of the track of the Roman road from Stretford to Newton-in-Bowland and Hornby, in a volume of the Proceedings of the Lancashire and Cheshire Historic Society, says:— "The public road through Stretford lies on the site of the old Roman road, so far as that continues straight, and runs hence to Manchester. Owing to the immense size of Manchester, and the thick population of its suburbs and vicinity, it is impossible to tell the direction of the line to, or near, the stations of Mancunium. It leaves Manchester sometimes upon, and if not, parallel with Strangeways, on the new line of road thence to Bury. Near Prestwich the lines of road again correspond. Thence, with evident remains at intervals, it continues its straight course till it falls in again with the modern road, passes the Dales, and then crosses the river Irwell. Throughout the parish of Radcliffe its remains are frequently evident, and occasionally very conspicuous. For some length it forms the boundary between the parishes of Radcliffe and Bury. Then it ascends the high grounds at Affetside, and falls in with Watling-street there. Here its course is evident through Edgworth, to the heights of Blacksnape, by falling in with the public road between Bury and Blackburn."

THE SAVINGS BANK.

A Savings Bank was established in the town on the 1st of April, 1822. At present the Savings Bank is in Silver-street, and is open at certain hours on Mondays, Wednesdays, and Saturdays.

PHYSIC AND LAW.

At one time all the physic in the town might have been put into a gallipot. There was but one attorney, and it is reported that he was starved to death. His office was in a room at the back of the Old Boar's Head, opposite to the church.

UNION SQUARE.

The first cellar sunk and the first stone laid in Union-square, was in 1784. There was one Lodge of Freemasons then in the town, and the ceremony of laying the first stone was performed with masonic honours by Mr. Robert Haworth, overseer of Bury. The mallet used on this occasion bears the inscription :—"First stone of Union-square, Bury, laid by Mr. Haworth, on Monday, July 4, 1784."

THE DISTRESS IN RUSSIA IN 1812.

On the 28th December, 1812, a meeting of the inhabitants of Bury and neighbourhood was held at the Red Lion Inn, for the purpose of raising pecuniary aid for the distressed in Russia. The chair was occupied by Edmund Yates, Esq. In opening the meeting, he said he was confident all who were present owing to the unexampled, patriotic, and successful struggle which the Russian nation had made, not only for their own liberty, but for the liberty of all Europe ; the privations and sufferings which they had endured in effecting this would, he was sure, excite in every British bosom the best feelings and the greatest desire to contribute to the alleviation of their miseries, which had exceeded anything that had ever been heard of before. After the necessary resolutions had been passed, and the thanks of the meeting unanimously voted to the chairman, the following sums were subscribed:

William Yates, Esq.	£500
Edmund Yates, Esq.	200
Lieut.-Colonel Yates	50
Thomas Hutchinson, Esq.	50
William Hutchinson, Esq.	15
Rev. James Hutchinson	10
William Walker, Esq., and Son	5
Mrs. Nuttall	1
Mrs. Andrews	1

Above one hundred ladies and gentlemen in Bury and its vicinity subscribed to this charity.

THE SPORTS OF THE EARLY INHABITANTS.

In 1775 the popular sports and merry-makings of the people had not fallen into such almost entire disuse as they have at present, and were generally of an innocent nature, with the exception of bull-baiting, which was much practised in the villages of Lancashire; and bear-baiting also, if a wandering bear-ward happened to bring his poor animal within ken. At Bury, for many years, the self-constituted master of the revels was Mr. Greenhough, a schoolmaster, keeping school down a narrow passage in the Wylde. On the 29th of May, two entire oak trees, of as large a size as could be obtained, were placed one on each side of the Wylde. The boughs above were entwined together, and a figure, dressed to represent King Charles the Second, was placed, with much rejoicing, amongst the branches, the school-master's brother always upon this occasion singing, with a very excellent voice, under the umbrageous arch formed by the united trees, in the open air, for the assembled company, the old song of the "Twenty-ninth of May," of which the burden is :—

> The bells shall in th' steeple ring,
> And music sweetly play;
> And loyal Churchmen ne'er forget
> The Twenty-ninth of May.

Another exhibition of "loyalty" was the bonfire on the 5th of November, also on the Wylde—perhaps as being more immediately within the schoolmaster's domain—to which a public donation of one load of coals was given, augmented by such others as people chose to give. The fire was lighted early in the day, and continued burning till the night was pretty well advanced, its light spreading far abroad above the thatch of the little low-roofed houses in the vicinity.

The crowning sport of the year was, however, that held in commemoration of Robin Hood; though after 1776 this festival declined from the importance it had heretofore held. It was not, as such exhibitions are at present, in connection with a society or order, but solely for the free pleasure of the people, and apparently one of the last, except the rush-bearings, of those out-of-door pageants, formerly so much delighted in by the people of England. Twenty, thirty, and sometimes more, if they could obtain accoutrements, of the handsomest and comeliest young men of Bury would be "disguised," as it was always termed, as foresters, woodmen, &c.. and a smaller number as sylvans, or other wild-looking objects. They were disguised, and some of them were most effectually so, by the strange, uncouth attire in which they were invested, and the frightful "vizards" worn over their faces. Robin Hood's band was made as complete as possible, and many of the actors were from year to year known and distinguished by the names of the persons they represented. Little John was invariably a personage of high importance, both from his high statue,—the most gigantic youth of the neighbour-hood being always selected—and the dignity he assumed in marshalling the forces. The habiliments of those who personated "wild men" were the most odd-looking and grotesque that could be conceived. It was not from book learning the idea of their dresses was ever suggested, but observance in such matters of the traditions regarding them, handed down from father to son from time immemorial. In one part of the "show" the young men were on horseback, and flowers and beautiful blossoming branches were carried in their hands; and the Wylde, which was, more especially, the head-quarters of the "outlaws," was made, by spoils from the woods and the gardens around, to resemble as near as possible, their greenwood home. These kind of sports faded away before the approach of trades and regular unremitting employment, for they were incompatible with it. On one of these occasions the good folks of Bury had to go without their customary supply of home-brewed ale, for, amid the frost of nine weeks' duration, nearly all the ale in the town was frozen in the barrels. With all this holiday rejoicing in the good old times excesses were committed that could not be suffered to pass unnoticed. This was more especially the case on "Mischief night," or "Maying night," the night of the last day in April, till at last it was deemed advisable to put a stop to its observance, and it is now seldom heard of. Of the notable exploits of a daring crew of "mischief makers," almost one of the last was this:—Johnny Stott, commonly called "Owd Nip-cheese," was a rather sharp-looking old man, who kept a small shop at the end of his cottage, and at the other was a weaving-shed communicating with the house. Johnny was not very popular, partly from his penurious, grasping disposition, and partly from his habit of interfering in the concerns of his neighbours, often giving advice in a very dictatorial manner, where it was neither welcome nor wanted. A party of "mischief" lads accordingly fixed upon " Owd Nip-cheese" as proper prey, and on the appointed evening as the old man was busy weaving in his shed, by the light of a candle fixed against the wall, he was suddenly startled by the report of a gun, discharged close to a small unglazed aperture, that served in the daytime for a window, and at the same moment received a smart blow upon his back from a well-directed pebble. This, coupled with an intimation he had previously received that somebody meant "to do for him," in return for his meddling propensities, made him at once conclude that he was shot; and overcome by fright, he fell down as if it were really so, uttering the exclamation, "Good Lorjus days; I'm kilt!" At the first call for assistance, a number of his persecutors rushed in ; and whilst raising the old man, and pretending to search for the wound, they managed to besmear his shirt with some blood they had brought with them in a small phial. This was displayed as confirmation strong of the injury he had received; and such was the poor man's consternation that he was for some time after-wards really ill in consequence, and Dr. Platt's bill for attendance and physic took, as he considered, so much "brass," that it was long before he could be reconciled to it.

BURY LANE.

Ninety-eight years ago, Bury-lane was a narrow thoroughfare, especially towards the top, and the old inn of the White Lion was one of the best specimens of the houses in the neighbourhood. Even then it was an old house, with thatched roof, from which the chamber windows projected, and bore the reputation of being haunted by a spirit so fond of beer, or mischief, that frequently on rising in the morning the host would find all the ale taps turned, and the contents of his casks flooding the cellar floor. At length so overbearing were the pranks of the goblin, that they could be borne with no longer, and a suitable person was found to lay the spirit. After many formalities, invocations, and charms, the spirit was driven from one scene of its playful tricks to another, and finally took refuge where it had done most damage, namely—the cellar. Here it was at length captured, its conqueror throwing a "silver cheyn" (chain) round its neck, and binding it by the most awful oaths never to disturb the peace of the house again, "so long as grass shall grow or waters run;" so when these natural phenomena cease, this imp or spigot may again re-visit the scene of his former doings !

Another boggart of the neighbourhood was the "Tuggin at th'Nook," the "Nook" being the corner of Bury-lane (now Bolton-street), turning towards the church. This innocent little sprite always first appeared in the form of a white rabbit, and, if followed, would either suddenly disappear or assume another shape, as that of a dog, &c. This appearance of a white rabbit is a general superstition, and many towns and villages formerly could speak of their good and evil spirits in the shape of a white rabbit.

THE WRECK OF THE "ROTHSAY CASTLE."

The loss of the steam-packet *Rothsay Castle*, in 1831, was an event which cast a gloom over Bury, and the details of the disaster will long be remembered. The following particulars of the event are from the Rev. Thomas Selkirk's "Record of the Loss of the *Rothsay Castle:*" "On the 17th August, 1831, the *Rothsay Castle* steam-packet, from Liverpool for Beaumaris, on an excursion of pleasure, having encountered a violent storm on her passage, struck on Dutchman Bank, at the entrance of Beaumaris Bay, about midnight, and the vessel being old, and of frail construction, became a complete wreck before ten o'clock in the morning. The horrors of the scene no pen can adequately describe; with extreme difficulty and hazard, about twenty passengers made their escape on fragments of the vessel, but, of the 150 persons on board, 128 perished, of which number no fewer than 21 of the sufferers were from the parish of Bury. Amongst the victims of this fatal night were Mr. William Tarrey, of Bury, land agent to the Earl of Derby, and his whole family, consisting of his wife, with five of their children, and a servant maid. This melancholy catastrophe was principally to be ascribed to the intoxication of the captain. The number of persons from Bury on board the vessel when she became a wreck is thus classified:—1. Mr. Wm. Tarrey ; Mrs. Tarrey, his wife; Betsey and Thomas Tarrey, his children by a former marriage; John Tarrey, his only son, by his wife who suffered with him ; Thomas and Mary Appleton, his son and daughter by a former marriage; and Rachel Howarth, their servant maid. 2. Mr. W. Walmesley and Mrs. Walmesley, of Seedfield, with their son, Henry; Miss Margaret Walmesley, of Boar Edge; Mr. James Fitton, of Seedfield, and Miss Selina Lant, of Bury. 3. *Mr. Robert Whittaker, of Bury, and James, his only child, and *Mary Whittaker, his sister, and Thomas, her son; and Mr. John Wilkinson, of Bury. 4. *Mr. John Nuttall, of Bury. 5. Mr. Thomas Charles, of Bury. 6. *Mr. John Duckworth, of Shuttleworth, and Mrs. Duckworth, his wife; *Mr. Lawrence Duckworth, of Edenfield, and Mrs. Duckworth, his wife; and Mr. Thomas Entwistle, of Edenfield.

THE PUBLIC CHARITIES.

Referring to the charities granted to the parish, Mr. Baines, in his " History of Lancashire," says :—

" The public charities in the parish of Bury are neither so numerous nor so important as in many of the other parishes of Lancashire. Amongst these parochial charities the Free School stands pre-eminent. It was established in May, 1726, when the Rev. Roger Kay, Rector of Tittleton, Co. Wilts, gave towards it 95 acres of land, with houses, and a rent-charge of £25 per annum upon the estate of Ewood Hall, in the township of Haslingden and parish of Whalley. He also left the residue of his real estate for the endowment, consisting of the freehold estate of Chadwick, or Chadwick Hall, in the parish of Rochdale. By the original statutes of the school, it is directed that the sum of £50 shall be paid annually to the head master for his services, and £20 annually to the usher ; but in consequence of the increased value of the property, the head master now receives £200 a-year, with an excellent house rent free,

---

* Those marked with an asterisk were saved; all the rest perished.

and the usher £100. It is further directed that the sum of £20 shall be paid yearly out of the rents of the school lands for two exhibitions, towards the maintenance of two scholars in either St. John's College, Cambridge, or Brazenose College, Oxford ; the scholars to be such as are born within the parish of Bury, or the founder's own relatives, born out of the parish, but educated or brought up at the school at Bury. These exhibitions are now advanced to £25 each, but they are seldom both claimed. The whole income of the foundation at the time when the Parliamentary Commissioners made their report in 1824, was £442, and the disbursements amounted to £383. A portion of the land is let on building leases. Dr. James Wood, a former exhibitioner, left by his will £500 for augmenting the exhibitions. The present annual value of the school property is £840 gross, £698 net. The objects of the trust are—For a free grammar school for the town and parish of Bury, for ever ; for providing two exhibitions of £20 per annum each, tenable for seven years, at St. John's College, Cambridge, or Brazenose College, Oxford, open to the founder's relations, and to boys living in the parish, with preference to poor boys ; for teaching ten poor girls ; and for apprenticing poor boys and girls. The subjects of instruction prescribed are Latin, Greek, and Hebrew tongues, writing and arithmetic, and all such good authors as are usually taught in schools for the better education of youth. The trustees (1867) are the Dean of Manchester, the Rectors of Bury and Prestwich, and four other clergymen and six laymen, residing within ten miles, having estates of £50 a-year, being members of the Church of England. They have to make rules from time to time, audit the accounts annually, to appoint and dismiss masters and boys, appoint examiners, and hold annual visitations. If the trustees neglect to appoint a master, then the Bishop of Manchester to appoint. The head master must be a graduate of Oxford or Cambridge, an orthodox member of the Church of England, and well skilled in the Latin, Greek, or Hebrew tongues. There are (October, 1867) 115 day scholars, chiefly under fourteen years of age, and within a radius of four miles. In the upper school the annual payment for instruction is eight guineas, in the lower school four. The present head master is the Rev. C. F. Hildyard, B.A., Oxford. In 1748, the Rev. John Stanley, Rector of this parish, and other inhabitants, founded a school here for the education of eighty boys and thirty girls, which has since been converted into a national school, and a spacious building erected by subscription, as a school-house, at a cost of £1,000, the land on which it stands being given by the Earl of Derby. This building is also used as a Church Sunday school. The other charities in this parish are, Tottington

School, built in 1715, and endowed with £12 per annum, together with the interest of £200. In 1737, James Lancashire bequeathed £50 to each of the schools of Unsworth Chapel, Heywood Chapel, and Walmersley. In 1749, James Starkey bequeathed £30 for the use of Heywood School. Edenfield School is entitled to an annual income of from £3 to £4. Baldingstone School, in Walmersley, is supported by the rent of a tenement called Bentley, augmented by the sum of £50. In 1778, Ann Bamford bequeathed £30 a-year, with certain premises, for a free school in Heywood, and also £1,000 for the use of such school, to be laid out in land ; but, dying within twelve months from the date of her will, the statute of mortmain took effect, and the bequest became void. According to a verdict returned 16th July, 1529, Ann Kay, of Bury, made a bequest to the poor of the parish, but no mention of it appears in the Commissioners' report. In 1666, Robert Shepherd granted a rent charge of £9, subject to a deduction of £1. 10s., to poor housekeepers of the township of Bury, and towards the expense of apprenticing their children ; and in 1810, William Yates bequeathed the interest of £400 to deserving persons of the same township. The parish tablets record several other bequests of small amount."

VICTORIES OF THE ARMY AND NAVY AND REJOICINGS AT BURY.

During the many troubled times of war, ranging from 1775 to 1815, occasions of public rejoicing were made whenever news of "another victory" arrived at Bury; and the firm at the Ground were never behind in their manifestations of gladness. The wars with France, Holland, Spain, and India each received appropriate commemoration at their termination; but the triumphs of the Nile, Trafalgar, and Waterloo eclipsed in demonstrative significance all the others. On each of these occasions many pieces of cloth were printed, as scarfs, sashes, flags, and escutcheons, containing, in gorgeous if not very delicate emblazonment, the names and titles of the heroes of the several fights, thickly enclosed with emblems, and encircled with mottoes relating to liberty and patriotism. On the pieces especially printed for flags and banners the Royal Arms were conspicuously displayed in all the glory of purple, red, blue, and yellow, the artists being left pretty much to their own devices in regard to form and colouring. Each workman that wished it could receive a banner or a scarf on application, the public display of which would take place in a procession organised by the men, the point of greatest attraction being the lawn in front of Chamber Hall. On each of these occasions the windows in front of Chamber Hall were fully illuminated at night; but after Sir Robert's departure the only incident

Derby Hotel, Town Hall & Athenæum, Bury, Lancashire.

of this kind that took place was that on account of the jubilee of King George the Third, when Mr. Edmund Yates, who had not yet left Bury for Tring Park, had the whole front of the building decorated with transparent lamps in many devices; the next and only demonstration afterwards proceeding from any member of the families of Peel or Yates being on reception of news of the victory at Waterloo, and entire defeat of Napoleon, when Mr. Thomas Yates, of Irwell House, had the windows taken out, and coloured transparencies, portraits of Wellington, Blucher, the King and Queen—George and Charlotte—and others, substituted in their place. This was the first exhibition of such a nature that had ever taken place in Bury, and we may say, in passing, that there seemed amongst the people a fanaticism of joy and enthusiasm at the downfall and subsequent capture of this their most dreaded enemy and opponent.

AN OVER-ANXIOUS BUTCHER.

A good many years ago, there flourished in Bury a very handsome butcher, with a very handsome wife, both of them very stout, and well remembered in the town. This man was accustomed to pray for whatever he wanted. On one occasion the family heard his great heavy weight drop down on his knees in the room upstairs, and being only a very thin floor, they heard the nature of his petition to Heaven, which referred to the cattle market at Manchester next morning. "Oh, Lord! let there be plenty of sheep; long-backed ones; square-tailed ones; and fat." He got into bed; but presently the family heard him come thundering down on his knees again, for he had omitted the most important part of his prayer, which he had jumped out of bed to supply, "And chep, O! Lord."

A HUSBAND'S LEGACY AND A WIFE'S OPINION.

Some years since, a legal man in Bury went to receive instructions from a client, who was suffering from "*delirium tremens*," as to the disposition of his property. "Moll mun have it o'," said he, meaning his property. On the professional man offering some remonstrance, and reminding him that he had children, he was again very decided that his wife, "Moll," should have what he possessed, saying, "Moll mun have it o'; hoo's been a good woife to me." Whereupon "Moll" interfered with "Thou'rt a greight foo'; thou'rt a greight foo'; as soon as ever thou'rt sodded awst wed again."

THE PUBLIC AMUSEMENTS, OR "ASSEMBLIES."

When, on the establishment of the calico printing business, trade and manufactures began to flourish in so unprecedented a manner in Bury,

the public amusements of the town kept pace with the increasing
prosperity of the inhabitants; and in these days the foremost place
must be accorded to the Theatre, and the Bury Assemblies. The
Assemblies were held at Mr. Boothman's, Eagle and Child Inn, an inn
taking first rank in the town, although far from being so spacious as it
afterwards became when rebuilt as the residence of Mr. Edmund Yates;
returning to its original use when he left it for "The Chamber," on Sir
Robert's departure for Drayton Manor; and again resuming its ancient
cognisance, the armorial bearings of the Derby family. These meetings,
in their earliest stage, closely resembled a family reunion; all composing
them were well-known to each other, but all were not the fortunate
possessors of a well-appointed carriage and horses; and for these, at
the close of the occasion which had called them together, a servant
would be in attendance with a lantern on those nights when the moon
did not shine, and no one dreamt of danger in returning home. The
especial favourite country dance at the Bury Assemblies was "Speed
the Plough," commencing from the time the dance and music were
produced in London, in the theatrical piece of that name. The
orchestra consisted of four musicians; the instruments, a violoncello,
pipe and tabor, played by Mr. Skelton, and two violins by the talented
young brothers, Thomas and John Hutchinson. Dancing commenced
at eight o'clock, the night's amusements terminating at one a.m., except
on some special occasions, such as when "Captain John," accompanied
by some of his gay companions in uniform, was at home on a visit.
Not a musical instrument, even the most simple, nor a sheet of music,
could be bought in Bury. These, if wanted for the Assemblies, were
obtained from Mr. Sudlow, of the Hanging Ditch, Manchester, proprietor
of the only music shop at that time Manchester could boast or support.

FALL OF MOSS-LANE THEATRE.

In these later days we have become accustomed to thrilling narratives
and astounding events, and such occurrences scarce make a tithe of the
impression they formerly did; but the fall of the Bury Theatre, situated
in Moss-lane, was long spoken of and remembered as an appalling
tragedy. It was a beautiful summer evening, July fourth, 1787, that a
company of players, who had been some time in the town, had fixed
upon as the occasion for an entertainment and exhibition of more than
usual attraction and splendour. Great preparations had been made, and
an overflowing house anticipated. The theatre was a barn in the lane,
not far from the Market-place, the best available building that had
offered for the purpose, and was ornamented and decorated in the

interior, until the awkward, rough walls of the barn scarcely knew themselves in the new dress they were made to assume. A gallery was
formed across one end, but its strength as yet had not been fully tested,
for on not one night hitherto had the house been so thronged as to put
its capability to the proof; but on this occasion an early and crowded
audience was expected, and every inch of room had been made available.
The play was Shakspere's, and was announced as "A Celebrated
Historical Play, called King Henry the Fourth, or the Humours of Sir
John Falstaff; by desire of the ancient and honourable society of Free
and Accepted Masons." After the song of Four-and-twenty Fiddlers,
by Mr. Levis, was the pantomime of Lord Mayor's Day, or Harlequin's
Revels. This little Moss-lane Theatre made no pretension to grandeur,
or even the most common-place assumption of being anything beyond
the rude and rustic edifice for which its builders had designed it; but,
on an occasion still earlier, its boards had been impressed by the stately
tread of the tragedy queen, Mrs. Mattocks, of Covent Garden, the rival
and contemporary in 1776 of Mrs. Yates, of Drury Lane. John Palmer,
also, who died August 2nd, 1798, whilst impersonating the "Stranger,"
in the recently-produced play, on the stage of the Williamson-square
Theatre, in Liverpool, and was accorded a most honoured funeral by the
townspeople, had made his appearance here, along with Mr. Betterton,
the father of Julia Betterton—Mrs. Glover. Mr. Palmer's last words,
occurring in his part, and uttered, as was believed, in deep emotion,
near the end of the play, being, "and in another and a better world,"
the realisation of which, to himself, was so exceedingly near at hand.
The audience looked upon his fall, and subsequent silence, as an artifice
to enhance the theatrical effect, whilst his fellow-players, doubtful of
interference with what might be acting, did not step forward to raise
him, and all in the house were very slow to receive, at last, an intimation from the manager as to the startling reality. The curtain fell
amidst deepest commiseration for the man who had yielded up his spirit
without a reassuring word of comfort in all that crowded assembly.
The lane in which stood Bury's Thespian temple could scarcely be over
fifteen feet in width between the banks of thick and clustering hedgerows at the bottom, or between the barn and the few low, old-fashioned
cottages running down some little distance from where the road began
in Silver-street. The accommodations of the theatre were as comfortable as the limited space allowed; excellent performers belonging to a
company at that time popular in the county. Many persons of rank and
fortune attended these entertainments, given in country towns, in
buildings which the same class of persons now would be far from

entering for that purpose. In a temporary theatre, of even humbler pretensions than the one in question, a family of ladies, bearing a proud name in Lancashire, came, evening after evening, to witness, with pleased attention, the efforts of the actors, attended by footmen bearing cushions and footstools for their mistresses' accommodation, and provided with lanterns to light them safely over the small distance necessary to be traversed after the performance. The "house" was entirely filled, and the most sanguine anticipations of the manager and company realised in the number of people assembled to witness the histrionic display. The play proceeded, came to an end, and the curtain fell amidst loud applause. Its next rising, after a longer cessation than usual, was hailed with almost breathless interest, for, fronting them, now on the stage, were the fathers, brothers, husbands, sons, and lovers of those forming the audience. The scenery and stage decorations were arranged to aid in the representation of a "Grand Freemasons' Meeting," by the brethren of the Lodge in Bury, this order at that time being extremely popular, and the institution held in high esteem by the townspeople. The "brothers" were dressed in the full regalia of their several offices, and as each individual on the stage became recognised by his friends in the body of the house, cheers long and loud repeatedly shook the walls of the building. As a conclusion to this part of the evening's amusements, several toasts were given, drunk, and heartily responded to by the audience; for, amongst all present none were strangers to each other. A number of masonic songs were sung by such of the brethren as had sufficient ability and confidence to put both to the test upon so public an occasion. After a masonic epilogue, spoken by Mrs. Clarke, the descending curtain fell amidst a "blaze of triumph," and the most unbounded cheers and congratulations, and concealed the Masons and their glittering paraphernalia from the admiring eyes of friends and kinsfolk there assembled. The entertainments of the evening had been announced as for the benefit of Mr. Bonville and Mr. Levis; and, before the commencement of the pantomime, Mr. Bonville came forward to sing, with Mr. Eyeley, the beautiful duet, "As I saw fair Clora walk alone," the words of which had been written in youth by Emanuel Swedenborg, as an English and Latin exercise, and were newly set to music by George Hayden. So much had now taken place that it was long past midnight; and as the songs, toasts, and cheers could be plainly heard outside the building—each aperture being open on account of the heat— a considerable crowd had collected on each side of the barn, or theatre.

The pantomime of "Lord Mayor's Day" was next in order. The "revelry now had begun," and with the mishaps of the lover, clown, and pantaloon, the mirth and fun grew fast and furious, whilst the easily elicited applause rang out on the still night air loudly and frequently, and, perhaps, by its vibrations, and the tremulous motion communicated to the timbers of the building by the repeated and continued movement, in unison, of a large number of people, was the means of hastening the catastrophe. Outside, the deadest hours of a midsummer night were passing away; within, all was eager expectation or gratified attention. Harlequin (Mr. Bonville) was bound down on the stage with strong cords—not fictitious bonds—all too real and firmly tied. But—interrupting sympathy for the prostrate hero—what sound is it that now strikes with the terror of death to the hearts of that closely compressed multitude? Sharp cracks and dull booms, as of rending beams and rafters, that appal alike weak women and strong-limbed men. Time seems annihilated, so much is felt in an instant of space; and then the fearful ruin crashes down upon that helpless multitude, pent closely up without chance of escape, and totally unable, in their horror-stricken fright, to avail themselves, even if it were possible, of the usual mode of egress from the doomed and shattered building. It was the unusual weight of people in the temporary gallery that had wrenched it from the walls into which it was fixed, and by which it had been believed to be sufficiently supported or sustained. This, with all it contained, was hurled with crushing violence upon the solid and compact mass of humanity that filled the whole area of the theatre below, every available nook in the walls, or, perhaps, more dangerous still, a perilous abiding place on the clumsy beams overhead, on to which men and boys had climbed in their efforts to secure an uninterrupted view of the proceedings. The gallery, as it fell, drew with it inwards most of the roof above, the whole of the gable end, and great part of the side walls; the weight of its living freight rendering its fall more fatally effective. As before mentioned, Mr. Bonville, the harlequin, for whose benefit in part the entertainment had been announced, was lying bound on the stage; but under the impulse of uncontrollable fear at witnessing in so unusually helpless a condition the unlooked-for avalanche—although the orchestra and stage, and consequently the actors also, escaped the danger and destruction which overwhelmed the audience—he, by an effort of strength for which he could not afterwards account, burst asunder the bonds which invested his limbs, and sprung to a place of safety, out of the blinding, smothering, whirlwind of dirt and rubbish that swayed like a funeral pall over the suffering, writhing mass of human beings beneath.

The view upwards, where sight was possible, was frightful. Stripped and naked joists and beams hung, threatening still further destruction.

The ornaments and hangings on those parts of the side walls still standing were dragged into dirty, tattered rags, which the former gay colours made appear more hideous. The circular frames supporting candles, which had depended from the rafters and the front of the gallery, were crushed down amongst the people; and in some instances smouldering under were still burning, setting fire to the clothes of sufferers unable to escape from their proximity. Still the place was almost entirely dark; for, although three frames of lights still hung from the uninjured portion of the roof, yet from the dense cloud of dust that filled the place their flame was only just visible, whilst the footlights in front of the stage were either extinguished by loose stones and falling rubbish projected upon them, or crushed out by those who at the first impression of danger dragged themselves up to the stage as a means of escape. Shrieks that resounded into the town and far over the fields towards Parkhills and Buckley-wells, and startled with a strange dismay the quiet of that beautiful night, mingled with the rattle of falling stones and timbers; but as all fell inwards upon the pent-up multitude the noise of the fall was not so great as might have been believed. After the first feelings of consternation had passed, and comprehension returned, the men and boys who had been endeavouring to obtain some knowledge of the theatrical proceedings by listening outside, set to, with hearty goodwill and indifference to danger, to rescue the inmates from their terrible position. Lights to work by were brought from all the dwellings in the neighbourhood; the number of helpers was increased, and no able-bodied townsman slept that night, but incurred danger as great almost as that already passed, in the effort to rescue the unhappy victims of this unforeseen tragedy. As the news of the accident spread throughout Bury, drawing men and women from their beds, hundreds more were ready and anxious to lend a helping hand; and the circumstance that almost each family in the town had a relative or friend present in the theatre this night, lent additional strength to the means and efforts used to extricate them. Many were found preserved in situations where, at first sight, it had appeared hopeless that their lives could be saved; and of these a large number was rescued from death. That appalling cry of anguish and of horror, aggravated by the darkness, confusion, and tumult, had gone forth through the Market-place and contiguous thoroughfares, piercing the dull ear of midnight with unwonted fear in a town where a danger of this nature had hitherto been unknown, or had such been the case most surely would have been recorded in some fireside narrative; and the first view of the shapeless heap of ruin excited greater apprehension than was afterwards found justifiable. Crushed, bruised, bleeding, and insensible, but still living, many were drawn out from under the gallery, after all else of the superincumbent weight had been removed, owing their safety to the slanting position in which the beams had fallen, but so deeply were these imbedded in rubbish that their removal was extremely perilous to the immured victims beneath. Dr. Platt, the "old doctor" of Bury, and Dr. Cunliffe, the more recent one, had been amongst the first to appear at the scene of disaster. Of all the people in the building, numbering over three hundred, not including the professional persons, who were in the safer end of the structure, few escaped unhurt, and many were maimed and crippled for life ; but, although the amount of suffering was great, yet, contrary to all expectation, the cases of actual death were fewer than could have been thought possible. Joseph Fitton, landlord of the Old Hare and Hounds, and Richard Booth, cabinet-maker, were got out dead; Mrs. Coup, wife of Adam Coup, and Miss Bentley, of Wood-road, died soon afterwards. In the case of Joseph Fitton the sorrow was enhanced by the condition of his wife, only lately confined, and so much grief did the shock of her husband's sudden death occasion that it led to the deprivation of reason, and, unable to endure the misery, she terminated her existence by hanging herself on Sunday, the 16th of December following. Amongst the multitude that had composed the audience, broken ribs, legs, and arms, dislocated hips and shoulders, were general, and the evidences of this night's trouble might be seen in limps, and distorted limbs, down until half a century afterwards.

SIMNEL SUNDAY.

This is a festive pastime, the observance of which is almost wholly confined to Bury. The sacred character of the Sabbath but ill accords with the sort of revelry and jovial feasting which takes place in Bury on the fourth Sunday in Lent ; for the great mass of those who love the simnel feast think much of cakes and ale, and very little of the Lenten holy day. But whatever may be the character of the revels which accompany the observance of the simnel festival, it is undoubtedly a high day to many of the dwellers in Bury, and the inhabitants of a wide surrounding district. If the weather is fine the population in the town is vastly increased on the day, and locomotion along the streets is no easy matter to pedestrians. Bury has long enjoyed a special reputation for the making of simnel cakes. These cakes have an antiquity which dates back much earlier than the time of Henry VII., but the origin of the festival is lost in the obscurity of the far past. It seems probable that the origin of the Simnel Sunday was the ancient Christian custom of making Lenten offerings on that day; and while losing its original significance the name has been maintained in the custom of "going a mothering," or making presents to one's mother on Mid-Lent Sunday.

The fourth Sunday in Lent coming between Quadragesima and Easter Sunday, is called Mid-Lent or "Mothering" Sunday, from the ancient usage of visiting the mother (or cathedral) churches of the diocese to make Lenten offerings. The public processions which were made on these occasions have fallen into disuse since the middle of the thirteenth century, but in their place the custom of "going a-mothering" has grown in Lancashire and some other counties. Though this custom is not now much practised in some districts, it seems to have found a congenial home in this locality, though with modifications from its original meaning, the practise now being to make presents of simnel cakes to relatives and friends at a distance.

There are many ways of accounting for the origin of simnels, and especially of their peculiar association with Bury, but a direct and reliable origin has not been handed down to us. One story goes, that in the old days a pilgrim of the name of Simnel was passing through Bury on Mid-Lent Sunday, and animal food being of course forbidden him by the canons of Holy Church, a rich cake was made for him in recognition of his many virtues. Thenceforth it became a custom to make a feast of rich cake on that particular Sunday, and the rich sweetmeat so prepared was called Simnel cake in honour of the pilgrim. Then there is another version, which may be as fully authentic as the last. It is related that Lancashire women living in these parts were once upon a time such deplorably bad cooks, that a wise and benevolent lady of the time hit upon a plan for removing the stigma by offering a prize for the best maker of a cake. Of course, the housewives, and the young women who expected to be housewives, were put to the test to produce a good cake, and many and various were the cakes sent in for adjudication. One of the lasses was, however, an inventor in her way, for she struck out in a new line of cake making, and made her cake rich with fruits and spices. The legend does not say whether she won the prize or not. Thus it came to pass that cake making became an annual event among housewives.

Some allege that the father of Lambert Simnel, the pretender to the throne in the reign of Henry VII., was a baker and the first maker of simnels, and that his son's celebrity shed lustre upon his father's cakes. It is related that long ago there lived an honest old couple in Shropshire, boasting in the names of Simon and Nelly, but their surnames are not known. It was their custom at Easter to gather their children about them, and thus meet together once a year under the old homestead. The feasting season of Lent was just ending, but they had still left some of the unleavened dough which had been from time to time converted into bread during the forty days. Nelly was a careful woman, and it grieved her to waste anything, so she suggested that they should use the remains of the Lenten dough for the basis of a cake to regale the assembled family. Simon readily agreed to the proposal, and further reminded his partner that there was still some remains of their Christmas plum-pudding hoarded up in the cupboard, and that this might form the interior, and be an agreeable surprise to the young people when they had made their way through the less tasty crust. So far, all things went on harmoniously; but when the cake was made, a subject of violent discord arose, Sim insisting that it should be boiled, while Nell no less obstinately contended that it should be baked. The dispute ran from words to blows, for Nell, not chosing to let her province in the household be thus interfered with, jumped up and threw the stool she was sitting upon at Sim, who on his part seized a besom, and applied it with right good will to the head and shoulders of his spouse. She now seized the broom, and the battle became so warm that it might have had a very serious result had not Nell proposed, as a compromise, that the cake should be boiled first and baked afterwards. This Sim acceded to, for he had no wish for further acquaintance with the heavy end of the broom. Accordingly, the big pot was set on the fire, the stool broken up and thrown on to boil it, while the besom and broom furnished fuel for the oven. Some eggs, which had been broken in the scuffle, were used to coat the outside of the pudding when boiled, which gave it the shining gloss it possesses as a cake. This new and remarkable production in the art of confectionery became known by the name of the cake of Simon and Nelly, but soon only the first half of each name was alone preserved and joined together, and it has ever since been known as the cake of Sim-Nel, or Simnel.

It has been stated by a Lancashire antiquary that the term "simnel cake" originally meant the *very finest* bread. *Plain demain* is another term for it, on account of its having been used as *Sunday bread*. The name appears in mediæval Latin as *simanellus*, and may have been derived from the Latin *simila*—fine flour. In Wright's "Dictionarius" of John de Garlande, compiled at Paris in the 13th century, it appears thus:—"*Simeneus—placentae*—simnels." At one time these cakes were stamped with the figure of Christ, or of the Virgin.

On the occasion of the marriage of the Prince of Wales, a large specimen of a simnel, mounted on a handsome gilt tray and stand, was forwarded to Her Majesty by the inhabitants of Bury. A letter, of which the following is a copy, accompanied the cake :—

Bury, Lancashire, 6th March, 1863.

Sir,—The committee for arranging a loyal commemoration of the marriage day of His Royal Highness the Prince of Wales in this town, bowing to the strongly manifested wishes of the inhabitants, are desirous of expressing to our gracious Queen, to His Royal Highness the Prince of Wales, and to his intended Princess, their feelings of devoted loyalty and attachment. They therefore ask, through you, the gracious acceptance by Her Majesty (if she will so far condescend) of a large cake, of a kind peculiar to this town, and with reference to which there is much interesting tradition. It is called a " Simnel," and is given as a token of good-will at this season of the year. The custom is very ancient, and has been handed down from our earliest Saxon forefathers. The gift—the acceptance of which is now most respectfully craved—may seem humble, and beneath the notice of royalty ; but it is our happiness to know that all that is interesting to any of her subjects, is also acceptable to our Queen. We most respectfully ask the acceptance of our humble offering.—I have the honour to be, sir, your most obedient servant,

Col. the Hon. C. B. Phipps, K.C.B., &c., &c.   J. S. WALKER, Chairman.

Some fears were expressed as to whether the simnel would reach Her Majesty. These doubts were, however, dispelled by the receipt of the following letter :—

Windsor Castle, March 11th, 1863.

Sir,—I have the pleasure to inform you that Her Majesty has been pleased to accept the simnel cake sent by the inhabitants of Bury. The deep and loyal interest shown in all parts of the country, in the auspicious event which took place yesterday, has been most gratifying to Her Majesty, as well as to the Prince of Wales ; and the feelings which dictate this offering from the town of Bury are fully appreciated.— I have the honour to be, sir, your most obedient humble servant,

J. Scholes Walker, Esq.   C. B. PHIPPS.

Originally, or in the palmy days of the Hutchinsons as simnel makers, that is about 1780, all of Lancashire and some neighbouring counties were supplied from Bury exclusively ; not another maker was known to exist. Men came to Bury for the holiday ; and returning home twenty, thirty, or forty miles, would carry, slung over the shoulder, a safely-packed "bundle" of the much-prized Bury simnel. The sale was so extensive for that period, and so many were required, that preparations for their manufacture were necessary to be made three months in advance. At that time, and afterwards, the making and selling of simnels, the consumption of " cakes and ale," or simnel and mulled ale or wine, has been " prodigious," and profitable to the vendors.

The materials of composition of the Bury simnel should be of the best quality, and the following is the proportion of each article ; whilst it may be said that, at the date above mentioned, most of the ingredients were more than double the price they are at present :—" Five pounds of flour, 4lbs. currants, 1lb. raisins, 1lb. sugar, 1lb. (or 2lbs.) butter—where too much butter is used, it is difficult for the ' knobs ' to retain their shape— ¾lb. barm (good brewer's yeast), ¼lb. blanched almonds, scraped or cut fine ; ½lb. candied lemon, ½ ounce cinnamon, ¼ ounce nutmeg, ten eggs, one gill of cream." The mixing of the ingredients, or " putting together," and setting to rise, should be done the evening before the day on which it has to be baked. When the dough is fully prepared, a portion of four or six pounds may be taken as an approved or convenient quantity, and must be rolled out to form a thick cake, with a " pretty considerable " elevation at the centre. The rolling out of the edge must be much larger than the cake itself is intended to be, and when spread out sufficiently must be doubled back, or returned upon the surface to the extent of about four inches, and as the circumference is of necessity considerably wider than the inner portion of the surface of the cake, it must be pressed down at intervals all round, when between each depression will be found an elevation or protuberance, which protuberances form the celebrated " knobs" of the simnel, by which the cut portions of the cake are always designated. When taken from the oven it must be " glazed," whilst hot, with a thick syrup composed of white of egg and loaf sugar, and afterwards covered with powdered sugar to the depth of a quarter of an inch. The simnel is better if made a while previous to being used, and the powdered sugar must not be put upon it until near the time of the cake being required for consumption.

BURY ARMOURY AND DRILL HALL.

——loyal of heart and liberal of hand
Were the gallant, the high-born, of England's fair land ;
But their glory is gather'd, their honours are told,—
Let the race of to-day match the good knights of old.

Before entering into a description of the Bury Armoury and Drill Hall, it may be stated that the 8th Lancashire (Bury) Volunteer Corps was formed in the summer of 1859.

The Armoury and Drill Hall stands on the vacant ground behind the Peel Monument, and formerly the site of the ancient feudal castle. The corner-stone of the building was laid by Mr. Philips, M.P., on the 22nd of August, 1868. The cavity in the stone contains several local newspapers, the current coins of the realm, a Waterloo medal (presented by Mr. George Booth, of Bury), and a parchment document, of which the following is a copy :—

This corner-stone of the Armoury of the Eighth Regiment of the Lancashire Rifle Volunteers was laid by Robert Needham Philips, Esquire, Member of Parliament for the Borough of Bury, on the twenty-second day of August, in the year of our Lord one thousand eight hundred and sixty-eight.

The Armoury is built upon the site of the ancient castle of Bury, and partly from the materials taken from the ruins. The ancient castle was built upon the still older Saxon fortress, and was destroyed during the civil wars between King Charles the First and the Parliament.

The following are the names of the officers of the Regiment :—John Hutchinson, lieutenant-colonel; O. O. Walker, major; John James Mellor, captain ; Charles Walker, captain ; William Harper, captain; Richard Kay, captain ; Samuel Kershaw, captain, William Hartley, captain ;

John R. Hutchinson, lieutenant; Edward Bland, lieutenant; Samuel Walker, lieutenant; Thomas Kay, ensign; William Ormerod Walker, ensign; William Plant Woodcock, ensign; Edward Lovelock, captain and adjutant; Thomas B. Bott, M.D., surgeon; Rev. Edward James Geoffrey Hornby, M.A., canon of Manchester, honorary chaplain.

James Farrar and Henry Styan, architects.

John Hall, Thomas Crossley, Thomas Cornall, Robert Edmondson, John Kay, and Joseph Downham, contractors.

Colour-sergeant James Shaw, honorary secretary.

A public procession took place before the stone was laid, and after the ceremony a large number of gentlemen sat down to a cold collation.

For some time before the erection of the Drill Hall, the want of such a building was felt, especially for drilling recruits, and for the protection of the whole corps during wet weather. They also required various accessories, which they could not obtain except by the erection of such a building. One drawback, if such it can be called, with regard to the edifice is that it is to some extent hid from public view, and its elevation is certainly worthy of a position to the front. It has, however, during the last few years been more exposed to public view, by the demolition of some old property, and who can say that, at some future day, it will not occupy as prominent a position as the property which now stands in front of it? Externally, the building has a formidable castellated appearance, the character of the architecture being Norman, liberally treated. The centre portion has a bold tower, with battered basement, turreted angles, and crenelated parapets. Under this tower is a Norman doorway, eight feet wide and very lofty, and is treated with appropriate ornaments. At the right hand side of this doorway is another, which leads to the staircase, reading-room, balcony, &c., and above is a small turret, carried up to a greater altitude than the tower itself, and which contains a three-dialled clock. On the left wing are two circular towers, projecting with the main tower, and provided with loopholes. On the right wing is another angle turret. The whole front is of Cumberland walling, and the length of the hall is 108ft. 6in. by 69ft. 6in., 20ft. high to the wall plate, and the walls are 18 inches thick. At the end of the shed, looking over the railway, there is a splendid view of the country, with Holcombe Hill in the distance, and at this end there is also a door admitting to an airing ground. The roof spans the whole width of the building, and is formed on the lattice-girder principle. There are 61 girders, the stoutest timber not being more than $1\frac{1}{4}$in. to $3\frac{1}{2}$in. These are firmly strapped to wall plates, which are secured by bolts running six feet down the walls. The hall is estimated to hold from 5,000 to 6,000 persons, and apart from the purpose for which it was specially erected, it is admirably suited for large public gatherings.

CHAPTER II.

Bury and Bolton Canal: the Upsetting of a Packet-boat—The "Old Hare and Hounds"—The name "Jane" and "Spinning Jennies"—Pedestrianism—The Second Theatre at Bury and Mr. Stanton—The Rev. John Wesley's Visit to Bury—"Jenny Roth'ell" and "Ivin Tree" Cottage—"Th' Paddle Wo'," or Paddle Wall—Bury and the Parliamentary Troops in 1648—Appearance of the Town in its Early Days—Mr. Frank Nuttall and Miss Yates—"Yorkshire Johnny"—Bury Bridge and the Ship Inn—The Wylde—Football Matches—"The Ginnel" and the "Crooked Billet"—The Dungeon—Drs. Bevin, Platt, Cunliffe, and Parks—The Pillory and the Old Cross—The Old Court House—Butcher-lane—The Old Boar's Head Inn—The Old Grey Mare Inn—Otter Hunting—Bury and her Patriots.

BURY AND BOLTON CANAL.—THE UPSETTING OF A PACKET-BOAT.

The formation of the canal between Bury and Bolton was considered a work of great importance, and the first boats that brought coal to Bury were hailed with much rejoicing. They were two boats belonging to Messrs. Craddock, and first came with their jetty freightage September 24th, 1796.

The catastrophe that took place one summer Sunday evening on this canal, by the upsetting of the packet-boat when near its landing in Bury, was the next fatal circumstance, after the Moss-lane Theatre, that made a sensation in Bury. It was caused by the insensate folly of a party of passengers, drunken men, numbering near twenty, who overawed the quieter portion on board, and persisted, for amusement and to frighten the women, in swaying the boat, heavily laden and overcrowded, from side to side, until the window-sills of the cabin, below the deck, were almost on a level with the water of the canal. The brutal wretches, maddened with drunkenness and riot, paid no heed whatever to the remonstrances of the captain, the shrieks and piteous entreaties of the women, or the tears and cries of children who were on board; for the journey was a favourite Sunday trip, many families going that day to visit friends or relatives in Bolton. Opposition led only to more strenuous efforts, and they were blind to danger ; and at length the dreaded apprehension was changed to reality.

The heavily-laden boat, urged by powerful impetus, gave one fatal dip below the water-line, turned upon its side, with its living freight, a helpless multitude, and rose no more. Amongst the drowned were the two young children of Mrs. Knight, afterwards the wife of Captain Chick, R.N. They had been taken in the packet to Bolton by a maid servant, without the parents' knowledge or sanction, Mr. and Mrs. Knight being absent from home at some distance.

THE "OLD HARE AND HOUNDS."

Two centuries ago, for certain, this time-honoured hostelry was built; as to how much earlier a date its establishment might reach cannot now be known, but Roundhead and Royalist must equally have clanked flagon or can under shelter of its roof, or loitered before its threshold discussing politics—so far as was safe—and the last brewing of mine host, until the curfew peal from the neighbouring steeple warned them of the closing day. Not much loitering in-doors at night in those times; tap-rooms were lacking in the brilliant illuminations we have at present. At this same old inn, February the 24th, 1762, being Shrove Tuesday, 72 persons met for to drink their Majesties' healths, and all the royal family (?), in which company there were 38 persons whose ages amounted to upwards of 3,040 years; being all of them residents within a mile of the said town of Bury. Explanatory of the above-mentioned meeting, it may be said that at this period George the Third, newly on the throne, still more recently married to the German Princess Charlotte, his first child yet unborn, King, Queen, and Government were in high favour with the majority of the people; whilst France, and Spain especially, were, in naval warfare, suffering repeated defeats at the hands of the British.

THE NAME "JANE" AND "SPINNING JENNIES."

Captain Peel, of Ardwick, the "Robert Peel, junior," of the firm, married Miss Jane Yates, only sister of Mrs. Peel, his cousin Robert's wife. Members of the Peel family have, in their alliances, shown a remarkable partiality for the name of "Jane," when it became a question of selecting a partner for life. In later times William Yates Peel, brother of the statesman, Sir Robert, married Lady Jane Eliza Moore, sister of the Earl of Mountcashel; Jonathan Peel married Lady Alicia Jane Kennedy, daughter of the Earl of Cassilis; Lawrence Peel married Lady Jane Lennox, sister to the Duke of Richmond; and another member of the family married Lady Jane Manners. It was in reference to these that George the Fourth—when a nobleman in attendance announced the two latter marriages—said, "Ah! my lord, you see these Peels cannot, even yet, do without their 'spinning Jennies.'"

PEDESTRIANISM.

Feats of walking were performed in the "good old days" in Bury and thought nothing uncommon. From Bury companies of men and women have set off, after six in the evening, to visit the Manchester theatre, returning after the performance; nor was it spoken of as meriting comment. Young women, anxious to secure some article of necessary adornment, have left Bury at five maybe in the morning, reached Manchester, spent two or three hours in making purchases, and been quietly seated at home again by three o'clock in the afternoon, with no appearance or mention of undue fatigue. Finished goods being despatched by waggons and carts from the Ground, seldom later than six a.m.—being loaded overnight—occasion often arose during the day for a message to the Manchester department requiring immediate attention. A lad would be summoned, and furnished with instructions; and, for the journey to Manchester, a shilling was added to his week's wages, with the privilege that, if accomplished before the evening bell, at six o'clock, such time was at his own disposal. It is said that some of these boys would accomplish most of the distance at a running pace. Before and after the year 1800, the distance to be traversed, including the return, was nearly twenty-two miles, a devious, ill-kept road; each little hamlet, or straggling collection of cottages, being recognised in its course. Buckley Wells, "Rediva'-lone," "Fishpoo-bruk," with its ancient "fowt," or fold; Hampson Mill, or Hampson's Mill—not then a printworks, as it afterwards became—but truly a mill, by which, at that time, the road passed, although afterwards, in the march of improvement and saving of time, so very considerably shortened and straightened out. Lily-hill, a terror to timid passengers in the first started twice-a-week coach; and, with its dangerous little bridge, a place of caution to the master wool manufacturers on horseback, going to or returning from the market at Manchester; in the latter case too often with brains not over steady, and riding in company as a measure of greater safety. Beyond lay "th'" Whitefield, Besses, Prestwich, and so on to Red Bank, and, through its unpicturesque locality, the business part of the town was entered in what was once the Miller's-lane, now Miller-street, in which stood the building popularly known as "Arkwright's Factory," with a chimney then considered so high that the townsfolk, in their Sunday walks, took that way to look at it, and it was spoken of as the "big chimney."

THE SECOND THEATRE AT BURY, AND MR. STANTON.

After the destruction of Moss-lane Theatre (elsewhere referred to) a new one was erected in Clerke-street, named after Sir William Clerke, the Rector, and was exactly opposite the Methodist Chapel, but no feeling of intolerance was ever entertained. The front and public entrance parts of the theatre were constructed of wood. For many years its performances were extremely successful ; the various allied families of the Peels and Yateses not only attending themselves, but purchasing tickets in a generous quantity, to be presented to the workpeople. Mr. Stanton and his company were well known and well liked in many of the towns of Lancashire, and in no town were their labours better appreciated than in Bury.

Mr. Stanton, besides being manager of the company, and an actor of tolerable eminence, was also a scene painter of considerable ability. He painted, for his theatre, the old market place of Preston, and it formed one of the most effective pieces amongst his scenic representations. He also, out of compliment to Mr. Peel and his family, painted for the stage a view of Chamber Hall, from the eminence at the back of the Grammar School ; whilst another member of the histrionic corps, a jovial fellow, wrote a song introducing local topics, and an enumeration of the night's entertainments, concluding with,

> The truth of my doctrine the more to enhance,
> In Bury to-night you shall see part of France ;
> And by way of farewell, all these pleasures to crown,
> We will bring Chamber Hall to the midst of the town !

The play was "King Henry the Fifth; or, the Battle. of Agincourt." Whatever the merits of "Chamber Hall" as a picture might be, in the crowded house that night there was no dissentient voice ; on its display the audience rose as one person, and shook the building with repeated cheers and exclamations loud and long, meant as fully for leading members of the firm then present, and the family at the Hall, as for its representation in mimic hues before them on the stage.

THE REV. JOHN WESLEY'S VISIT TO BURY.

When the Rev. John Wesley was in Lancashire, in 1787, following his usual practice of preaching in the open air whenever he could collect a congregation, he came to Bury, and, as the most notable place, to the Ground, and, inquiring for Mr. Peel, requested his permission to converse with the workpeople, and inquire into their spiritual condition and the state of their religious knowledge. The request was granted ; and, much pleased with Mr. Wesley's conversation

and his evident sincerity, Mr. Peel invited him to spend the evening at his house, where he also had breakfast the next morning. The house was not Chamber Hall, but that which was afterwards the counting-house, fronting the small bridge of the dam. This was in July, and Mr. Peel did not enter upon Chamber Hall until the new part of the building was completed, which was not until the close of January, 1788, the old farmhouse that gave its designation remaining at the back, almost entirely in its original condition, a structure mostly stone and timber; the new part, containing more modern accommodations, being of brick, and presenting, in place of that removed, a somewhat longer front than the old dwelling had done. The family was settled in the new home barely in time for Mrs. Peel's confinement of her eldest boy. Of this visit to Bury Mr. Wesley himself makes the following entry:—
"A few years ago Mr. Peel began business with £500, and is now supposed to have £50,000." Availing himself of the privilege accorded, Mr. Wesley passed freely about the works, addressing himself to the people of the different shops, in words clothed in the garb of simplicity, but often carrying conviction, and spoken as with the voice of one having authority to make known the commands of his Divine Master.

"JENNY ROTH'ELL" AND "IVIN TREE" COTTAGE.

The "Ivin Tree," or Ivy Cottage, was a very old dwelling, one of the most ancient around Bury, and was situate a little below Castlecroft-lane. Here was born and lived with her aged mother and grandmother—who had likewise spent the whole of their quiet and uneventful lives within its precincts—"Jenny Roth'ell," a blackworker by profession; not a witch, or practiser of the black art, but a most expert maker of the black mode silk bonnets worn before the general introduction, at a later day, of straw. Her "honeycombing" was something marvellous. A spinster to the end, she was the best example that could be found, in humble life, of the kindly, cheerful, useful, and industrious old maid. She was selected by young women as first counsellor and adviser in all cases pertaining to matrimony, living to caress the grandchildren of many whose marriage she herself had promoted. No wedding, christening, or burying, was complete without Jenny; and of her it might be said that in youth she was an old-fashioned young woman, and in age a young-hearted old woman. The roof of her cottage was completely covered by the growth of an immense ivy tree, as well as the front and one side. The door, two or three little orifices for windows, and the chimney, being all that was distinguishable out of the evergreen foliage, except a few patches of

D

ragged brown thatch, visible here and there; a few old trees stood around, and a little irregular garden straggled down the steep hillside behind.

" TH' PADDLE WO'," OR PADDLE WALL.

This was a long, low, stone wall in Bury-lane; a protection to way-farers from the dangerous bank descending to the field or croft on the level plain below, which intervened between the high range of ground surmounted by the wall and the " great lodge" or reservoir beyond. This reservoir was constructed in the year 1792, in what was, previously, only a worthless piece of wet and marshy land. Still further than the reservoir, the highfield, and then the extensive pasture known as the downbottoms, forming the limit of the land owned by the firm of Peel and Yates in this direction. Paddle Wall was said to be the haunt of beings of a demoniacal nature, and not only children but grown up folks were afraid to pass along the extent of its path after nightfall; for, when darkness settled so as to render natural objects indistinguishable, then would fearful influences be discerned, exerting a power transcending nature, but only for malevolence and horror. If it was needful to pass the wall during the night, company would be sought in order to keep up mutual courage; whilst the terrors of the Paddle Wo' were so undisputed and so generally recognised that an acknowledgment of them has survived almost to our own times. Down to some years preceding the use of gas in the town, the odium of a haunted spot continued attached to the place; but at length, vague and undefined, this became forgotten and known no more; whilst, for the *first time*, between 1823-25, the whole extent of the Wall was built upon and rendered habitable. Paddle Wall is a corruption of Battle Wall. How many or how few have knowledge that one of the fiercest conflicts between Englishmen, during the civil wars, had here its theatre?

BURY AND THE PARLIAMENTARY TROOPS IN 1648.

The battle of Ribblesdale, or Walton-le-Dale, on the south of Preston, took place August 17th, 1648; the army, on the Parliamentary side, being arrayed against Scottish soldiers under the Duke of Hamilton, and English Royalists under General Langdale; and it was three days prior to this that a detachment from the army of the Parliament entered Bury. There is no mention that Cromwell himself ever entered or stayed in the town—its Royalist proclivities might prevent that—but on the night following the engagement at Preston the successful soldier and patriot slept at Astley Hall, Chorley, an ancient seat of the Charnocks—

at the Restoration in possession of Sir Peter Brooke, Knight—and from thence into Staffordshire. The assaulting troops advanced from Yorkshire into Lancashire. For the reduction of Bury approaches were made under Major-General Lambert, strengthened by a brigade under Major Ashton, leading upon the town from the level and favourable plain of Cockey Moor. Entering the town on that side the river offered good means to the Royalist defenders of opposing their passage, and possibly no means were left untried to do so, as this part of the river was the only place, for some distance, where the aggressive forces could cross with advantage; and the first building of the bridge must have been determined by this natural situation. It may have been simply a ford, for traffic and travel alike were limited. On one hand, up the river, marshes and undrained land; on the other, downwards, elevated banks that could well be defended. This contraction of available space would render the encounter at the passage of the river more close and deadly. Could the contest that took place on what was then, or afterwards, named Bury Lane, have been made visible to us, we should most likely have seen it equally well sustained. The fight raged up the road or along the crest of the high land extending from the river, and reaching its extreme altitude at the hill on which the Castle then stood. The line taken, ultimately becoming the main street of the town, after the remunerative business had commenced below the Mill Brow, could be traced by its sanguinary evidences to the Market-place, or open space of ground between the ancient fortress and the church, where the last and most fearful open conflict had its closing struggle on that tragical August day. The knowledge here obtained is traditionary; no written record exists. And on the stage of history at this time, about the period 1648, a glance of recognition at the condition of Charles and Cromwell,—each a true and fitting representative of the opinions and principles he advocated—would show Cromwell advancing to success, and the reforms he aimed at; Charles's life and kingly supremacy drawing near to its end upon the scaffold. At the close of the day's encounter the Royalists—those who could enter—sought shelter in the Castle; the Parliamentary troops, breathing awhile, took cognisance of the evidence, so far, of victory, in the bloodshed and slaughter that had taken place since forcing the passage of the river. Between the upper and the lower parts of Bury Lane were some few enclosures for grain, orchard, or garden; but open pastures intervened, and the tumult of the affray quickly extending over these, soon burst through the frail defence of orchard or paddock, and corn that could not be garnered since word came of the probability of attack, lay crushed and soaked in blood, the owners or defenders of the place dying on their own desecrated lands ; or those who survived, maimed and suffering, dragged themselves, as best they might, to their homes around the town, unobserved, if possible, for that night the conquering party held possession of the area in front of the entrance to the Castle ; whilst the morning following, August the 15th, the siege of the fortress, and its consequent demolition, began, its destruction occupying two days, or until the close of the 16th.   For a century and a half afterwards the fields adjoining Bury Lane, once drenched with so sanguinary a baptism, were pointed out and made memorable as having overflowed with human blood, that for many following successive years caused all grain there grown to be streaked as if with gore, being thereby popularly supposed to indicate an excess in the soil of that unwonted rain with which their roots had been nourished.

APPEARANCE OF THE TOWN IN ITS EARLY DAYS.

From ancient houses remaining in the town at the middle of the last century it was apparent that Bury had never, at any time previously, extended much beyond the neighbourhood of the church.   Until the establishment of printing and the cotton manufacture, the whole compass of the town was very small indeed, the "Lane," being the only avenue in which the houses continued for any distance from the central part around the church and Market-place ; and no other thoroughfare from the town having even an appellation.   At a somewhat earlier day all the ways from town had soon ended in moorland, or wild uncultivated tracts ; hamlets or villages seeming isolated and far between; trade, as yet, having scarcely centred in any of them, although many were of undoubted antiquity.   The loneliness of the roads, and the little communication between habitable parts at a former period, may be imagined if it be remembered that so lately as 1796 a stage coach travelling through Bury, between Manchester and Rochdale, was discontinued through lack of patronage, although it passed but twice a week.   Before the occupancy of the Ground, the neighbouring marsh land had formed a natural withdrawing reservoir for floods and inundations, and at the place where the bridge was established the river was neither deep nor dangerous at any time, besides being the first available firm ground in the course of the river on this side, after passing the marsh, and the commencement of hilly land embanking the river for a short distance downwards.   From Bury, in the time of the civil wars, there could have been, after passing the river, no rightly defined road to any other place.   Moor and wild lay before the traveller where to choose. The only recognised route would be that over Cockey Moor, and leading to "Bolton in the Moors." In these days of acknowledged safety and mathematical precision in laying out a highway, we remember little of the uncertainties and troubles to be encountered by foot travellers of a former time.

MR. FRANK NUTTALL AND MISS YATES.

This gentleman, long afterwards most extensively known as "Old Frank," was the last link connecting our later days with the flourishing times of the Print Trade, and Bury, in the era of the earlier "Masters;" and his memory is inseparably connected with the rise and prosperity of the Ground, and its great and extended business relations. From his house, before the intervening plantation was fully grown, looking over the lodge, Chamber Hall was in view. This strip of plantation was not only needful and ornamental, but intended also to form the dividing line separating the lawn and shrubberies of the Hall from what more strictly pertained to the business part of the estate ; the line being, until the trees were sufficiently grown, marked out only by white posts connected by chains. Long afterwards, when Mr. Edmund Yates resided at the "Chamber," with his amiable and accomplished daughter, totally blind— she lost her sight consequent upon a dangerous illness in early youth— her favourite walk, alone, and one which she could not be persuaded to forego, although its vicinity to the water made it dangerous, was from the Hall through the shrubberies and plantation, and by the side of the lodge to Mr. Nuttall's, there to await the anticipated happiness of her father's afternoon leisure ; and no other sound could deceive her ear as to the footfall of this beloved parent, who bestowed upon her the most affectionate and watchful care, all the more devoted because his afflicted girl was motherless; almost her only other companion, besides her father, being her accomplished friend and governess, Miss Wallis, afterwards Mrs. Howarth. Mr. Nuttall's house was the depository of all the keys for each "shop" on the works ; and the sheltering porch and hospitable hearth were a pleasant sight at evening to the foremen or others of the various thronged departments, who entered, bearing each one or more bunches of ponderous keys clasped in their heavy iron ring, and destined for the night to be hung upon a strictly allotted hook, high up on the old-fashioned mantel-piece, where, to the practised eye, a glance along its wooden front would detect, by vacancy, which places were open and what men were still employed. For forty-years this was the abode of Mr. Nuttall, a man of the most sterling worth and integrity ; entirely in the confidence of the first masters, through life retaining deep attachment to them, and the scene of their earliest business venture; and clinging to the place long after its greatness had departed. His connection with the firm was established when quite a youth, that is in 1774, he being then fifteen years old; born 1759. In 1834, Mr. Nuttall removed from the works to a house he had lately built, but did not long survive the change. During over fifteen of the first years of his residence at the Ground, there was held at his house, on some specially-appointed day during Christmas, what might be called a cabinet council of the firm, all the masters being present, in deliberation or conclave, assembled in the "house part" or parlour; whilst in the kitchen, during the morning, each person holding an office of trust or being overseer of the labour of others, either in the print business or the cotton manufacture, was required to present himself and answer any needful questions.

The gentlemen partners first partook of breakfast as Mrs. Nuttall's honoured guests; then, the table being cleared, books and documents of importance were produced and commented upon, and all the leading transactions of the past year brought forward, reviewed, and discussed; whilst in the closely neighbouring kitchen refreshments were supplied to all, but most especially to those coming from distant establishments, come of them outlying from Lancashire into Yorkshire. At this period the waggons of the firm traversed, several times a week, the distance between Bury and Halifax, or Clayton Heights. As the distance was considerable, and the roads bad, the waggoners were allowed, in winter, a stout pony to ride at discretion. Mr. Nuttall repeatedly let pass opportunities of acquiring a great fortune, and guarded the interests of others much more than his own. Thomas Norris, of Redivals, and Howick Hall, near Preston; and Richard Hamer, of Bury Lane, with numerous others, all men of extraordinary business capacity, began their career under his authority and fostering superintendence.

"YORKSHIRE JOHNNY."

One of the most odd-looking objects to be found upon the Bury Ground in the days of Messrs. Peel and Yates, was "Yorkshire Johnny," an old man employed on the Ground exclusively to carry coal and make up the fires in the print shops. Originally Johnny came from Halifax, but his surname was unknown, and he never answered to any other appellation than "Yorkshire Johnny." He was one of the most crooked and diminutive men ever seen, and seemed to embody in his person some monstrous imagination of romance. His neck, arms, legs, fingers, and toes were each, individually, the subject of a grotesque and singular distortion, and he was bowed down almost literally to the earth, not from age or infirmity, but from actual conformation. He was double-jointed ; and, either from hard living or natural defect, the sensation of touch in his fingers was so obtuse or deficient that he could not distinguish a substance by that sense, or take up any small object from a flat surface. His wrinkled skin was like shrivelled parchment, and of the colour of mahogany ; whilst it is not doubtful that Johnny never knew the meaning of personal cleanliness. His attire every day in the week was the same, with the exception of doffing his " brat," or apron, to distinguish the day of rest. He had no home or dwelling off the works, but for many years slept in the " white-room," a room for white pieces, across the dam that flowed before the counting-house, to which he gained access by crossing the water on two narrow planks, supported on piles. In bad weather Johnny would take his night's rest in the watchman's place at the foot of the Mill Brow. He was never known to undress, except when he cast away some worn-out garment to replace it with another almost as bad, come to share the comfort and warmth of the place. The only absences he was ever known to make from Bury, were to Halifax, whither he would adventure, leaving the Ground about four o'clock on Saturday afternoon, at the close of working hours, and returning through the night of Sunday—performing the journey thither and back on foot—in readiness for his accustomed work on Monday morning.

No person who had once seen Johnny could ever forget him. His height, at its fullest extent, and when standing as upright as he could, was under five feet; his fingers were so curved that they resembled the talons of some monstrous bird of prey; his hair, ragged and unkempt, of doubtful hue, but not doubtful dirtiness; whilst it seemed probable his skin was innocent of an ablution since infancy or childhood. He never entered into conversation, not even over that only indulgence, his ale, which he called for sitting in a nook of the chimney-place in the kitchen or taproom of the old Hope and Anchor, stone built and old fashioned, and possessing a sovereign attraction for the topers of the day; its only neighbouring inns on either hand being the Ship, the Nancy Frigate, at the Bridge; and the Hare and Hounds and White Lion at the top of the Lane. This thoroughfare did not receive the title of Bolton-street until the commencement of widening the upper part took place about 1821; and until later than 1823 the old signboard of "Bury-lane" was suspended against a building lower down, till it finally dropped from the wall through age and decay. Yorkshire Johnny never wore stockings, winter or summer, and his legs, as well as his arms and chest, were well covered with hair, rough and coarse as that of an ourang outang; whilst his shapeless feet were thrust into clumsy clogs. This dwarfed and stooping figure might have been seen at all hours of the day traversing the Ground, bearing a burden of coal upon his back, in the old-fashioned wicker coal-basket, and tending fires with commendable assiduity in each direction. He rarely spoke or looked up to recognise any one who crossed his path, unless it might chance to be "one o'th' maisters," when his poor, bent frame would be elevated to its utmost height, for the joke, good-humoured reprimand, or word of kindness he might receive; Johnny's ambition reached no further. In order to perpetuate the singularity of his appearance, at Mr. Yates's suggestion William Murray, the talented animal painter, was sent for to take Johnny's portrait when at his daily labour, though the old man was not aware of it. As throughout the day Johnny was continually crossing from one part of the works to another, attending to his numerous fires, a "special sitting." was not required; and the artist, of whom Bury may be justly proud, has faithfully depicted "Yorkshire Johnny" as he then appeared.

BURY BRIDGE AND THE SHIP INN.

Of the structure of Bury Bridge as it now stands the two oldest houses on the nearer side were all that occupied any position so low down the road ; of these the most noted being the old " Ship Inn," so long in the occupation of the Fletcher family, whilst almost opposite stood the pleasantly-appointed house of Robert Braid, the dyer, and his comfortable wife Susy. Samuel Fletcher, who first set up the sign of " The Good Ship Nancy," a counterpart of the vessel in which he had longest seen service, was a jolly old sailor, although, according to the " custom of the country," some of his most habitual visitors bestowed upon him the additional cognomen of " Owd 'Says I' " on account of the frequent use he made of that expression when telling about naval adventures, sea fights, and seamanship.

THE WYLDE.

The site and neighbourhood of the Wylde comprises the most ancient, and undoubtedly the original portion of the town. The antique, time-honoured dwellings of the earlier people of Bury had clustered, as much for safety as proximity, around its area ; this space, in the olden days, forming a green or common ground between the houses of the townsfolk, the church, and the embattled buildings on the brow of the hill, over-looking the lower lands and crofts belonging to the Castle. This green, or allotted piece of public land, was to the inhabitants of those times all that our parks, recreation grounds, or gardens are to us. Here, seeming to have been the custom for centuries, on each favourable evening after labour, were all accustomed to meet; sitting, even upon the ground, if a stone or wooden bench was not attainable; and so confirmed had this nightly convocation become that until 1820, if any one wished to see a person, and inquired at his habitation, the answer would be that " he was up th' street "—" up th' street," in whatever direction the inquirer might be, invariably signifying the spacious, inexpensive, and democratic place of meeting. Quarrels or disturbances but seldom occurred, and the unwitting temperance of such an open-air assembly may have contributed to this; whilst an hour or two after the curfew had spread its well-known vibrations on the air, in the soft summer twilight, friends and fellow-workmen would stroll home in companies of a dozen or more, rendered wiser perhaps, and may-be more charitable by the association of the last few hours.

FOOTBALL MATCHES.

The great and established amusement—reaching apparently from a remote time—of men and boys in Bury, at Easter, was football playing. Christmas, Shrovetide, and Good Friday, had each special matches, but the early days in Easter week decided pre-eminently for the championship of the year. Matches were formed by the best players being selected from two general divisions of the townsmen, and the place where the final struggle for victory had to be decided was the Wylde and the close adjoining neighbourhood of the church; the enclosure of the churchyard, the erection of iron railing and gates, and the uniform levelling of the Wylde being of comparatively modern times. In winter the football matches would be played upon the ice, if strong enough for the purpose, and when it happened that the waste lands were overflowed and frozen, the satisfaction of the combatants was considerably increased.

"THE GINNEL" AND THE "CROOKED BILLET."

Beyond the garden hedge fronting Radcliffe Wrigley's house on the Wylde, and leading to the Grammar School, was the extremely straitened thoroughfare of the "Ginnel"—its name signifying its capacity. Across the Ginnel were what might be spoken of as two enclosed courts, consisting of old, very old, low-roofed cottages, in any of which a person of tolerably tall stature would have found it difficult to stand upright. Some of these dwellings had back doors opening freely into the churchyard itself, being built, apparently, about two hundred years before the graves had an enclosure to themselves. Others, lacking doors, had windows, or old-fashioned casements, through one of which, belonging to his cottage, a later sexton of the church, William Crompton, frequently made way to his customary employment, in order to save himself the trouble of passing around. The Crooked Billet public-house stood here, and encroached far upon what should have been churchyard ground; a close narrow passage, barely sufficient to allow entrance or egress, followed by another public-house extending to the old gates, formed a complete boundary to the sanctuary of the dead on that side; the last-mentioned inn being exactly opposite the bellhouse of the church, and, like its neighbour, the Crooked Billet, having convenient and authorised entrances from the churchyard, it formed a convenient and much appreciated mode of obtaining refreshment for the bellringers. To judge by old time encroachments of habitations for the living upon needful space allotted to the dead, our forefathers would seem to have courted rather than shunned their vicinity.

THE DUNGEON.

Closely neighbouring the houses of entertainment was the Dungeon, the public prison of the town, and the only building recognised as having a judicial capacity. Access was gained to it by a low, dirty, covered passage opening on the Wylde, and called the Dungeon entry. This prison was in such close proximity to the church that persons traversing the churchyard could, at times, hear the oaths and imprecations of those who might at such period be the inmates of that wretched place. It was a dismal, dark, damp, old stone building, altogether unfit to be made, for even a short time, the abiding place of a human being.

DRS. BEVIN, PLATT, CUNLIFFE, AND PARKS.

One resident in the Wylde, living there, an aged man, until 1780, was Dr. Bevin, a solitary bachelor, who, keeping no assistant, was accustomed when called to pay a professional visit so far as was then considered out of town, to inscribe in large characters, with chalk, upon his closed door, the place of his destination and probable time of his return. Fronting upon the Wylde were two houses of more modern style and far better condition than any of the others. In one of these lived the eccentric Dr. Platt, a greatly respected surgeon and physician; at one time, with the exception of Dr. Bevin, who was old and unambitious, the only medical man practising in Bury, so small were its population and requirements. An old-fashioned, kind-hearted man, a naturalist, and, for his time, of considerable scientific information. Dr. Cunliffe established himself about 1780, and almost at once succeeded to the best patronage of the town; his professional life there was during the best period of Bury's transition from its former quietness and thrift, to activity and the moderate but general enrichment of all who had either talent or business qualities to recommend them. The proclivity of Dr. Platt as a naturalist—so little was the science then known or estimated—of making all possible inquiry into habits or formation of fishes, birds, beasts, and insects, subjected him frequently to the infliction of jokes of a good-humoured, satirical character, such as is instanced in some verses commemorating the destruction of the "Holcombe Monster," an enormous otter troubling and depopulating the waters of Holcombe and elsewhere near upon five generations ago. The otter, after much trouble and many pursuits, had at length been captured; and an assembly of "Th' Wise Men of Howcome" having been convened to sit in judgment upon the creature, their united sapiency was unable to determine whether such an "unlikely thing" was to be pronounced as "fish, flesh, or fowl." In this emergency it is requested that Dr. Platt, of Bury, be sent for, and urged to give them the benefit of his knowledge upon the subject.

> Gossip Platt, his spectacles did put on,
> Paused a moment, and thus begun.

Here followed a long and learned harangue by the worthy doctor, which, instead of enlightening his hearers, left them in greater doubt and darkness than before.

When Dr. Platt left his house in the Wylde, which he had occupied very long, the person to succeed him as tenant was a young man, Dr. Parks, the first of that name in Bury, who, on establishing himself in the town, commenced business in the old doctor's house as a druggist, making a daring innovation by taking out the front of the private residence and sufficiently altering it to suit a public business. The new shop, with its elegant fittings, good lights, and beautiful many-coloured glasses, was considered very grand, and a great novelty and improvement, especially when contrasted with the little, dim, and dusky place heretofore known as a druggist's shop by the townspeople, Mr. Parks being fittingly rewarded for his enterprise by a considerable share of public patronage and appreciation.

THE PILLORY AND THE OLD CROSS.

Near to where the church gates now are stood the Pillory, which was used about the year 1800 for the last time. Near the centre of the Market-place stood the old Cross, which has long since been removed. At its base, which was for a long time in a crumbled and broken state, crowds at times used to assemble to discuss the various topics of the day, to narrate their experiences, and to crack their jokes at the expense of many an innocent passer-by.

THE OLD COURT HOUSE.

This building formerly stood near the old Cross in the Market-place. It is recorded that a poor woman was once brought before the court for a misdemeanour. The sentence was that she should be whipped at the Market Cross till blood was seen to gush from her back. The woman was brought forth, and stood in the presence of a large concourse of people. For some time no one could be found to execute the law, but at last Old Hector Brown volunteered to inflict the punishment. Before commencing he took the whip to a slaughter-house and dipped it in blood. When the woman turned her back to Hector, he drew it across and said, "Here is blood at the first lash, make off!"

BUTCHER-LANE.

This lane, although not very wide at present, was at one time much narrower. An old report as to the origin of the name is as follows:— In the time of the civil wars there lived a butcher near to this place, who made himself noted by many brave exploits for the King's army. At one time being closely pursued in Leister-field by a dragoon, the butcher struck spurs into his horse, and leaped over both of the hedges that divided the lane and made his escape. The lane has ever since been known by the name of Butcher-lane.

THE OLD BOAR'S HEAD INN.

Mention has already been made of an attorney, the only one then resident in Bury, occupying a room at the back of this inn, and also of a member of the Pilkington family amassing a large fortune within the house now occupied by Mr. James Hayward. It ought, however, to be stated that a former landlord of this house once bought a silver tankard at a Mr. Hamer's sale at High Crompton, near Bolton. This tankard was christened "Hamer," and was constantly kept upon the table in the principal drinking room. Out of "Hamer" the masons, carpenters, and slaters, when engaged in building St. Mary's Church, drank many a quart of liquor. It is recorded that Messrs. Joseph and James Tootil, along with their labourer, Harry Wood, tossed "Hamer" about much to the benefit of the rising family at the Old Boar's Head.

THE OLD GREY MARE INN.

The ancient hostelry of the Old Grey Mare Inn has disappeared, but it was once of considerable reputation for conviviality and good cheer. On Mid-Lent Sunday, so highly were its comfort and accommodation appreciated that it was almost impossible for another person to enter its doors when once it had become thronged; or, if once within, a matter also of considerable difficulty to squeeze out again. Its old rafters had re-echoed to songs and jovial scenes of merriment for more than a hundred years. Besides Mid-Lent, the Grey Mare, along with the other public-houses around the church, was accustomed to receive a large accession of company on occasion of weddings, christenings, and burials.

OTTER HUNTING.

Otter hunting used to be a favourite sport in the neighbourhood of Bury. Whenever a huntsman was fortunate enough to obtain a knowledge of an otter being about, Mr. Edmund Yates, who was an enthusiastic votary of what is denominated "sport," would send a messenger, not trusting a letter, to his friend Squire Lomax, of Clayton Hall, who was said to possess the best pack of hounds in Lancashire, informing him of the discovery and the anticipation of a triumph in the prospective hunt and capture of the predatory otter. The Starkies of Huntroyd—or, as it was commonly pronounced, "th' Huntrid"—were also never backward at such summons, Le Gendre Pierce Starkie being a well-known follower of the hounds around Bury; and when, by his devastations, an otter was believed to lurk in the neighbourhood, many a country lad would spend hours in traversing the banks of a river or brook in order to engross the glory of being the first to give intimation of the otter's retreat. The kennel of the Bury Hunt was placed at Crostons, near Woodhill, and on still evenings the deep-mouthed baying of the hounds could be distinctly heard for a considerable distance, often accompanied by the strenuous efforts of the huntsman to control his noisy four-footed pack of obstreperous pupils.

BURY AND HER PATRIOTS.

War opinions were raging in the year 1792, and the discordant sound of the drum was heard in every corner of the parish of Bury. The divine right, and legitimate power of kings, were much disputed by loyal Churchmen, Presbyterians, and different grades of Dissenters, who were all struggling to grapple the power of the " loaves and fishes," popularity, and fame. During the French wars there were in Bury four sorts of soldiers, viz.:—Bury Loyal Association (referred to in another chapter), Bury Cavalry, Bury Riflemen, and Bury Pikemen. By the aid of drums and fifes men were being enlisted as soldiers to discomfit the great Napoleon. Ministers of the Church of England might be seen among gentlemen in Bury, and other parts of Lancashire, parading the streets with bands of music, and cockades in their hats.

CHAPTER III.

The Discovery of Roman Relics at Walmersley—The Old Bury Constables—Ox Roasting at Bury Old Cross—The Yates and Peel Family—The Black Bull Inn, Blackburn—One Hundred and Three Years Ago—The Mistress of the Black Bull Inn—Dress of the Period—Mrs. Yates, the Maternal Great-grandmother of the late Sir Robert Peel—The Young Traveller's Visit to Darwen—Brinscall, Anglezark, Horwich, &c.—Cockey Moor—Pedlars and Pack Horses—Brooksmouth—The Hope and Anchor—The Claytons of Bamber Bridge—Home Weaving—Mr. Peel's Survey of the Site of his Future Printworks—Old Mill—The Miller's House—Doctor's-lane and Mansion—The "Ground"—Mr. William Yates—First Workshops—Fires—The Partnership—The Bleachworks—A Thief with Horns and Tail—Price of Calico—Apprentice Children.

THE DISCOVERY OF ROMAN RELICS AT WALMERSLEY.

Early in July, 1864, James Nuttall, farmer, Throstle Hill, Walmersley, discovered a quantity of Roman coins, which at the time created some interest to antiquarians. Soon after the " find " James Nuttall became somewhat celebrated, and envied by a few. He and his wife (an aged couple) had resided alone upwards of three years in the house on the hill, and eked out a scanty subsistence by the products of their labour on the farm and at the handloom. Even this secluded pair was seriously affected by the cotton crisis, and, in addition to this, a few months before they were bereft of one of their beasts. They now lost all hope of ever recovering from the effects of the sad blow ; and, for want of the " needful," wreck and ruin seemed to be the fate of all. Many times had the old woman, almost sorrow stricken, driven the only two cows they possessed up the moor to the shippon ; and as often had her husband totteringly wended his way to Holcombe and Ramsbottom for the purpose of disposing of the milk. The by-path to the farmhouse had for some time on Sundays been frequented by a number of youths, from a neighbouring village, and they, regardless of the day, amused themselves by gambling, pitching and tossing. Mrs. Nuttall had often remonstrated with these gamblers, and, finding that they would persist in their unholy occupation, threatened to inform the police. On the evening of the eventful day—the day of the " find "—the careworn couple, in company with their nephew, took a stroll down the hill, and, on returning with the beasts,

Mrs. Nuttall drew attention to the place which the "pitchers and tossers" frequented.   She had on previous occasions observed some "buttons" on the slope, and believing that they were "mots," had kicked them out of the way. On this particular Friday evening she again perceived some "mots," and pointed them out to her nephew and husband. The latter proceeded thither, picked up a handful of earth, and, after a minute examination, came to the conclusion that the "buttons" were ancient coins. Nuttall made a further search, and, having removed a small quantity of earthwork from the road side, which is supported by some huge pieces of stone, was successful in coming upon the earthenware jar, which fell into fragments as it was dislodged from the place in which it had been so long embedded.   The farmer, anxious to obtain some information about the treasure, soon made the discovery known; and subsequently sold a number of the coins at 1d. each.   Other curiosities were at first sold proportionately cheap; and, as the news spread, his house was literally besieged by gentlemen and others, who offered a much higher price for some of the articles. Many of the coins were in a good state of preservation, the heads of some of the emperors being perfectly plain. The "image or superscription" on the coins left no doubt as to the skill of the coiners of those by-gone ages. The market soon became brisk, and very high prices were asked for objects even of a valueless description. There can be no doubt these relics would, in proper quarters, have demanded more than their weight in gold. An antiquarian, writing at the time, upon the discovery, says: "The urn or small earthen vessel, in which the coins, &c., were deposited, was found buried in the earth near a modern occupation road, leading to a farmhouse, occupied by a Mr. Nuttall, on Throstle Hill, in the township of Walmersley.   The locality is situated about three miles to the north of Bury, and about half a mile to the east of Grant's Tower. It is distant about three miles, on the map, from the nearest point of the Roman highway, which leads from Manchester, by Cockey Moor, Edgeworth, and Blackburn, to Ribchester. The vessel was buried on the edge of the moorland overlooking a well-cultivated, but secluded and picturesque valley. The old road, from Bury to Burnley and Colne, passes near the spot. The earthen vessel which contained the hoard was covered by a small flag. It contained from five to seven hundred bronze coins, chiefly of the small or 'third brass,' and all of which belong to what is termed the 'lower empire.' None that I have seen, however, are earlier than the time of Gallienus and his wife Salonica (A.D. 253-268). The latest in point of date are coins of Maximianus (286-310), and Carausius (287-293). I noticed others of Posthumus (260-267), Victormus

(265-267), Claudius Gothicus (268-270), Tetricus (267-272), Quintilius (270), M. Claudius Tacitus (275-276), and M. Aurelius Probus (276-282). The following articles were deposited with the coins :—A pair of silver bracelets, slightly, not elaborately ornamented, one with the vine leaf, the other with bunches of grapes. The latter was broken, the former perfect. The workmanship is not of a very superior character. A plain bracelet of massive silver, broken, about one-third of an inch in breadth. Two armlets, one about an eighth of an inch thick, of twisted silver cord ; the other about one-tenth of an inch thick, formed of a single wire fashioned so as to resemble the one formed of two twisted cords. Two fragments of another armlet, about a quarter of an inch in diameter, formed of thick silver wire twisted round a bar of bronze. Three silver finger rings, one with a red stone attached. Several pieces of broken silver rings, like wedding or ear rings in form ; some pieces of a thin bronze armlet, and a small bronze hinge. The blade of a bronze spoon, elegantly shaped, rather more than one inch and a half in length, by a little over half an inch in breadth. Perhaps the most interesting relic is an amulet of amber, richly streaked with orange-coloured veins, and pierced so as to be suspended alone, and not so as to form a portion of a continuous string of beads. I am inclined to think that the treasure recently discovered may have been deposited in the earth during the troubles attendant upon the usurpation of Carausius, the admiral of the Roman fleet stationed to protect the coasts of Britain from the ravages of Saxon pirates. The coins I have enumerated do not extend over a period of fifty years ; and the most numerous and most recent are those of Carausius. He was slain, after a reign of six years, by his lieutenant Allectus, who continued the usurpation about three years longer, when he succumbed to the Emperors Dioclesian and Maximianus. During this period, many parties would have become obnoxious to the Imperial Government, and like their successors about 418, would seek safety in flight. A few of the coins of the reigns of Tacitus, Probus, Maximianus, and Carausius are base, being formed of bronze, and afterwards silver-plated ; a practice not uncommon in the troubled times in which they were coined."

THE OLD BURY CONSTABLES.

Formerly, two constables were chosen annually from Bury, as the magistrates resided at Bolton, and the constables had to go to Bolton to attend all petty cases from this district. As the population of Bury increased, it was agreed that a Bolton magistrate should occasionally visit Bury, and hold his court at the Ship Inn, Bury Bridge. Some time

Rock & C? London. N? 6561.

1 Jan? 1877

New Bank. Bury. Lancashire.

afterwards, these petty sessions were removed to the Red Lion Inn, near the churchyard. Mr. Baker was the first superintendent appointed by Captain Woodford for the Bury district. When he left the force he was succeeded by Mr. Grove, who was not as popular or respected by the inhabitants as his predecessor. Mr. Burredge succeeded Mr. Grove, but he was discharged from the force by Captain Woodford for misconduct. Mr. Henshall was next appointed superintendent. Mr. A. Milne is now the superintendent, and has discharged the duties thereof for a considerable number of years.

OX ROASTING AT BURY OLD CROSS.

On the occasion of the visit of the Earl of Derby, the Right Hon. Charles James Fox, and other noblemen, to Bury, a stage was erected around the Old Cross. Below the stage was a large ox, stuck upon a strong spit, with its inside full of potatoes. The spit was turned round by a number of men, before two or three loads of coals, which were kindled into a large fire. Barrels of ale, and abundance of soft oat cakes, were put upon the stage. The ox was turned and roasted all night, and on the following day the inhabitants assembled in large companies. When the noble visitors arrived, they and the gentlemen of Bury walked round the stage and bowed to the surrounding multitude. When the visitors retired, the butcher and the people set at the half-roasted ox, tore it into pieces, and threw it, as well as the potatoes, oatcakes, and beer, up and down the Market-place. Some of the beer was drawn out of the barrels into large cans, and great numbers ran with cans full of beer up Dungeon-entry into the churchyard. Drinking, shouting, and all kinds of lewdness, was carried on all night, and it was far more than the two constables (Mr. Mangnall and Mr. Jacob Warburton) could do to keep the peace. Mr. Mangnall died a few days afterwards, and it was said that the day's revelry killed him. Mr. Warburton fell into a state of habitual drunkenness, spent his property, and died in poverty.

THE YATES AND PEEL FAMILY.

One hundred and three years ago—that is, about the year 1770—a low thatched public-house, that had apparently been built many years ago, bearing the name of the Black Bull, stood in the most frequented thoroughfare of the town of Blackburn. The sign-board hung creaking from a projecting post in front. The small diamond-shaped panes, divided into compartments by deep stone mullions, emitted on winter

E

evenings a pleasant light, that augured well to the tired rider or weary
pedestrian of the active hospitality and abundance that reigned within.
The mistress of this abode was, in appearance, as cheerful and comfortable looking as the mansion over which she presided.   Her countenance
was extremely mild and pleasing, her carriage upright and rather
dignified.   Her unvarying costume for " wharly," as workdays were
called in this part of Lancashire, was composed of a now almost obsolete
sort of worsted stuff for women's gowns, called camblet, or camlet,
which name is derived from a kind of cloth first brought from Palestine
by those who returned from the holy wars. This cloth was composed
of camel's hair, and often, as a sort of penance, formed the under
garment of persons residing in religious houses.

At the period now alluded to, and long before, such dresses for
females had invariably been made by men, the stiffness of the sewing
being supposed not to be adapted to fingers less strong ; and, notwithstanding the present great number of dressmakers, milliners, &c., who
sew by hand, and more recently by machinery, one hundred years ago it
was only in the great towns and cities that female sewers were to be
met with. The tailor measured the dame or mistress of the house for
her new gown, which often lasted half a lifetime when he visited the
place to receive orders for the " maister's " Sunday suit, or a new coat
and breeches for the lads; and many now living would smile were
they to behold what were then the habiliments of a boy just breeched.
Loosely-fitting single breasted coat and vest, often, amongst the wealthy,
of scarlet or some other gay colour, and richly embroidered ; breeches
of a strong, fine sort of jean or velvet, for the sons of the gentry ; and,
amongst the poorer, or more homely, the same garment of leather, or
homespun grey woollen cloth ; knitted stockings ; shoes with large
buckles; shirt frilled, and falling low at the breast; felt hat, with a
broad brim, and hair, straying in curls down the neck from under it, is
the appearance a boy would then present.

To return to the hostess of the Black Bull.   Her dress, of sober-
coloured camlet, was open in front, and when not covered by her
household apron of blue-checked linen, displayed as she moved a lining
of a thinnish sort of yellow worsted taffeta, which at the inner edge was
sewed on in deep Vandykes. The dress was full and flowing, and its
multitudinous plaits taxed the skill of the tailor to collect all into the
compass assigned for them. It was pointed at the waist, before and
behind.   The sleeves were tight, and only just turned at the elbow.
The dress was cut low round the bust, and, at the breast, the stays, of
very stiff material, projected somewhat outwards, to prevent pressure

upon the bosom ; and could any of our modern young ladies see a dress of their great, or great-great-grandmother's, they would acknowledge it to be much of a coquettish appearance. Calico, so named from Calicut, in the East Indies, from whence some of our supplies of cotton were derived, was then almost unknown in that region which, as time rolled on, was to hear the hum of millions of spindles, and the booming sound of the genii-like labours of machinery ; while its valleys should be intersected, and its hills cut through, by railways. A silent but mighty change in the textile industry of man was in progress. John Kay had given the first intimation of what ingenuity, guided by intelligence, could effect in relation to the old machines employed in the production of cloth. John Kay, of Bury—the town that was soon to witness the enterprise of the Peels, &c.; and their attention was directed to all then known in science or art that could be brought to bear upon the, to them, momentous question of improving and expediting the various processes in the manufacturing of cotton cloth or calico, especially as regarded its connection with printing. In 1769 and 1770 two great advantages had been gained, namely, in spinning cotton by rollers, and the invention of the spinning jenny, but still amongst the people English-woven cotton cloths were far from being in general use.

As regarded Mrs. Yates, her neckerchief, at that time no inconsiderable article of female attire, was of India muslin, brought low, and the ends crossed over the bosom. When young, her hair fell behind in flowing curls, but was now brought to the front of the brow, and turned back over a roll or pad. Her neat mob cap, with one border, was of linen, bleached to a snowy whiteness on the grass of their own croft, near the orchard ; and this same cap, as she advanced in years, was always covered with a black silk neckerchief, tied down closely just above the neatly-plaited border. This custom of wearing a neckerchief on the head, formerly so general in Lancashire and all our northern counties, was the only thing left to show the use of the coif and wimple by our Saxon and other foremothers ; and in relation to the person of Mrs. Yates, it formed her only head gear, when her presence was required not very far from home ; but when business, pleasure, or regular attendance to the Sabbath call of the old church bells, claimed a more particular covering, a hat of felt was worn, with a broad brim and low round crown, encircled with a quilled ribbon, and fastened, not with ties of ribbon, as at present, but by two silver or iron pins, six inches in length, with large heads or knobs. This custom arose and prevailed when ladies' hair was worn raised up in a large *toupie ;* and these pins were used by being drawn, one on each side, through the hat, and the hair also on the crown of the head.   This was all the fastening employed, and from the high position of the hat, it left the ears and low part of the face free and open to observation ; whilst the younger portion of those who wore them added to their gaiety of appearance by ribbons, which floated behind like streamers.   Bonnets of straw, as we now occasionally see them, were at that time entirely unknown in this part of England.   The Sunday or visiting dress of Mrs. Yates consisted of a thick sort of silk, or in summer weather of linen, printed in a large chintz pattern on a white ground, in which butterflies and flowers, of unknown and fantastic varieties, predominated.   This dress was made with a train, often tucked up through the pocket holes, and displayed the broad-striped dimity petticoat beneath, of a strength and stiffness before which the modern texture which bears that name would shrink into insignificance.   Long silk mittens were drawn up her arms to meet the gown near the elbow, and from her waist depended a rather voluminous apron of embroidered muslin.   Over her shoulders was thrown a scarf, or cloak, as it was styled, of black mode, trimmed with lace, of a price which would startle the present purchaser of a similar article ; but it should be remembered that then the best suit was seldom brought forth from the recesses of the dark carved oaken kist, or chest, except for church or occasions of great importance.

Such was the appearance in costume of a kind and good woman, Mrs. Yates, landlady of the Black Bull, in Blackburn, who moved respected and esteemed in her station of life ; and this lady was the maternal great-grandmother of the late Sir Robert Peel.

In the year 1770 a young man, mounted upon a horse, more remarkable for strength than elegance of shape or limb, was seen proceeding through the, at that time, strictly rural country, lying to the south of Blackburn.   Although young, being only twenty years of age, his countenance, of a heavy cast, was remarkable for its thoughtful, solid expression ; and an intelligent observer would have thought that its owner possessed good powers of observation and reflection, and be inclined to believe that he would do nothing without mature considera-tion.   But when once a course of action was resolved upon, it must be a weighty influence indeed that could cause him to alter his plans.   His head was large, his forehead broad, and his whole bearing indicative of the appearance which, in after years took the form of massiveness rather than corpulence.   His attire was neither costly nor elaborate, being remarkable rather for inattention to personal appearance than the contrary.   His dark brown hair fell loosely over the collar of his widely-fitting riding coat, and his blue eyes had a look of steadiness and good-nature that impressed the beholder in his favour. Altogether, ho might be pronounced for what he was, the son of a country yeoman, or small landowner in easy circumstances.

In the early morning he had left his father's home, a farm which had been long in the family's possession, and derived its name from them, and where the labours of the loom alternated with the pursuits of husbandry and the care of cattle. His route had been devious, over a tract of country at that time of considerable difficulty to horsemen. Three days previously, his nag had been in a contrary, or northerly direction, but the object of his journey, which was the same as at present, had not been attained. Before the glittering dew was exhaled from the pastures and moorlands, he had visited Darwen and Moulden Water; and travelling westward, had traversed the country lying extended in front of the rising ground, surmounted by the ancient tower belonging to the Hoghton family. On arriving at the little hamlet of Brinscall, which then consisted of only two or three neighbouring farms, he surveyed the capabilities of the ground with attention; his observation being, in every instance, particularly directed to the numerous springs and brooks with which the country adjacent to, or lying on the slopes of the long line of the Lancashire hills abounds. To the numerous streams which take their rise in this ridge of hills, along with the coal mines of the same district, the lead which this county has taken in the great branches of manufacturing industry may, in a great means, be ascribed.

Passing onwards, he once more pursued a southerly direction. Along the banks of pleasant rivulets, through the green and shady coppice, up the stern ascent of the Nabb, and the solitary gray heights, and across the high grounds of Anglezark, with its ancient Saxon appellation; almost all at that time unenclosed, even by the rude, loosely-built gray stone fences by which they are at present partly intersected. Below the elevation he traversed lay Hartwood Green—a name suggestive of a period when the deer roved free over these wild bleak moors, cropping the scanty herbage, or, from the high eminences, snuffing the summer gale, redolent with purity and fragrance.

Over our traveller's head the noonday sun was beaming in unclouded brilliancy, as he stopped to refresh himself and his horse in the pleasant vale of Horwich. Twenty-five years before the whole country side had rung with alarm at the advance, through this part of Lancashire, of the Highland army under Prince Charles; but the mission of the solitary equestrian was destined to work as great a revolution, in another form, as that attempted by Charles Stuart. Old Rivington, in hoary majesty, frowned above, whose beacon-light had often been kindled to give the alarm to the watchers on other hills, during the troubled period of the civil wars. Proceeding onwards, he turned across the moors, then rarely trodden, in the direction of the place which now bears the name of Belmont; thence, through the ancient village of Bradshaw; and, after diverging to several rather unfrequented places lying around, the setting sun of a long summer's day beheld him slowly proceeding across Cockey Moor, on the road to Bury.

At that time the road between Bury and Bolton lay across Cockey Moor, by Ainsworth Hall, and was little better than a bridle-path, carts not being then much in use; and the only thing that could be considered an indication of traffic between the two towns, with the exception of wandering pedlars, who carried frames resembling camp-stools, on which they exhibited their wares when an opportunity offered of displaying them to advantage, was the appearance of a long string of pack-horses, the foremost being the bell-horse, with a collar of musically-sounding bells round his neck, by whose tinklings the movements of his followers were regulated, and also gave notice of their approach—a matter of some moment in places where the road was so narrow as scarcely to allow room to pass them. The bales which these pedlars and pack-horses generally carried on their route through Cumberland and Westmorland, contained chiefly Scotch linen and other coarse goods, on the sale of which they purchased the woollen cloths of Yorkshire, and at Manchester a miscellaneous stock, consisting chiefly of gay-coloured shawls and neckerchiefs, Nottingham hosiery, and Coventry ribbons. The manufacture of checked and corded muslins and fine ginghams was attempted at Chorley as early as 1665. That town afterwards became famous for these goods, and they soon formed a considerable portion of the pedlar's pack. A number of such horses as these were now before the young traveller, as he arrived at the entrance of Cockey Moor lane, leading in the direction of Bury.

The line of pack-horses could be descried, stretching down the road, along whose sides the bramble and honeysuckle shot forth their long branches, covering rich blossoms, which filled the dewy air with sweetness, and he slacked the rein of his weary horse, and followed in their rear, until emerging into the Smithy Lane, he passed them at as sharp a trot as his horse was capable of, calling the attention of the smith from the forge, in his rudely constructed place of labour, who cast a workmanlike glance at the horse in passing, and, no doubt, wished it had required his aid. Some years later, at this same forge, a smith n a fit of madness, killed his child by dashing its head repeatedly against the anvil.   And now the horse is cooling its feet in passing through the mouth of the brook that here entered the river—Brook's Mouth, as its name indicates—and the next moment is clattering over the bridge, and up Bury Lane, at that time almost entirely bordered by hedgerows, except in places where some ancient thatched cottages presented their fronts or gables to the road.   This was the termination of his journey ; and on entering the front of the low stone-built inn, bearing the sign of the Hope and Anchor, he received the respectful greetings of the landlord, and entered the house to take up his abode for the night, before proceeding with the investigations which had brought him into this part of the country.   The Hope and Anchor seemed then a much more substantial building than any of the houses in its immediate neighbourhood, and was kept by an honest childless couple, named George and Betty Wood.

It was Sir Robert Peel, the future baronet, printer, and statesman, and whose gains, during the course of his life, amounted to millions, who took up his abode on the evening last mentioned, at the roadside inn of the old Hope and Anchor.   This house was, latterly, the Bury Dispensary.   Most of the houses and buildings which then constituted the town were situated at the top of Bury Lane, in the immediate neighbourhood of the Church, and usually designated as " up the street."

Printing which, for some time after becoming known in England, was confined to linen and foreign muslins, was first introduced into Lanca-shire by Messrs. Clayton, of Clayton Green, or Bamber Bridge, near Preston, in the year 1764 ; and their success was considerable, though ultimately surpassed by that of the Peels.   This enterprise of printing at Bamber Bridge made much talk among country people, who frequently got pieces of their own weaving printed at the works belonging to the Claytons.   This was the case of the Peels, of Peel Close, or Fold, near Blackburn.   They had looms fixed at one end of the low-ceiled, but roomy " housepart," as the principal apartment for the family was called ; and wove, during the year, a tolerable quantity of home-carded and spun woollen cloth, for family use, which was afterwards bleached on the grass.   In the south-eastern districts of Lancashire, large looms for woollen weaving, were more in use ; but in either case, the men of the household, as well as the women, were often employed in the labours of the loom, especially at those seasons when the weather prevented them from pursuing their work in the fields. Old women or girls generally carded the wool ; and the verse of an old song in use at that time, says :—

Here comes the pedlar with his pack,
Peg jumped off the card-stock in a crack;
He comes, he says, "My pretty lass,
Hast thou provided me that brass?"

Young Peel rose early in the morning following his arrival at the Hope
and Anchor; and, after making a few inquiries from the host as to the
low ground lying extended in the rear of the inn, and stretching far into
the distance along the banks of the Irwell, he set out upon the business
that had brought him to Bury, which was to survey the capabilities of
the site in question for the establishment of a printworks.   It was for
this purpose he had visited each place that seemed to combine the
requisites he sought along the track of his previous journey, in order to
examine and ascertain which possessed the most advantageous position,
especially as regarded the supply of water in its immediate neighbourhood.
The young man stood at the top of the brow that overlooked a considerable
portion of the land below, upon which their works were soon to be
erected.   Its appearance pleased him.   In front, down the short but
rather rugged descent, lay the ancient mill.   The miller was a man
well-to-do ; for besides the mill, he owned a considerable portion of land.
The kiln, where the grain for the mill was dried, stood higher up in the
lane, a little before the commencement of what was known as the
"paddle wall."   This wall served as a parapet to the road on this side ;
for, without it, the bank fell ruggedly and abruptly down to the fields
beneath.   The miller's house was situated on the rising ground above
the mill, towards the lane, and for the convenience of the millers who
had ever held the place, a path had been formed down the grassy bank,
in the rear.   Even at that time the dwelling was near a century and a
half old.   It was extremely rude in the internal construction, but of good
strength, the beams employed consisting of trunks of trees, not planed,
being used simply as they had been felled in the woods, except that the
branches were lopped away ; though, in one instance, from a huge beam
overhead, a single arm, that had been suffered to remain, protruded its
naked and skeleton-like limb, and was used by the family as a convenient
rod, from which might be suspended many an implement of labour, when
not immediately required for use.   Blocks of rough-hewn stone formed
the walls, though some of the inner partitions consisted of wattled
wicker-work, covered with clay mixed with broken straw.   There were
no upper rooms, the limited skill of the architect not permitting their
construction ; for, in increased height, the rude and ponderous materials
would have required as much support as they gave, so the "chambers,"
as the sleeping rooms were called, were on the ground floor.   In many
of the older dwellings of the people of Lancashire at the time, there was

only a sort of loft over the house part. It would be open overhead to the beams and thatch, lighted by a little window deep set in the wall of the gable end, or in the thatch; and so low, that it was only in the centre of the floor a person could stand upright. Access was, in most instances, gained either by a ladder inside, or steps of solid blocks of stone outside. Some of these outside staircases were so massive, that a modern builder could have made the same quantity of stone answer the purpose several times over. Down the capacious chimney of the miller's house—where often hung a dozen flitches to season in the smoke of the fire beneath— the light of day fell on the ample hearth. Coal, then, was very far from being so generally obtainable as at present; besides, wood in the neighbourhood was rather plentiful, and near at hand. The energies of steam had not yet been called forth to dive into the bowels of the earth, to bring its treasures to the surface, and increase the comforts of the people. The old mill has given its name to the brow, but the ancient building disappeared long ago, to make room for another erection. On the other side of the brow leading to the mill stood another cottage or two, fronting the lane; and at the end of Doctor's-lane was a gate, from which a wide and sunny path led, between well-kept hedgerows, to the once pleasant stone-built mansion, that lay immediately at the top of the walk. The lady who, in 1756, resided here for the first, and for many years the only person who kept a carriage in Bury; her doing so was a proof of consequence, for they were then extremely rare, sedan chairs being in use; and great was the wonder of the dwellers in the lane, and " up the street," when Madam's coach, after emerging from the seldom-opened gateway, bore her along, to pay a visit of ceremony or friendship in Bury or its neighbourhood. About one hundred and twenty-five years since there was not a house but this along that part of Bury, reaching from the bridge to the upper end of Bury-lane, in the town; and the residence of " Madam," as she was always styled, was situate entirely alone in the fields, which stretched far behind and on either hand. The gardens and enclosures for fruit trees belonging to the house were old-fashioned, but kept in good order, and were then deemed rather extensive. Her nearest neighbours, in rank approaching to herself, were the residents of Chamber Hall, the front part of which was taken down in 1786-87, and upon the site the present edifice of that name is erected; a very different looking structure to its predecessor.

The young traveller, as before stated, stood on Mill Brow, and after surveying the ground lying extended beyond, set off at a quick pace to explore it more nearly. Although the business in which he was about to venture, and in which the Messrs. Claytons had led the way in

Lancashire, was not familiar to him, yet his sound judgment and previous observations enabled him at once to perceive the capabilities of the locality now presented to his view. The name of the "Ground" was given to it in the first instance, and it has retained the appellation under all changes. In fifteen or twenty years after its establishment, Bury Ground had attained a celebrity scarcely calculated upon by its masters, and the early history of its productions will ever be remarkable in the annals of the printed calico trade in England. No sooner was the question settled in the mind of Mr. Peel as to the eligibility of the site in question, than, after noting down its most remarkable features, he returned home to communicate the result of his observations to his father, to whose foresight and sagacity the son was first and principally indebted, as regarded the full and practical development of the idea of embarking in a business almost unknown, and entirely different to their previous pursuits. The idea of printing had first been started from their having a proof of the great profits realised in the business, by getting a piece of cloth, spoiled in the weaving, printed for them as handkerchiefs by the Messrs. Claytons, which handkerchiefs they readily disposed of, at a good profit, amongst their friends.

But another person was also a sharer in these plans. This was Mr. William Yates, the son of the hostess of the Black Bull, previously referred to. He was considerably older than the younger Mr. Peel, and had at his command the disposal of the property his parents had already acquired; though it has been said that the sum used at first to commence the works was only £500. Let this be as it may, it is certain that, after embarking, it did not long remain at so low a quotation, and its increase could soon be reckoned by tens. As it was an object to establish as early as possible, the workplaces at first consisted mostly of wooden sheds, or rooms ; these, as circumstances offered, were replaced by more substantial erections, but fire often caused a change in the material of their structure much sooner than would else have happened. In some instances, no doubt, these fires arose from carelessness, at a time when such things were not so well regulated as at present; but after, from the great heat maintained in buildings not always suited to the purpose, it was extremely difficult to prevent their recurrence ; and from 1770, the date of the commencement of printing at Bury, to past 1800, the workpeople who had retired for the night to their homes in the town or the neighbourhood, would be dismayed by the glaring reflection of light in the sky, that told that a fire was raging in some of the numerous workshops at the Ground.

It is to the circumstance of building upon no uniform plan, but erecting them near, or at a distance, just as occasion required, that the straggling far-extended area of the Bury works must be attributed. One of the largest drying-houses, heated by stoves, was burnt down about 1780. From the great quantity of candles used to work by on the winter evenings, the workshop windows had all the effect of an illumination. Gas was not then dreamt of, and oil was too expensive, except in some cases.

The first partners were Robert Peel, William Yates, before-mentioned, and soon afterwards Mr. Tipping. The connection with them of the latter was not, however, of very long duration; but still the names of Peel, Yates, and Tipping were widely known, from the excellence and variety of the work produced. The number of partners was afterwards, at such times as appeared advisable, increased to six—all men of great talent and aptitude for business; and the designation at this time was "Peels, Yates's, Halliwell, and Warren," the individuals constituting the firm being Robert Peel, William Yates; Edmund Yates, of Bury, eldest son of the preceding; James Halliwell, of Manchester; Henry Warren, of Bury; Robert Peel (commonly called Captain Peel, and cousin of the first-mentioned Robert Peel), of Ardwick, Manchester; and (on the withdrawal of William Yates) Thomas Yates, of Bury, brother to Edmund Yates. Mr. Thomas Yates, before entering as a partner, served a regular apprenticeship in the drawing-shop on the Ground. Jonathan, the brother of Mr. Peel, was in business for himself, as a printer, at Church Bank, near Accrington.

In three years after commencing printing, that is, in 1773, the firm embarked in the cotton manufacture; and this affords proof of the facility with which money was then made. They soon had, in the neighbourhood around Bury, what were then considered immense establishments, as the Radcliffe Mill, Makin Mill, Hinds, The Burrs, White Ash, and Summerseat; and employed weavers in Yorkshire and over a large portion of North and East Lancashire. They had also a printworks—afterwards purchased by Messrs. Grant—at Ramsbottom, in connection with the works at Bury; and a bleaching and chemical works situated between Bury and Radcliffe; besides which, the extensive grounds and crofts around their printing establishment, and in front of Chamber Hall, to the extent of many acres, were covered with pieces stretched to bleach. To persons unaccustomed to the sight of these white fabrics in great numbers side by side, and length by length, overspreading and completely hiding the green grass, they have all the effect at a distance, especially in sunlight, of extensive and brilliant sheets of water. Many little boys were employed, whose duty it was to peg these pieces to the ground at each end, and afterwards pin them together, side by side, to stretch and expose the surface to the sun and air. Our improvements in chemistry have now almost entirely superseded this slow and tedious process of grass bleaching, which, besides being inconvenient was also expensive, from the great surface of grass land required for the purpose.

It was at the bleachworks mentioned, that in the winter, about the year 1803, several pieces had, at times, been missed from the "dryhouse," and the thief could not be discovered, at least no thief in a human form, for many were the stories afloat of a hideous monster having been seen, by different persons, in the dead of the night, prowling around the place. The descriptions of the form were various, but all agreed it was an evil spirit in the form of a beast. That it was no *real* beast, was, in their opinion, sufficiently proved by the unearthly artifices wherewith it eluded their nearer approach, though, no doubt, its escape was as often to be attributed to the cowardice of the watchers as to any other cause. Many were of opinion that it was the famous Radcliffe "shag," which, after a rest, was come to revisit once more the scene of some former exploit. Be this as it may, after some consultation, a strong, robust man, a returned soldier, who declared he feared neither man nor devil, was appointed in the room of the former watchman. He took his station behind a pile of pieces, in a corner of the drying house, which was easily entered. It was a fine, frosty night, and any sound around the place was distinctly audible. A little after twelve o'clock the barking of a dog was heard, which gradually approached nearer. This was interpreted as a contrivance to ascertain if any dogs had been placed upon the premises, as in that case they would reply with an answering bark. After awhile shuffling movements were heard outside, as if some awkward animal prowling around in search of an entrance ; and shortly, some fastenings were removed, and, as the night was clear and bright, sufficient light was admitted through the wooden bars forming the walls of the drying-house, for the sentinel distinguished an animal of large size moving on all-fours about the floor. But when the same animal proceeded to select a number of pieces, and fasten them into a bundle, preparatory to carrying them away, the watchman was no longer in doubt as to the spirituality of the intruder. He had a loaded gun, but thought it would be a more merciful and glorious capture to conquer the ghost without resorting to its aid. Accordingly, spying a favourable opportunity, he sprang upon the nocturnal visitant, who was totally unprepared for a surprise from such a quarter ; and, being a powerful man, after a little resistance, succeeded in securely tying the limbs of the thief with the very pieces he had appropriated as plunder. On examination, the disguise was found to consist of the skin of a sheep and a bull's hide, the horns and tail of the latter being retained to assist in striking fear into the hearts of the beholders. It was thought the idea of stealing the pieces originated from first wearing the disguise in a frolic to frighten the country folks ; for the delinquent proved to be a poor, weakly, ill-fed weaver, in the neighbourhood ; and, after terrifying him, with a view to prevent his again resorting to so nefarious a means of living, consideration of his poverty, and, in other respects, harmless mode of life, induced the masters to pardon the offence.

In 1775, an improved system of carding was brought out by the firm, but cotton cloths were still very expensive. In 1776 the price of common-fine calico pieces, manufactured by Thomas Duxbury, of Rishton, near Blackburn, for Jonathan Peel, of Church Bank, was £2. 14s. each. In 1829, pieces of the same description sold for 6s. each. The year 1779 saw the mule jenny brought into operation. So rapid a growth of business at Bury, &c., caused for many years a large influx of people into this part of Lancashire ; and, in many instances, persons from opposite sides of the kingdom were associated in the same work. Many people were taught employments which they now saw for the first time ; for in the earlier stages of the printing business, comparatively few were acquainted with the various processes. As regards the cotton mills, children of both sexes were procured from the London workhouses in large numbers, and trained for the labour required. They were well treated, every consistent regulation for their comfort being made by their masters.

A 'prentice house for boarding the children was opened at Radcliffe, and another at Hinds, each under the superintendence of a "mistress," strict attention being paid to their health, cleanliness, and clothing. The apprentices, on first coming from London, often seemed a singular set of little folks, many of them wearing the peculiar garb of the charitable houses from whence they had come; and at first forming a peculiarity in the places of labour to which they were attached, mostly from the difference in their speech to the little rustics of Lancashire, to whom they were subjects of raillery, and who did not spare "nicknames" for them. They were some days and nights on their journey northwards, and travelled in a large covered carrier's waggon, until, on arriving at Bury, they were at once consigned to the person appointed to receive and take care of them. One of the boys thus brought down bore the name of Alphonso Adolphus M'Gelland Hill, and afterwards proved either weak in intellect or of very eccentric notions. He wrote many verses, for which he could never find a publisher ; and believed himself to have discovered the principle of perpetual motion, though his poverty, he said, prevented him from deriving any benefit from it.

CHAPTER IV.

Conduct and Character of Mr. Peel—Early Patterns and Prints—Pencillers—Female Designers—Pinners—Engraving—Beggars—Long Jack o' Booth—Mr. Yates—An Ounce of Tobacco—Sir Robert's Infancy—Mrs. Peel—Confidence between Parents and Children—Boyish Sports and Recreations—Handsome Present to the Government—The Exportation of Machinery, &c,—The Bury Loyal Association of Volunteers—Presentation of Colours to the Volunteers—Speeches of Lady Clarke and Lieutenant-Colonel Peel—Volunteer Field Days—Names from the old " Roll Call "—An old Volunteer Song.

Mr. Peel was a man of large sympathies and judicious benevolence; and it was his pride to see his people comfortable and happy. To this, no doubt, may in some measure be attributed the great number of excellent, trustworthy persons in his service, many of whom have since risen to eminence and wealth in the county. So long as their establishment was in a moderate compass, he personally exercised a great deal of superintendence about the works; and when the great lodge (reservoir) was in formation actually assisted to dig some part of it himself—perhaps to expedite the workmen; for, whatever was in progress, seemed as if it could scarcely be completed fast enough for the requirements of the business. And "Mr. Edmund" would walk round and say to the spadesmen, not "navvies," "Come, come, lads! what are ye doing? Come, get on, lads!" With all this energy and despatch, over-hours were, at that time, almost unknown. The people worked hard during the regular hours of labour, and after that the Ground was quiet, except when the carts or waggons came in, heavily laden with cotton, drugs, and other stores, which they brought back in place of piles of printed pieces taken to Manchester in the morning. For many years after the commencement of the works at Bury, there was no " drawing-shop," in the general sense of the term; their first, and for some time only, pattern designer, or drawer, from London, occupying a small room set apart for him,—soon afterwards burnt down, with all the buildings adjoining,—near what was afterwards known as " Old Frank's place;" many of the workshops on the Ground being distinguished by the names of those who worked in them, some retaining the name long after the original occupier had left it. Besides other articles of moment consumed in this fire, were the designer's favourite china cup, knife, fork, and silver spoon; for he took his meals "all alone" in his neat and pleasant little workroom; and the quietness and elegance of his manners impressed all who knew him in his favour; a proof of which is shown in his being addressed by the title of "Mr.," such a mark of respect being then observed to no other person on the works with the exception of the masters themselves.

The simplicity, and stiff, awkward appearance of some of the earliest patterns designed and used at the Ground would now excite a smile, and are such, both as regards position and colouring, as the merest tyro in the art would now scarcely think of executing. Yet these things sold high; and for one description of work alone there was, for many years, a regular demand of 20,000, the profit on each piece being one guinea clear. The firm early began a foreign trade, and kept a shipping warehouse in Liverpool. It was the chintzes of Peels and Yates's, amongst others, that, previous to the League of Boston, the good citizens of the city prohibited their wives and daughters from wearing; and many American ladies, in the height of their enthusiasm for the public cause, burnt their stock of English printed gowns, rather than wear an article of British taxation. The style of the earlier patterns continued the same, almost invariably, from year to year; the high price readily obtained for them making it not so strictly essential to obtain newer, richer, or more original designs. The patterns generally consisted of leaves, variously disposed, some circles, pippins, clubs, dice, diamonds, and spots, and flower heads of a daisy or buttercup form, which mostly presented, not a delicate profile view, but, disposed over the calico, stared the beholder full in the face—what are called " set " patterns, trails, &c., not being then in use; while, on the "furnitures," some fully opened-sunflowers were five inches across, and the thorns of rose stalks most palpably displayed, as if the artist conceived that was very true to nature. But, notwithstanding the inferiority of the patterns, the price of the garment piece of goods, of the above description, containing twenty-eight yards, was from £4 to £5, or 3s. to 3s. 6d. a yard, and even more. Many years later, the very commonest print possible to purchase was 1s. 6d. a yard; and down to 1810, good prints of one or two colours only, on a white ground, were 2s. 6d. or higher, muslins 3s. 6d. per yard, and printed furnitures the same price.

Until a regular supply of calico could be procured, much of the fine printing was on linen, of rather coarse texture; and it was the very limited supply they were able to obtain of this material that principally directed the attention of those who could estimate the capabilities of the printing trade, to the much more extensive manufacture of cotton into calico. Prints, at first, received from the hands of the printer only an impression from the block, or one colour, which was generally an outline of the object, if more colours were to be laid on. This laying on of colours was done by women, of whom a large body were maintained called "pencillers;" and long ranges of workshops were set apart for their use, as those of Peel-street and New-street, now divided into dwellings, but which were built for pencilling shops, and mistresses appointed over them. The number of pencillers was very great, and the work most delicate and beautiful, as may be seen upon an inspection of any of the best old pieces of print so treated. One then considered very costly and beautiful was a chintz pattern, upon a white ground, the outline of white purple was laid on by the block, the remaining colours, two greens, two reds, two blues, a drab, and a yellow, being pencilled upon the cloth by the women ; and, it must be remembered, that every single leaf or object all over the work, had to be separately touched with a pencil of the colour required. Thus, it will be found, the surface of the cloth required passing over nine times previous to the completion of the pattern. Sometimes, in a great press of business, pencilling was given out, to be done at home, apart from the works ; but this was rather inconvenient, on account of the pieces having to be drawn upwards from the work-table, for the colours to dry. In the shops, each woman had the piece suspended before her, with a supply of hair pencils, of different degrees of fineness, according to the size of the figure or object to be touched, and saucers containing colours—of red, green, blue, yellow, &c., of each variety of shade, according to the pattern required. When the outline only required filling up with the appointed tint, the work was easily and expeditiously performed, and a good workwoman might sometimes earn £2 a week. In this state of things there was no lack of suitors, and a young woman had no more to do than to signify whom she would choose.

A number of females were employed also at Bury Ground as " block pinners," and apprentices were received regularly for the business, which consisted in inserting small lengths of brass wire, or pins, of different degrees of fineness, into a wooden block, to form the pattern required, which was delineated upon the block by a " putter-on," or dresser. Sometimes, rollers of lead or boxwood were used to receive the pinning pattern, but from the hardness of the metal or wood, these were more difficult than the common block, whose surface was generally plane tree. A block, of an extra size, contained no less than 60,000 pins. The smaller sizes of pins were numbered as " dust," or "O," from their fineness.

F

The character of Mr. Peel was, like his appearance, commanding and impressive. His walk, when in the prime of manhood, was slow, dignified, and majestic. His dress was of good material, but worn in a careless and slovenly manner, as if it occupied little share of his attention. His hands were often crossed behind his back, under his coat; and, unless engaged in conversation, his attention and thoughts appeared almost always pre-occupied. He was a man whom no one would venture lightly to accost, nor upon a trifling subject. Simplicity of manners pleased him, but worthlessness was soon detected; and his strict justice was known and trusted in by all. Though he scarcely appeared to notice many of the people in his employment, yet circumstances often occurred which proved that their individual interests and welfare were objects of consideration with him; and so great an impression did the favourable word or opinion of Mr. Peel make upon any one happy enough to obtain it, that after a lapse of fifty or sixty years, the very words he has used upon such occasions have been repeated with tears by those to whom he had then spoken in terms of commendation. He was deeply conscious of the responsibility of his situation as a master, controlling the livelihood and comfort of a number of persons greater than had hitherto been brought together as the workpeople of one firm. His kindness to children was great; but it was not always that he had leisure to observe these little folks, from being often busily engaged. One day, during a heavy thunderstorm, he overtook a group of children, bewildered with fear, and with gentle words drew them towards him; and although the rain was fast falling, went some little distance out of his way to see the terrified children safe to their parents' door.

Mr. William Yates, and his son Edmund, were both men of a dignified appearance and nature, but not approaching to the impressiveness of manner which characterised Mr. Peel; and so much more did his presence inspire awe, that although his benevolence and kindness were widely known and appreciated, yet any of the workpeople and others could use more freedom in offering a remonstrance or soliciting a favour from old Mr. Yates or Mr. Edmund. So freely did some of the older workpeople, in his absence, speak of Mr. Yates, that some of them did not scruple to name him as "Billy fro' th' Bull," in allusion to the inn his parents had kept at Blackburn. They were often plagued with importunate beggars, many of whom, from long standing, seemed to consider themselves as privileged beings. It should be remembered that at that time closed gates, and such notices at places of employment as "No road," or "No admittance except on business," were unknown and unthought of; and at Bury, persons entered and moved freely about the extensive works. Consequently, beggars, often in numbers, made their way upon the ground towards the counting-house whenever it appeared probable they could meet with the masters. One of these individuals was long an annoyance to Mr. Edmund, though he continued to tolerate him. He was a tall, gaunt man, of rather imbecile intellect, known by the name of Long Jack o' Booth, and each time he begged a donation he promised it should be the last. Mr. Edmund, when he again perceived the man, would pretend to put himself in a towering passion, and exclaim, " Jack! Jack! art thou here again ? "—at which, with all humility, Jack would say, " Bless yo', Mesthur Edmun', iv ye'll gi' meh a shillin' this toim, awl non come again, yo'll see ;" which promise was only kept so long as Jack saw no opportunity of asking for another. There was often great good humour in these encounters, and on one occasion, when an old man thought his work deserved a little more remuneration, he placed himself in Mr. Yates's way, resolved to crave the favour of some little addition; but, in the flutter of his spirits at speaking with " th' maister," he transposed the order of his request, and, instead of asking for " moor wage for his work," solicited to have " moor work for his wage." Mr. Yates perceived the mistake before the poor man himself did, and laughingly told him his request should be complied with. However, the change was such as the aged labourer wished.

When any of the boys employed on the ground performed a service for Mr. Yates, he would give him a shilling, *if he happened to have one*, and, if not, would tell the lad to remind him of it, *next time*, to do which, however, required more courage than the poor lads were able to muster; and, in this manner, many of them had large outstanding accounts against " th' owd maister," which were destined never to be settled. On one occasion, he wished for a messenger to take a note to Mrs. Haworth, in the Square, and the boy was told to take it, and " bring an answer back ; " but, from the rapidity of Mr. Yates's utterance, the order was understood to be " bring an ounce o' 'bacco back." The Square was reached, and the note presented to the servant, who was informed that " it was for her mistress, and she must send an ounce o' 'bacco back." The astonished girl went to acquaint Mrs. Haworth with this unusual demand, and that lady herself came to interrogate the messenger, but to all her inquiries, she only received the oft-repeated information, " that Mr. Yates had ordered him to bring the note, and take an ounce o' 'bacco back." " I cannot understand this," said Mrs. Haworth ; " but, at all events, give him what he requires, and I will see Mr. Yates afterwards." The boy, who had been uneasy at all this questioning, and was afraid to present himself before Mr. Yates with his errand unperformed, felt rejoiced at this determination—although he began to feel some misgivings as to his own correctness—and hurried back to the Ground. Appearing before the gentleman who had sent him, he gravely presented the tobacco. Mr. Yates received it with surprise, and after examining it, asked whence and why it came. "Why, sir, you told me to give the note, and bring some 'baccy back." After a little reflection, the misapprehension was evident, and "th' maister," Mr. Yates, laughing heartily, made his way to the other members of the firm, to relate the adventure, in corroboration of which he produced the unlucky ounce of tobacco.

Although much consideration, from the moment of his birth, was bestowed upon the young heir of the Peel family, it is not left on record that he differed much from any other of the many hundred thousand wonderful and beautiful children born to doting papas and mammas. What, perhaps, gave him a little more importance was that some time elapsed between the births of the first two children (daughters) and that of Robert, the third child; and there was more of distance between Elizabeth—Mrs. Cockburn—and her brother Robert, than was the case with any of the eight children who succeeded.

Mr. and Mrs. Peel were, as regards the treatment of their young family, among what might be termed the most sensible of parents. Mrs. Peel was a true example of a noble-hearted English mother and matron ; and it is a happy remembrance for those who have seen her at Chamber Hall, in the midst of her children, all of whom in their infancy received their natural nourishment from her own breast. Robert was a stout, healthy boy, as active and as fond of play as any other boy would be possessing the same advantages, and surrounded by the same happy circumstances. Mr. Peel was a high-minded man, and most excellent father. Robert was much with his parents, being, even in boyhood, very often the associate of his father ; and, from the peculiar nature of each, the most intimate confidence and friendship subsisted, without, in the least, breaking up the respect and filial reverence the one should entertain towards the other. Accustomed, on all occasions, to apply to his parents, or grandfather, Mr. Yates, for advice or assistance on any doubtful point or emergency, he was much in the habit, when quite young, of being their associate at home ; and, if appealed to, he would give his opinion with a judgment and reason that, even so early marked the depth and comprehensiveness of his mind. But Robert Peel, although a studious boy and naturally of a quiet, retiring disposition, was, nevertheless, at Bury, no laggard in his play, as many a well-contested game at bandy-cad, or hockey, and football, in the field before Chamber Hall, bore witness. Nothing pleased his grandfather more than to join him in his sport ; and when coming across the croft from the works, so soon as he caught sight of the juvenile players he would exclaim—loudly enough, in order to make himself heard—" Come hither, Bob! give me thy football, let's have a kick ! " And much would the old gentleman enjoy the fun for a while, for he was an excellent football player, and could send the ball higher and further than many younger men were able to do. Mr. Yates encouraged the efforts of William and Edmund to join in the play with great glee, and laughed merrily to watch the attempts of the youngsters. Sometimes he would send a favoured lad or two from the Ground to share with his grandsons in the pleasure of this hardy and healthy amusement ; and many such instances of kindness and consideration to poor lads employed upon the Ground have been recorded by persons who worked upon the spot. One of the most animated sights it was possible to see was when, in winter, the great lodge was frozen over, and crowded " i' th' bell-hour" at noon, or in the evening, with hundreds of men and boys, sliding, skating, or snowballing ; while Mr. Yates, standing by, would be pleased at the diversion, and encourage them in their well-contested matches. This sight, to a stranger, would convey some idea of the populousness of the workshops, and the great number of people employed.

Robert, William, and Edmund often went from the Hall over the croft to their grandfather, in the counting-house, especially when they required his influence or mediation in any matter. But, upon one occasion, this was insufficient to save one of the younger of these from punishment by his father, for a juvenile delinquency, and the counting-house was the scene of its administration. The fault was, that the boy had disposed of a number of beautiful and favourite doves without permission.

In 1797, Messrs. Peel and Yates contributed £10,000 sterling to the Government, in aid of the national embarrassment, which was then caused by the stoppage of the Bank of England. A subscription for the same purpose was also got up for such of their workpeople and friends as chose to contribute.

In 1782, an Act was passed which prohibited " artificers in printing calicoes, muslins, or linens, from leaving the country," and the " making of implements for exportation used in their manufacture," or for printing purposes, was forbidden. By this Act the interests of Robert Peel were benefited perhaps more than those of any other person in the kingdom, because his business in these departments was the largest then known. There can be no doubt that these Acts were passed in a spirit of jealousy towards, and had particular reference to, the Republic of the United

States, which was at that time fast rising into note. Considerable feeling had previously been manifested towards the Republic, indeed, to such an extent that prints from England had been sent back from Boston, which was the principal seaport and maritime emporium of the British colonies, " Peel's chintzes " being particularly noticed.

In 1798, Messrs. Peel and Yates announced their intention of forming a volunteer corps, to consist of people in their employment, and any others who might be inclined to serve. This opportunity for obtaining drills and playing at soldiers was eagerly taken advantage of both by middle-aged and even elderly men. To witness the jovial good humour and alacrity with which the quickly formed bodies of volunteers entered upon the duties of their new profession of arms, it would not have been concluded that the occasion of their enrolment was a very terrible one. There was more fun bandied about, more jokes cracked and played, and more incentives to laughter than else might have been the case during the many years as the months they were thus occupied. No one could, at first, say that his military duties sat lightly upon him ; and many who thought to carry it off quite pompously unwittingly found themselves voted as members of the awkward squad by the rigid disciplinarian who had the task of reducing their limbs and movements to the required formality. Then there was the appointment of sergeants, adjutants, and other officers, and the particular days for donning the new accoutrements and exercising made a glorious holiday. When the number of men to be enrolled was ascertained, Mr. Peel sent orders for the necessary implements, adornments, and coverings wherewith his warriors should encase their doughty limbs ; and soon the men of Birmingham and Sheffield, as well as more peaceable artisans, were set to work in their behalf. During the early part of the proceedings the excitement upon the hitherto peaceful Print Ground was tremendous. Then were conveyed, from one shop to another, mysterious instuctions, dark hints and surmises, also rumours to the effect that some one or other had seen unwonted bales arrivè that were not publicly opened in the warehouse as usual, but submitted to the inspection of " the mesturs " and a few others, in some place apart. Then strange legends got abroad that dangling sabres, flashing swords, had been seen ; guns, bayonets, buckles, straps, gloves, belts, in bewildering quantities ; red coats, and whole boxes of feathers, supplemented by the military cap or hat of the day ; sword-knots, sashes, pipeclay ; in short, all that could be thought of to complete the equipment of a soldier and transform the hitherto peaceful and soberly-clad civilian of Bury and its Printworks into a fierce-looking, sabretached hero. Despite much good-humoured criticism, the men and officers looked well in the regimental full dress ; the knowledge of which seemed to administer pretty strongly to the owner's vanity and self-satisfaction, and the admiration of all the women of his acquaintance. This "dress" attire consisted of a scarlet coat—of much ampler cut than was afterwards the case—faced with white, white waistcoat, and, for officers, commencing with the sergeant, white kerseymere breeches, and gaiters, or leggings ; a crimson sash, or leather shoulder-belt, buckles in the shoes, and a hat of the required shape, with a cockade and feather on one side.

This band of Britons received the title of "The Bury Loyal Association of Volunteers," and the initials " B.L.A." were impressed upon buttons and other articles manufactured expressly for their use. The " drill " of the Bury Volunteers took place almost every evening in Chip Field ; but the more perfect " exercise " on only two afternoons during the week ; and no expense or trouble was spared to make the condition and appearance as perfect as possible ; each one of the body holding any rank above that of " private " often, at some particular " day," having his hair powdered, and tied behind with a ribbon. When all were considered to be trained into something like military discipline, so that they could, at least, move and march in tolerable order, the 18th October, 1798, was appointed on which Lady Clerke, wife of the rector, Sir William Clerke, presented appropriate " colours to the " Loyal Association," in the then newly-formed Union-square. A husting was erected, and on presenting the flags Lady Clarke said :—

I have the honour of presenting the colours of the Bury Loyal Association, at the request of the ladies of this town and neighbourhood. I hope you will receive these banners as a testimony of our loyalty, and as a token of the entire confidence we place in the zeal and public spirit of this corps, who have so laudably come forward in defence of our king and country.

Three cheers followed Lady Clerke's speech, after which Lieutenant-Colonel Peel spoke as follows :—

To Lady Clerke and other Ladies.—The ladies of this town and neighbourhood have conferred an unspeakable obligation to our Loyal Association in presenting us with these colours ; a gift greatly enhanced in value by coming from the hands of a lady in whom is united every female accomplishment. I receive them with the greatest satisfaction, from an assurance that this pledge of approbation and confidence is not misplaced,—that these colours will be guarded with religious care, and will be neither wrested from us by an enemy, nor stained by misconduct.

Gentlemen Volunteers,—The ladies of Bury have enrolled themselves members of our association, and through the medium of these colours have afforded us a striking proof that we shall ever be accompanied by their best wishes and prayers. Under such patronage we shall ever be rendered invulnerable ; their example will preserve unanimity, their smiles and confidence animate us to exertions worthy of their good opinion. I will give way to the patience you evince of expressing your gratitude by cheering our fair companions. (Three times three cheers rang through Union-square for Lady Clerke and the Ladies.) I shall be extremely wanting in justice to you and your feelings if I did not embrace this opportunity of testifying the high sense entertained by myself and brother officers of your soldier-like behaviour and good conduct. No words of mine can convey an adequate idea of your merit. At a time when the British shores were darkened by a threatened invasion, when our rapacious enemies thirsted for our blood and treasure, and doomed to plunder alike the palace and the cottage; whilst they were feasting on the promised destruction of our religion, government, and commerce, and appointing taskmasters to be stationed in our workshops, to seize the fruit of our industry, and subject us to perpetual bondage; whilst thus employed a spectacle presented itself new to the slaves of despotism. Men forced into the service by fear of the guillotine were palsied at the appearance of British Volunteers serving His Majesty without pay. Citizens turned soldiers. The mechanic, supporting his family by labour in the day, and learning the use of arms by night, at once dissipated every apprehension at home, and penetrated with despair the rulers of France. Notwithstanding that every praise is due to His Majesty's regular forces, the contest for a time might have been unequal when opposed by the armies of France and the disaffected in this country. I claim for you, therefore, and your brethren in arms, a victory the most complete, without the loss of blood, without a struggle. Intent on plunder, these enemies of mankind turned their backs on Great Britain, and hastened to perpetrate new enormities in a part of the globe where the people are disunited and defenceless. Egypt, that ill-fated country, is doomed a second time to be devoured by locusts,—a plague more afflicting than that of Pharoah. The hand of the Almighty is visible here, the crimes of Bonaparte and his followers seemed reserved for a punishment much greater than that of visiting England as prisoners. Our immortal Nelson, by an unparalleled victory, has deprived them of their ships, and exposed them to the vengeance of an injured people, without hopes again of seeing their native land. Conscious that we have rendered our country good service, let us unite heart and hand in giving long life to the Bury Loyal Association. (Loud cheers.) Having the honour of being placed at the head of this highly respectable corps, and considering you as a part of my own family, may I be allowed the liberty of calling your attention to the discharge of those duties which our new situation has rendered indispensable. This address is much shortened in consequence of a most excellent sermon we have just had from our worthy chaplain, Sir William Henry Clerke, Bart., and I have only to lament that it cannot be preached by him to every Volunteer corps in the kingdom. Continue your attendance at the times appointed for drilling; avoid bad company; and having raised yourselves to a situation commanding respect, preserve it by good behaviour in every situation of life; attend to your officers, and you will experience from them a return of kindness and friendship. With regard to myself, I wish to be considered rather as your parent than your commander, and in cases of sickness and distress I shall ever feel happy in affording assistance to yourselves and families. As you have engaged in the honourable service of His Majesty, you will never forget that any attempt to injure his person, character, or government, is an insult offered to yourselves. Unlike the five Tyrants of France, who consult their own safety in the destruction of their countrymen, I have had many proofs of His Majesty's warm attachment to the lower orders of his subjects. He rejoices in your prosperity, and is grieved at your misfortunes. Being truly the father of his people, let us with one voice address Heaven, saying, God bless the King, with three times three cheers.

In the evening of this military day, Lieutenant-Colonel Peel and the officers offered the sergeants to allow their men to drink as long as they pleased at the different public-houses in the town, where revelry and wantonness, dissipation and drunkenness were carried on through the night.

On these "days" the newly-formed military companies of other towns, Bolton or Rochdale, would be invited; and then again these towns returned the compliment by inviting their Bury compeers upon similar festive or warlike occasions. Some length of time following the enrolment and operation of this first body, a company of younger men, emulating the martial ardour of their sires, was formed and designated "The Rifle Corps;" including many "bucks" of the period, who were not at all unwilling to enhance their manly charms by wearing the very becoming allotted uniform of dark green, braided with black. The previous warfare in North America had largely stimulated practice in this particular department, and the riflemen—or sharpshooters, as they were almost exclusively termed—of Bury numbered in their ranks the finest young men to be found in the town or in its vicinity. Like their predecessors, the " B.L.A." they also must have "field days;" and on one of the early days of its embodiment an invitation was accepted on the occasion of such an exhibition being held by brother riflemen in the neighbouring town of Rochdale, and in which the visitors were expected to take a prominent part. At a time when all the soldiers were considered most efficient, the best review of the period took place in the " Croft" and grounds in front of Chamber Hall. The plantations did not then intervene so much as afterwards, and the display was considered, even by critical judges, to be excellent and extremely satisfactory. Ladies and gentlemen of many families most distinguished in Lancashire graced that day the house and grounds of the " Chamber;" whilst, from every point of 'vantage on the land around numerous spectators of another class participated in the exhibition. Castle Croft, that day for the first day since the destruction of the castle, re-echoed once more to the tramp of armed men and horses; but, unlike that, this procession was peaceful, and only delayed from time to time by the passage of some well-appointed carriage belonging to the " gentry."

The collected armament had formed in the Square; marching thence, with colours and music, to the appointed rendezvous; and not only on the works, but throughout the whole town, was the holiday kept, for there were numbers from far and near, drawn by the celebrity of the occasion. All the open hilly ground from School Brow lengthwards to the Paddle Wall was early filled with an expectant audience, and the free road past the Hall was similarly thronged.

Excepting Manchester and Liverpool, Bury held pre-eminence in Lancashire for a most soldierly and excellently equipped body of men, perfect in all appointments, so far as money and painstaking could produce that result; and Captain Starkie's company of five hundred picked men, mounted and caparisoned, defied competition throughout the length and breadth of Great Britain.

The following are a few names taken from the " roll call" belonging to Lieutenant-Colonel Peel's company, in 1799, all or most of these being now time-honoured in Bury and its neighbourhood :—

William Barnes	Thomas Coup
James Barrett	Henry Coup
Robert Barlow	Ralph Crompton
Samuel Bentley	Thomas Davenport
Thomas Bridge	Thomas Gee
James Brook	John Hamer
Thomas Dawson	John Hope
James Holt	James Kenyon
Samuel Kay	William Kenyon
James Lomax	Samuel Meadowcroft
Robert Openshaw	John Pollitt
Anthony Preston	John Ramsbottom
Robert Spencer	Samuel Taylor
Jacob Watson	Richard Whittaker
Richard Wolfenden	John Whitehead
Edmund Whitehead	William Whitworth
William Butterfield	Samuel Pollitt
Holker Wilson	John Turner
Thomas Hutchinson	Thomas Norris
Richard Hardiker	Benjamin Riley

Of the *six* military companies formed in and around Bury, commencing in 1798, that raised, equipped, and paid by gentlemen of the Starkie family, and commanded personally by Captain Starkie, of Redivals, stood high for the excellence of all pertaining to its appearance and completeness. A principal training ground for the troop was in a large field off " Redival Lone," and it would now seem as if all memory of the gay and stalwart band has totally passed away from the scene where it originated.

The following song, written for this company, was a favourite with women who had a kinsman or sweetheart in the troop :—

I.

Ye gallant sons of Britain,
    I pray you lend an ear;
Stir up your manly courage,
    And enter volunteer;
And enter volunteer, my boys,
    To lead our foes a dance,
And drive the mounseers back again,
    Unto the soil of France.

II.

It's of brave Captain Starkie,
    Was born in Lancashire,
Near unto loyal Bury town,
    If you the truth inquire.
He raised both men and horses,
    So valiant, brisk, and young,
Five hundred lads of Lancashire,
    A present to their king.

III.

Their coats they are of blue, my boys,
  All turn-ed up with red;
A gallant cap and feather
  To wear upon their head;
A gallant horse to ride, my boys,
  Ten guineas in advance,
To go with Captain Starkie
  To quell the pride of France.

IV.

There's many brisk young weavers
  Left their sweethearts and their looms,
Likewise their tender parents,
  To join these bold dragoons.
They will leave their native country,
  For the royal British Crown,
And never to return
  Till th' *Convention* is put down.

V.

Then get your courage up, my boys,
  Prepare to stand and fight;
We'll ride along to battle,
  And may God defend the right!
With the Light Horse of England
  So merrily we'll go,
Along with Captain Starkie,
  That valiant hero!

CHAPTER V.

Captain Starkie's Troop—Mr. Yates and Horse Racing—The Profits on Bury Ground
—Mr. Peel's Baronetcy and Mr. Halliwell—Mr. Edmund Yates's Marriage: his
Illness: Death of Mrs. Cunliffe—Mr. William Yates and His Family—Irwell
House and "The Tenters"—Messrs. Hardman, Norris, and Hamer—The
Extension of the Firm—The Genealogy of the Peel Family—Burrs Mill: An
old Wages or Mill Book—Benevolence of Sir Robert Peel and the Firm—Sir
Robert Peel and the Representation of Drayton Manor—Handsome Contribution
to the Government—The Second Lady Peel—Death of Sir Robert Peel—Lady
Peel and Preston Guild—"Syphax" and "Nero"—Mr. Smiles' Account of Sir
Robert Peel—Testimonies as to the Character of Sir Robert Peel—William
Yates Peel—Sir William Peel, K.C.B.—The Right Hon. F. Peel—A Cock
Fight—Captain Yates and the Dinner Party—The Old Residence of the
Wrigley Family.

Invocations to British loyalty were then very much in vogue, and it
might have been held to include a national virtue. As the companies
formed at the expense and under the supervision of Mr. Peel embraced
mostly his own peculiar workpeople, so, as is intimated in the song,
Captain Starkie's troop included many weavers—home-working hand-
loom weavers—men following a profitable occupation, often earning from
two to three pounds weekly, and drawn from a district extending six or
eight miles from where the seat of the organisation lay. There were
besides many sons of farmers or countrymen, few townspeople or tradesmen. Radcliffe, Stand, Ramsbottom, Prestwich, Unsworth, Saddle-
worth, Turton, Walmersley, Heywood, Cockey Moor, all found representatives, a strong feeling uniting them in firm companionship, and the
fame of "Captain Starkie" and the "Starkie troop" spread over Lancashire, and extended into each of the neighbouring counties. Some
recruits from even farther away than the places enumerated made perfect
the complement of five hundred; and amongst them were yeomen "stout
and true" from the neighbourhood of The Huntroyd, the family seat of
the Starkies. They assembled from distances as far as it was possible
to traverse, in order to meet the requirements of the enrolment. They
were sturdy and independent men, mostly inhabiting home-steadings,

scattered at intervals throughout the beautiful and romantic scenery of this part of Lancashire; and how rarely beautiful, sequestered, and wild many portions looked at the period of these events this generation may never know.

MR. YATES AND HORSE RACING.

Mr. Edmund Yates had a passion for horse racing. One year his favourite mare, Bonny Grey, ran at Kersall Moor races and won. To describe the enthusiasm of the people of Bury that night would be simply impossible. Men of all classes and employments, down to the lowliest "tier-boy," identified themselves with the glory of Bonny Grey's victory; and during the ensuing summer and winter a song, of which the following is a verse, held pre-eminence in the town and workshops for some miles around :—

> Come, all you Bury heroes,
>   Of courage stout and bold ;
> Come, go with me to Kassy Moor,
>   And venture all your gold.
> Come, venture all on Bonny Grey ;
> Whene'er she runs she wins the day,
> And she has beat the Oldham Bay ;
>   Huzza ! huzza ! huzza ! boys.

The glory of beating the Oldham Bay added a double wreath to Bonny Grey's laurels.

THE PROFITS ON BURY GROUND.

Although the years previous to 1800 were stirring times in the world of war and politics, these same politics oftener bringing on a war than averting it, yet business at Bury continued to advance prosperously, and during these times the profits to " Peel and Co.," of Bury Ground, from the print trade alone, continued, almost without abatement, at £70,000 per annum. Mr. Peel had the lion's share of this, as had been the case from the first ; and though in the beginning he had little money to commence with, yet he brought what, in the end, proved more conducive to his interests, namely, sound judgment, just discrimination, and good sense. It was once a common saying in Bury that " though others browt th' money, Peel browt th' wit ;" " wit," in this sense, meaning a right use and understanding of the means.

MR. PEEL'S BARONETCY AND MR. HALLIWELL.

Mr. Peel's baronetcy was confirmed on the 29th of November, 1800, and from thence, in all documents relating to law or business, the firm was named as consisting of " Sir Robert Peel, of Drayton, in the county of Stafford, baronet ; Edmund Yates, of Bury, in the County Palatine of Lancaster ; James Halliwell, of Manchester ; Henry Warren, Robert Peel,

junior (cousin to Sir Robert), of Manchester ; and Thomas Yates, of
Bury, all in the county of Lancaster aforesaid, calico printers and
co-partners." Mr. Halliwell lived in Manchester ; the town department
of the business being confided, almost entirely, to his very able
management. It was this ability that had led to admission with the
firm. Halliwell-street (Long Millgate), Manchester, and Halliwell-lane,
Cheetham Hill, take their names from having been his property.

MR. EDMUND YATES'S MARRIAGE—HIS ILLNESS—DEATH OF MRS. CUNLIFFE.

Mr. Edmund Yates, Lady Peel's brother, was twice married, his second
wife being the daughter of Jonathan Peel, of Church Bank, near Accrington;
Jonathan being Sir Robert's brother, in this case Edmund Yates married
a lady to whom his sister Ellen was aunt. Before his first marriage he
had a severe attack of fever, and when partially recovered Dr. Cunliffe
judged it well for him to be driven out as much as possible in order to
facilitate his recovery. A trained nurse for a sick person was at that
time impossible to be found, and it was requisite that a sensible, careful
woman should accompany him in these airings. But who would undertake that office in a close carriage, and with a patient so circumstanced ?
Mrs. Cunliffe, the young wife of his medical attendant, herself volunteered
to do so; and fell a sacrifice to her disinterestedness, leaving two infant
sons to feel the want of a mother at an age when they most required
maternal aid and guidance. This happened eighty years ago; John
Cunliffe, Esq., of Myerscough House, Garstang, and but recently deceased, being one of these sons. Mr. Edmund Yates, shortly after his
marriage with Miss Haworth, his first wife, occupied the then new and
finely-built house in Silver-street, afterwards Mrs. Wilding's, Eagle and
Child Inn, where the Bury Assemblies were long held. His father, Mr.
William Yates, by far the eldest member of the firm, had been the first
of the company to retire from the ranks of business men, and enjoyed
life and leisure in his quiet home, the Rectory. He was four times
married; his last wife, Miss Ursula Robinson, of Newcastle, surviving
him.

MR. WILLIAM YATES AND HIS FAMILY.

Mr. William Yates, before and long after the marriage of his daughter
to his partner, Robert Peel, lived at Woodhill, and from thence he saw
his family of sons go forth into the world, all men of mark and ability.
Edmund and Thomas, the eldest and youngest, were printers like himself, Thomas Yates serving a previous apprenticeship to pattern designing
in the " drawing-shop " on the Ground. " The Colonel," Jonathan,

afterwards General Yates, entered the army during the troubled times following the French Revolution, and saw service in Egypt and elsewhere against the aggressive power of the "First Consul." Colonel Yates would speak of the period of greatest privation and suffering during his travels and campaigns, as that passed in Egypt, including the year 1798, when rain did not fall once during sixteen months; and, away from the great source of refreshment, the Nile, the sole water available to satisfy thirst, would be found a corrupt mass of insect life. The mementoes brought to England, from the then almost unknown countries he traversed, were at that time regarded with almost unbounded wonder and admiration. After attaining the rank of General, he died at a very advanced age about twenty years ago, and some twelve years afterwards was followed by the last surviving brother of Ellen, Lady Peel, the Reverend William Yates, Rector of Eccleston, near Chorley, Lancashire. John, a captain in the army, like his brother Jonathan, also served abroad. He died in the prime of manhood, fulfilling his own prediction that his life would be "a short and a merry one."

IRWELL HOUSE, OR "THE TENTERS."

Irwell House was built for Mr. Thomas Yates, and locally known as "The Tenters," from the circumstance that it was erected on ground previously occupied by the frames for "tenter hooks," whereon woollen cloth was stretched to dry—a process seldom now required. Of his children four were daughters, Sarah, Jane, Catherine, and Elizabeth. The eldest died in youth, after a marriage engagement long opposed by her family, but chiefly by her uncle and guardian, Colonel Yates. The opposition ceased too late to save her life; and she died, sincerely mourned by many besides her despairing lover, Lieutenant Vandaleur. Mrs. Thomas Yates—neé Miss Sarah Craven—long outlived her husband: her sister, Mrs. Brocklehurst, and family, also resided in Bury, near Redivals.

For a long time no place upon the works of Messrs. Peel and Yates could be spared wherein to pay the "tier-boys," themselves a host, so a treaty was entered into with Betty Booth, mistress of a cottage in the Mill Brow, and it was agreed that her house should be the future pay shop of the little and rather unruly band of labourers, and in recompense of the inconvenience it might occasion her, each boy or girl, that could conveniently carry it, was allowed to bring a "cob" of coal to replenish Betty's fire and stock, chiefly with a view to the night in question; and this primitive mode of recompense was legitimately sanctioned by the authority of the masters.

MESSRS. HARDMAN, NORRIS, AND HAMER.

In course of time Messrs. Peel, Yates, and Co., gave up their works to Messrs. Hardman, Norris, and Hamer, and though these gentlemen had realised great wealth in the employ of the Peel and Yates' families by perseverance and industry, they took the works, paid for them, and began to work for themselves, for the advantage of themselves and families. Mr. Norris afterwards retired, as will be seen in the notice of that gentleman's life, and the works were carried on by Messrs. Hardman and Hamer.

THE EXTENSION OF THE FIRM.

When Sir Robert Peel was in the height of his splendour, and in his loftiest station in Bury, he often said, " The farther a man is in debt and the richer he is." The extensive capital and influence of the company was at one time almost incredible, and at another time they could not tell whether the works would go on or not. At this time another partner was called in, whose name was Tipping (previously referred to), and he advanced some thousands of pounds. Money then came pouring in upon them, and riches overflowed their coffers. The company, at this stage, established printworks at Ramsbottom, and they took other partners in the firm, namely, Hollowell, Warren, and Kay; the two latter gentlemen superintended the works at Ramsbottom, and according to the little capitals they advanced, received proportionate profits. From 1773 to 1790 the rising of the Peels and Yates's was the most astonishing in Bury, and from 1790 to 1812, such was their influence, power, and popularity in Bury, that they governed every institution, public and private, in town. Sir Robert Peel, when he resided at Chamber Hall, was often heard to say, " Whoever lives to see it, my son Robert will one day be the Premier of England."

THE GENEALOGY OF THE PEEL FAMILY.

The Peel family became court favourites; they married and inter-married with the first nobility and gentry of the land, as the following will show :—

Sir Robert Peel married, for his first wife, Ellen, daughter of William Yates, Esq., by whom he had issue :

First.—Mary, married to George Dawson, Esq.

Second.—Elizabeth, married to the Rev. William Lackburn, Dean of York.

Third.—The second Sir Robert Peel, married Julia, only daughter of General Sir Edward and Lady Floydd.

Fourth.—William Yates Peel, Esq., married to the Hon. Lady Jane Moore, daughter of the Earl of Mount Cashel.

Fifth.—Edward Yates Peel, Esq., married to Amelia Maria, second daughter of John Swenfern, Esq., of Swenfern.

Sixth.—The Rev. John Peel, LL.B., married to Augusta, fifth daughter of John Swenfern, Esq., of Swenfern.

Seventh.—Colonel Jonathan Peel, married to the Hon. Alicia Jane, daughter of the Earl of Lascelles.

Eighth.—Lawrence Peel, Esq., married to Lady Jane Lennox, daughter of the Duke of Richmond.

Ninth.—Henrietta, youngest daughter of Sir Robert Peel, married to the Hon. Robert Eden, afterwards Lord Henley.

BURRS MILL: AN OLD WAGES OR MILL BOOK.

At a meeting of what was called "The Brotherhood," held in Manchester in 1858, a general wages or mill book was shown of work done, and payments, &c., made by and to the workpeople at Burrs Mill, then in the occupation of Messrs. Peel, Yates, and Peel. The work-book is for the year 1800, and it shows not only the very low money rate of wages, but also the larger portion of what was due was settled not by cash but by a species of truck system, the manager giving the hands orders for bread, flour, or meal, for butcher's meat, for groceries and general provisions, and even for drapery, on some shopkeeper in Bury, the draper patronised by the firm being Mr. Grant (father of the Messrs. Grant Brothers), who then kept a drapery and smallwares shop in Bury. Wages were lower and hours were much longer than at present. Amongst other hand processes was that of "batting cotton," the scutcher not being then invented. Batting was paid for at the rate of 1s. per 100lb. of cotton. Each folio contains a sort of family account with a father and mother, or one of them, and several children.

THE BENEVOLENCE OF SIR ROBERT PEEL AND THE FIRM.

Sir Robert Peel took many men by the hand who were in cases of poverty and distress, both in the cotton and woollen trades, about Bury. If tradesmen saw a bargain to be made in the above businesses, in corn-dealing, or other trades, it was not uncommon for them to go down to Peel's counting-house and draw a bill for a hundred or a thousand pounds. They then went and bought the raw material, or business, worked it, and sold the goods in the market before the bills became due. By this means many gentlemen in Bury began to rise, and amassed large capitals. The firm of Peel and Co. endeavoured, among other ways, to benefit the working classes, by establishing sick clubs, &c., in Bury, paying them five per cent. interest for the sums collected, and they made presents to these institutions annually, while they traded throughout the year with the surplus money.

SIR ROBERT PEEL AND THE REPRESENTATION OF TAMWORTH.

The intelligence and immense wealth of Mr. Peel being a matter of notoriety in Lancashire, he was solicited and induced to become proprietor in a bank at Manchester; but he did not continue long in this establishment, for he resigned it to the conduct of his brothers, and those friends with whom the speculation had originated. Being placed securely out of the chilling atmosphere of poverty, rewarded for years of virtuous industry by boundless wealth, and enjoying every domestic happiness, he purchased Drayton Manor, near Tamworth, as the future seat of the Peel family. His actual territorial possessions, added to the establishment of an extensive factory, gave such a preponderance to his influence in Tamworth, that Mr. Peel and his son William were returned to Parliament for that borough, to the exclusion of the former patrons, the Townsends. This privilege, however, with much generosity, he again shared with the rejected family, contenting himself with retaining one seat only in Parliament for his own family. The following address, issued to the electors of Tamworth by Sir Robert Peel, on his acceptance of office, in 1834, will no doubt be read with interest:—

Gentlemen,—On the 26th of November last, being then at Rome, I received from His Majesty a summons, wholly unforeseen and unexpected by me, to return to England without delay, for the purpose of assisting His Majesty in the formation of a new Government. I instantly obeyed the command for my return, and, on my arrival, I did not hesitate, after an anxious review of the position of public affairs, to place at the disposal of my Sovereign any services which I might be thought capable of rendering.

My acceptance of the first office in the Government terminates for the present my political connexion with you. In seeking the renewal of it, whenever you shall be called upon to perform the duty of electing a representative in Parliament, I feel it incumbent upon me to enter into a declaration of my views of public policy—as full and unreserved as I can make it, consistently with my duty as a Minister of the Crown.

You are entitled to this from the nature of the trust which I again solicit—from the long habits of friendly intercourse in which we have lived—and from your tried adherence to me in times of difficulty, when the demonstration of unabated confidence was of peculiar value. I gladly avail myself also of this, a legitimate opportunity, of making a more public appeal—of addressing, through you, to that great and intelligent class of society of which you are a portion, and a fair and unexceptionable representative—to that class which is much less interested in the contentions of party than the maintenance of order, and the cause of good government, that frank exposition of general principles and views, which appears to be anxiously expected, and which it ought not to be the inclination, and cannot be the interest, of a Minister of this country to withhold.

Gentlemen, the arduous duties in which I am engaged, have been imposed upon me through no act of mine. Whether they were an object of ambition coveted by me—whether I regard the power and distinction they confer, as any sufficient compensation for the sacrifices they involve, are matters of mere personal concern, on which I will not waste a word. The King, in a crisis of great difficulty, required my services. The question I had to decide was this : Shall I obey the call, or shall I shrink from the responsibility, alleging as the reason that I consider myself, in consequence of the Reform Bill, as labouring under a sort of moral disqualification which must preclude me, and all who think with me, both now and for ever, from entering the official service of the Crown ? Would it, I ask, be becoming in any public man so to act upon such a principle ? Was it fit that I should assume that either the object or the effect of the Reform Bill has been to preclude all hope of a successful appeal to the good sense and calm judgment of the people, and so to fetter the prerogative of the Crown that the King has no free choice among his subjects, but must select his Ministers from one section, and one section only, of public men?

I have taken another course ; but I have not taken it without deep and anxious consideration as to the probability that my opinions are so far in unison with those of the constituent body of the United Kingdom, as to enable me and those with whom I am about to act, and whose sentiments are in entire concurrence with my own, to establish such a claim upon public confidence, as shall enable us to conduct with vigour and success the Government of this country.

I have the firmest conviction that that confidence cannot be secured by any other course than that of frank and explicit declarations of principle ; that vague and unmeaning professions of popular opinions may quiet distrust for a time, may influence this or that election, but that such professions must ultimately and signally fail, if, being made, they are not adhered to, or if they are inconsistent with the honour and character of those who make them.

Now, I say at once that I will not accept power on the condition of declaring myself an apostate from the principles on which I have heretofore acted. At the same time, I never will admit that I have been, either before or after the Reform Bill, the defender of abuses, or the enemy of judicious reforms. I appeal with confidence, in denial of the charge, to the active part I took in the great question of the currency, in the consolidation and amendment of the criminal law—in the revisal of the whole system of trial by jury—to the opinions I have professed, and uniformly acted on with regard to other branches of the jurisprudence of the country. I appeal to this as a proof that I have not been disposed to acquiesce in acknowledged evils, either from the mere superstitious reverence for ancient usages, or from the dread of labour or responsibility in the application of a remedy.

But the Reform Bill, it is said, constitutes a new era, and it is the duty of a Minister to declare explicitly, first, whether he will maintain the Bill itself; and, secondly, whether he will act upon the spirit in which it was conceived.

With respect to the Reform Bill itself, I will repeat now the declaration which I made when I entered the House of Commons as a Member of the Reformed Parliament, that I consider the Reform Bill a final and irrevocable settlement of a great constitutional question—a settlement which no friend to the peace and welfare of this country would attempt to disturb, either by direct or by insiduous means.

Then as to the spirit of the Reform Bill, and the willingness to adopt and enforce it as a rule of government. If by adopting the spirit of the Reform Bill it be meant that we are to live in a perpetual vortex of agitation—that public men can only support themselves in public estimation by adopting every popular impression of the day, by promising the instant redress of anything which anybody may call an abuse, by abandoning altogether that great aid of government, more powerful than either law or reason, the respect for ancient rights, and the deference to prescriptive authority ; if this be the spirit of the Reform Bill, I will not undertake to adopt it ; but if the spirit of the Reform Bill implies merely a careful review of institutions, civil and ecclesiastical, undertaken in a friendly temper, combining with the firm maintenance of established rights the correction of proved abuses and the redress of real grievances, in that case I can, for myself and colleagues, undertake to act in such a spirit, and with such intentions.

Such declarations of general principle are, I am aware, necessarily vague, but in order to be more explicit, I will endeavour to apply them practically to some of those questions which have of late attracted the greatest share of public interest and attention.

I take, first, the inquiry into Municipal Corporations.

It is not my intention to advise the Crown to interrupt the progress of that inquiry, or to transfer the conduct of it from those to whom it was committed by the late Government.

For myself, I gave the best proof that I was not unfriendly to the principle of inquiry, by consenting to be a member of that Committee of the House of Commons on which it was originally devolved.

No report has yet been made by the Commissioners to whom the inquiry was afterwards referred, and until that report be made I cannot be expected to give, on the part of the Government, any other pledge than that they will bestow on the suggestions it may contain, and the evidence on which they may be founded, a full and unprejudiced consideration.

I will, in the next place, address myself to the questions in which those of our fellow-countrymen who dissent from the doctrines of the Established Church take an especial interest. Instead of making new professions, I will refer to the course which I took upon these subjects when out of power. In the first place, I supported the measure brought forward by Lord Althorp, the object of which was to exempt all classes from the payment of Church rates, applying in lieu thereof, out of a branch of the revenue, a certain sum for the building and repair of churches.

I never expressed, nor did I entertain, the slightest objection to the principle of a Bill, of which Lord John Russell was the author, intended to relieve the conscientious scruples of Dissenters, in respect to the ceremony of marriage. I give no opinion now on the particular measures themselves. They were proposed by Ministers in whom the Dissenters had confidence. They were intended to give relief, and it is sufficient for my present purpose to state that I supported the principle of them.

I opposed, and I am bound to state that my opinions in that respect have undergone no change, the admission of Dissenters, as a claim of right, into the Universities; but I expressly declared, if regulations, enforced by public authorities superintending the professions of law and medicine, and the studies connected with them, had the effect of conferring advantages of the nature of civil privileges on one class of the King's subjects from which another class was excluded, those regulations ought to undergo modification, with the view of placing all the King's subjects, whatever their religious creed, upon a footing of perfect equality in respect to any civil privilege.

I appeal to the course which I pursued on those several questions when office must have been out of contemplation; and I ask with confidence, does that course imply that I was actuated by any illiberal or intolerant spirit towards the Dissenting body, or by an unwillingness to consider fairly the redress of any real grievances?

In the examination of other questions which excited public feeling, I will not omit the Pension List. I resisted, and with the opinions I entertain, I should again resist a retrospective inquiry into pensions granted by the Crown, at a time when the discretion of the Crown was neither fettered by law nor by the expression of any opinion on the part of the House of Commons; but I voted for the resolution moved by Lord Althorp, that pensions on the Civil List ought for the future to be confined to such persons only as have just claims to the Royal beneficence, or are entitled to consideration on account either of their personal services to the Crown, or of the performance of duties to the public, or of their scientific or literary eminence. On the resolution which I thus supported as a private Member of Parliament, I shall scrupulously act as a Minister of the Crown, and shall advise the grant of no pension which is not in conformity with the spirit and intention of the vote to which I was a party.

Then, as to the great question of Church Reform, on that head I have no new professions to make. I cannot give my consent to the alienation of Church property in any part of the United Kingdom, from strictly ecclesiastical purposes. But I repeat now the opinions that I have already expressed in Parliament, in regard to the Church Establishment in Ireland, that if by an improved distribution of the revenues of the Church its just influence can be extended and the true interests of the established religion promoted, all other considerations should be made subordinate to the advancement of objects of such paramount importance.

As to Church property in this country, no person has expressed a more earnest wish than I have done that the question of tithe, complicated and difficult as I acknowledge it to be, should, if possible, be satisfactorily settled by the means of a commutation founded upon just principles, and proposed after mature consideration.

With regard to alterations in the laws which govern our ecclesiastical establishment, I have had no recent opportunity of giving that grave consideration to a subject of the deepest interest, which could alone justify me in making any public declaration of opinion. It is a subject which must undergo the fullest deliberation, and into that deliberation the Government will enter with the sincerest desire to remove every abuse that can impair the efficiency of the Establishment, to extend the sphere of its usefulness, and to strengthen and confirm its just claims upon the respect and affections of the people.

It is unnecessary for my purpose to enter into further details. I have said enough with respect to general principles and their practical application to public measures, to indicate the spirit in which the King's Government is prepared to act. Our object will be the maintenance of peace, the scrupulous and honourable fulfilment, without reference to their original policy, of all existing engagements with Foreign Powers, the support of public credit, the enforcement of strict economy, and the just and impartial consideration of what is due to all interests, agricultural, manufacturing, and commercial.

Whatever may be the issue of the undertaking in which I am engaged, I feel assured that you will mark, by a renewal of your confidence, your approbation of the course I have pursued in accepting office.

I enter upon the arduous duties assigned to me, with the deepest sense of the responsibility they impose—with great distrust of my own qualifications for their adequate discharge, but at the same time with a resolution to persevere, which nothing could inspire but the strong impulse of public duty, the consciousness of upright motives, and the firm belief that the people of this country will so far maintain the prerogative of the King, as to give to the Minister of his choice—not an implicit confidence—but a fair trial.

> I am, Gentlemen, with affectionate regard, most faithfully yours,
>
> (Signed)   ROBERT PEEL.

HANDSOME CONTRIBUTION TO THE GOVERNMENT.

The independence of his position left him leisure to reflect upon the political difficulties which closed round England; and when contributions were asked for the maintenance of the war, Mr. Peel presented to his country the munificent sum of £10,000. In the year 1798, he had embodied a corps called the Bury Loyal Volunteers; he subsequently formed the Lancashire Fencibles, and organised the Tamworth Armed Association, all at his own individual expense, and under his own personal surveillance. It was for these acts of loyalty, prudence, and patriotism, these eminent public services, these unparalleled examples of a noble generosity, that he was created a baronet on the 20th of November, 1800.

THE SECOND LADY PEEL.

It should be here stated that two years after the death of Lady Peel, Sir Robert made an offer of his hand to Miss Susanna Clerke, of Coventry, sister of Sir William Henry Clerke, rector of Bury, and who was then living at Springside. The characteristics of Sir Robert's marriage with Miss Clerke were far from being so happy or propitious as those of the union with the wife of his youth, his first and best-loved choice, Ellen

Yates. During the period that elapsed between Lady Peel's death and the fulfilment of Sir Robert's second engagement, Miss Peel was undisputed mistress of Drayton, and when once assumed it is seldom found an easy requisition to give up the reins of government, although in this case the stepdame to whom her father presented her was thirty years older than herself, and in that way might take precedence even of her own mother had she lived. Robert, the second baronet, was married at the age of thirty-three, to Miss Julia Floydd, the daughter of General Floydd. Things passed on for some time at Drayton and in London during Sir Robert's second experience of married life, but it was apparent that the occurrence of a very trivial cause might give rise to important consequences. The occasion that was taken for a final disruption may seem disproportionate to the importance of the question, but previous estrangement and contrariety of opinion had prepared the way for it, and should be taken into consideration before judgment is pronounced. The immediate cause precipitating a catastrophe long impending was this: the family carriage, with its full and imposing equipment, had been ordered by Lady Peel at a particular hour, for the inspection by her ladyship of some charitable projects in which she was immediately interested. Miss Peel had also specially retained the same dignified vehicle of travel for herself, at exactly the same period of time as had been done by her stepmother, the new mistress of the mansion, Lady Peel, to pay a visit upon which she had set her mind, to friends a dozen miles distant, and when upon going forth the ladies met upon the threshold, Lady Peel was astounded and indignant, and Miss Peel resolved to carry her point and bring the question of supremacy to an end, which she did by entering the carriage and giving orders for the drive. It was a gratuitous insult to the lady who occupied her dead mother's place, and after this no middle course could be taken. Sir Robert was finally appealed to, but Lady Peel found, or imagined, that in her husband's opinion of the matter, and the way in which he expressed it, there was a shade of preference for his daughter. This she could not brook, and calling another carriage, her own, left Drayton never to return. She died in 1824, at the age of seventy-two.

DEATH OF SIR ROBERT PEEL.

Having reached the summit of worldly ambition, obtained the reward of untiring industry, received that distinction which alone was wanting to illustrate the liberty enjoyed under the English constitution, he withdrew from public life, and devoted himself to the care and education of his numerous family. By his second marriage he left no offspring, but he was spared to see eleven children, the issue of the first, all united in marriage with members of the ancient aristocracy, and all distinguished by the possession and practice of those virtues of which he had so diligently given them an example. As the vale of years closed in, and the shadow of death fell darkly about it, this venerable man prepared for his approaching change; he directed the residue of his years to the happiness and comfort of the many friends and relatives his philanthropy had gathered around him. On the anniversary of his nativity, which saw him attain his seventy-eighth year, he presented a medal commemorative of the day to each of his fifty grandchildren, whom he had invited to Tamworth. Drayton Manor continued to be his constant residence, and there he expired, on the 3rd of May, 1830, in the 81st year of his age, leaving amongst his children, his relations, and some public charities, the large sum of three millions sterling!

LADY PEEL AND PRESTON GUILD.

During the residence of the family at Drayton Manor, Lady Peel came several times to Bury to see her father. The last time but one that she came into Lancashire was on occasion of the Guild at Preston, in 1802, when she was to take a public place in the Civic Procession of that fair town of the County Palatine, as became her rank and title. Lady Peel took the place becoming her rank amongst these fair and noble women; and most truly did she adorn and lend additional grace to the eminence and station, now for the first time so publicly asserted, in that native county which had witnessed the worth, talents, and industry of her husband, and whose reputation, and still increasing trade connections, bore testimony to the soundness of the business principles he had established. Lady Peel's dress, for this ceremony, was manufactured expressly for herself, the fabric being composed of a transparent material, striped and checked with threads of silver.

" SYPHAX " AND " NERO."

It should be here stated that a few years after his daughter's death, Mr. Yates left the Rectory for Springside; and, on his decease, Mrs. Yates went to reside at Everton, near Liverpool, accompanied by a faithful and attached man-servant, Syphax—one of the two negro boys Colonel Yates had purchased in Egypt during his first campaign abroad; long his own personal attendant, but afterwards transferred to the service of Mr. and Mrs. Yates. Nero, the companion of Syphax, was married from this household, finding a suitable helpmate in one of the female domestics, who declared that, although black, he was " a knowledgeable man, and gradely good;" whilst Syphax, either unfortunate in wooing, on account of colour, or, like his first master, the Colonel, preferring a life of celibacy, remained a bachelor in the family to the end.

MR. SMILE'S ACCOUNT OF SIR ROBERT PEEL.

Mr. Smile, in his interesting work entitled " Self-Help," thus refers to Sir Robert Peel and the first Lady Peel :—

Sir Robert Peel, the first baronet and the second manufacturer of that name, inherited all his father's ability, enterprise, and industry. His position, at starting in life, was little above that of an ordinary working man ; for his father, though laying the foundations of future prosperity, was still struggling with the difficulties arising from insufficient capital. When Robert was only twenty years of age, he determined to begin the business of cotton printing, which he had by this ti ie learnt with his father, on his own account. His uncle, James Haworth, and William Yates, of Blackburn, joined him in his enterprise ; the whole capital which they could raise amongst them amounting to only about £500, the principal part of which was supplied by William Yates. His father kept a small inn in Blackburn, where he was known as " Yates-o'-th'-Bull;" and having saved money by his business, he was willing to advance sufficient to give his son a start in the lucrative trade of cotton printing, then in its infancy. Robert Peel, though comparatively a mere youth, supplied the practical knowledge of the business ; but it was said of him, and proved true, that he " carried an old head on young shoulders." A ruined corn mill, with its adjoining fields, was purchased for a small sum, near the then insignificant town of Bury, where the works long after continued to be known as " The Ground;" and, a few wooden sheds having been run up, the firm commenced their cotton-printing business, in a very humble way, in the year 1770, adding to it that of cotton-spinning a few years later. The frugal style in which the partners lived may be inferred from the following incident in their early career :—William Yates, being a married man, with a family, commenced house-keeping on a small scale, and to oblige Peel, who was single, he agreed to take him as a lodger. The sum which the latter first paid for board and lodging was only 8s. a week ; but Yates, considering this too little, insisted on the weekly payment being increased a shilling ; to which Peel at first demurred, and a difference between the partners took place, which was eventually compromised by the lodger paying an advance of sixpence a week. William Yates's eldest child was a girl, named Ellen, and she soon became the especial favourite with the young lodger. On returning from his hard day's work at " The Ground," he would take the little girl on his knee, and say to her, " Nelly, thou bonny little dear, wilt be my wife?" to which the child would readily answer, " Yes," as any child would do. " Then I'll wait for thee, Nelly; I'll wed thee, and none else." And Robert Peel did wait. As the girl grew in beauty towards womanhood, his determination to wait for her was strengthened; and after a lapse of ten years—years of close application to business and rapidly increasing prosperity—Robert Peel married Ellen Yates when she had completed her seventeenth year; and the pretty child whom the mother's lodger and father's partner had nursed upon his knee, became Mrs. Peel, and eventually Lady Peel, the mother of the future Prime Minister of England. Lady Peel was a noble and beautiful woman, fitted to grace any station of life. She possessed rare powers of mind, and was, on every emergency, the high-souled and faithful counsellor of her husband. For many years after their marriage, she acted as his amanuensis, conducting the principal part of his business correspondence, for Mr. Peel himself was an indifferent and almost unintelligible writer. She died in 1803, only three years after the baronetcy had been conferred upon her husband. It is said that London fashionable life—so unlike what she had been accustomed to at home— proved injurious to her health; and old Mr. Yates was afterwards accustomed to say, " If Robert hadn't made our Nelly a lady, she might ha' been living yet."

TESTIMONIES AS TO THE CHARACTER OF SIR ROBERT PEEL.

Sir Lawrence Peel, late Chief Justice of Bombay, in a sketch which he wrote of the life and character of the late Sir Robert Peel, says :—

" The name of the late Sir Robert Peel is indelibly inscribed on a glorious page in the history of England. The study of his character is exceedingly important, whether considered with regard to his individuality or his political life—whether viewed as a man or as a statesman." To us it appears that his near relative has here presented the public with a fair and impartial statement, from which it can form a just estimate of him in both of these capacities. There may be a natural leaning to the favourable side, and a liberal construction of disputed passages in party warfare ; but if so, the counterbalance of candour in narrating the circumstances and conditions of the case, and the sound judgment in drawing the conclusions, afford to equally candid and judicious readers a perfect assurance of the general truth and justice of the whole.

In his mid-career Sir Robert Peel was accused of duplicity and cowardice. He was said to be the Blifil, or Joseph Surface, of diplomacy and intrigue. But his memory has never been disparaged by such suspicions as were cast into his teeth by the heat and strife of the struggle in which he was so heavily engaged. The grave and a very few years have toned down the language of disappointment and exasperation, and the person and the minister stand before us in a more sober and far clearer light than when looked at through the stormy clouds which enveloped no inconsiderable portion of the living presence. Sir Robert's posthumous memoirs have furnished his own explanation of his conduct whilst thus exposed to censure ; and the volume now given to the world supplements that publication so ably that, in our opinion, there can be little left for future writers whereon to vary the decision we may honestly arrive at on the premises before us.

The three grand events—the epochs of twenty-five years—which link the measures of the politician with the destinies of his country, and having profound influence upon those destinies, were the re-adjustment of the currency, the removal of Roman Catholic disabilities, and the enactment of Free Trade. In the two latter, especially, he severed himself from the great Conservative body with which he had previously acted, not only in the most cordial manner, but with the hot zeal of a leader, and it is to account for such striking changes of policy that the true character of the individual becomes so essential to be ascertained.

Sir Robert Peel inherited from his forefathers—or, as it is commonly said, it ran in the blood—an immutable self-reliance and almost extreme caution. These were the elements of his mental constitution. " His mind (says his biographer) was well gifted, but not richly endowed with rare gifts : a sound mind in a sound body : a fair jewel in a fine setting." His father educated him distinctly with the object of another William Pitt, and the author observes,—"Here, then, was the fortunate, it may be the wise, union of high culture with a fitting nature. Next came the higher advantage of an early aim : culture steadily directed to one certain and not unreasonable end." That end was accomplished, but not without sacrifices. First of all was the " divorce from childish nature which is inseparable from all early culture severely applied. That mind treated as the hand of the artisan, and forced overmuch on one application ; the faculties strained to one absorbing pursuit ; a reason, in its infancy, put to man's work ; a memory over cultivated ; a fluency of speech too early acquired, brought their ordinary results : an imagination starved, a diction correct and flowing, but without stops of varied beauty—the level lawn of language." What, asks Sir Lawrence, was to be foreseen from this condition of things? Nothing lofty, nothing impassioned, coolness, calculation, and changes, of course, according as the weighing-machine varied, and the balance inclined one way or other. " Change, then, was inevitable ; but in such a nature as his it was also sure to be timid and reluctant ; no new birth or sudden conversion, but the gradual slow development of a growing stature. An honest conformity to a growing world." Guizot has said of him, *Il naquit Tory*—and so he did ; but it was in moderate Toryism, and his disposition was so deeply tinged with what is, perhaps, untruly deemed the opposite principle, that Sir Lawrence draws his portrait with perfect fidelity when he says that he was "tentative, laborious, cautious, slow in adopting, but steady in the pursuit of adopting a new course; fearful lest the new wine should burst the old bottles; standing on the old way; proud to be of the people—their friend and never their flatterer; justly sensible of the value of due gradations; a new man, but clinging to prescription and ancient usage; a mixture in his origin and fortune of two conditions in life; a Tory and a Democrat in one; and, adds our author, "no uncommon or unnatural union."

In a production of this class, when the chief bearing lies in the moral example and the political interest, we are not called upon to go into the family history and antecedents of the Peels. They were substantial yeomen—the writer's father was wont to "pish" to himself over the superscription of his letters, half playfully and half peevishly muttering to himself, "a pretty Esquire, truly!" and they sprung up and rose with cotton to be magnates in the land, to refuse garters and peerages, and to hold calico, industry, self-reliance, and integrity, to be above ancestry, and the noblest legacy they could leave to their descendants. Yet, observes the author, "I am unable to ascribe to industry alone all that the late Sir Robert Peel became. The raw material was more than commonly good—it was excellent. He was a quiet clever boy, and also a thinking boy, naturally observant and reflecting. He was no prodigy, certainly. His parts and his promise were such as many boys have and give"—nothing, however, is more deceptive than the early promise of a youth. A girl commonly beats all her brothers in her early lessons, and I have seen no young people so quick of apprehension as the young Hindoo [could not a valuable application be made of this sub-stratum in forming our Indian Governments?] though the after progress is not proportionate to the early excellence. Byron seems to have given a correct account of his school-fellow. He nowhere speaks of Peel as a genius, neither does he describe him as a boy of moderate capacity, and superior only by dint of fagging. He was never in scrapes, and always knew his lesson. But unquestionably the severe discipline had also some drawbacks. Peel seems never to have tasted the sweets of childhood, nor enjoyed the careless pastimes of boyhood. "The originality and freedom of his mind, though not destroyed, were impaired by it. He grew up graver than becomes a boy. His thoughts, as his manners, were cast too much in an artificial mould, and were tinged by a certain formality." In short, geniality was wanting. His youth was overstrained, and his early induction into office confirmed his aptitude to become too much of a case statesman." Yet he was ever the friend to progress, and when once quite sure of his footing he advanced, even sacrificing, most painfully, his personal and party connections, for that line which a sense of his duty pointed out as a national benefit.

On the occasion of the inauguration of the statue to the late Sir Robert Peel, in 1852, at Bury, elsewhere referred to, the London *Times* thus alluded to the deceased baronet:—

It is a common complaint of the age that titles and honours are no longer the meed of excellence, but are filched from the rightful owners by wealth or intrigue. There are, however, other rewards, other adjudications, than those which issue from Downing-street under the Royal sign manual; there are other ranks of nobility than those that sit in Barry's gorgeous halls; other titles than our modern Burke telleth of; and other perpetuations besides embalmments and porphyry sarcophagi and marble mausolea. Public opinion can recognise all sorts of merit, and mankind are not ungrateful for actual services; so, if men will be content to walk in the path of utility and honour, they will not lose their reward. . . . We saw the solemn inauguration of a costly memorial to mark the virtues and the services of a lately departed statesman, in the place of his nativity, among many that remembered his family and his education amongst them, and, still more, that were deeply sensible of the benefits they and the empire had received from his measures. . . . We have the great statesman who pursued with far ken and steady aim the ultimate good of his country, and who, for this, sacrificed party, consistency, and self; insomuch that while his statues are inaugurated, and while every cottage confesses him its benefactor, his bitter foes and incessant detractors are actually installed in his room.

Providence seems to have withheld all personal rewards, and to have surrounded the close of Sir Robert Peel's career with clouds and darkness, with loss of office, with estrangement of friends, with calumny, and even with public calamity, as if to set off, on that dark foil, the enduring splendour and increasing success of his political achievements.   The testimonies that now flow in to his memory must be sincere, for they have no other reason or motive but the truth of his merits, and the sensible reality of his services.   The multitude made a holiday at Bury, and walked reverentially round the newly-uncovered statue, and pointed out, with pride, to strangers the house where Peel was born. and where he first went to school, and every spot touched by his infancy, for no other reason—they could have no other reason, except that Sir Robert, as they knew and felt, had filled their houses with plenty and gladness, and had overthrown the envious barriers that so long interposed between their own honest labour and the full garners of the far west.   They knew that the great measures of which Providence and his own virtues had made him the author had crowded our ports, kept our factories at work, and conciliated all classes in this country at a time when plague, pestilence, and famine, and the worst horrors of revolution and of war, were about to be let loose on devoted Europe. . . . Popular honours derive all their efficacy and meaning from the will and act of the people.   It was not Mr. Baily, the sculptor—not a select circle of wealthy and admiring friends—but THE PEOPLE OF BURY that gave this statue its true value and significance.   It is a true and faithful expression of the feelings with which they and the country at large regard the memory of our great statesman.   Such a spectacle we cannot but consider is sufficient to silence all the idle complaints that patriotism has not its honour and reward in these days.   What has the State, what has Royalty, what has fortune, what has fashion, to do with these public testimonies, which are simply the honest thanks of the people for the benefits they have actually received?

WILLIAM YATES PEEL.

The Right Hon. William Yates Peel, was the second son of the first baronet by his first wife, daughter of Mr. William Yates, of Bury, and was born in 1789, at Chamber Hall. He married, June 17, 1819, Lady Jane Eliza Moore, second daughter of Stephen, second Earl of Mount Cashel, and Lady Margaret, eldest daughter of Robert, second Earl of Kingston, by whom, who died in September, 1847, he had a numerous family. The right honourable gentleman was for a long series of years a member of the House of Commons. After completing his studies at Harrow School, he removed to St. John's College, Cambridge, where he graduated B.A. in 1812, and M.A. in 1815, and in June, 1816, was called to the bar at Lincoln's Inn. In the following year he was returned to Parliament for the borough of Bassing, but only represented that constituency a few months, for in 1818, he was chosen member for his father's borough of Tamworth, for which he sat continuously up to 1830. He was then elected for Yarmouth, Isle of Wight. In 1831, he was returned to the House of Commons, in conjunction with the late Right Hon. Henry Goulburn, for the University of Cambridge, defeating Viscount Palmerston and Mr. William Cavendish (afterwards Duke of Devonshire). In 1835, he was again elected for Tamworth, which he represented up to the general election in 1837. From that time up to 1847, he remained out of Parliament, when he was again returned for

Tamworth. The loss of his wife in that year so affected him, that mentally he was unable to attend to any public duties, and consequently resigned his seat in the House of Commons. He held several official appointments, having been appointed a Commissioner of the Board of Control in 1826, Under Secretary of State for the Home Department in 1828, and a Lord of the Treasury in 1830, and again held the same office in 1834, to April in the succeeding year. He held the same Conservative politics as his distinguished brother, Sir Robert Peel, and was a willing supporter of that eminent statesman's free-trade policy. His death took place at Baginton Hall, Warwickshire, on the 1st June, 1858.

SIR WILLIAM PEEL, K.C.B.

The gallant and heroic conduct of Sir William Peel, K. C. B., third son of Sir Robert Peel, Bart., will long be remembered by the inhabitants of Bury. He was born on the 2nd November, 1824. In April, 1838, he entered the navy as midshipman on board the Princess Royal, Captain A. Fanshaw, flag of Sir Robert Stopford, and took part in the bombardment of St. Jean d'Acres. From this ship he removed to the Monarch, and afterwards to the Cambrian, in which ship of war he served in the China seas. In 1844, he passed his examination in such a brilliant manner, that he called forth the warm eulogiums of Sir Thomas Hastings and Sir Charles Napier, and was forthwith promoted to the rank of lieutenant. In May, that year, he was appointed to the Winchester, 50 guns, on the Cape of Good Hope Station, and shortly after removed to the Cormarant, steam sloop, in the Pacific, and subsequently to the Thalia, 42, on the same station. Sir William was promoted to the rank of Commander, 27th June, 1846, and was appointed to the command of the Daring, on the North American and West Indian Station. During the interval which ensued, prior to the breaking out of the Russian War, Sir William held several minor appointments, and filled up his leisure time in foreign travel. In 1851, he travelled through Egypt and Nubia, and in the following year he came with his brother to Bury. At the outbreak of the Russian War he was appointed to the command of the Diamond, and joined the Black Sea Fleet, under Admiral Dundas. His restless activity, when it was apparent that no naval operations of any extent would take place, led him to join the naval brigade in front of Sebastopol, where he greatly distinguished himself. His exploits in the Russian War were alluded to by the correspondents of the London *Times*, and a " Post Captain," writing under date of January 27th, 1858, thus alludes to Captain Peel's distinguished services :—" It was universally considered by both the army and the navy that no officer distinguished himself more, or rendered more valuable service from the very commencement of the siege of Sebastopol. Lord Raglan and Lord Lyons made frequent mention in their despatches of ' the chivalrous bravery of Captain Peel,' and your able correspondent during the siege often alluded to the ' conspicuous gallantry and unwearied perseverance of Captain Peel.' He gained the Victoria Cross for throwing a burning shell out of the battery during a bombardment. He led the ladder party at the assault on the 18th of June, where, although severely wounded, he remained on the field to the last. He fought ' sword in hand' in the then red line which rallied round the two-gun battery at Inkerman. No naval officer has ever exposed his life more fearlessly or distinguished himself more eminently than William Peel, who is as modest as he is brave, chivalrous, and good—the Bayard of the British Army—' Sans peur et sans reproche.'

The name of Captain Peel will ever be associated with that of the Diamond Battery, which did such good service to the Allies during the siege. He did not witness the fall of that redoubtable fortress, for wounds and over-exertion did their work on his weak frame, and he was compelled to return to England to recruit his health and renovate his shattered frame. He was made a Companion of the Order of the Bath for his services in the Crimea, and for his eminent services in India nominated a Knight Commander of that Order of Knighthood. He was also an Officer of the Legion of Honour of France, and of the Imperial Order of Medjidie, and received the Sardinian war medal. He died on the 27th of April, 1858, and the London *Times'* special correspondent (Dr. Russell) at the seat of war in India, paid the following just and interesting tribute to his memory :—" The electric telegraph has carried its brief announcement of the sad news we heard this morning to England some days before the letter I am now writing can reach you. But I can add no details to the brief statement of the event, which must cause such grief to every English heart. The death of Sir William Peel at any time would be a national loss. Despite the theory that there is no such thing as a necessary man, I believe that at this particular juncture his death is a national calamity, and it is one for which I see no reparation. His gallant comrades in the noble profession which was the joy of his life will be the readiest to admit that the foremost naval officer of the day lies in the grave which contains his body. It is not of mere personal gallantry that I speak, although in his career he astonished great men by glorious recklessness of his own life whenever the smallest benefit to the service was to be gained by braving

danger, or of the contempt of death he exhibited wherever and whenever
by example, he could encourage his men to greater emulation of his
own calm courage ; but I allude more to the largeness of conception, the
mastery of detail, the great professional zeal, the consummate skill, the
ingenuity and incessant activity of acquaintance in all that related to
moral questions and tactics, and the shrewd watchfulness with which
he regarded every matter affecting the condition of our fleet and the
efficiency of the service, which he justly regarded as the noblest development of the power and might of England.   In the march from Lucknow
to Cawnpore he was carried down in a dooly, or litter, as he was unable
to ride owing to his wound, but he could limp about, and just before we
entered Cawnpore, he was able to walk a little when we halted, without
the aid of his stick.   Morning after morning, as our letters were laid
down beside each other, he talked to me of the various news which
came to us from home, and I well remember the light which was in his
eye, as he said, speaking of the Conspiracy Bill, ' I am delighted at it,
not from any sympathy with the rascally assassins who flock to England,
or from any feeling against France or the Emperor, whose orders I
wear, but because my instinct tells me, as its instinct told the House,
that it was the right thing for an English Parliament to do, reason or no
reason.   We must never take a step in that direction, even if one came
from the dead to tell us to do it."   It was probably in the litter he
contracted the fearful malady which cost him his life ; for, if I am not
misinformed, it was obtained by him from the hospital at Lucknow,
where several cases of smallpox occurred before we left.   On the day
after his arrival at Cawnpore, he was seized with sickness and feverish-
ness, from which he recovered, but the symptoms of smallpox were
soon exhibited, and when I mentioned the news to Dr. Clifford that he
had it, who had been one of his attendants, the latter said he feared it
would go hard with Sir William, owing to his irritability of constitution,
and to the debility arising from his wound.   It was one day's march
from Futtehghur that I heard of his illness, and on my arrival I tele-
graphed to the Rev. Mr. Moore, the chaplain at Cawnpore, to know how
he was.   Next day I received the reply ' Sir William is doing as
favourably as can be expected in a case of bad confluent smallpox.'
This morning, on the line of march, we heard he was no more ; it flew
from mouth to mouth.   Sir Colin Campbell showed the grief that was
felt by every officer in the force.   Over and over again, all this morning,
' Peel dead !   What a loss to us !   It will be long ere the services see
two such as Adrian Hope and Peel !' mingled with expressions of regret
and sorrow."

Birthplace of the late Sir Robt. Peel, Bart. Bury, Lancashire.

THE RIGHT HON. F. PEEL.

The Right Hon. F. Peel married, on the 12th August, 1857, the only daughter of Mr. John Shelley, of Avington, Hants (brother of the poet, Percy Bysshe Shelley). She died on the 30th of July, 1865, in the 27th year of her age. In 1852 he contested Viscount Duncan in the representation of Bury, and was returned by a majority of 62. He was defeated at the election in 1857, the present member (Mr. R. N. Philips) being returned by a majority of 35. In 1859 he again contested the borough, along with Mr. Thomas Barnes, and was returned by a majority of 156. Again, in 1865, he contested the borough, along with Mr. Philips, and was defeated by a majority of 23.

CHAMBER HALL.

The birthplace of the late Sir Robert Peel is now devoted to a very important object. It is used as a Baptist College, and was opened for that purpose by the Rev. H. Dawson, on the 3rd of October, 1866. Prior to the hall coming into the possession of the Peel family, it was occupied by Mr. Taylor, who carried on business as a cotton manufacturer. One of Mr. Taylor's daughters married Mr. Scholes, also a cotton manufacturer, who resided in a mansion in Stanley-street. Richard Walker, Esq., the first M.P. for Bury, married one of Mr. Scholes's daughters, and the Rev. Mr. Potter, of St. Mary's Church, married the other. When the late Sir Robert Peel succeeded to Chamber Hall he built a modern front to it—grand in those days. Edmund Yates, Esq., succeeded Sir Robert Peel at Chamber Hall, and Mr. William Hardman succeeded him. Edmund Hardman, son of William, next took possession. Upon the establishment of Chamber Hall as a residence, it became an unbroken custom for all the partners to meet and breakfast there each Monday morning throughout the year ; and, from the general success of business, these meetings were often extremely agreeable ones—those residing at a distance coming over on horseback.

A COCK FIGHT.

When William Yates, Esq. (grandfather to Sir Robert Peel) resided at the Rectory House, three of the sons played many a curious prank. Being full of frolic and cruel sport, one day they brought twenty fighting cocks to the house, all provided with silver heels, and turned them down on the green flat before the front door. Nineteen of the birds fought till they expired, whilst the odd bird never entered the battle, but gazed on as though commander-in-chief of the affray.

CAPTAIN YATES AND THE DINNER PARTY.

Captain Yates (captain of the old Bury Rifle Corps), together with his officers, soldiers, and band, once took a trip to Bolton. When they arrived there Captain Yates sent an order to the landlord of the Commercial Inn to get ready speedily the best dinner and wines he could possibly set out. Dinner being nearly ready, the landlord said, " Who is to pay for this dinner ? " This got whispered to the ears of the captain, and he stormingly said, " Tell the landlord to be handy, and I will let him see who is to pay for it." The dinner being richly set out, the captain and officers were called into the room, all standing round the table, longing to pitch their knives and forks into the dainty dishes, but, alas ! Captain Yates, at one fell sweep, tossed the table over and its contents. He then said to the landlord, " Now, sir, bring in your bill, and I will pay the cost," which he did accordingly. The Captain repaired with his officers and band to another public-house, where they got a lunch, and after going through their varied evolutions in Bolton with other rifle corps, returned to Bury.

THE OLD RESIDENCE OF THE WRIGLEY FAMILY.

On a portion of the townward boundary of the outer walls or defines of the old Bury castle was, in former times, situated the gardens and old-fashioned farmhouse long in possession of the family of the Wrigleys. This house was one of the best specimens in Bury of the old style of dwelling for a substantial farmer or yeoman. Its long, low, diamond-paned windows, divided by massive stone mullions, deeply set within the rugged wall ; its two antique porches, with stone seats ; the doors deeply clubbed with grim-looking nails, giving access to the house in its principal parts ; and the outside staircase of heavy masonry, which led to the upper rooms, there being no inside staircase, for the best sleeping and other apartments extended over the ground floor ; all these would in our day have rendered the house of Radcliffe Wrigley extremely picturesque, if not extremely habitable. Its situation was unrivalled around Bury. The property was freehold, and is said to have been in the family from the building of the house, which might have been antecedent to the destruction of the castle. Of this desirable central property, now bearing increased value from the successful printing enterprise carried on upon the Ground below, Mr. Johnson, the steward, on behalf of his master, the Earl of Derby, earnestly desired to obtain possession, and at length, after many years' waiting, and by means not very creditable, the steward's object was attained. The story, as recorded, is that Radcliffe Wrigley, the last possessor of that name, was purposely stupified with drink, and in that condition, on documents previously prepared, induced to sign away, for a most inadequate sum, what he had sacredly promised his wife should never be alienated from them, namely, the homestead of his fathers, and lands by birthright pertaining to his children, as faithfully as he had received them from his ancestors. The destruction of the old house was accomplished, and the land sold or leased to Mr. Charles Openshaw, who built the house afterwards occupied by Mr. Edmund Grundy. It was a tradition of the neighbourhood, from times long past, that under some nook of the stone flooring of Radcliffe Wrigley's house, a vessel containing money—silver coin—had been buried at some period of danger during the troubled days that followed the Commonwealth ; but if such was found at the demolition of the building, its lucky possessor never made it known. In the garden of this place, when digging for a well in 1740, an under-ground passage was discovered. The excavators entered upon it by breaking through the stone roof which had impeded their labours, finding that the subterranean way led, as nearly as could be ascertained, towards the Church or Rectory on one hand, and on the other directly to the hill beneath the boundaries of the ancient castle. From the Church, or vicinity of the Rectory, this passage, or a similar one, must have been continued for some distance, as is proved by the following incident. About twenty-six years ago, the pavement in front of houses the property of Mr. Francis Nuttall, near the Rectory gates, and opposite a building once occupied as the post-office, was obliged to be removed, in order that the workmen of the Improvement Commissioners might open the ground to form a sewer ; and in this, as in the former case, they came upon the stone roof of an under-ground passage, widening into an apartment a little more spacious than the passage itself. It was well built, of solid masonry, and seemed to have been either the substantial deep cellar of some long-ago removed house, or the probable termination of the subterranean avenue from the Castle. It was well floored with flag or stone, and with a doorway at one side, which had apparently formed another communication. The thoroughfare through the doorway was practicable for some inconsiderable distance, leading under the foundations of the buildings above; and, if it were possible to judge, seeming also to lead towards the Rectory or its adjacent grounds, or, at least, occupying that direction. Further research was impossible, not only from the fallen rubbish that impeded, but also from the fact that the structure, so lately discovered, must again be lost, either by its destruction or by its closing up. Such portions of the cavity as it was not found necessary to demolish were not again to be left vacant, but were filled up with earth after being

H

open to inspection for only a short interval; it being said to be impossible to keep so public a street in an obstructed condition, or to delay the work merely to gratify antiquarian curiosity. It may not be improbable that, at some time previous to the Reformation, a Religious House existed here in connection with the Church, when its situation would be upon the ground upon which the present Rectory stands. Within this century it was a current tradition in the town that one or more passages existed underground, leading from the depths of the foundations of the old Castle, under the Rectory, and outward through a portion of its gardens; but the termination was forgotten, or had never been made public.

CHAPTER VI.

" Circumstances alter Cases"—Cockey Moor-lane—Witchcraft or "The Black Art"—The Plumber and Sir Robert Peel—Gas Making—Thomas Openshaw, Esq.—James Clerke, Esq., and Sir William Clerke—Hutchinson Family—Tharcake and Parkin—Mr. Ellis Cunliffe, surgeon—John Warburton, Esq.

" CIRCUMSTANCES ALTER CASES."

When Messrs. Peel and Yates occupied the Ground in Bury, Mr. Yates ordered Mr. Hope, of Woodhill, to take a load of cannel as a present to the Rev. Henry Unsworth, the incumbent of St. John's. The carter took the cannel to the rev. gentleman's house, and he said to Mr. Unsworth, " I have brought you a load of cannel." The rev. gentleman, in a loud tone of voice, said, " I have no room for any cannel." " Ah!" said the carter, " Mr. Yates has made you a present of this." Mr. Unsworth then said, " That alters the case, bring it forward."

COCKEY MOOR-LANE.

Cockey Moor-lane was rather celebrated for the number of singular individuals that at different times had their dwelling-place there. In this lane there was a mean collection of houses known by the appellation of the " Job." In Cockey-lane stood an isolated little wooden hut named the " Cabin," its occupier, an old man named Bobby, surname unknown, also designated as " Bobby Cabin," and the " Cabin Doctor," a dealer in herbs and simples ; a stunted, rather deformed, strange-looking old man, bearing a staff, and wearing invariably a dark grey, long skirted coat. Poor as he must have been, and very restricted as were his means of subsistence, the old man craved no charity, and the few pence he received as a professional fee seemed to be satisfactory and to supply his limited wants. His days, in fine weather, were mostly spent in wandering over the country, generally in lonely places, seeking the plants he used as remedies ; and his time in the cabin seemed most frequently employed in drying and assorting them. He lived alone, and died alone. Another celebrity was Johnny Gorton, a " curer of childish diseases by blowing into the mouth," who spoke of himself as the " seventh son of a seventh son." For diseases of the throat and lungs, " thrush," or whooping cough, Johnny's blowing or breathing was held to be infallible, and his services were in request not alone amongst families that might have been considered the poorest or most ignorant. Johnny owned a little cart and a donkey, and in his small way could always find employment by carting coal from Hinds to the Ground.

WITCHCRAFT, OR " THE BLACK ART."

A notable fortune-teller in Bury, not professional, was Leah Bentley, a young woman working in a small building known as the " Glory Hole," the work of which consisted in stitching and examining unprinted pieces. Leah's particular forte lay in being able to discern in the ball, or oblong transparent substance named a " crystal," the fortunes or bearing of the especial object for which she was consulted. The power of the crystal at times became exhausted, when it would require to be once more charmed, or " charged," though how this was effected was not publicly made known. Her character was above suspicion, and many believed in the truth of the visions she declared she beheld in the magical glass, and placed confidence in her representations. The most remarkable, or best remembered of these is when, upon one occasion, she was requested to leave the works and cross the Croft to the Chamber Hall, as the family wished to make trial of the power of her crystal. Jonathan, the brother of Mrs. Peel, being then engaged with the army in Egypt under Sir Ralph Abercrombie, no letters had been received from him for some time, and apprehensions were entertained as to his safety. Leah, in ignorance of their motives, was desired to consult the crystal, and upon doing so proceeded to speak of what she saw therein. Out of the misty cloudiness, after a little while, the figure of Colonel Yates seemed to emerge, and she described him as looking healthy and well; he was in uniform, and apparently in conversation with others, for gradually the appearance of several gentlemen, also in uniform, was mentioned, seemingly in debate, and following this, the scene immediately surrounding the group also became visible. It was the quarter deck of a man-of-war, although the woman was ignorant of much that she described quite sufficiently for the recognition. She could not retain this power of penetration very long, and by-and-by all objects in the glass receded into the original condition of cloudy indistinctness; but note was taken of the time and situation, and the next letters abroad asked information of the Colonel's doings at that particular period, which, when the answer arrived, was found to corroborate Leah's account of his appearance, the presence of naval and military officers, his companions, in consultation, and the ship whereon the scene was represented to have taken place.

THE PLUMBER AND SIR ROBERT PEEL.

A most respectable plumber in Bury, when a young man, presented an invoice, for work done, to the first Sir Robert Peel, before he was made a baronet. Considerable time was occupied in reading it. "You will excuse me, Mesther Peel; I am but a very poor writer," said the young man. "I don't know what sort of a writer thou art, but thou art a good figurer," was the expressive reply.

GAS-MAKING.

Mr. Benjamin Bassett was the first to make gas in Bury, and light up his foundry with it. That was in the year 1818. He made it at his own works, which were beside the Shakspeare Inn, Rochdale-road. There were then no iron pipes, and the pipes required in the making of the gas and in conveying it to where it was required were made of lead.

THE LATE THOMAS OPENSHAW, ESQ.

This gentleman expired at his residence, Primrose Hill, Bury, on the 10th of May, 1869, in the 79th year of his age. His useful career, together with some facts connected with the early history of this old and respected Bury family, deserve more than a passing notice. The birthplace of Mr. Openshaw was a house which still stands near Pimhole Bridge, in Pimhole Fold. It is an unpretending structure of brick, having an oval stone, a little ornamented, inserted over the door, bearing this inscription :—

G: E:

O P E N S H A W ,

ANNO

1775.

From this it appears that the residence was built by Mr. Openshaw's grandfather. Pimhole at that period bore quite a different aspect to that which it presents at this day. John Ainsworth, who was commonly termed the Bury poet, and who wrote under the *nom de plume* of "Veritas," alludes to Pimhole in his "Walks round Bury for sixty years and upwards" in the following terms :—"The land around Pimhole was beautiful ; neither pen nor pencil can delineate correctly this once happy and rural place." And the etymology of the word Pimhole would confirm Mr. Ainsworth's remarks. The first syllable, it is conjectured, is a corruption of Prim, and the latter of hall. It is thought that Pimhole is a corruption of Primrose Hall; and it is a fact that that beautiful flower once grew in great luxuriance at Pimhole. In the brook which ran before his father's door, and which, it is believed, was once overhung with trees, Mr. Openshaw indulged in his favourite pastime of fishing. When he plied the "gentle craft" in the local rivers or elsewhere he was often accompanied by a person named Jonathan Clough. His education was well cared for. Miss Longworth introduced him to the mysteries of the "three R.'s," and subsequently he was sent as a boarder to a school in Ardwick. From thence he was taken to engage in the more serious affairs of life. He learnt the manufacture of woollen goods under his father's tuition, and subsequently became the travelling partner of the firm of John Openshaw, Son, and Co. Although necessarily much engaged in trade, and often away from home by reason of the nature of his employment, he invariably succeeded in returning on the Saturday evening, so as to be able to perform the duties of the Sunday school. A natural inclination led him to undertake this onerous office. The first Church Sunday school that was opened in Bury was in the Wylde, and it was afterwards removed to Butcher-lane. A person named Robert Howorth kept a day school there, and the wardens of the Parish Church secured the use of the room on Sundays. About 1820 the Sunday school was removed to a house in what is now called Cross-street, opposite to what were then termed "'torney Parker's gates," which still exist. It was here that Mr. Openshaw commenced teaching, which employment he carried on for about fifty years. After a time he devoted his attention more particularly to Pimhole, and used to assemble the children of the village at his father's residence, which was situate at the top of what is known as Garden-street, Pimhole. But the number of scholars increasing, the upper rooms of a tenement in Pimhole Woollen Fold were secured in 1828. This school, like its more modest predecessor, in the course of eight years proved to be inconveniently small, and Pimhole Sunday Schools were then built, principally at Mr. Openshaw's expense. He conducted and taught these schools until 1864. During this long period he was remarkably regular in his attendance twice a day, and was never absent unless compelled to be so by unavoidable circumstances. He had always the patriarchal way of leading his scholars to church, and was never deterred by inclemency of weather, and never could be persuaded that he had caught cold from sitting in church in damp clothes. He also conducted the singing. He had a good tenor voice, and was passionately fond of glee singing, a taste for which he had probably acquired from mixing with his father and his father's friends, who met at each other's houses to cultivate this class of music. Nor did he confine himself to these labours of love. Twice each Sunday he gave an address to the scholars, and he devoted much time to forming and carrying out schemes of charity, and means of inculcating education. One of his undertakings was a Dorcas society, which he liberally supported. Once each month he gave materials for various articles of wearing apparel required in a family to the young women of the village, who were taught at the society's meetings by qualified persons how to cut out and make the garments. A peculiarity of these gatherings was that the young women sang while at their work, and to listen, or even to join in, the singing was one of Mr. Openshaw's greatest delights. Up to about fifteen years before his death the articles were bestowed according to the wish of the maker, provided of course that the proposed recipient met with Mr. Openshaw's approval. But as the population of the village increased it became a necessity to confine the donations to people connected with Pimhole, and Mr. Openshaw made the following rules, which we find written in one of the society's books in his own remarkably neat hand :—

Rules for Thomas Openshaw's Dorcas Society.

1st. No family to have aid from the society unless all or part of its members work at the cotton or woollen concerns at Pimhole.

2nd. No family to have any article of clothing from the society unless the members of it attend some place of worship; especially the father of the family.

To carry out what seems to have been one of his plans to make good housewives of the young women of Pimhole, he called together those of the first class in the school, as well as the teachers, twice each year, and supplied them with materials with which to make substantial potatoe pies for the consumption of their respective families. He also commenced free night schools, which he regularly attended. Some evenings, as if in furtherance of the before-mentioned object, were devoted to teaching the young women to knit and sew ; and it is a well known fact that the Pimhole women were eminently skilled in the first useful accomplishment. Other evenings were set apart for reading, writing, arithmetic, and explanations of the Scriptures. Mr. Openshaw also held quarterly meetings of both the married and single. To the former, whom he used to address as the " heads of families," he tendered many valuable suggestions regarding the management of their families, and earnestly exhorted them to keep out of debt. And the young people he was wont to warn against " early marriages" and " foolish courtships." Mr. Openshaw approved of the method now in vogue of creating emulation, as well as giving an inducement to perform the labour of learning, and accordingly gave prizes. For many years previous to 1848 he presented, each November, top-coats and cloaks to deserving scholars. After that he offered them the option of blankets, umbrellas, or money. Each prize-winner also received a suitable book and a small donation of money in the following March. Some of the scholars have received more than twenty of these books, and show them with evident pride and pleasure. In order to foster a love of horticulture and to find rational, healthy, and profitable employment for leisure hours, Mr. Openshaw had about forty gardens laid out, which he let at the sum of one shilling each per annum as an acknowledgment, his practice being to return the money at once, besides giving prizes to those who had the best-tilled ground. He was fond of observing old customs, and on the 5th of November gave to each girl who attended the night school a cake of parkin. That delicious compound of sweetmeats, the manufacture of which, as already stated, is peculiar to Bury, was similarly dealt with. At each of the three annual fairs he caused to be distributed to every child who was in any way connected with Pimhole, a penny or a halfpenny. He was always fond of children, and would spend hours in watching them play. It was a pleasure to him to secure them for an auditory, and he would relate to them interesting tales of former years. At the fairs held in September and March he gave the teachers a tea party. In addition to other means of instruction, Mr. Openshaw some forty years ago commenced a day-school, and had it carried on at no little cost to himself. Throughout the long course of his life he thought that it was the duty of a master to care for and promote the earthly as well as the eternal welfare of his workpeople. Just as the father is to some extent responsible for the morality and prosperity of his offspring, so Mr. Openshaw conceived was a master placed towards those whom he employed.

Mr. Openshaw was not without visible testimonies of the high esteem in which he was held by all with whom he was brought in contact. In 1838 he was presented with a beautifully-chased silver cup by the people of Pimhole, in acknowledgment of his efforts in furthering the cause of education. The gardeners also testified to his kindness by offering him a snuff-box. The young men of the Saturday Night School also presented him with a Bible, bearing the following inscription :— " To Thomas Openshaw, Esq., of Primrose Hill.—As a token of affection and gratitude for his unwearied exertions in the education of the young men on Saturday evenings. For his good qualities as a man and his virtues as a Christian, this volume is humbly and affectionately presented by the young men of Pimhole." The young men of the first class in Pimhole Church Sunday School also presented him with a Bible on November 5th, 1857, in which was inscribed, "Presented to Thomas Openshaw, Esq., of Primrose Hill, by the young men of the first class in the Pimhole Church Sunday School, as a token of affection and gratitude."

A natural modesty of disposition prevented Mr. Openshaw from becoming a public man. He was pressed to accept a magistracy, which he declined, as well as the honour of being nominated as a member of Parliament. He was in politics a consistent Conservative, but never took a very active part in electioneering movements. He, however, considered that it was his duty to serve the town in some measure, and filled the offices of guardian of the poor and churchwarden. Indeed, he was the first person who was appointed to the latter office by the late rector, the Rev. G. Hornby. He was an active and a generous supporter of our local charities.

Mr. Openshaw's characteristics were punctuality, neatness, and perseverance, and his charity was unbounded. Not content with his large benefactions at home, he was equally generous towards those who resided on his valuable estates in Wales, and was a liberal subscriber to many of the charitable, missionary, and other beneficent institutions of the country. Nothing could be more characteristic of the man than the following letter, which was addressed to a friend, and which was written so late as March 24th, 1869 :—

Dear ———,—I am always very glad to relieve any poor person you may wish to bring under my notice, for I am sure it will always be very far from your wish to recommend any but those who are deserving or those who have been unexpectedly deprived of work through no fault of their own. I have been mostly confined to the house so far this week by a copious bleeding from my nose, and this morning when just about to go to church for morning prayers, another bleeding prevented me, but it was not so serious. I will most willingly assist ——— as you state, or any other person you may name (either personally or by your usual and best manner of sending a note) and this week, from the unexpected breakdown, I doubt not you will have other applications. Dear ———, "err on the soft side," in such cases, is my old lesson, you know; and this, I believe, you have a great wish to follow.

Mr. Openshaw could not rest contented until he had erected to his God a house of prayer; and he caused to be built the beautiful structure of St. Thomas's Church, at a cost of above £8,000, as will be seen in the historical notice of that church in another page. His remains were interred in the family vault at St. Paul's Church, on the 14th May, 1869.

> He sleeps—yet little of him sleeps below,
> Earth has its share, dust unto dust we throw;
> His soul is in its native heaven, his mind
> Remains with us, to benefit mankind.

The will left by Mr. Thomas Openshaw was proved, shortly after his death, in the registry at Manchester, under £30,000. He left liberal legacies to his sister, nephews, nieces, and others, and to his servants, as well as the following charitable bequests:—To the National school at Bury, £100; and to six district Sunday schools, each £25; to the Bury Dispensary, £500; and £200 for the poor of Bury; to the district of St. Thomas's, £1,000 for the poor; and to the districts of All Saint's, St. Paul's, Holy Trinity, St. John's, and Redvale, each £600 for the poor, to be called "Openshaw's Charity." The residue, real and personal, he left to his brother, Oliver Ormrod Openshaw, absolutely.

JAMES CLERKE, ESQ., AND SIR WILLIAM CLERKE.

At the time the Americans were shaking off the British yoke, General Burgoyne was sent with an army to quell the rebellious, and bring them back to be liege subjects to the King of Great Britain. James Clerke, Esq., was General Burgoyne's aide-de-camp. He was killed, and the British army discomfited, while the General came to England on a parole of honour. James Clerke, Esq., was brother to Sir William Clerke, and when dying he requested General Burgoyne, if he came to England, to use his influence to obtain his brother a situation in the Church. His brother was at that time going through his studies at college. General Burgoyne, having married a sister of the Earl of Derby, applied to the noble Earl for the preferment of Sir William. When the Rev. John Stanley died, the General's request was granted, and Sir William Clerke succeeded the Rev. John Stanley as Rector of Bury. He was well received by the parishioners when he arrived at the Rectory, which was then surrounded by beautiful lands. Smithy Field, Chip Field, Leister Field, and Church Field, lay on the south-east side of the Rector's house. Sir William was fond of agriculture. He often took an active part at the plough, and in the time of harvest he was busily employed among the hay-makers, shearing and housing corn into the tithe barn that lay below the Rectory House. Subsequently he removed from the Rectory House to Gooseford, for some time the residence of William Grant, Esq. Here he entered largely into the agricultural line. He pulled down the old farmhouse at Gooseford, and built a good mansion on the site, which he called Spring Side. His farm and land extended from Spring Side to the Nubbs, and from the Nubbs to the Lumm, &c. He had possession of the corn mill at the Lumm, and became one of the first-rate corn dealers in the country. Many men were employed upon his farm, but they sought by every means to plunder him. He sold meal, flour, malt, &c., through the country, as far as Affetside. It is said that through the dishonesty of the persons to whom he sold produce, Sir William passed from one embarrassment to another until he became in a straightened condition in his financial affairs. He was ever goodnatured and kind to the poor, and though he could not lessen human woe generally through his living, he had a good name among those who often felt the benefit of his temporary charities. Sir William was also a great trader in lime. He had limekilns at Clitheroe, and had ponies travelling with lime from town to town and village to village. Sir William's difficulties gradually became more apparent—entanglement followed on the heels of entanglement, until at length he became enveloped in the intricate meshes of the law. His affairs were such that he had to call to his assistance the money-mongering Jews, with whom he trafficked for a loan of £10,000 at sixteen per cent. The interest for this sum was annually paid out of the rent belonging to the Rectory. He was compelled to leave his newly-erected mansion at Spring Side, through trouble which his generous nature had brought upon him. The stock and interest of the Jewish money-mongers were lost when Sir William died. In all his public actions he appears to have been actuated by the highest moral feelings, though not always controlled by prudence. No difficulty could vanquish him, and no danger surprise him. He was constitutionally active and enterprising, and his only failing was that he was not sufficiently cautious. He could not subdue the promptings of his restless nature. He was tried in every station of life—the heaviest and most responsible. He was at court, in consultations, in commissions, in arbitrations, at public meetings, indeed, every moment of his life seemed to be occupied. Loaded, as it were, to the earth with papers, accounts, and lawsuits, he applied all his energies to his overwhelming matters; but, after all, sunk under them, while enduring the privations of incarceration in a prison, in the year 1818. Sir Robert Peel and William Yates, Esq., contracted for and took possession of the whole of Sir William's property in the Rectory of Bury. Spring Side, with all the lands and gardens surrounding the hall, likewise fell into their hands. Lady Clerke and her family withdrew from Bury, and resided with friends in different parts of the country.

THE HUTCHINSON FAMILY.

This family, believed to have come out of the parish of Pilkington, amassed considerable wealth in Bury during the early stages of manufactures. Mr. Thomas Hutchinson and his son, Mr. William Hutchinson, were among the first founders of the National School. Mr. John Hutchinson, brother to Mr. Thomas Hutchinson, resided in an old-fashioned residence at the further end of what was then termed Manchester-street. He married a daughter of William Walker, Esq., father of Richard Walker, Esq., M.P. For a long time the Hutchinson family followed the woollen business in Bury. Mr. William Hutchinson occupied a mansion in Bolton-street. James Hutchinson, of Woodbank, was one of his sons; and Thomas Norris, Esq., of Limefield, married one of his daughters, by whom he had a large family. Mr. and Mrs. Norris had a considerable share in the management of the Free Grammar School and the Girls' School in Bury, and were related to the Rev. Roger Kay, founder of the Grammar School. The Hutchinson family, which are noted in Bury to this day, were inhabitants of Bury thirty or forty years before the appearance of the Peel family.

Lydia Hutchinson, and afterwards her daughter Mary, never known except by the name of " Mally," was, commencing about 1788, the only confectioner or professed pastry-cook in Bury. The Hutchinsons, who gave great celebrity to the Bury Simnel, of which they were for a long time the only makers, occupied three distinct dwellings, fronting the street continuously, the centre one being the part first occupied as a shop by " Lydia," and when her sons Thomas and John reached manhood, the confectionery, being their sister Mally's department, was removed into the upper dwelling, the large room of which had heretofore constituted the parlour or house-part for the family, and the brothers commenced business on their own account as grocers; whilst the small cottage next below the shop was occupied as a dress-making room by the younger sister, Elizabeth, or " Betty" Hutchinson. The father of the family, Robert, husband of Lydia, was one of the most thorough and scientific musicians of his time, an enthusiast in his love and practice of instrumental music of the highest order. To his training his sons Thomas and John owed their special excellence on the violin, but Robert Hutchinson's favourite playing for himself was on the harpsichord, which instrument, before the house-part was taken for the confectionery shop, was placed there; and afterwards, until the old ˙man's death, stood in the small room behind, which space it almost filled, and where, from his easy chair, in almost his last sickness, he could conveniently touch the keys. Until under his wife's management the shop in Bury-lane was opened, he had from his youth upwards walked in all weathers from his home at the Wharf, near Openshaw Fold, to Ardwick Chapel, Manchester, in fulfilment of his duties as organist. His musical taste, had been developed, even in boyhood, by playing upon the virginal, and the antiquated instrument of his early life was kept by him until the last. At the time when his harpsichord was purchased, those made by Rucker, the most celebrated maker, cost one hundred guineas, the double key-board peculiar to the instrument proving often a sore puzzle to country folk who obtained a surreptitious peep at Robert Hutchinson's " music," as the harpsichord itself was always termed. His sons were splendid violinists and scientific musicians like himself; and love of the art and ability to conquer its difficulties seemed component in their nature. In that department they were the most accomplished of their time in Bury. At stated seasons, Thomas—known invariably as Tommy—walked to Manchester with his violin, to attend, as a player, at the Subscription Concerts, which were then established ; and at the Bury Assemblies the brothers always led the music for dancing. John, the younger brother, was also an industrious entomologist. Mally, Betty, Tommy, and John died unmarried ; a sister married and left children. The " bakehouse " of the Hutchinsons was a memorable place of merry-making to many in the bygone times, serving alike for kitchen, parlour, and reception-room ; always comfortable, but especially so in winter ; roughly constructed, low, and open to the rafters ; a place where the greatest fun could prevail secure from old Robert's hearing or condemnation. All these meetings took place without premeditation, for there was no set time appointed for company, and none came unless ready to contribute to the general stock of amusement and good spirits. The most enjoyable part of the night commenced when Tommy and John took their violins to play country dances for the assembled company ; and then, apparently in the most careless and unstudied manner, would the brothers " discourse " music so exquisite that it was in itself a sufficient treat to hear it.

THARCAKE AND PARKIN.

There was a kind of cake made in Bury and its neighbourhood during the first five days of November each year—and at no other time—the use of which has not been discontinued more than forty years; but at a period still earlier, each family, rich or poor, felt it as a social obligation to continue the practice, and accepted the custom without inquiry as to its origin or signification. This bread was designated " Thar-cake," a mispronunciation of " Thor-cake," and as Thor-cake it was made and greatly relished by all children and young people and also by some older people. In modern days it became a compound of oatmeal, butter, and treacle ; anciently it was made of coarsely-ground or pounded grain, kneaded to a consistency with honey. The honey in the cake was indispensable, but in more degenerate times treacle became the substitute. Thar-cake, as made in Lancashire from fifty to one hundred years ago, had in its composition oatmeal, a goodly proportion of butter, and as much of good thick black treacle as made it up ; no water was requisite or allowed. After this period began its decadence. Its use had been carried to Manchester, and the little town-bred children entirely within this century corrupted its ancient designation to "Parkin," and now, still further to extend and confirm this perversion, a well-known firm of biscuit makers in Glasgow announce the sale of " Parkin," or what is intended for it, under the same dishonoured appellation.

MR. ELLIS CUNLIFFE, SURGEON.

This gentleman, who was well known in Bury as a skilful and active surgeon, died on the 21st December, 1821. His dress a blue coat with brass buttons; and top boots. He wore his hair powdered, and a pigtail, which hung over his coat collar. He almost never went anywhere on wheels, but accomplished his very extensive practice, which embraced Clitheroe, Whalley, Heywood, Middleton, Stand, Radcliffe, Tottington, Holcombe, &c., on horseback. On going to an evening party he asked those present to guess how far he had ridden that day. He said, " I mounted ' Bolus ' this morning. I rode him to Preston, I fed him. I rode him on to Lancaster, when, just as I entered the Court, I heard Ellis Cunliffe called. I said, ' Ellis Cunliffe is here, sir '; and having given my evidence I re-mounted ' Bolus,' and rode him to Bury." Not a bad day's work, ninety miles for man and horse. He was master of the hounds, and a capital rider. He had a groom whom he always designated, with his usual dignity, as " Richard," and to whom he left, by his will, an annuity. This man, commonly known as " Dick," was proverbially not fond of drinking pure water; on one occasion he could not be found; however, the Doctor thought the cellar might " not be a bad cast," so down he went, and discovered Dick, just draining the last drop of beer out of a quart pot, holding it with both hands, his elbows in the air. " Richard! Richard!" the Doctor exclaimed. The culprit exclaimed, " Eh! Mestur, yo han catched me, neaw;" as if the first time he had ever done so, because the first time he was caught in the act. Dick acted as waiter in the house, on special occasions, when Mr. Cunliffe had friends, and once when he ought to have exhibited his more polite qualities he spoiled his manners. Mr. Cunliffe had invited the first Sir Robert Peel to meet an eminent dignitary of the Church at dinner. The latter asked, during dinner, for a glass of water. Dick, who could not believe that anybody would be such a heathen as to drink water, went up to the rev. gentleman, and said, " Th' ale's very good, mestur." The reply was, " I prefer water, thank you." Dick could not imagine that he had heard correctly, so he brought a great foaming pot of porter, which he presented close under the visage of the astonished clergyman, who, in a loud, somewhat irritated tone, exclaimed, " *Water*, I said, man!" Then Dick, with characteristic anxiety that the visitors should have what *he* thought was good for them, being convinced that the water was to have spirits mixed with it, went up and inquired, " Win you have your waetur whut or cowd?" On one occasion the gig was at his door, and the doctor was just on the point of stepping into it, along with the late Mr. Edmund Grundy, having Preston races in view, when up came a man on horseback at great speed, with " Doctor, yo mun goo to Middleton directly, as quick as ever yo con, to so-and-so," &c. " Oh! very well," said the Doctor, " I will go at once." " The horse shall be put into the stable," remarked Mr. Edmund Grundy. " Oh! dear, no," quickly answered the Doctor, " just throw a cloth over the horse, I shall not be many minutes." He jumped upon a fresh horse, rode from Bury to Middleton and back, besides doing what was professionally required, changed his top boots, and the cloth being removed from the horse in the gig, the two friends drove away to Preston races. Mr. Edmund Yates having a grey horse, an excellent hunter, but too high-spirited for him to manage, made a present of him to the doctor, by whom the horse was soon taught manners, and will be still remembered by some as the old white horse ridden by Mr. Cunliffe. Mr. Grant, of Nuttall Hall, had the skin of this horse preserved, to cover an easy chair. This horse, " Catfire," was very sagacious; he had become blind from inflammation in the eyes, consequent on being put into a cold stable, yet he would gallop round a field not far from Buckley Wells, jumping a ditch, which crossed the field, each time he came to it.

JOHN WARBURTON, ESQ.

Mr. Baines, in his " History of Lancashire," says :—" The worthies of the parish of Bury have been sufficiently numerous, but their biographers have been very few. The talented but eccentric Warburton, Somerset Herald, has, however, escaped the common oblivion."

John Warburton, Esq., F.R.S. and F.S.A., Somerset Herald, a persevering and indefatigable antiquary, was the son of Mr. Benjamin Warburton, of Bury, by Mary, eldest daughter, and at length heiress, of Michael Buxton, of Buxton, in the county of Derby, gentleman, and born on the 28th of February, 1681. He was a man of inferior education, but possessed of great natural abilities, and made his first appearance before the public in 1716, by compiling, from actual survey, a map of the county of Northumberland, followed soon after by others of Middlesex, Essex, Hertfordshire, and Yorkshire. In 1719 he was elected Fellow of the Royal and Antiquarian Societies, and continued in the latter body till his death, but was ejected from the former in 1757, in consequence of having neglected, for a great number of years, the completion of his annual payments. On the 24th of June, 1720, he was created Somerset Herald, by Benjamin Bowes-Howard, Earl of Berkshire, Deputy Earl Marshal, having previously received his patent, dated on the 18th. In 1722 he published, in four closely-printed quarto pages, "A List of the Nobility and Gentry of the counties of Middlesex, Essex, and Hertford, who have subscribed for, or ordered their coat of arms to be inscribed on, a new map of those counties, which is now making by John Warburton, Esq., F.R.S., and Somerset Herald." In August, 1728, he gave notice that "he keeps a register of lands, houses, etc., which are to be bought, sold, or mortgaged, in England, Scotland, or Wales; and, if required, directs surveys thereof to be made; also solicits grants of arms, and performs all other matters relating to the office of a herald. For which purpose daily attendance is given at his chambers in the Herald Office, near Doctor's Commons, London. He answers letters, post-paid, and advertises, if required;" which quackery did not raise him very high in the opinion of his brethren. In 1749 he published a map of Middlesex, on two sheets of imperial atlas, with the arms of the nobility and gentry on the borders. But the Earl Marshal, supposing them to be fictitious, by his warrant commanded him not to take in any subscribers for arms, nor advertise or dispose of any maps, till the right of such persons respectively was first proved to the satisfaction of one of the kings-of-arms. In his book of "London and Middlesex Illustrated," after observing on the Earl Marshal's injunction respecting the submission of his maps to one of the kings-of-arms, he subjoins, "which person's (Anstis) partiality being well known to the author, he thought it best to have another arbitrator joined with him, and therefore made choice of an impartial public, rather than submit his performance wholly to the determination of a person so notoriously remarkable for knowing nothing at all of the matter." After censuring the notion that trade and nobility are incompatible, as a doctrine fitted only for a despotic government, and judiciously remarking upon the moral impossibility there would soon be of proving descents and arms, from the want of visitations, he returns to attack the heads of the college by saying that such proofs are obstructed by the exorbitant and unjustifiable fees of three heralds, called kings-of-arms, who receive each £30 for every new grant. In this book he gives the names, residences, genealogies, and coat-armour of the nobility, principal merchants, and other eminent families, emblazoned in their proper colours, with references to authorities. That Warburton was often in distress for money, and at such times had very little delicacy in relieving himself from his embarrassments, appears but too true. Mr. Gorse, the Richmond Herald, and his contemporary, gives the following circumstance, as proof of his readiness to catch at any time an opportunity of imposing on the unwary:—" Walking one day through the streets of London, he passed by the house of Mr. Stainbank, a rich merchant, over whose door he saw an achievement or hatchment, on which were painted three castles, somewhat like those borne in the arms of Portugal. He went immediately home and wrote a short note, begging to see Mr. Stainbank on very particular business. The gentleman came, when Warburton, with a great deal of seeming concern, told him that the Portuguese ambassador had been with him, and directed him to commence a prosecution against him for assuming the royal arms of Portugal, and, besides, meant to exhibit a complaint against him in the House of Lords for a breach of privilege. Mr. Stainbank, terrified at the impending danger, begged his advice and assistance, for which he promised to reward him handsomely. Warburton, after some consideration, said he had hit on a method of bringing him out of a very ugly scrape, which was that he should purchase a coat of arms, which he would devise for him as like as possible the achievement, and that he would show it to the ambassador, to confirm its being the legal coat of arms, and say that the similitude complained of was owing to the blunder of the painter. The arms were granted in due form, and paid for, when Warburton, over and above his share of £40, asked and obtained a particular reward for appeasing the representative of the Portuguese majesty." Mr. Gorse adds to this laughable and scandalous story, that, " notwithstanding this and many like dirty tricks, he clearly proved the truth of the proverb which says that ' honesty is the best policy,' by dying a beggar." He expired in his apartments at the College of Arms, on the 11th of May, 1759, aged seventy-eight, and was buried on the 17th, in the south aisle of St. Bennet's Church, Paul's Wharf. A remarkable circumstance occurred at his funeral. Having a great abhorrence of the idea of worms crawling upon his body when dead, he ordered that his body should be enclosed in two coffins, one of lead, the other of oak ; the first he directed should be filled with green broom, heather, or ling ; and, in compliance with his desire, a quantity was brought from Epping Forest, and stuffed extremely close round his body. This fermenting, burst the coffin, and retarded the funeral until part of it was taken out. Mr. Warburton was a diligent antiquary, and his manuscript collections were very great. In the " Sketch of the Materials for the County of Chester, by an F.A.S., in a letter to Thomas Falconer, Esq., of Chester," it is noticed that " his indefatigable labours have greatly contributed to the ornament and illustration of almost every county in the kingdom. His method was, perhaps, singularly sensible,—to glean up everything, either in print or manuscript, which had the most

I

distant relation to that particular county he had intended to elucidate.
The scattered fragments, like the Sibyl's leaves, he bound up into volumes,
suitable to the size of the papers he had collected, either folio, quarto,
or octavo." For Cheshire alone he had five volumes. The manuscripts
are particularised as comprising " A Calendar of the Manors of
Cheshire, with the several fees the Lords of the said Manors paid to the
Earl of Chester, and the names of proprietors, to the year 1710, 4to.—
An account of the principal Families in Cheshire, with the lands they
held in the said county, from 33 Edward III. to 24 Henry VII., folio.—
A Register of the Black Prince, and Homage due to the Earl of Chester,
with the names of the principal Families, Lords of Manors, Lordships,
etc., from 3 Edward III. to 29 Eliz., folio.—A variety of Maps, Plans,
and Prospects, with MS. notes, by Plot, Warburton, and others, and
whatsoever is curious in the repositories of the Herald's Office, the
Harleian Library, and the Office of Records, relative to the County
Palatine of Chester." He was remarkably unfortunate in his disputes
and squabbles with his brethren, by whom he was despised and detested ;
yet Mr. Toms, Rouge Dragon, says, that " though his conduct was
faulty, yet he was extremely ill-used, especially by the younger Anstis,
who was of a violent, tyrannical disposition." That Warburton was
vindictive and scurrilous, however, is undoubted. Mr. Warburton was
the author of " Vallum Romanum, or the History and Antiquities of the
Roman Wall, commonly called the Picts' Wall, in Cumberland and
Northumberland, built by Hadrian and Severus, the Roman Emperors,
seventy miles in length, to keep out the Picts and Scots, in three books,
with a letter from Roger Gale, on the Roman antiquities in the North of
England, the whole illustrated with a map and other plates ; " London,
1753, 1754, 4to.—" Roman History, continued from the Second
Century of the Christian Æra to the Destruction of the Greek Empire by
the Turks ; " London, 1794, 12mo. These, with some prints, are the
whole of his publications, but he had also a valuable collection of old
dramas, a catalogue of which, with some remarks, appear in the
Gentleman's Magazine for September, 1815. A Plan of Helston's Loch,
in Cornwall, was engraved by Mr. Warburton ; and two instruments for
drawing up tin out of the lake, invented by him, but never published.
" Proposals relative to his Mines, called the Silver Mines of Penrose,"
were also among his papers. He had likewise " Notes relating to several
Monasteries in Devonshire, in the handwriting of Lord William Howard,
of Naworth, temp. Eliz." His " Essex Collections " fell into the hands
of Dr. Gower, of Chelmsford ; and his other MSS. were used in
" Hasted's History of Kent."

CHAPTER VII.

" Cheshire Shore's Neezing Club:" its History and Doings—The Whitehead Family—The Walker Family—The Nuttall Family—John Partington—Mr. Samuel Smith—Bury Grammar School—The Coaching Days—Mr. Thomas Norris—The Athenæum—The Ragged School—The late Mr. John Hall.

" CHESHIRE SHORE'S NEEZING CLUB:" ITS HISTORY AND DOINGS.

" Lancashire Folk Lore " can give us nothing funnier than the tale we have to tell. " Owd Cheshire Shore" would have told it much better, only as that captain of the " Royal Woodrangers' Association " isn't here to tell the tale in his own way—having resigned his " captaincy" at the bidding of a dread spectre who shall be nameless— we must give the story as we got it. Cheshire Shore is dead: long live old " Cheshire." He sent in his resignation about a month ago, and there was a large gathering of the " Royal Woodrangers" to see the old man's bones laid in that bed from which there is no rising till the " crack o' doom." For Cheshire was much respected by his " lads," the rangers, whom he captained for many a year, and had led victoriously through more than one hard-fought fight. They would have done any-thing for Cheshire, and they do seem to have been very anxious at time and time to keep his whistle wet and his " clay" well soaked—no easy matter for the lads to do, for Cheshire was blessed with a wife whose tongue was a terror to all tipplers and " nowts," and he could seldom escape from her apron-string. Well, about the " Royal Woodrangers." Although Cheshire Shore, *alias* William Jones, may not for certain be that " oldest inhabitant" whose authority upon everything local is held in so great respect, yet he was a very old inhabitant, and has cobbled shoes and waxed his tatchin'-end in Bell-lane for something short of a century. Of that we are sure. Cheshire was always " fond o' childer," and it was his custom about fifty years ago to go to Ashworth Wood, for a stroll on sunny Sundays, and especially on Palm Sunday, when Cheshire looked like a patriarch who had taken all his tribe out for an airing. On that day all the juvenile population of the neighbourhood of Bell-lane turned out to go with Cheshire to the wood, when they had a sort of woodland carnival, Cheshire joining in their little games and frolics like a Gulliver among the pigmies of Lilliput. He never failed to bring each mother's child safe home, so that the gathering waxed greater as the years went by. No doubt Cheshire looked upon Ashworth Wood as his own particular right by length of user, a position that seems to have been disputed, for some twenty-five years ago a quarrel arose between Cheshire's band and a rival clan from Heywood for the possession of a spring in the wood, called Jacob's Well. They could not all drink at it at once, and very likely there was a little of the dog-in-the-manger business about it. Well, old Cheshire brought his bairns and his grievance back to Bury, and Bell-lane grew wroth at this infringement upon its rights and customs. The following Sunday saw a formidable gathering of the hobbledehoy population of Bell-lane, who were burning with a fierce desire to clear the wood of the Heywood "varmint;" and the expedition started under the direction of Cheshire Shore as Captain-Commandant. These warlike preparations must have got wind in the meantime, for Heywood also mustered strong, and was first at the well. A flying helter-skelter sort of skirmish ensued, many being frightened but nobody hurt. Cheshire's band returned crestfallen and vanquished, but only for a time; for the fierce feud raged for two succeeding Sundays, the result being that Heywood was at last "gradely licked," and had to sing small ever after. Cheshire Shore was henceforth Captain Shore, and wore his honours like a hero. The expedition on Palm Sunday became a great affair from that time, and was no longer confined to "childer" of small growth. In course of time the sylvan pic-nic degenerated into a "neezing" expedition, otherwise called birdnesting, and the lads who looked to Cheshire as their captain styled themselves members of the "Royal Woodrangers' Association." After holding the office for forty-three years, Old Cheshire resigned his captaincy in the manner aforesaid; and as Palm Sunday was again hard upon them, the "neezers" determined, in conclave, to have another captain to stand in Cheshire's shoes. So they prepared to appoint his successor by election conducted with due form, and the candidates issued their addresses to the "neezing" constituency, who were apprised of these things in the manner following, the "writ" being printed and posted in the form of a placard:—

Electors and Non-Electors.

Notice.—Isaac Bridge and James Chadwick are coming out as candidates for the forthcoming election of a head president to the Royal Woodrangers' Association. The seat is vacant by the death of the late Cheshire Shore, who has been returned without opposition for the last thirty years. All voters will have to appear before the revising barrister, Jeff Kershaw, who will sit every evening from seven till ten o'clock at the Central Committee Rooms, 73, Bell-lane, and if any flaw is found against any voter he will be struck off the list.—Returning officer, John Rawson; clerk to the returning officer, Thomas Mitchell. Captain Wild, senior judge and senior secretary; George Kearsley, treasurer; William Skitter, chairman; James Rothwell, vice-chairman.

The election took place on Saturday last, the "polling booths" of the respective candidates being the Royal Oak beerhouse—better known as the Cock and Trumpet—and the Church Inn, both in Bell-lane, of course. Chadwick *alias* Jemmy Boo was declared duly elected by the returning officer, he having a majority of six; but the Bridge party demanded a "scrutiny," on the ground that Boo had recorded 13 votes from Radcliffe who voted by proxy, contrary to rule. Boo's return is therefore being petitioned against because of "illegal practices," and as he is expected to be "unseated" the two candidates already in the field are the defeated Bridge and "Roary." But the election was allowed to stand for the following Sunday, when the rangers gathered in great force under the new "head president," and repaired to Ashworth Wood as aforetime to declare the grounds duly opened. The captain delivered the usual oration on Windycliff Bridge, and there was much cheering; and after him came the defeated candidate, who considered himself their captain *de jure*, and who was determined to have his "blow." He said that if he were not elected their lawful captain he would make the woods to tremble before him, and would cut down every tree, and cause a famine to fall upon the wood so that birds should not build their nests there for seven long years, and the "neezers" would have no sport because of this evil thing which they had done unto their lawful captain. Much shouting followed this oracular outpouring of righteous wrath, and the "Royal Rangers" adjourned to the Chapel-house to discuss the matter over a good dinner and "summat to sup."

THE WHITEHEAD FAMILY.

This family are of long standing in Bury, and it is said that they were settled here at the time Prince Rupert passed through the town, on his way from York to the siege of Lathom House, and that the Prince stopped with the family. One branch of the family were barbers in Bury before the Peel family came upon the scene ; indeed, they were the principal barbers in the town, and the whole of the wig men had their wigs dressed, pomatumed, or perfumed by the Whiteheads. A description of the toilet of great people in those days, at balls or parties, would appear rather ludicrous now-a-days, ridiculous as some may at present appear ; suffice it to say that when these festive occasions took place, Mr. Whitehead (father of Mr. Henry Whitehead, formerly postmaster) was called in to see that everything was done in proper order, and if his family could not perform the duty in due time, he called in assistance from the neighbouring barbers. It is said that Mr. Whitehead has at times called to his assistance Mr. Arkwright, afterwards known as Sir Richard Arkwright, the inventor. It is certain, however, that Sir Richard Arkwright did visit Mr. Whitehead in his carriage as a brother barber. Some idea of the labour of a barber in those days may be gathered from the fact that it took three hours to curl dress wigs, powder them, &c., for every lady or gentleman that attended a ball or festive gathering. At that time many gentlemen gave one guinea a year to have their pates powdered. The ladies, gentlemen, and soldiers had their hair tied behind, friseared, and powdered, but afterwards, what was called the Prince of Wales' dock (having the hair cut close to the head behind) was introduced in Bury, and Mr. Whitehead's business and that of other barbers began gradually to decline. Mr. Henry Whitehead often went long journeys for the Peel and Yates' families,— to London and other parts of the country,—on horses, in carriages, and on foot. As a pedestrian he had scarcely an equal in England, for it was not uncommon for him to go at the rate of six miles per hour. On one occasion he walked for a wager on the Manchester road twelve miles in two hours, and won the bet with ease. On another occasion Mr. Whitehead and several gentlemen went from Bury to York races. After the races were over twelve of them agreed to walk from York to Bury in one day. Mr. Wolfenden, then nearly eighty years of age, was one of the party, and the party did their best to persuade him not to try to walk with them, for they felt sure that he would not be able to keep up with them. All, however, set out together, and travelled on till they arrived at Halifax. Here Mr. Whitehead and Mr. Wolfenden began to leave their companions, who could not reach any further than Rochdale the same evening, while Mr. Whitehead and Mr. Wolfenden arrived in Bury the same day. Mr. Whitehead filled many public offices in Bury, much to the credit of himself and the satisfaction of the town. Besides officiating as postmaster, he was the first deputy constable of the parish, for which he received £30 per annum. When he resigned this post he was succeeded by Mr. Andrews, at a salary of £100 a year.

THE WALKER FAMILY.

Mr. Richard Walker, grandfather to Richard Walker, Esq., M.P., was an extensive cattle dealer in Bury. His wife was a near relation to the Openshaw family. Mr. Walker was much respected in this town, and here he accumulated considerable property. Afterwards he removed to

Besses-o'-th'-Barn, where the Walker family originally resided. On returning to Bury he took up his residence in a neat cottage in Manchester-street. On his death, he bequeathed handsome property to his family. Mr. William Walker carried on the woollen dyeing and milling businesses. He had a mansion at Moorside, Bury, and had warehousing upon each side of the street, and works in Walmersley. At his death he left many sons and daughters. Richard Walker, Esq., was his eldest son, and was long connected with his father in business. Subsequently he entered into the iron trade along with his brother, Mr. John Walker. These works, as is well known, have long been successfully carried on, and find employment for a large number of workmen. In 1832 Mr. Walker was returned to Parliament (see report of borough elections) by a triumphant majority. Oliver Ormerod Walker, Esq., of Chesham, was the third son of William Walker, Esq., who resided in Stanley-street. He was born on the 2nd December, 1794, it is believed, in the house now occupied by the Bury Improvement Commissioners. He was educated at the Bury Grammar School, and subsequently became a pupil of Dr. Hood, who was at that time curate of the Parish Church, and at a later period incumbent of Heywood. He set himself to learn the manufacture of woollen goods in which his father was engaged, and was abroad for some time on business. Changing his mind, however, he began to study surveying, and was for many years with Mr. Harper, but ultimately became a cotton manufacturer. About 1826 he went into partnership with Mr. John Lomax and his brother William. They then built a portion of Messrs. Walker and Lomax's mill, and commenced the manufacture of cotton goods. From that time his life was one of continued prosperity. He was a Liberal-Conservative in politics, but it was not until the year 1859 that he came prominently forward in the political world in his native town. Still it cannot be said that he did not take his share in public business. He acted as a trustee of the Bury Grammar School, and filled many similar posts. He was placed on the commission of the peace for the county of Lancaster, on the 24th October, 1853. He was twice married, his first wife being Miss Haslam, by whom he had one daughter, Mary, who married Mr. Wanklyn, and died some years ago. He died on the 20th of April, 1870, aged 75 years, and was interred in the Bury Cemetery. At the present day the Walker family are extensive employers of labour, and occupy a very influential position in the town.

THE NUTTALL FAMILY.

Long before the appearance of the Peels, this family was one of wealth and influence in Bury. Their rising to affluence was originally

through the instrumentality of the Openshaws. The old mansion and
warehouse belonging to the Nuttall family were situate at the top of
Moss-lane, in what was then called Manchester-street. Their foreign
and domestic trade as woollen manufacturers was very extensive. The
establishment of the Nuttall family was splendid; they had men and
maid servants, horsemen and carriages, while their power and name had
great influence in Bury. The grandmother of Robert Nuttall, Esq.,
before her marriage, was Miss Kay, a near relation of the Rev. Roger
Kay, the founder of the Free Grammar School in Bury. Many members
of this family now reside in the town; and are either more or less
concerned in business or professional pursuits.

JOHN PARTINGTON.

At one time the most remarkable place of business established in the
Wylde, and it was also the first by a very long interval, was the shop
of John Partington, commencing something prior to 1760. John was a
pattern of economy, frugality, untiring perseverance, and industry. He
was a bachelor throughout life, and was, by profession, a woollen
weaver—the established trade of Bury before printing was introduced.
A poor lad, thrown early on his own resources, and, since the death of
father and mother, without relatives or any near kinsfolk, he had from
the first practised a self-reliance and abstemiousness that marked his
habits as out of the ordinary path. Humble-minded, strictly honourable,
temperate in supplying his own wants, but generous to aid when it fell
in his power, John Partington, even whilst still a young man, had made
many friends in that sphere of life wherein God had placed him. Seldom
seeking outward modes of recreation, he plied the loom in his little
" house-part" from morning till night, declaring that he was kept too
busy to consider whether he was tired or not. In process of time,
feeling lonely, John began to debate whether he might not enliven his
solitariness and also add a little to his gains, by throwing open the small
" front place," as a shop. After much deliberation with himself, as
usual, consulting no other, he fixed upon purchasing a small quantity
of groceries to commence with; also an extremely limited assortment of
the common kinds of thread and buttons. Time passed; he increased
his stock in each department; and whatever small quantity of any article
was required, John had no objection to weigh or measure that quantity,
even if it were so small as threepennyworth of tea, a pennyworth of
sugar, or a still more infinitesimal division to suit the purse of the purchaser; tea, sugar, and all foreign articles of consumption being then
extremely high-priced and costly. Much later than this, in 1804,

common sugar was elevenpence a pound, and loaf sugar double that amount. If a commodity was inquired for that he did not possess, and probably then heard named for the first time in his life, he would good-naturedly say that he happened not to have the article at present, but would certainly offer it the next time they came; and he never was known to break his promise, or fail to procure, often at great inconvenience to himself, whatever his customers had desired to obtain. To supply an unwonted thing may seem an easy matter now, but was certainly difficult then. The post was slow, expensive, and uncertain; there was no business stir in the town; and no coach, cart, or other vehicle ran, as public accommodation, between Manchester and Bury, or any of the neighbouring towns. However, in spite of every difficulty, the shop prospered wonderfully, and John Partington had fewer obstructions to contend with; whilst each evening he punctually wrote down the name of any unknown article, in his way of trade, that he had heard mentioned during the day, or that it seemed advisable to add to his store. He continued weaving also until the increased business and profits of his shop warranted his giving it up; and at the same time he took as assistant or apprentice, to participate in his enterprise and share the comforts of his home, a friendless, unprotected lad, who, it was said, had travelled alone and on foot either from Scotland or some distant part of Yorkshire. Coming to Bury in his wanderings, a total stranger to all, the kind, the generous John Partington gave him rest, food, and shelter, and thenceforward treated him as a son. This boy was the gentleman known afterwards as Mr. Richard Mc.Millan. Years passed, and in course of time the good old frugal master died, with an accumulation of honestly-acquired wealth and stock, which in his youth the ancient woollen weaver would have deemed impossible, all left freely and unreservedly to the youth, now recognised as " Mr. Mc.Millan," whom he had brought up and protected. Although presumedly of humble origin, his manners were quiet and dignified, and his countenance pleasant. He wore his hair powdered, in accordance with the prevailing fashion for gentlemen. Nor must the tidy, busy, respectable, and provident housekeeper be forgotten, for she seemed part and parcel of the thriving, contented bachelor's well-ordered establishment; and lady customers were always pleased to exchange a word with Molly. The little shop in the Wylde had far outgrown its circumscribed antecedents, and numerous and expensive alterations and enlargements had quite changed the appearance and condition of the original structure. Mrs. Peel and Mrs. Edmund would sit and take a chat with Molly in the interval of purchasing or giving orders; and the shop proved a

favourite resting-place, especially after Mr. Mc.Millan rendered his large
business still more extensive by entering upon the sale of all beautiful
and fancy articles, comprising also some books. Bury Fair had, from
time immemorial, been held in the Wylde, and it was to the windows
of the parlour upstairs that the juveniles of the families of Peel and
Yates were brought to witness the antics of the showmen and the
general diversions of the day, as well as to replenish their stock of toys
from the assortment displayed in a room adjoining the front and principal
place of business. Besides the sales in tea and grocery, his trade in the
department of toys, children's books, and many elegant articles hitherto
unseen in Bury, became after a while almost incredible, and eventually
he removed to more commodious premises near the Old Grey Mare Inn.
After his death, at a good old age, about 1830, the sale of the stock-in-
trade, principally of toys, took place at the Red Lion Inn, and occupied
several weeks. As intimated, like his predecessor John Partington,
Richard Mc.Millan lived and died a bachelor, and also, like his old
master, left all accumulations and acquired property to his own assistant
and former apprentice, William Searles.

MR. SAMUEL SMITH.

This gentleman, who officiated as a commissioner for nine years, died
on the 28th September, 1869, in the 59th year of his age. He was a
regular attender at the Brunswick Chapel, and for many years taught in
the Sunday school connected with it. He laid the foundation-stone of
the new chapel. In business he was successful, and was a good steward
of the wealth entrusted to his care. His characteristics were strict
integrity, punctuality, and diligence.

BURY GRAMMAR SCHOOL.

In the year 1726, the present Grammar School was founded by the
Rev. Roger Kay, M.A., then prebendary of the Cathedral Church of
Salisbury, who assigned to trustees valuable landed property in his
native county of Lancashire, for the re-establishment of a " Schole for
teaching grammar" in Bury. There had been a previous foundation,
dating from the year 1748, when the Hon. and Rev. John Stanley,
rector, and other inhabitants, founded a school for the free education of
80 boys and 30 girls ; but even the names of the feoffees who were
entrusted with its management had been lost. Of course, whatever
funds there were originally had followed the example of the feoffees ;
and this excellent man determined to restore to Bury what it had so
unaccountably been deprived of. Acting on a broader and wiser prin-

Grammar School, Bury, Lancashire

ciple, he so contrived his admirable statutes that there should be a perpetual power in the hands of the trustees of electing into their body, whenever a vacancy occurred, a successor who should be equally capable with themselves of directing and furthering the best interests of the school he had founded. He directed also that on the 6th of May in each year, the "visitation day," as he terms it, there shall be a general gathering of the trustees ; that a sermon shall be preached at the parish church by the Rector of Bury, or one of the trustees in holy orders, "if they shall so please; " and that the principal subject of the sermon shall be "the usefulness of public benefactions of this nature, as a means to induce and move others to add to this, my charity." He foresaw the positive and lasting advantages which his liberality would insure to the inhabitants of Bury, and expresses a modest hope that those who, either in their own persons or those of their children, have benefited by his bounty, should, when God has blessed them with competence, help forward the work of education in the town by similar acts to his own.

Referring to this school in the year 1869, the report of the Assistant Commissioners to the Schools Inquiry Commission, states :—" This is one of the wealthiest and one of the most recent grammar school foundations in Lancashire. The trustees take more interest in it than trustees usually do. Although the Bury school receives a larger proportion of children of wealthy townspeople than do most of the Lancashire grammar schools, very few boys think of proceeding to the universities, and there is often a lack of candidates for the exhibitions. From 1844 to the time of my visit none have been given away. This may partly be due to the small value of the exhibitions, which, even with the addition made by Dr. Wood's bequest, would go but a very little way towards the expenses of an Oxford or Cambridge education. Nor in the Bury school, where so few of the boys remain long enough to get high in classics, and where the master's attention is necessarily so much absorbed in the work of the lower boys, would it be easy even for so excellent a scholar as the present head master to prepare any but a very clever boy to win an open scholarship at one of the better colleges. Having hardly any boys intended for the universities, and comparatively few intended for the professions, having to send out most of its scholars to business at 14 or 15 years of age, Bury school cannot carry either its classical or its mathematical teaching very high. What is given, however, is good of its kind, and is happily combined with a thorough handling of the ' commercial' subjects. Bury, although it has grown apace during the last 50 years, is by no means so new and rough as some of the other manufacturing towns. There is, I was told, fewer very large fortunes here ; there is less social separation between classes, and the wealthy manufacturers are more willing than their brethren in Bolton or Rochdale to send their sons to a day school where they will meet the children of shopkeepers or clerks. Hardly any grammar school in Lancashire has succeeded so well in recommending itself to parents of different social ranks as this of Bury. There are a good many children of millowners and professional men, a good many of shopkeepers and other tradesmen ; all mix freely together in school and at play, and all, if they stay long enough at school, learn Latin in due course, the parents making little or no objection, because they see that arithmetic and writing are duly cared for. . . . The difficulties under which it labours, and which prevent it, in spite of its fine endowment, from giving what may be called a high education, are difficulties incident to its local position among a population whose sons it receives, ill-prepared, at nine, ten, or eleven years of age, and is forced, by the pressure of business, to send into the world at fourteen."

THE COACHING DAYS.

Before the country was crowded as it is at the present time with a network of railways, Bury was not ill provided with the means of travelling by coaches, as will be seen from the subjoined list of coaches, which was published in 1824 :—

From the Grey Mare Inn, Market-place.

LEEDS AND YORK.—" The Royal Mail," every night at 9, through Heywood, Rochdale, Halifax, and Bradford. The " Neptune" by the same route, every day at 12.

LIVERPOOL.—" The Royal Mail," every evening at 7, through Bolton, Wigan, and Prescot. " The Neptune," every day at 1, through Bolton, Leigh, Newton, St. Helens, and Prescot.

MANCHESTER.—" The Traveller," every Sunday and Monday morning at 10, and on Tuesday, Wednesday, Thursday, and Saturday mornings at 7, returning the same evenings, and proceeding immediately through Haslingden, Accrington, and Whalley, to Clitheroe. " The Commercial," every Sunday and Monday at 10 in the morning, and on Tuesday, Thursday, and Saturday mornings at 7, and a coach every Monday evening at 7.

From the Eagle and Child Inn, Silver-street.

MANCHESTER.—" The Comet," every Tuesday and Saturday mornings, at half-past seven. " The Alexander," every Tuesday, Thursday, and Saturday mornings, at 8. A coach every Sunday, Wednesday, and Friday mornings, at half-past nine, and every Saturday morning at half-past seven. A coach every Tuesday morning at a quarter before eight. A coach every Monday afternoon at three, and at half-past five.

SKIPTON, BY BURNLEY AND COLNE.—" The John Bull," every Sunday afternoon at 2, and Monday, Wednesday, and Friday afternoon at 3, and every Saturday afternoon at half-past 3, and every Tuesday evening at half-past 5, through Rawtenstall.

From the Old Boar's Head, Fleet-street.

COLNE.—" The Union," every Sunday, Thursday, and Friday afternoons, at 2, every Monday evening at 7, every Tuesday evening at 6, and every Wednesday and Saturday evenings at 5, through Rawtenstall and Burnley.

MANCHESTER.—" The Union," every Monday afternoon at 4, Tuesday and Saturday mornings at 7, and Wednesday and Thursday mornings at 9.

From the White Lion, Millgate.

MANCHESTER.—" The Favourite," every Tuesday, Thursday, and Saturday mornings at 8; and " The Lark" every Tuesday and Saturday mornings at half-past 7.

Conveyance by Water from the Canal Warehouse, Bury Bridge.

MANCHESTER, LIVERPOOL, and all parts of the Kingdom.—The Old Quay Company, every Monday, Wednesday, and Friday.—Thomas Cooke, Agent.

MR. THOMAS NORRIS.

This gentleman, who died at Howick House, near Preston, in 1852, on the completion of his 87th year, may justly be termed one of the celebrities of Bury. He was born at Croston, on the 18th of January, 1765, of respectable parents, his father being a small landowner in that township. He received a good education, but was not attached to any particular pursuit until he was twenty years of age. He then went to fulfil the duties of under-bookkeeper at Ramsbottom, in one of the branch concerns of Peel, Yates, and Co. After being at Ramsbottom, his industry and general business habits led to his promotion to a confidential position in the calico printing works of the same firm, at Bury. At this time the cotton trade was being rapidly developed in various parts of England. The value of Mr. Norris's services was seen, appreciated, and acknowledged by his employers, and, after various promotions, he was at length made a partner. His career then, of course, partook of the prosperity which at that time so largely crowned the efforts of cotton-spinners. He continued, in a comparatively retired position, to amass money, and to enjoy the confidence and esteem of his partners and his workpeople until the year 1814, when the heads of the firm, Sir R. Peel and Mr. Yates, withdrew from business; at least, they very materially diminished their stake in the concerns, and their names were removed from the firm, though they actually retained an interest in the works for about seven years longer. From 1814, the works at Bury were carried on by the firm of Howarth, Hardman, Norris, and Hamer. Success continued to attend the operations of this firm, as it had done those of its predecessors; so much so that Mr. Norris, in 1821, retired from business in the possession of a very large fortune. Sir R. Peel and Mr. Yates then withdrew from it altogether, as did also Mr. Hamer. Previous to Mr. Norris's retirement from business he had in the little leisure he had allowed himself, cultivated a taste for the fine arts. Untrammelled by the cares of the counting-house, he had now greater opportunities of indulging his refined taste. His judgment in matters pertaining to the arts was great; and the very large and valuable collection he has formed, more especially of the *chefs d'œuvre* of the old masters, attests the correctness of his taste. He was also an accomplished conchologist and entomologist, and his cabinets contain one of the best private collections of shells and insects in the kingdom. He also indulged his taste in numismatology and botany, and was fond of astronomical investigations; in short, science generally found him a devotee. The very long connection he had had with the Peel family did not terminate with the close of their business engagements. It was continued with the first baronet until his death, in 1829, and Mr. Norris was appointed by him one of his executors; Mr. Yates, his partner, also evincing his confidence in Mr. Norris by a similar trust. The second baronet, the lamented and distinguished statesman, often corresponded with the subject of our notice, whom he highly regarded; and it is somewhat remarkable, that in the year 1837 he acceded to a request of Mr. Norris to sit for his portrait for him. This was a mark of favour which Sir Robert had declined to many of his most intimate friends, including even some of the most distinguished of his contemporary statesmen, and members of his cabinet. So averse was the deceased statesman to these " sittings," that we believe there were only two paintings in existence for which he sat,—the fine portrait by Sir T. Lawrence, painted when Sir Robert was comparatively a young man, and the one in the late Mr. Norris's gallery, which is by Linnel. It is much to be regretted that Linnel's portrait is not at all a happy effort of the artist. Mr. Norris, after he had attained a substantial position in life, occupied the house of Redvales, where he lived until the year 1845; when the formation of the railway required his property, he purchased, and removed to, Howick House. The deceased gentleman was of very retiring manners; he mixed little in public life, preferring to gratify his tastes in private. He was much esteemed and respected by all who knew him, and he was exceedingly benevolent and liberal in deeds of charity. A consistent member of the Church of England, he was anxious to extend her usefulness, and he contributed largely from his ample means towards increasing the number of her places of worship. In the neighbourhood of Bury, where he had derived his fortune, he was especially anxious to extend her ministrations; but he did not confine his liberality to any particular district. In his charities he was, as in most of his other transactions of life, remarkably unostentatious. He had enjoyed very good health, and up to a short time before his death was in the full possession of his faculties.

THE ATHENÆUM.

In 1836 a mechanics' institution was commenced in the town, the first meetings being held in small schoolrooms in Silver-street. It was removed in 1844 to a woollen warehouse in the Wylde, the use of which was granted gratuitously by Mr. Edmund Grundy. Owing to the rapid increase of members the erection of a new building was resolved upon, and a canvass for subscriptions was at once set on foot. The Earl of Derby gave a donation of 100 guineas, and also a piece of land in Market-street. When the subscription had amounted to about £3,000, the erection of the building which is now called the Bury Athenæum was commenced. The corner-stone was laid by Lord Stanley, on the 3rd October, 1850. In character the building is Italian: it is 122 feet long, 44 feet high, and 43 feet deep, consisting of a basement and two storeys. The total cost of the building was about £4,000, and to it 250 members of the old Mechanics' Institution brought 1,000 volumes of books. The subscription is 2s. 6d. per quarter, and the institution is tolerably well supported. There are classes in it for the study of various subjects in connection with the Science and Art Department. The library contains a large number of volumes. Of late considerable improvements have been made in the assembly and other rooms.

THE RAGGED SCHOOL.

The Bury Ragged School is situated in George-street, and was established in November, 1859, in the Temperance Hall, Agur-street. Its object, according to the first report of the promoters, was to benefit the poor and neglected children of the town ; to teach them reading, writing, arithmetic, and sewing; to give them religious instruction ; and also to provide food and clothing in extreme cases. The building in which the children meet presents a neat and very substantial appearance : it is lofty, commodious, and well ventilated, and in every way suitable for the purposes for which it was erected. There is a large schoolroom, 42 feet by 26 feet, with lavatories on each side of the principal entrance for boys and girls, over which is a gallery capable of holding about 80 persons. At the other end is a vestry 13 feet by 11 feet, with separate access from the outside ; alongside this room is the kitchen, the same size as the vestry, and extending over both rooms is the infant schoolroom. The corner-stone of the school was laid on the 11th September, 1869, by James Barlow, Esq., who was then Mayor of Bolton. The total cost of the building, with the furniture and fittings, amounted to £800. The opening services of the school were preached on Sunday, March 20, 1870, by the Rev. John Guttridge.

THE LATE MR. JOHN HALL.

One gentleman who left his "footprints on the sands of time," and who was resident in this district, was John Hall, Esq., of Holly Mount. He died at the ripe old age of fourscore years and ten, on the 13th September, 1870. His parents occupied a middle-class position in society, his father, William Hall, having rented a farm at a place known as "Bottom of the Roof" (Gorsey Brow), at Chesham. He was the second eldest of four sons, and was born on the 12th December, 1780. Agricultural industry was his first pursuit in life, but cotton manufacturing was to all intents and purposes his destined business. In 1820 he betook himself to the manufacturing trade at Mount Pleasant, where he all along remained, and where, by his indomitable perseverance, great frugality, and sterling genius, he amassed an enormous fortune. Handloom weaving was in those days universal, but when the steam age set in, and power-looms were invented, Mr. Hall applied his faculties to the construction of machines for fancy twilling, and his fertile imagination conceived an ingenious invention for the manufacture of this class of goods. He caught the tide at the flood—his manufactures were in great demand in the market—and he earned a high reputation as a manufacturer. As business increased, he increased the size of his premises, and this, in like manner, found employment for a greater number of hands. His wealth accumulated, and he erected mills in Bolton, in conjunction with his brother, and purchased several large estates, including a very extensive and valuable one in Gloucestershire. He was a bachelor, and lived retired in a plain but commodious house situate in close proximity to his factory. His mode of living was of the plainest character, and notwithstanding he abounded in wealth he never deviated from his homely ways. It was not a spirit of niggardliness that caused him thus to spend his life, but it was one of the peculiar—if we may be allowed the term—characteristics of his life. He was quite the reverse of being parsimonious; thoroughly liberal in the distribution of his charity in a tangible form, and after that truly Christian fashion of not letting his right hand know what his left hand had done. Although a staunch and consistent adherent of the Established Church of England, he could not be called a bigot in the way of relieving those of a similar religious persuasion with himself, for his philanthropy extended to the distressed and unfortunate of any and every sect— Establishment and Dissent alike. To those of his workpeople whom he could not find employment during the cotton famine, he allowed one-third of their previous earnings, and in addition paid the rent of their cottages. His business he attended to solely himself, and frequented the Manchester market for the long period of seventy years. Before the railway era, and when only one coach ran between Bury and Manchester, he was in the habit of walking three days a week to Manchester, and continued his pedestrian journeys till he had reached considerably beyond threescore years. He afterwards walked three days every week to Bury and took train from there to Manchester, returning by train to Bury and walking home to Mount Pleasant. He was seventy-five years of age when he shortened his journeyings on foot. As a pedestrian he was unexcelled, and many incidents are told of his performances. At the age of eighty-four he walked four miles in an hour, and appeared quite fresh at the end of his journey. It was his regular custom to go to bed at about eight o'clock at night, and get up at four on the following morning, proceed at once to the warehouse, and have a quarter of a day's work done before his employés had arrived to commence their day's labours. It was his wont, until he was eighty-six years of age, to mow the grass on his estate at Mount Pleasant, and it was often remarked that he could keep pace with the best mower that came alongside him in the field. Geology was his favourite study, and few men knew the Lancashire coalfields better than he did. He was also widely known as an electrician. He bequeathed freehold property to the value of £15,000, and left in various bequests to relatives and friends cash also amounting to £150,000. He did not forget the poor of his own and adjacent parishes. He bequeathed £500 to be invested in the Funds, the interest thereof to be divided for ever in the following manner:—One-third among the poor of Walmersley, and one-third among the poor of Tottington, every Easter Tuesday; and the remaining one-third among the poor of Tyldesley Banks and Astley every alternate year. His remains were interred in Walmersley churchyard.

In 1860 Mr. Hall invited the members of the Manchester Geological Society to pay him a visit, and in the "Transactions" of that society for May of that year the following account of their visit is recorded:—

EXCURSION TO BROOKSBOTTOMS AND THE NEIGHBOURHOOD.

At the last meeting of the society it was announced from the chair that Mr. John Hall, of Mount Pleasant, near Bury, had invited the members of the society to make a geological excursion into this district, which affords some of the best natural sections of the lower coal measures, described in the paper read at our last meeting, to be found in the county of Lancaster; and Wednesday, the 9th of May, was fixed for the occasion.

Accordingly, on the 9th inst., a party, consisting of Mr. Alderman Harvey, and Messrs. Binney, Darbishire, A. Knowles, Barr, Atkinson, Diggle, and Taylor,

K

proceeded by train to Summerseat station, on the East Lancashire Railway.   Here the party was met by Mr. Hall, and his brother, Mr. Willam Hall, Mr. Ramsbottom, of Elton, and Messrs. Wild and Whittaker, of Burnley.

Mr. Hall first explained to the party the great fault from north-west to south-east, in line running from below Holcombe Hill, passing through Summerseat, Pigslee, and Chesham.   It is above 300 yards in extent, and brings the strata below the Dogshaw or Arley coal in contact with the upper millstone ; thus showing that the Bury coalfield has been thrown up to that extent to the north-east, and since removed by denudation.

After looking at the fault—which is seen on the banks of the Irwell, just below the Summerseat station—we examined the upper millstone, and walked over a considerable thickness of it shown in the Holcombe Brook, until we reached the weir, just below Holcombe.   Here we saw the lowest of the three coals lying on the upper millstone, and known as the Brooksbottom series.   It is about 14 inches in thickness, and has a rock roof and a warrant floor.   In the latter the roots and rootlets of stigmaria, together with leaves of ferns, were met with.   In some flaggy beds of sandstone we saw certain oval-shaped bodies, resembling the casts of a bivalve shell.   On proceeding further up the valley to Ridge we observed the second of the seams of coal, which is about six inches in thickness, and has a hard floor, and afterwards the highest seam, which is near ten inches in thickness.   In the black shales lying immediately above the last named coal, the party found plenty of the fossil shells of the genera *aviculopecten, goniatites,* and *posidonia.*   Here Mr. Hall pointed out the section exposed on the side of Holcombe Hill, above the shales with the fossil shells previously named; and informed us that it contained the Rochdale and Haslingden flag beds, capped with the rough rock (the upper millstone of the geological survey) at the top of the hill.

The party then returned to Summerseat, and went over the coals and shales of Brooksbottom, past Bass-lane, over the Haslingden flags, to Mr. Hall's house, at Mount Pleasant, near which place they examined some interesting specimens of boulder stones, consisting of granite, syenite, and greenstone.

After partaking of lunch with their host, the party inspected the rough rock seen in the quarry at Baldingstone, and then crossed over the country to the large quarry at Top-o'-th'-hill, where the Featheredge coal, 16 inches in thickness, was seen embedded in the midst of a thick and very coarse-grained sandstone (rough rock), with five or six yards on the top of it, and seven or eight below it.   The feathery character of the edges of the coal from whence it derives its name was examined.   The position of the coal embedded in rock, which was equally coarse both above and below, showed how difficult it was to make the rough rock, or its seam of coal, a line for the division of the lower coal measures from the millstone grit of the Geological Survey.

They then went over the district to Chesham Brook, near which Mr. Hall was born ; and he there pointed out the strata and coals which he had examined between 50 and 60 years ago.   In this interesting section he again directed our attention to the great fault which he had pointed out at Summerseat ; and showed on the deep side of it a foot coal in two beds, something like the Smith coal at Wigan; then eight yards below the last seam, another little bed of coal ; and 60 yards deeper, the Dogshaw or Arley mine, which had been worked to a considerable extent in that district.   The fault here is much wider than at Summerseat, and the strata appear to have been disturbed for a much greater distance.   On the up side of the fault we saw the positions of the 40-yards and foot mines before we came to the gannister coal, which here showed its hard floor from which it derives its name, as well as the white clay lying under it, in all their characters.   We then saw the Quarlton and Darwen mine, called by Mr. Hall the " Spanish juice coal," from the circumstance of its breaking with a conchoidal fracture ; and the New Mills Seam, called by Mr. Hall the " Salts coal," from its fracturing like Epsom salts.   In the roof of this last-named coal, the party found remains of fishes of the genera *rhizodus, palæoniscus,* and *platysomus.*   We then went up to the quarry where the Woodhead rock is worked.   The stone here is coarser in grain than usually seen ; but it appears to be a strong and useful building stone.

We now crossed over the country to the fire-clay works at Boaredge, on the old road from Bury to Rochdale.   Here in an open cutting we found the bed of fire clay forming the floor of the foot coal, 10 inches in thickness, lying about eight yards above the Featheredge coal, which in this part, instead of having a rock roof, has one block of black shale. In the black shales comprising the roof of the foot coal, we found plenty of the remains of shells of the genera *aviculopecten, goniatites,* and *posidonia.*

After leaving Boaredge we saw the rough rock with the Featheredge coal, coming from under the last described strata. We then passed Birtle Colliery, where the gannister coal is wrought. Turning a little to the right, we came to a quarry where the Upper or Upholland flag is worked.

After leaving the last-named place we walked direct over to the Birtle valley, near Messrs. Ramsbottoms' works, and examined the fine section of the Rochdale series of coals there shown. In the bottom of the valley the Featheredge coal had been wrought, with a black shale roof, containing *aviculopectens, gomatites, orthoceratites,* and *posidonia,* mixed with numerous coal plants. Above it had been found the foot coal, containing fossils of the like genera. These two seams we did not see, the workings having been finished some years.

On ascending the south side of the valley we saw a fine section of the salts mine, which showed the bright layers of coal parted with darker laminæ, so characteristic of this bed. In the roof we found a few remains of *goniatites,* which had not been previously seen in such positions in this neighbourhood, remains of fish of the genera *megalichthus* and *palæniscus* were also found. On proceeding up the hill side we found the gannister coal of about 16 inches in thickness, showing its hard floor and white fire clay. After proceeding past Messrs. Ramsbottoms' works, we saw a fault running south-east and north-west, which brought the rough rock up to a level with the gannister coal, thus showing the upthrow to be about 100 yards. We then crossed over land chiefly composed of rough rock, past Cobhouse, to Mr. Hall's house, at Mount Pleasant; our worthy host, who is in his 80th year, having effectually used a pickaxe, such as few of our modern geologists handle, to bare the strata, and kindly explained to the party the position of the respective beds, which he had been familiar with for the last sixty years.

After dining at Mount Pleasant, and enjoying such a geological treat as few men in Lancashire can afford their visitors, and experiencing the Lancashire hospitality of a man such as nature and fortune have rarely blessed, we left the Summerseat Station by the nine o'clock train, and reached Manchester about a quarter to ten, highly delighted with our journey, and hoping again to have the pleasure of visiting our kind host, and obtaining from him some more of the valuable geological information respecting the Lancashire coal field, which he is so willing to communicate to all who ask his assistance.

CHAPTER VIII.

The National School—The Cemetery—The Greenhalgh Family—The late Mr.
Charles Openshaw—Richard and James Pilkington—The Dispensary—The
Union Offices—The Shrievalty—Co-operation—The Grant Family.

THE NATIONAL SCHOOL.

This was originally a charity school, and was founded in 1748 by the
Rev. John Stanley, who was then the rector, along with the Openshaws
and the Hutchinsons and other principal inhabitants in the town and
neighbourhood, for the instruction of 80 boys and 30 girls. The trustees
of the school distributed three prizes annually to the best writers: the
first prize was 2s. 6d., the second 2s., and the third 1s. 6d. In the year
1815 this charity was augmented very much by a numerous list of
annual subscribers, and the school was changed into a National Charity
School, during which time a spacious and commodious building was
erected as a school-house, at an expense of £1,000. The land on which
it stands was given by the Earl of Derby.

THE CEMETERY.

This is situated a little over a mile from the centre of the town, and a
short distance off the main road to Manchester. It was formally opened
on the 21st of May, 1869. The grounds contain 33a. 1r. 27p. statute
measure: 20 acres of which are devoted to the burial of the dead, and
the remaining 13a. 1r. 27p. are set aside for walks for the use of the
inhabitants of the town. The whole site of the Cemetery and walks is
surrounded by a boundary wall of parpoints backed with rubble. This
includes a fine bold stone and weathered coping, finely tooled, with four-
feet piers at intervals. Between these piers and extending all round the
grounds is an ornamental railing of wrought-iron vertical bars, fitted in
with cast-iron tracery. There are three entrances to the grounds, the
principal one being of bold and massive proportions. On each side of
the gateway are side entrances for foot passengers, in character with the

Rock & Co. London. No 6556.

1700. 1875.

Cemetery Bury Lancashire.

major entrance. The Established Church, the Dissenters' Chapel, and the Roman Catholic Chapel are prettily designed, and altogether form a picturesque appearance. The registrar's house is situated to the right of the main entrance, and appears to be unique in every respect. The grounds and walks have been carefully and artistically arranged, and are much frequented by visitors, especially in the summer time. The total length of walks and roads is 4,745 yards, or nearly three miles. The designs were made by Mr. James Farrar, borough surveyor for Bury, and by Mr. Henry Styan, architect, Manchester.

THE GREENHALGH FAMILY.

A brief account of this family cannot fail to be interesting, exemplifying, as it does, the result of small beginnings, combined with perseverance and diligence. The family originally resided at Freetown. In his young days, Thomas Greenhalgh was a cordwainer. He was possessed of a strong enterprising mind, and commenced business as a cotton spinner in Union-square. Mr. John Baker made him what was called in those days a "roving Billy" and two frames. The frames consisted of about 90 or 100 spindles, and cost from £90 to £100 each. The cotton he fetched from manufacturers at Bolton, and, with the aid of two operatives, spun it into forties and fifties weft, and took it back to Bolton. By this means the family accumulated a little capital. They were ambitious to rise, and embarked in the cotton trade. Improvement succeeded improvement in cotton spinning, and as Mr. Greenhalgh's machinery became of little or no value for the purpose for which it was intended, he sold the brass and iron work to Mr. Baker as old metal; the woodwork belonging to the frames he sold for cotton looms and bedsteads. Having accumulated a pretty large sum of money, he went into partnership with Mr. James Kay, in a cotton mill near Heap Brow. Their machinery here was on an improved scale, and both of them having a good knowledge of buying and selling, the concern went on very well for years. New inventions rapidly increased, and the machinery of Greenhalgh and Kay became of little use. Seeing that other small mills in Bury were rapidly progressing, it was mutually agreed that their partnership should be dissolved. The Kay family built a large factory at Heywood, and this concern became so prosperous that they either purchased or rented the ancient mansion of James Starkie, Esq., of Heywood Hall. Mr. Greenhalgh took Knut Bank, near Rochdale, for a term of years. It consisted of an old farmhouse, farm, and other outbuildings; and he erected a large mill on the river Roch, in the valley below the old house. Here Mr. Greenhalgh took two partners into the concern for a short time, Messrs. Spencer and Kay. After they withdrew, he carried on the whole concern, and became very wealthy. Two of Mr. Greenhalgh's sons were educated at Cambridge, where one of them took the title of LL.D. and M.D. When his term had nearly expired at Knut Bank, he bought some freehold property in Freetown, where he erected a family mansion. He also built a large factory and loom-shed in Freetown, as well as numerous cottages.

THE LATE MR. CHARLES OPENSHAW.

This gentleman, who died a few years ago, at the age of seventy-eight years, was the last survivor of twenty-one brothers and sisters, who filled a large space in the annals of Bury. His father, Thomas Openshaw, was the youngest of four brothers, born at Pimhole, all of whom have figured in the history of, and laboured for the advancement of the manufacturing industry of this country, as spinners of woollen goods. One, George, remained at Pimhole; another, John, went to Starkies; the third, James, went to Openshaw Fold; and Thomas, the youngest, and father of Charles Openshaw, went to reside in Stanley-street, occupying the house and workshop, afterwards taken by Messrs. Norris and Harrison. Thomas was first married to Margaret, aunt to the late Mr. W. Walker, Stanley-street, secondly to Miss Powell, and had twenty-one children—Charles being the youngest son by the latter wife. Charles learned spinning with his father-in-law, the late James Elton, Esq., and manufacturing at Tottington-lower-end. He commenced business as a manufacturer of dimities with the late Mr. Peter Rothwell, of Pot Green, Holcombe Brook. After some years they separated, and Mr. C. Openshaw then commenced making velveteens, cords, &c., and soon became eminent as the producer of a first-rate article. At this time he employed several hundred hand-loom weavers, for the first time bringing Bury into notoriety for that manufacture. Many anecdotes are told of his kindness and cordiality of feeling towards his workpeople which it is here needless to recapitulate, but at the annual Christmas Festival, fifty years ago, he was in the habit of giving his weavers a quart of ale and a good dinner when they brought their work home. Such was his feeling towards his workmen that he was one of the last to exchange his hand-looms to power-looms, and allowed others to precede him in weaving fustians by power before he adopted that improvement, though afterwards he succeeded in establishing a large number of power-looms, which were eminently successful. He married Alice, eldest daughter of the late James Elton, Esq., before mentioned, by whom he had five sons and four daughters. Throughout his long life, marked as it was by strict integrity and honesty of purpose, he upheld his favourite motto and toast at public meetings, " Honour and Honesty." His remains were interred at Holcombe.

RICHARD AND JAMES PILKINGTON.

Richard and James Pilkington were formerly well-known woollen manufacturers in Bury. One of them married a daughter of Mr. George Openshaw, of Pimhole, grandfather of the late Thomas Openshaw, by whom he had children. One of these children was named Robert, and soon after he was born his mother said that his name would be spoken of, and would resound throughout England. This was, however, true, for he was imprisoned in Lancaster Castle for two years for combining with hand-loom weavers against their masters for an advance of wages. After his liberation the Radicals of Bury sent him as a delegate, with others, to London, on the Reform question, where he had many interviews with Sir Francis Burdett, M.P., and other popular statesmen. To equip Robert for this expedition, the Radicals of the day borrowed for him a pair of boots, and collected for him ten pounds. He remained in London about three weeks, and when he returned home he gave up the boots to the proper owners. The Radicals examined his accounts, and told him that he had made a very expensive journey ! Mr. Pilkington was a very busy politician, till at last he was imprisoned in Horsemonger-lane Gaol, London, together with the late Mr. Samuel Bamford, of Middleton, and others, for political offences, under the administration of Lord Sidmouth. After his liberation, he took his departure for the United States of America, where he died. Besides these Pilkingtons, there was a Mr. George Pilkington, who lived in an ancient house in Redvales, where Basset's foundry once stood, and near to Belle Vue. This old mansion was a beautiful residence, close to the old road leading to Manchester. One of his sons, Mr. Thomas Pilkington, was a woollen manufacturer in Bury. Mr. George Pilkington had a brother (Mr. Thomas Pilkington) who was a very eccentric man. He was a very officious and orderly character in Bury, and resided in a neat little cottage in the Wylde. He married a sister of the late Mr. Robert Battersby, a cordwainer, who, failing in business, kept the Old Boar's Head, opposite the church, where he became very rich.

THE DISPENSARY.

In 1829, a number of gentlemen in Bury and its vicinity, called a public meeting to consider the propriety of establishing a dispensary, which resulted in that institution being formed. The Rev. G. Hornby was the first president, and the Rev. H. C. Boutflower secretary. It is now situated in Knowsley-street, and the president is the Rev. E. J. G. Hornby, the rector.

THE UNION OFFICES.

The Poor-law Union Offices, in Parson's-lane, were opened at the end of August, 1866. The architecture of the building is in the Italian style, of brick and stone combined. The architect was Mr. Farrar, the borough surveyor. The building has a neat and bold appearance, and the interior arrangements are very complete.

THE SHRIEVALTY.

In the spring of 1872, the dignity of High Sheriff of the county was conferred upon Thomas Wrigley, Esq., an appointment which was followed by great rejoicings at Timberhurst and in Bury. Mr. Wrigley was the second High Sheriff appointed from this town and district, for we find that in 1668 and 1669, Thomas Greenhalgh, of Brandlesome, near Bury, Knight, held the office, and passed through Bury with his retinue, on his way to meet the judges of assize at Lancaster. We also find that Thomas Hopwood, of Hopwood, Esq., passed through Bury on his way northward in 1726, at a time when all the assize business was transacted at Lancaster. And in 1824, John Entwistle, of Foxholes, Esq., also passed through Bury in his shrieval procession, going through Union-square.

CO-OPERATION.

In the town of Bury co-operation has been so eminently successful, that a history of the borough could scarcely be considered complete if it did not allude, however briefly, to the rise and progress of this movement. Many years ago an association was formed in Bury, the title of which was the General Labour Redemption Society, and it had for its object the social advancement by means of co-operation of the working classes. This society had a shop in Stanley-street, near to St. John's Church, and here they soon began to do a flourishing business, numbering very shortly upon their books no less than 400 members. The capital was composed of £1 shares. The success of the society, however, soon received a serious check, for jealousy crept into the ranks of the members, and most of the men who had taken the most active part of the business began to withdraw. Those who were left continued to carry on the business for some time longer upon their own account, but owing to some misunderstandings the association was at length broken up. This attempt to form a co-operative society did not result in any loss to the members, for at the dissolution of the association a large surplus remained, chiefly owing to the stock of goods on hand, and these were divided amongst those who remained. During the time the society was in existence a public meeting was held in the Town Hall in favour of co-operation, on which occasion the Rev. Charles Kingsley, Mr. Vansittart Neale, and other advocates of co-operation delivered addresses ; and when the association above referred to first became disunited these gentlemen counselled the members to remain united, if they could do so by any means. Before the association became finally broken up, a deputation from Bacup waited upon the committee to inquire into the operations of the society, with the view of obtaining such information as would enable them to commence a similar association in Bacup ; and the earnestness of the deputation from Bacup is evidenced by the fact that they purchased groceries from the shop in Stanley-street, with which goods, it is stated, they commenced the co-operative movement in Bacup. So successful was the movement in that town that the members were induced to build a co-operative mill out of the profits they had realised upon provisions and other departments. When the mill was built and ready for stocking with machinery, a number of persons connected with the movement visited the ironworks of Messrs. Walker and Hacking, Bury, with the intention of ordering machinery from that firm, and as they were going through the works they came in contact with Mr, Richard Sulley, who was much struck with the success of the movement in Bacup as detailed to him by the co-operators whom he had thus accidentally met with. This was in 1855, and he grew anxious to make another attempt in Bury, the more as an exposure of the system of adulteration was then going the round of the press. He conferred at the end of the week with the late Mr. John Muir, who had been connected with the previous movement, as to the advisability of making another attempt, and the two agreed to canvass their acquaintances and report their success. Mr. George Rastrick was the first gentleman spoken to by Mr. Muir, and he consented to join them in the movement. Their first meetings were held in a summer-house in Mr. Sulley's garden, and though quiet and retired as their meeting-room might be it was soon found to be too small for the accommodation of those who swelled their ranks. They then began to meet at the house of Mr. Mayor, in Paradise-street, and continued their meetings there until they decided to stock a shop. Before, however, commencing business operations, Mr. Muir and Mr. Rastrick visited Bacup, to examine the mode of conducting the stores there, and they purchased a few articles from the Bacup committee. Having purchased scales and weights, and a small stock of groceries and flour, they began to sell flour to one another at Mr. Rastrick's, and the groceries at the house of Mr. Muir, in Wyndham-street. As their business soon became somewhat extensive, a shop in Market-street, formerly occupied by Mr. Stout, earthenware dealer, was taken, and business operations were opened there with a very small capital, the promoters of the movement acting as shopmen, weighing and making up all the goods ready for sale, keeping the accounts, and performing all the multifarious operations incident to such a business after they had done a hard day's work, until such time—which was not very long after they removed into Market-street—as they could afford to keep a regular shopman. In the book containing a record of the first transactions of the society, under date of November 10th, 1855, there is a list of contributions amounting to 9s. 6d.; on the 17th, to 11s.; on the 24th, 17s.; and two payments of 1s. each. Such payments continued up to December 29th, when the total amounted to £6 9s. 6d. On the debtor side of the book the transactions, including purchase of scales, goods, &c., amounted up to January 5th, 1856, to only £3 19s. The first sale of goods recorded in the book is on December 29th, 1855, to the amount of £2 6s. 9d. At this time Mr. Smithson, a Quaker gentleman, had such faith in the society's success, that he gave them twelve months' credit for goods, and promised them discount on their transactions at the end of the year. By the end of January the transactions had amounted to £25 0s. 5d.; and on February 9th the total income was £76 4s. 1d., including contributions, and the expenditure of £48 19s. 2½d., leaving £27 4s. 10½d. in hand. With this balance the expenses up to February 14th were £12 6s. 5d.; February 15th, £15 6s. 2d., when there was a balance in hand of £40 7s. 2½d. On the 26th February there was a balance in hand of £51 13s. 5½d. Thus the sales went on increasing, until on the 22nd of March the day's sales were set down at £16 5s. 1d. In July the transactions had increased to such an extent that in one week the business done amounted to £32 4s. 7½d., and by the end of October to £83 18s. 6d. After this the movement proceeded with rapid strides, and as time rolled on and business and capital increased it was decided to erect the commodious building in Knowsley-street, known as the Co-operative Hall. This building was formally opened on the 9th of January, 1869, by a tea party and public meeting, which was presided over by Mr. R. N. Philips, M.P. It was erected from designs prepared by Mr. E. Simpkin, at a cost of about £6,000. The exterior of the building is very plain but substantial. It has three storeys above the ground, and cellaring extends under the whole of the building, occupying a space of 480 square yards. On the basement storey there is a passage for waggons and carts carried through the building on iron beams and brick arches. Upon the ground floor the offices are situated, and either side of the waggon-way a platform for loading goods, each of 150 yards area. The warehouse, situate on the first floor, is 350 yards square, and there are also the committee room, ante-room to lecture-hall, &c. The large hall is 74 feet by 60 feet, and has up to recently contained a gallery, which ran the whole length of one side. For some months back, however, workmen have been engaged in erecting a gallery along three sides of the hall : the platform or stage has been removed to the side of the room next to Knowsley-street, and retiring rooms erected at each end of the platform. The alterations are a great improvement to the room, and will make it more suitable for entertainments and large public gatherings. Its total elevation from floor to ceiling is 30 feet. The ceiling is divided into nine panels, each marked out with enriched mouldings. A similar moulding runs round the room, and also an ornamental frieze. Addresses were delivered at the opening ceremony by Mr. Philips, Mr. Hilton, Mr. J. R. Cooper (Manchester), the Rev. W. R. Thorburn, and Mr. E. Hooson (Manchester).

From that time to the present the Bury District Co-operative Provision Society has had a most successful career, comprising at the present time no less than 24 branches. Some idea of the amount of business done by the society may be gathered from the following general statement of the accounts, which was published in the 70th report for the quarter ended September 9th, 1873 :—

	£	s.	d.		£	s.	d.
To Members' Capital, as per Ledger	79291	5	3½	By Stock on hand	20002	12	11
„ Accounts owing by the Society..	1487	0	3	„ Cash in District Bank	3271	5	6
„ Reserve Fund	1952	12	7	„ Cash in Bury Bank	21294	19	1
„ Balance	7018	3	2	„ Rochdale Corn Mill Society	273	19	4½
				„ Sowerby Bridge Flour Society..	50	0	0
				„ Building Account	13651	14	6½
				„ Building Cottages Account	7722	12	10
				„ Fixtures Account	1192	0	0
				„ Cash paid for Checks	16	11	6½
				„ Bury Co-operative Manufacturing Co.	14000	0	0
				„ Interest on ditto	166	19	1½
				„ Bury and Elton Commercial Co.	7000	0	0
				„ Interest on ditto	61	18	7
				„ Accounts owing to the Society..	308	18	10
				„ Cash on hand	735	8	11½
	£89749	1	3½		£89749	1	3½

In June, 1873, the Education Board of the society issued a circular which stated that the library contained 7,045 volumes, and that the circulation for the year then ended amounted to 19,584 volumes. The newsrooms are supplied with 62 daily newspapers, 122 weekly newspapers, 65 monthlies, and four quarterlies. Lectures and entertainments are got up by the Education Board, and their efforts to afford good sound information, by securing talented lecturers during the winter months, are certainly deserving of better support than they have hitherto, as a rule, received.

THE GRANT FAMILY.

For some time the Grant family resided in Bury. They lived in a small cottage near the top of Bury Lane—then very narrow, and consisting altogether of old houses—about the place where later was formed the garden of Mr. Hutchinson. The family consisted of father, mother, their four sons, William—never named by his relatives other than as Wully—John, Daniel, Charles, and two daughters, Elizabeth, (Bessie), who was lame, and always wore a "patten," and Isabella (Bella). Both were thorough Scotch lassies in conversation and appearance, and Isabella was placed to learn the dressmaking business with Betty Hutchinson. Mr. and Mrs. Grant spoke with such a strong native accent or pronunciation of "brode Scotche," that it was scarce possible for Lancashire folk to understand their meaning, the words being entirely unintelligible to most of their neighbours. On first entering public business, as drapers and haberdashers, they occupied a shop in the Wylde, afterwards inhabited by Mr. Spencer. Soon after reaching Bury, one of the children was drownéd; and so low were the finances of the family, that a collection was made in order to inter the boy with decency. The elder brothers soon obtained employment at the newly-established works of Hampson Mill; and in the evening, after his daily labours were closed, William Grant went round the town, and to many adjacent hamlets or villages, with a pack of goods for sale, consisting of low-priced waistcoat pieces, handkerchiefs, and hosiery for the men, and a few gaudy ribbons or cotton dress pieces for the women who might be attracted by his wares. After a while the family removed to a dwelling in Silver-street, and at this time tea was added to the abiding stock of the perambulating salesman. But it was not the evenings alone that were turned to such profitable account; whenever awaiting what is technically called his "turn for a job" during the day, the enterprising chapman was accustomed to sally forth at those hours which many similarly circumstanced would have devoted to recreation or idleness. The fruit of this persevering and self-denying industry and economy in the course of time began to be apparent, and, as a higher venture, the shop in the Wylde was taken, and furnished with as useful and tempting an assortment of goods as the acquired experience of the brothers induced them to select. Owing to unremitted effort and attention, the business was soon as prosperous and the shop as well attended as they deserved to be ; although their brethren of the counter intimated that the arguments of the proprietors were altogether unprecedented, and the attractions of the establishment not altogether what would be considered legitimate in the profession. For instance, the Messieurs Grant would come out to some considerable distance upon the pavement to address passengers or loitering country folks, to point out, to extol, to expatiate upon the beauty and excellence of the goods displayed in the window, and upon the counter and shelves. Nor was this all, for the culminating aggravation to the "trade" consisted in the introduction of a goodly-sized, full-toned hand organ, which, on market-days especially, was almost continuously kept playing by one stationed for the purpose, to the wonder and amusement of little boys, and maybe the annoyance of more sober folks, although it answered its purpose, for to "country" customers its music proved singularly attractive ; the amateur organist being generally old Mr. Grant, who was greatly pleased to aid, in this artistic manner, the more active mercantile transactions of his sons. A song, written at the time, makes mention of it thus :—

> Willie Grant is a grinder, we know;
> He rises at two in the morning,
> And keeps the whole town in a row
> By grinding his d——d barrel organ.
> Tally hi ho ! hi ho ! hi ho !
>
> Tally hi ho ! the grinder ;
> And if by his window you pass,
> He runs out to catch each parishioner ;
> You scarcely can peep in the glass,
> He is such a clever musicianer, &c.

The imputation of getting up betimes was true enough, for the whole family was seldom to be found in bed later than four o'clock in the morning, and the shop was invariably opened the earliest in the town. In spite of the objurgations of rival tradesmen, it would have been pleasant to know a little more of the characteristics, at this early period of their prosperity, of these amiable and persevering brothers. Of the father no information is afforded, except that he came from Morayshire, in Scotland ; and, what speaks well for the paternal guidance and authority, is the fact that all his children were brought up, unlettered though they were, perfect exemplifications of Scottish thrift, industry, and integrity.

When Mr. William Grant had performed his daily work at Hampson Mill, he went to Unsworth, and bought cotton fents from handloom weavers. These he got whitened and printed into fashionable waistcoat pieces, and went on Saturday evenings into Bury to different public-houses to sell them. This plan he followed regularly for some time till he formed a little capital. The family at this time lived at Haslam Brow, but as Mr. Grant proceeded step by step they removed into Bolton-street. Here he sold linen, cloth, checks, prints, &c., and continued to travel on Saturday night, and at holiday times. He worthily took the lead of his family, Mr. John, Mr. Daniel, and Mr. Charles being most actively employed under their brother, while he (Mr. William) admitted them into partnership, and they traded under the name of William Grant and Brothers.

They behaved in a most handsome manner to country people, for, after buying what they wanted, they had free access to their increasing and plentiful table.

The Grant family stood for years the scoffs, scorn, and rebuffs of what was at that day called the Bury gentry, by whom they were abused with virulent language, and every attempt made to prejudice the people against them. All the spite, envy, and malice put together could not hinder the rising of this remarkable family, for their philanthropic dispositions, and good behaviour in the parish, brought them into great repute and high respectability.

As their business got on rapidly, Mr. Daniel received the appointment of traveller for the company in various parts of the United Kingdom. He made several journeys into Scotland, and on one occasion he called at one of the largest houses in the printing business in Glasgow, and there showed samples of prints, &c. The gentleman belonging to the house said, "We have no need of any of your goods." Mr. Daniel said, "Perhaps, sir, you would take the trouble to look through my samples; I am certain these cannot fail to please you, for these are the newest, neatest, and most tasteful fashions." The gentleman remarked, "I want nothing that you have, nor shall I give you an order." Mr. Daniel persevered in pressing his goods, but the gentleman as strongly resisted him. The gentleman's patience being exhausted, he seized hold of Mr. Daniel's pattern-book, and threw it into the street. Mr. Daniel gathered up his book and the scattered fragments, and cleaning the filth therefrom, he walked very patiently back again to the gentleman, and said, "Sir, I am confident you will now give me an order." The gentleman, overcome by Mr. Daniel's address and command of temper, looked him steadfastly in the face, and said, "I will give you an order because of your patience and perseverance." From that day the greatest confidence was established between them, and thousands, if not tens of thousands of pounds, changed hands between the gentleman and the Grant Brothers.

Two persons were one day conversing in the White Lion Inn, Bury, respecting the behaviour and accommodation of the Grant family in their shop. One said he would bet a wager with the other that if he went for a pennyworth of anything they sold, they would thank him afterwards. The other man said, "Done." The stakes were deposited in the landlord's hands; one of them went to Mr. William Grant's shop, and asked to look at several pieces of print, check, linen cloth, &c. Many pieces were turned over. At last the man pitched on a piece of linen cloth, and said, "Be kind enough to measure one pennyworth from this piece." Mr. William took the penny and laid it on the cloth, cut a round piece therefrom the size of the penny, gave it him, and then said, "Thank you, sir!"

As regards the success of this remarkable family, their secret was a united purpose as to the attainment of one object, and that was the acquisition—denied as they were the advantages of capital and education, otherwise than natural shrewdness—by perseverance, economy, industry, and steadiness, of at least a competence and fitting reward for their labour and forethought. The old-fashioned fable of the father, his sons, and their bundle of sticks, is an apt illustration of the early career of the Grants in Lancashire; the strength and ability of the brothers united led to the conquest of difficulties that might have proved insuperable to others less favourably situated. After a course of successful business at the shop in the Market-place, the time arrived when a higher step was taken; this was commencing printing at Ramsbottom, at the works previously occupied and established by the Peel firm, but of which, being given up, Messrs. Grant became purchasers and proprietors; William Grant buying also the estate and mansion of Springside, formerly the residence of the elder Mr. William Yates. Any person afterwards visiting and inspecting their extensive and well-regulated works would have evidence of the thorough working and practical minds of the masters; their beautiful teams of grey horses and well-appointed waggons were the admiration of the day; whilst, as the Cheeryble Brothers, the fame and character of the Grants has gone over the world; and in their own immediate neighbourhood, sympathy for such of their brethren as were less fortunate than themselves in the march of life, and a wise benevolence towards all whom they believed deserving, is for ever recorded by the angel of universal charity.

Nuttall Hall has for some years been the residence of the remaining members of this noted family. Mr. John Grant died a few years ago, and his brother William, the last of the lineal descendants of the family, died on the 30th of May, 1873, at Grange. He left a widow, but no offspring. His remains were removed to Nuttall Hall, and were interred under the communion in St. Andrew's Church, Ramsbottom, on the 5th of June. His widow at the present resides at Nuttall Hall, of which allusion is made elsewhere.

Mr. Smiles, in his interesting work, entitled " Self-Help," thus refers to this family :—" William and Charles Grant were the sons of a farmer in Inverness-shire, whom a sudden flood stripped of everything, even to the very soil which he tilled. The farmer and his sons, with the world before them where to choose, made their way southward in search of employment until they arrived in the neighbourhood of Bury, in Lancashire. From the crown of the hill near Walmersley they surveyed the wide extent of country which lay before them, the river Irwell making its circuitous course through the valley. They were utter strangers in the neighbourhood, and knew not which way to turn. To decide their course they put up a stick, and agreed to pursue the direction in which it fell. Thus their decision was made, and they journeyed on accordingly until they reached the village of Ramsbottom, not far distant. They found employment in a printworks, in which William served his apprenticeship ; and they commended themselves to their employers by their diligence, sobriety, and strict integrity. They plodded on, rising from one station to another, until at length the two sons themselves became employers, and after many long years of industry, enterprise, and benevolence, they became rich, honoured, and respected by all who knew them. Their cotton mills and printworks gave employment to a large population. Their well-directed diligence made the valley teem with activity, joy, health, and opulence. Out of their abundant wealth they gave liberally to all worthy objects, erecting churches, founding schools, and in all ways promoting the well-being of the class of working men from which they had sprung. They afterwards erected upon the top of the hill above Walmersley a lofty tower in commemoration of the early event in their history which had determined the place of their settlement. The brothers Grant became widely celebrated for their benevolence and their various goodness, and it is said that Mr. Dickens had them in his mind's eye when delineating the characters of the brothers Cheeryble. One amongst many anecdotes of a similar kind may be cited to show that the character was by no means exaggerated. A Manchester warehouseman published an exceedingly scurrilous pamphlet against the firm of Grant Brothers, holding up the elder partner to ridicule as 'Billy Button.' William was informed by some one of the nature of the pamphlet, and his observation was that the man would live to repent of it. 'Oh ! ' said the libeller, when informed of the remark, ' he thinks that some time or other I shall be in his debt: but I will take good care of that.' It happens, however, that men in business do not always foresee who shall be their creditor, and it so turned out that the Grants' libeller became a bankrupt, and could not obtain his certificate and begin business again without obtaining their signature. It seemed to him a hopeless case to call upon that firm for any favour, but the pressing claims of his family forced him to make the application. He appeared before the man whom he had ridiculed as ' Billy Button ' accordingly. He told his tale, and produced his certificate. ' You wrote a pamphlet against us once?' said Mr. Grant. The supplicant expected to see his document thrown into the fire, instead of which Mr. Grant signed the name of the firm, and thus completed the necessary certificate. ' We make it a rule,' said he, handing it back, ' never to refuse signing the certificate of an honest tradesman, and we have never heard that you were anything else.' The tears started in the man's eyes. ' Ah ! ' continued Mr. Grant, ' you see my saying was true, that you would live to repent writing that pamphlet. I did not mean it as a threat—I only meant that some day you would know us better, and repent having tried to injure us.' ' I do, I do, indeed, repent it.' ' Well, well, you know us now. But how do you get on—what are you going to do ? ' The poor man stated that he had friends who would assist him when his certificate was obtained. ' But how are you off in the meantime ? ' The answer was that, having given up every farthing to his creditors, he had been compelled to stint his family in even the common necessaries of life, that he might be enabled to pay for his certificate. ' My good fellow, this will never do ; your wife and family must not suffer in this way ; be kind enough to take this ten-pound note to your wife from me. There, there, now, don't cry, it will be all well with you yet ; keep up your spirits, set to work like a man, and you will raise your head amongst the best of us yet.' The overpowered man endeavoured with choking utterance to express his gratitude, but in vain ; and putting his hand to his face, he went out of the room sobbing like a child."

CHAPTER IX.

The Parish Church—Rectors of Bury from 1507— The Rector's Power to Grant Leases of Glebe Lands—St. John's Church.—St. Paul's Church—St. Thomas's Church—Holy Trinity Church—St. Peter's Church—St. Mark's School.

THE PARISH CHURCH.

The history of the Parish Church, which is dedicated to St. Mary, has not been handed down to us in as successive and complete a manner as the history of many other parish churches; but from what details are recorded there is proof that the church existed in the reign of William the Conquerer, 800 years ago. A survey of the whole country was made at the order of William the Conqueror, and information gathered respecting the various estates, churches, &c. The Doomsday Book contains all the information so obtained, and it is therein stated that the patron of the church at Bury was one Roger de Poictou. Subsequently the patronage became a right of the family of the Lacies, who were also lords of the manor of Tottington, of which Bury was a part. The Pylkington family afterwards obtained the advowson from the Lacies, and in 1386 John de Pylkington became rector of Bury. From the Pylkingtons it passed, with the manor, to the Derby family. This change took place in the year 1485, at which time the representative of the family (Sir Thomas Pylkington) had his family residence at Stand. In the time of Sir Thomas Pylkington the long-continued struggles for the Crown of England between the Houses of York and Lancaster, commonly known as the "Wars of the Roses," were ended by the victory of Bosworth Field. It is almost needless to state that in this battle, King Richard III., of the House of York, was killed, and the kingdom passed to the Lancaster family, in the person of the Duke of Richmond, who was crowned on the field of battle and hailed as King Henry VII. by Sir William Stanley, the brother of Thomas, Earl of Derby. There seems to be little doubt that Sir Thomas Pylkington took part in this struggle on the side of Richard, as he was attainted by Henry, who granted his estates to the before-mentioned Earl of Derby. The right of the presentation of the church became in this manner the property of the Derby family, and has ever since been retained by them. At the period of the Great Rebellion, when the Puritan party, as they obtained power, showed the one-sidedness of their views about religious liberty, by ejecting from their livings all those clergymen who, being duly ordained by the bishops of the Church, remained faithful to their ordination vows, and, notwithstanding threats of fines and imprisonment, continued to use the Book of Common Prayer. Among these was the Rev. Peter Travis, B.D., Rector of Bury. By an order of Parliament, bearing the date of April 24, 1645, he was "sequestered as a delinquent and disaffected to the Parliament." The rectory of Bury was sequestered from him, as well as that of Halsall, which he seems to have held in conjunction with, and likewise his own private estate. In his place were appointed to officiate two Puritans, William Alt and Andrew Latham; and on the death of Latham, Tobias Turner succeeded him. Although these men received the income of the living they did not allow one penny to Mrs. Travis and her six children, who were consequently reduced to great poverty. During this period banns of marriage were published from the Market Cross by two of the magistrates of the district. At the restoration, in 1660, the use of the Prayer Book in public worship was enjoined by Parliament, by an Act called the "Act of Uniformity," and the church livings were given again to the rightful owners. The Rev. John Greenhalgh, S.T.B., was appointed to the rectory of Bury by the "good Countess" of Derby, Charlotte de la Tremanille. In the year 1764, the Rev. John Stanley, rector, obtained an Act of Parliament for the improvement of the living by granting leases of the glebe land for terms of 99 years, for building purposes. The church became so dilapidated about the middle of the 18th century that it was deemed necessary to rebuild it. About 1773, the whole of the building, with the exception of the spire, was pulled down and rebuilt. An amusing story of an attempted imposition by some of the workmen engaged in the work is told by Baines in his "History of Lancashire." It seems that a gentleman offered a guinea for the discovery of a date, but the workmen sought in vain. Disinclined to lose the reward they selected one of the roof-timbers, technically termed a "pan" (or "purlin"), and inscribed upon it, in rude Roman characters, the letters. "DCLXXV" (675), to which they contrived to give an appearance of antiquity. The artifice was found out, and the exact date of the church was not discovered. In 1843 the old tower and spire was razed and the present tower and spire erected.

Towards the latter end of 1869, or at the beginning of 1870, it was found that the woodwork of the church of 1780 was rotted to such an extent that it was unsafe to hold service therein, and steps were taken with a view to rebuilding the sacred edifice. After some deliberation, it was decided to pull down the body of the church, but to leave the spire standing. On the 5th of July, 1870, the operation of pulling down the chancel was commenced, and the first stone of the new chancel was laid on the 28th of September, in the same year. The last service in the church of 1780 took place on the 27th of August, 1871. The services were then removed, and are now held in the Town Hall, the first of which in that building took place on the 3rd September, 1871. On the 20th of the same month the workmen commenced to unroof the church, and on the 25th of June, 1872, they began to pull down the nave. The first stone for the foundation of the new nave was laid July 9th, 1872. The new edifice is being erected from designs prepared by Mr. J. S. Crowther, architect, of Manchester. It is upon the site of the old edifice, and will accommodate about as many worshippers as formerly. They will be seated upon the ground floor, for the new church, unlike its predecessor, will not be provided with galleries. It is being built of parpoints, with Hollington stone dressings, the style of architecture being geometric Gothic. It will contain several stained glass windows, the positions for many of which having already been taken up. The chancel will be covered with a groined roof, while the other portions of the church will be open-timbered. The interior of the chancel, as well as the reredos, will be richly carved, and contains several marble columns. The roof is very lofty, and every attention has been paid in order to secure to the building good acoustic properties. It is very probable that the seats will be in the form of open benches, now so much adopted in places of worship, in lieu of the old-fashioned pews, but this point, as well as several other matters of detail, have not yet been decided upon.

RECTORS OF BURY FROM 1507 TO 1873.

Instituted.	Rectors.	On whose Presentation.	Cause of Vacancy.
Oct. 21, 1507	John Nabbes Richard Smyth........	Henry Halsall and John Ireland, Knights......	Death of John Nabbes.
Feb. 4, 1557	Richard Jones	Hugh Jones, for this turn only, by permission of Earl Derby............	Death of last Incumbent.
Aug. 18, 1568	Walter Kenny	Earl of Derby	Death of Richard Jones.
1599	Thomas Dearden	Earl of Derby.	
	Peter Shawe	Earl of Derby.	
July 6, 1608	Hugh Wattmoughe	John Favour, Vicar of Halifax, for this turn only	Death of Peter Shawe.
Aug. 23, 1623	George Murray	Earl of Derby	Death of H. Wattmoughe.
Mar. 16, 1633	Peter Travis	Earl of Derby	Death of George Murray.
April 24, 1645	Walter and A. Latham	Parliament	Sequestration of P. Travis.
Aug. 28, 1648	Tobias Furness........	Com. of Plundered Ministers	Death of Andrew Latham.
1660	John Lightfoote	Earl of Derby.	
Feb. 20, 1660	John Greenhalgh......	Countess of Derby	Resignation of J. Lightfoote.
Feb. 26, 1674	Thomas Gipps	Earl of Derby	Death of John Greenhalgh.
March 5, 1712	James Bancks	Thos. Bancks, by virtue of a donation from William, Earl of Derby, dated June 12, 1676....	Death of Thomas Gipps.
July 19, 1748	John Stanley..........	Earl of Derby	Death of James Bancks.
Feb. 6, 1778	Sir W. H. Clerke, Bart.	Edward, Earl of Derby ..	Resignation of John Stanley.
Sept. 23, 1818	Geoffrey Hornby	Earl of Derby	Death of Sir W. H. Clerke.
1850	E. J. G. Hornby	Earl of Derby	Death of Geoffrey Hornby.

The Rector's Power to Grant Leases of Glebe Lands.

During the time that the Rev. John Stanley was Rector of Bury, that was from 1743 to 1778, an Act of Parliament was passed giving the Rector of Bury power to grant leases of the glebe lands. The following is a copy of the Act:—

An Act to enable the Rector of the Parish and Parish Church of Bury, in the County of Lancaster, for the time being, to grant Leases of the Glebe belonging to the said Rectory.

WHEREAS, John Stanley, Rector of the Parish and Parish Church of Bury, in the County of Lancaster, and Diocese of Chester, is, in Right of the said Rectory, seized of certain Glebe Lands, Part of which are in the Town of Bury, and are already built upon,

AND WHEREAS, the Right Honourable Edward Earl of Derby is Patron of the said Rectory:

AND WHEREAS it is apprehended that many Houses would be added to the said Town, if Land properly situated, and fit to build upon, could be obtained, but that there is no such Land contiguous to the said Town, except the said Glebe,

AND WHEREAS great Benefit would accrue to the said Benefit, if Power was given to the Rector for the Time being, to grant a Lease, or Leases, of the said Glebe Lands and Premises, for a Term of Years, sufficient to encourage persons to build upon and improve the same:

May it therefore please your Most Excellent MAJESTY,

at the humble Petition of the said John Stanley, that it may be ENACTED AND BE IT ENACTED, by the King's Most Excellent Majesty, by and with the Advice and Consent of the Lords Spiritual and Temporal, and Commons, in this present Parliament assembled, and by the Authority of the same, That from and after the passing of this Act it shall and may be lawful for the Rector of the Parish and Parish Church of Bury in the County of Lancaster, for the Time being, by Indenture or Indentures duly executed, to demise or lease all or any Part or Parts of the said Glebe Lands and Premises, and of the Buildings standing thereon, unto any Person or Persons who shall be willing to take, build upon, and improve the same, for any Term or Number of Years, not exceeding Ninety-nine Years: Which Lease or Leases shall be renewable at any Time and shall commence and take Effect in Possession, and not in Reversion; with Liberty for the Lessee or Lessees to take down all or any part of the buildings now standing thereon, in such Lease or Leases to be comprised; and to convert or dispose of the Materials thereof to such Uses and Purposes as therein shall be mentioned and agreed upon; so as in the said Lease or Leases there be reserved the best and most improved Ground Rent or Ground Rents that can be had or obtained, for the Benefit of the said Rector and his Successors, to be paid quarterly, without taking any sum of money, or other Thing, by way of Fine, Income or Foregift, except as hereinafter is excepted; and so as the Lessee or Lessees execute a Counterpart or Counterparts thereof, and enter into Covenants to build and keep in Repair the Messuages or Buildings intended and agreed to be built and to surrender the same at the expiration of the Term by such Lease or Leases to be granted; and so as in such Lease or Leases there be contained a Power of Re-entry for Non-payment of the Ground Rent or Ground Rents thereby to be reserved.

AND BE IT FURTHER ENACTED, by the Authority aforesaid, that it may and shall be lawful for the said John Stanley to take and receive of and' from any Person or Persons, to whom he shall grant a Building Lease or Building Leases as aforesaid, any Sum or Sums of Money, by way of Fine, Income or Foregift, not exceeding in the whole the sum of One hundred and Fifty Pounds, and to apply the same to reimburse himself such Sum or Sums of Money as he shall have expended in obtaining this Act.

PROVIDED NEVERTHELESS, AND BE IT FURTHER ENACTED, by the Authority aforesaid, That if at any Time hereafter it shall be thought necessary or expedient, for the Conveniency of the Inhabitants of the said Parish, to build and provide a Chapel of

Ease to the said Parish Church, contiguous to the said Town, it shall and may be lawful for the Rector of the said Parish for the Time being, and he is hereby authorised and required, by Indenture or Lease duly executed, to demise or lease, for any Term or Number of Years not less than Nine hundred and Ninety-nine Years, such part of the said Glebe, not exceeding ten thousand eight hundred feet, and at such Time, and to such Persons, as the Rector for the Time being shall think most expedient for the Purpose of building a Chapel of Ease to the said Parish, and for providing a Cemetery thereto ; but that the said Rector shall not receive, or be entitled to any Fine, Income, Foregift, Ground Rent, or other Rent or Payment of any Nature or Kind whatsoever, on account of any such Demise, or Lease ; any Thing hereinbefore contained to the contrary in any wise notwithstanding.

AND IT IS HEREBY DECLARED AND ENACTED, by the Authority aforesaid, That all and every Lease or Leases to be made of the said Glebe Lands and Premises, in Pursuance of this Act, shall be good, valid and effectual in law, to all Intents and Purposes.

PROVIDED ALWAYS, AND BE IT FURTHER ENACTED, by the Authority aforesaid, That nothing herein contained shall extend, or be construed to extend, to impower the said John Stanley, or his successors, Rectors of the said Rectory, to grant any Lease or Leases, by Virtue of this Act, of the Parsonage House belonging to the said Rectory, or of the Gardens adjoining to the said House, or of the Plot of Ground whereon the said House stands.

SAVING ALWAYS to the King's Most Excellent Majesty, his Heirs and Successors, and to all and every Person and Persons, Bodies Politic and Corporate, his, her, or their Heirs, Successors, Executors, or Administrators, other than and except the said Earl of Derby and his Successors, and the said John Stanley and his Successors, all such Estate, Right, Title, Interest, Claim, and Demand, of, in, and out of and all and singular the Glebe Lands and Premises so to be leased as aforesaid, as they every or any of them respectively had, before the passing of this Act, or could or might have had, held and enjoyed, in case this Act had not been made.

ST. JOHN'S CHURCH, BURY.

In the year 1767, in accordance with an Act of Parliament previously passed, the Rev. John Stanley, then Rector of Bury, made over to eight trustees a portion of the glebe land as the site of a church, which was to be a chapel of ease to the Parish Church. Upon this site, part of a field called " Listerfield," the present church was built by public subscription, the Earl of Derby and the Rector being among the contributors. The church was consecrated by the Bishop of Chester, on Friday, the 8th day of June, 1770. The right of appointing the incumbent was vested in the Rector of Bury, who also enjoyed the right of appointing the chapel-warden from three candidates elected by the seatholders. By the deed of consecration, certain pews were assigned and appointed in perpetuity to the subscribers to the building fund and their representatives, on the condition of their paying an annual rent of not more than 12d. for each " sitting-place " in such pews. Other pews were allotted to the minister, " to be let to the inhabitants of the parish of Bury, and those of neighbouring parishes, who choose to take the same, at the best rents he could get for them, for his better support and maintenance." Others, again, were assigned to the churchwardens, the rents to be applied for the necessary warden's expenses. Twenty six open forms at the west end were set apart and reserved for the poor. Among the donations to the chapel were :—The font, given by Mrs. Stanley ; the cup and paten, by the Hon. and Rev. John Stanley, rector ; the sounding-board, chain, and candlestick at the pulpit, by the Rev. John Campbell, minister.

1783. A grant of £100 from Queen Anne's Bounty, and £100 raised by subscription—of which the Rev. Henry Unsworth gave £60—were invested in the purchase of a farm at Westhoughton, called by the name of Baldwin's, in augmentation of the living of St. John's.

1789. The chapel-yard was enclosed by a wall and iron fence, the cost being met by a rate or ley upon the seats. To this, Mr. Unsworth gave £15.

1792. An organ erected by public subscription, at a cost of £228 18s. At the same time there was collected by public subscription—to which Mr. Unsworth gave £100—the sum of £170, which was invested as an endowment for the organist's salary. In 1805 this fund was augmented by a further sum of £130, and the total income now arising from it is £177.

The churchwardens' account book contains the accounts for every year since the foundation of the church. For many years the accounts are very similar, with here and there an investment for a new bell rope, a mousetrap, mending fences, &c. The first chapel-warden was Mr. John Openshaw.

In the year 1797, the Rev. John Stanley granted a portion of the Listerfield for enlarging the burial ground, and this grant was confirmed by his successor—the Rev. Sir W. H. Clerke.

During the baptism of an infant in this church in 1777 a terrible shock of earthquake was felt. The Rev. Mr. Campbell was officiating at the time, and the congregation broke everything in their way, rushed out into the chapel yard, in spite of the rev. gentleman's assurance that there was no danger, and his request that they would sit still.

The year 1821 was marked by the visit of Dr. Law, Bishop of Chester, who does not seem to have found the chapel in a very satisfactory condition. He ordered the Bible to be re-bound, a new Prayer Book to be provided for the minister, certain matters connected with the graveyard to be improved, and the church to be whitewashed. In the same year the Rev. Thomas Selkirk appears to have succeeded the Rev. Henry Unsworth as minister of St. John's Chapel, and he seems to have commenced by a series of innovations on the established order of things. The chapel was " thoroughly whitewashed and coloured," the pillars painted, and the pews and galleries " well cleaned ; " a " Venetian blind " was procured for the " altar window," and green blinds for the rest. " Thomas Turner was appointed to serve the office of beadle, with a salary of 26s. per annum, and a new hat and coat when necessary." The warden was " recommended to make the vestry comfortable," and the clerk " requested to clean the pews every Saturday." Transparencies of the Ascension, &c., were placed in the altar window by public subscription, at a cost of £24 8s. 2d.

In 1826, stoves were erected at a cost of upwards of £17.

In 1831, Mr. William Tarrey was elected chapel-warden. In the registry is the following entry :—" The above-named Mr. William Tarrey was lost, together with all his family, by the wreck of the *Rothsay Castle* steam packet, on the night of the 17th of August, 1831, near the Puffin Island, on the coast of Anglesey."

1833. A silver-headed staff, engraved " The Warden of St. John's, Bury," procured for the warden. In the same year Mr. William Walker and others raised a sum of money sufficient for a new organ, which was accordingly placed in the church and the old one disposed of.

1834. The Rev. Henry Crewe Boutflower succeeded to the incumbency.

1839. The two childrens' galleries on each side of the organ erected ; the cost defrayed by £50 contributed from a bazaar in Bell School, £53 from Mrs. Boutflower realised by the sale of work, and collections amounting to £29 9s. 6d. on the day of opening.

1849. The chapel underwent considerable repairs, a new ceiling, &c., being put up.

In the year 1852, Mr. Richard Norris being chapel-warden, an important alteration was effected. In consideration of an annual payment out of the income of the Parish Church of £58 a year, the seats appropriated to the minister's maintenance were given up, and some of those belonging to the warden. By this arrangement the seats on the north and south sides of the chapel were made free, the proprietors of seats in those places exchanging them for others which had belonged to the minister in the centre of the church.

The Rev. E. J. Smith, the present minister, was appointed in 1858. By an Act passed two years ago the living became a vicarage.

The schools which are in connection with St. John's Church, are situated in Hornby-street, and were opened on the 16th December, 1869. The total cost amounted to about £3,000. They are in the Gothic style of architecture, and are fully adapted to the requirements of such a building. The plot of land on which they are erected contains about 2,000 square yards, which allows ample space for playgrounds.

St Paul's, Bury, Lancashire.

ST. PAUL'S CHURCH, BURY.

The land for the site of St. Paul's Church was given by the Earl of Derby, father of the late Earl, and it includes not only the churchyard but the parsonage grounds and the fields adjoining. The building fund was·raised by public subscription. The foundation-stone was laid on October 3rd, 1838, by the late Earl of Derby, then Lord Stanley. The work was completed in 1841, the progress having been retarded by the fall of some of the pillars with a portion of the clerestory. It was first opened for Divine service on May 26th, 1841. The church was not consecrated until the following year, namely, June 29th, 1842. The first incumbent was the Rev. Hugh Allen, whose name was so prominently before the public a few years ago in connection with the proceedings at St. George's-in-the-East. The patronage of the church was vested in five trustees, four chosen by the seatholders, and the Rector of Bury, by virtue of his position. The organ was given to the church by one of the original trustees, the late John Lomax, Esq., of Springfield. In 1851, the church was licensed for the solemnisation of marriages. In 1848, the Rev. John Walker was appointed to the living, which he held until 1862, when the Rev. James Chell received the appointment. The church underwent considerable alteration in 1868. The unsightly gallery in the chancel was taken away, and the chancel opened out by the removal of the huge pulpit and reading-desk. The altar was raised considerably above the level of the church, and a *quasi* chancel, with choir stalls, reading-desks, and lectern formed outside the chancel arch. These alterations, together with the painting and decorating of the church, cost upwards of £600, which was raised by subscription. St. Paul's was the first church in Bury to introduce the weekly offertory. The choir first appeared in surplices on Advent Sunday, 1869.

In the summer of 1869 two handsome mural monuments were placed in the church. They are each Gothic in character, and are very highly enriched with ornament and carving. They are placed on either side of the chancel arch, looking toward the nave. One is to the memory of John Lomax, Esq., of Springfield; and the other to that of the late James Openshaw, Esq., of Lower Chesham. They are from designs prepared by Mr. L. Booth, of Bury. Upon the monument to the memory of Mr. Lomax is the following :—

Sacred to the memory of John Lomax, Esq., of Springfield, Bury, and Badfach, Llanfyllin; justice of the peace and High Sheriff of Montgomeryshire in the year 1862 ; born 28th November, 1801 ; died September 2nd, 1862.

As an originator and a trustee of this church, he was ever ready to promote its welfare.

This tablet is erected by his sorrowing children as a small tribute of their love and esteem.

Upon the other monument is inscribed :—

In affectionate remembrance of James Openshaw, Esq., of Lower Chesham, Bury; born April the 20th, 1814; died November 16th, 1867.

He was for many years a trustee and warden, and an earnest supporter of this church.

This tablet is erected by his sorrowing widow and children.

In 1872 Lawrence Booth, Esq., of the firm of Messrs. Blackwell, Son, and Booth, architects, of Manchester and Bury, was entrusted with the superintendence of the work of restoration of the church, and the edifice now presents a most chaste and beautiful appearance. In the place of the old oak pulpit, one of stone and marble, executed by Mr. J. Rawson, of Bury, was erected. It is supported upon five pillars, the centre one being of red Mansfield stone, and the outer ones of Sienna marble with carved capitals, from which four figures project to support four angles. On each face of the pulpit is a geometrical Gothic panel with background of red marble, with a white cross in the centre, inlaid with malachite, and having a precious stone in the centre. At each angle of the upper portion of the pulpit there is a pillar with carved capital and moulded bands and leases of statuary marble, the whole being surmounted by a moulded and indented cornice. The reredos is painted in delicate tints and gilded. All the old pews, which were in the ancient style, were taken out and replaced with open benches of pitch pine and walnut. The whole of the woodwork was executed by Mr. John Smith, of Bury. The flooring is composed of Minton tiles. Instead of there being two aisles, as formerly, there is now a wide centre aisle, and an aisle at each end of the church. The painting of the edifice was executed by Messrs. Berry and Sagar, of Bury, in a most admirable manner. The cost of the alterations amounted to about £600, the altar alone costing nearly £120 of that sum.

HOLY TRINITY CHURCH.

This church is situated in Spring-street, and was opened for divine service in October, 1863. The schools in connection with the church were erected about fifteen years before that date; and for about thirteen years, the scholars, at the close of the duties at the school, proceeded to divine service on Sundays to the Parish Church. During the two years immediately preceding the opening of the church, service was conducted in the schoolroom, the Rev. F. Wilson, the present pastor, being the officiating clergyman. The church is a plain stone building, without tower or spire, the external walls presenting little in the way of ornamentation. The interior has a somewhat naked and cold appearance, partly from the unplastered walls, and partly from the degree of light-

Rock & Co. Lond. Aug. 26. 1857.

2830 ⸗ 2872

St. Thomas Church, Bury, Lancashire.

ness imparted by the use of chairs in place of open benches or pews. The only part of the interior presenting any particular features of ornamentation is the communion, which is decorated somewhat after the Ritualistic fashion with devices, flowers, large candelabras, &c. The Rev. F. Wilson has been the vicar since the erection of the church, and resides in the parsonage house contiguous thereto.

ST. THOMAS'S CHURCH.

This sacred edifice is situated at Pimhole, bounded on the northerly side by Rochdale-road, and on the westerly side by Pimhole-lane. The site was the gift of the Earl of Derby, and contains over 8,000 square yards. The church is the gift of that venerable benefactor to his kind, the late Thomas Openshaw, Esq., and is the noblest of his many acts of charity. It is rectangular in form, and has a tower and spire 120 feet in height, a nave and side aisles, a chancel containing stalls for the choir, and the sacrarium, an organ chapel and vestry. The total length internally, from west end to east end, is 108ft. 6in., and the total width, 58ft. The width of the nave, from centre to centre of the aisle columns, is 29ft. 9in., and the width of the aisles 14ft. 1½in. The organ chapel and the corresponding chapel on the south side are divided from the aisles by means of a screen of open woodwork with metal work introduced therein. The pulpit is on the north side, and the reading desk on the south side of the chancel arch. The principal entrance into the church is through the tower at the north-west angle of the nave. The nave and aisles are fitted up with benches, as also the chapel on the south side, mentioned above, affording accommodation for about 650 worshippers. The church is in the Mediæval style, or that period of Gothic architecture known as " Early English," which prevailed in Europe during the 11th and 12th centuries. The east end appears to be peculiarly chaste and pleasing, as also the elegant south porch and the coupled lancet lights of the clerestory. The materials for the facing of the main body of the outside walls are parpoints of the Horncliffe stone ; the dressings round the windows, quoins, sills, and strings, being of the Fletcher Bank or Birtle stone. A very pleasing effect in colour is obtained with these stones, the former being of a greyish green and the latter of a warm, light buff colour. Internally, a few self-coloured materials have been used, such as wall tiling above the wainscoting red Mansfield stone in the shafts of the nave columns, and also in the small columns supporting the roof principals. The roof is open timbered, stained and varnished, and plastered between the spars, except in the chancel which has a carved and panelled ceiling. The height of the nave internally is about 48 feet. The whole of the woodwork, with one or two exceptions where oak is used, is of red deal, stained and varnished. The coupled shafts in the chancel are of Cornish serpentine, and the floor of the sacrarium, chancel, and the steps leading thereto are laid with Minton's encaustic tiles, as also the porch, space round the font, and tower. Some carving is judiciously introduced, and the effect both internally and externally is very satisfactory.

The church was consecrated on the 10th of December, 1866. The present vicar is the Rev. Thomas Atherton, who has officiated as minister since the erection of the edifice. After the church was built, day and Sunday schools were provided, principally by members of the Openshaw family, aided by grants from the Committee of Council on Education, and the National Society. They also provided for the erection of a parsonage house, which is contiguous to the church.

ST. PETER'S CHURCH.

This edifice is situated off Manchester-road, and near to the Cemetery. The foundation-stone was laid on the 23rd August, 1871, by Bishop Fraser. The style is the transition of the Early English, or pointed, into the Geometrical. The material of which the church is built is, on the exterior, parpoint walling, with Yorkshire stone dressings, &c., and bands of Runcorn stone. The interior is faced with red pressed brick of a superior kind, with several bands and patterns in black brick. The columns are in alternate bands of blue Burnley and Bath stone. Lofty traceried windows in pairs are placed over each arch in the nave. A stone and marble reredos, with gold mosaics, is placed behind the altar. The pulpit and font are executed in stone and marble. The ceiling is in the form of a pointed arch. The principal entrance is through the tower, which forms a narthex or vestibule. The west gable is pierced with a five-light traceried window, and door under. The architects were Messrs. C. J. Maycock and A. P. Bell, of Manchester. The church will accommodate 500 persons, and the cost, exclusive of tower and carving, £4,500.

ST. MARK'S SCHOOL, FREETOWN.

The Church Sunday School in Freetown is among the oldest in the town, having existed for a period approaching half a century. About the year 1826, when there was neither church nor school in what is now the parish of St. Paul's, Mr. Haslam, of Chesham, the owner of the Hudcar Mill, encouraged the opening of a Sunday school, and allowed a room in his mill to be used as a school in which to assemble the children of the neighbourhood. Mr. Richard Norris was the superintendent of this school, which flourished under Mr. Haslam's patronage. The mill afterwards changed hands, and Mr. Gregg, the next proprietor, did not belong to the communion of the Church of England, but, with true Christian largeness of heart, he extended to the school his patronage and support. From the room in the mill the school was removed to a cottage in Hudcar Row, and afterwards to the old building still standing near the brook, in Bridge-street. For upwards of twenty years the school was carried on without a permanent school building, but about the year 1850 it was determined to make an effort to raise a building adapted to the wants of the school. By the energy and perseverance of Mr. Norris, and those associated with him, a fund was raised, and a site obtained from the Rector of Bury for the purpose of building a school. Mr. Greenhalgh, of Chesham Fields, contributed a quantity of bricks, and G. Walker, Esq., Chesham, John Lomax, Esq., Springfield, and T. Openshaw, Esq., Pimhole, were among the most liberal contributors to the building fund. The result of this effort was the present school in Brook-street, which is known by the name of the Hudcar School. This school was opened about the year 1850, and was afterwards licensed for service, the Rev. Thomas Wolstencroft officiating there. For some reason or other the service in the school was discontinued until the present year (1873).

On the 5th of January, the school having been again licensed, service was held in it. The stipend for a curate in charge having been provided by the Church Building Society, the Rector of Bury and two gentlemen resident in the district, Freetown was made into a conventional district, and the Rev. Bigland Withers was entrusted with the pastoral care of it.

Owing to the increased population, the old school was found inadequate for the wants of the district, and steps were immediately taken to provide further accommodation. The Rev. Canon Hornby, Rector of Bury, has given a plot of ground as a site for church and schools, and a handsome school for about 300 children is being erected upon it. The design of this school provides for future extension when the necessary funds can be procured. The end of the first quarter of a century in the history of Freetown school found it entering upon a new phase of its existence, taking possession of new and more commodious premises. It is to be hoped that the end of the second quarter of a century will find it again advancing and taking up a more permanent position, and adapting itself to the altered condition of the neighbourhood.

CHAPTER X.

The Chapels, &c.— Temperance Hall—The Market—The late Edmund Grundy—John and Robert Kay—The Riot of 1826—The General Elections in 1832, 1835, 1837, 1841, and 1847.

THE CHAPELS, ETC.

The Dissenting places of worship in the town are—Baptist Chapel (Ebenezer), Knowsley-street; Baptist Chapel (Providence), Freetown; Catholic Church (St. Marie's), Manchester-road; Catholic Chapel (St. Joseph's), Peter-street; Christian Church, Rochdale-road; Free Gospel Church, Freetown; Independent Chapel (Bethel), Henry-street; Independent Chapel (Congregational), Castlecroft; Independent Chapel (Congregational), New-road; Independent Methodist, Henry-street; Methodist New Connexion Chapel, Bolton-street; New Jerusalem Church, Walmersley-road; Presbyterian Chapel (Unitarian), Bank-street; Primitive Methodist Chapel, Walmersley-road; Wesleyan Chapel, Union-street; United Methodist Free Church (Brunswick), North-street. With regard to the Silver-street or Bank-street Chapel, it may be stated that the Rev. Henry Pendlebury, M.A., being ejected from Holcombe Chapel in 1662, the meeting-house was afterwards built for him in Bass-lane, Bury. After his death, in 1695, the Presbyterian place of worship, called Dundee Chapel, on the opposite side of the brook to the Episcopal Chapel whence Mr. Pendlebury was ejected, was built for his successor, Mr. E. Rothwell, and in 1719 that part of the congregation who resided in Bury erected the chapel in Silver-street or Bank-street. Mr. Braddock was the first minister of this chapel; on his death, in 1764, he was succeeded by Mr. John Hughes, who, after occupying the pulpit about thirty-five years, was succeeded by Mr. Allard at the beginning of the present century. The old chapel of 1719 was replaced by a more modern building in 1837. The present handsome edifice in Bank-street, near the railway station, was opened in 1852. The exterior is very beautiful. It is in the late Pointed, or Perpendicular style, and

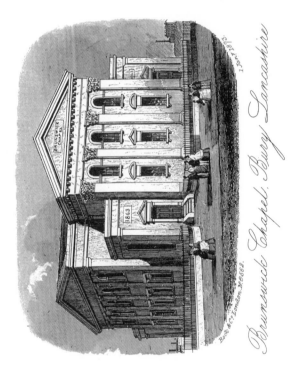

Brunswick Chapel, Bury, Lancashire

consists of a nave, chancel, and two transepts. The chapel seats about 700 persons, and cost £6,000. The schools at the back of the chapel were built in 1866, and are of two storeys. There is a very ornamental tower over the entrance, and the exterior is in excellent keeping with that of the chapel. Both chapel and schools were paid for by the voluntary contributions of the members of the congregation. Connected with the chapel is a small cemetery, with a neat little mortuary chapel, outside the town.

The ceremony of laying the corner-stone of the new and enlarged Brunswick Chapel, near the site of the old chapel in North-street, took place on Thursday, the 12th of June, 1862 (Whit-week). The lower storey of the edifice, now used as a Sunday School, was then erected, and the corner-stone represented, in fact, the first stone of the chapel walls on the first storey. The weather was most unpropitious for the procession of school children, which extended fully a quarter of a mile in length, the schools in connection with the United Free Methodist Churches of Limefield, Elton, Ramsbottom, and Heap Bridge, furnishing their quota to the ranks. The stone was laid, amid a drenching shower of rain, by Mr. Samuel Smith, who was presented with a handsome silver trowel and mallet, immediately after which the company adjourned to the old chapel, where the remainder of the " programme of the day's proceedings was gone through." In the evening, a tea meeting took place, under the presidency of Mr. S. Smith, and addresses were delivered by Mr. John Stockdale, Revs. M. Miller (Heywood), John Peters, E. Wright, (Louth), William Stott and J. H. Cuttell, and Messrs. J. Hacking, R. Lord, D. Smith, and R. Hall. The building, including the chapel and schoolroom, is built of stone, and is, on the ground plan, in the form of a cross, 100ft. by 70ft., with four entrances and vesti-bules, two from the street, and two from the schoolroom underneath. The floor of the schoolroom is on a level with the adjoining grounds, and is 18ft. 9in. below the chapel floor, which is nearly in a line with the street in front. The total height of the building is about 60 feet. Each of the four sides are finished with a pediment, cornice, and pilas-ters, of the Grecian style of architecture. The chapel was opened for Divine service in December, 1864. The cost of the erection was £7,250. It is in the Grecian style of architecture, with Doric pilasters at the back and sides, and Corinthian pilasters at the front. It will accommodate 1,200 persons, and is built of millstone grit dressings, and Horncliffe parpoints. From ground floor to ceiling it is 40ft. high, and 100ft. in length, by 75ft. in breadth. The collections at the opening services amounted to £244 0s. 10½d.—The United Methodist Free Church

Schools, Bank Top, which serve for the purposes of a chapel, are situate at Warth-fold, contiguous to the river Irwell, and near to the East Lancashire Railway Company's Line. They are of recent erection ; the corner-stone being laid on the 1st August, 1869, by Mr. R. Lord, of Union-square, Bury. The school is within five minutes walk of an old building, off Bank Top, belonging to the farm occupied by Mr. Joshua Bentley, and which was used as a school by the United Methodist Free Church denomination for 14 years. Mr. J. H. Riley, of Rochdale-road, was the architect for the present schools, which are plain and substantial, and cost £600.

The Methodist Chapel, Openshaw Fold, erected in connection with the United Methodist Free Churches, was opened on Wednesday, February 16th, 1870, the sermons on the occasion being preached by the Rev. John Adcock, of London. The building is of brick, with stone dressings, and is carried up to the height of four feet from the ground line in stonework, on the top of which the brickwork begins, and is carried to the height of 18 feet. The floor was raised on account of the site being occasionally liable to flooding. The front elevation has a neat and substantial look about it. The door is reached by five stone steps. The windows to the front are two in number, one on each side of the door, ten feet six inches by four feet broad, with stone sills and stone keys in the arches. Above the windows, and at the square of the roof, a stone string course is carried across, with a band or two of ornamental brickwork beneath. The name of the building—"Zion"— is inscribed on a square stone, with the date of 1869 upon it, and set in the front gable between the string course and the highest point of the ridge. A neat stone coping is laid on each gable end, finished off by moulded feet. To the top of the front gable is a small carved finial. There are to the sides four windows in each, the same height as the front. The whole of the outside of the chapel is faced with stock bricks. The interior is provided with a porch, having a door on each side leading into the chapel, which is of the following dimensions : 48 feet long, 32 feet wide, and 17 feet to the outside of the principals. The roof, being open, gives in the centre the height of 24 feet. The place will seat about 250 persons. There is a gallery at one end, and the space underneath has been utilised by making two vestries, one used as a class-room, and the larger as a minister's vestry. Under the vestry is a cellar, in which the warming apparatus is placed. The building is well lighted by two sunlights, in ornamental shells, depending from the ceiling. The pewing, forms, gallery front, and the principals of the roof, are of pitch pine, lightly stained and well-finished.

The top of the porch is well finished off with an ornamental railing, bronzed and gilt. The pulpit is of the platform shape, plain and unpretentious in design, of pitch pine, stained and varnished like the rest of the fittings. The total cost of the building was about £640 ; and the architect was Mr. J. H. Riley, of Bury.

TEMPERANCE HALL.

On Saturday, the 21st June, 1873, the corner-stone of a new Temperance Hall was laid in Henry-street, by James Barlow, Esq., of Greenthorne, Bolton, and is now in course of erection. The plan of the building comprises on the ground floor a lodge room for Good Templars, with raised seats all round, in the form of an amphitheatre, and all the requisite furniture for carrying out the ritual of the Order. In connection with this room there will be gentlemen's and ladies' retiring rooms. The large room for public meetings will be on the first floor, and will be approached by stone steps. There will be a gallery across one end, and a platform across the other, with cloak room, tea room, and two retiring rooms connected. The space under the platform will be utilised as a sewing room, whilst a large space under the floor will admit of all the seats and tables being stowed away when not in use. The exterior of the building will be very simple, being of brick with Burnley stone dressings. The building will be completed with thoroughly good but plain materials. The cost of the edifice and furnishing will be nearly £1,600. The architects are Messrs. Maxwell and Tuke, Peel Chambers, Bury.

THE MARKET.

In 1841 the market was erected where it now stands, upon the land and at the cost of the Earl of Derby. As great inconvenience was felt in consequence of the open area of the market not being protected from the weather, it was determined in the summer of 1867 to cover the whole with a roof of iron, and to have a large portion of the same glazed, to give ample light to the area. The plan of the work was entrusted to Mr. Green, civil engineer and architect, Portsmouth, near Todmorden (who was also architect for the Earl of Derby's estate workshops at Redvales). The market was closed while the work was going on, but was re-opened, with the alterations completed, in the first week in April, 1868. The roof is constructed chiefly of wrought-iron on the tie and tension principle, and has a central roof of 60 feet span, with two side roofs of 50 feet span each, with hipped sides at the angles. The form of the market, being an irregular triangle, presented many

M

difficulties in covering over the area without disturbing the existing shops, &c., but these were overcome in such a way that the whole presents a light and commodious appearance, and affords accommodation for 146 stalls—many more than previously. The contract for iron roofs, pillars, and gutters was taken by Mead, Wrightson, & Co., of the Teesdale Iron Works. The cost of the iron work alone was about £1,400, and the total cost was between £4,000 and £5,000.

THE LATE EDMUND GRUNDY.

This gentleman who contested the first election in Bury, was born at Cinderhill, in the township of Pilkington, in 1781. He was the seventh son by the third wife of Mr. Denis Grundy. Mr. Denis Grundy, who did not possess such a princely fortune as many manufacturers can boast, was nevertheless reputed to be wealthy, and was familiarly known as "Golden Denis." At his death he left upwards of £20,000 to his children. He entered the business at an early period in life as a calico printer, and continued in that business until 1820. In 1821 he and his family went to America, but he only remained there one year, during which time he neither entered into business nor purchased land. He was induced to visit America with the intention of settling there, from the impression that the course of legislation in this country at that time was calculated to destroy real prosperity. On his return from America he set his son, Mr. Thomas Grundy, to the study of the law, and Mr. Edmund Grundy to the practice of physic. His other sons were too young for business and they were sent to school. He became a coal proprietor, and continued in the coal business until he gave it up to his sons. Mr. Grundy was well known as an arbitrator and valuer. His mode of life was of a simple character; he neither fed nor clothed extravagantly; and he was a really industrious man. During a period of more than 20 years he was a total abstainer from intoxicating drink. At one time he was president of the Temperance Society, and continued to be devoted to its principles and a supporter of the cause. For many years he was a member of the Board of Guardians, and for some time was chairman of the Board. He was not a penurious man, but was known to be hospitable and kind. and loved to have his friends around him at his residence at Park Hills. That residence was built in 1825, and he continued its occupant for 32 years. He was a great admirer of the late Mr. Henry Hunt, at the time private meetings were being held among the Radicals. He was not at Peterloo, but found bail for Mr. Hunt, and was also examined as a witness on behalf of Mr. Hunt, when that gentleman was tried at York on a charge of treason. He was ardently attached to Mr. Cobbett, M.P. for Oldham, and that gentleman came occasionally to Park Hills to see Mr. Grundy. In the year 1832, when the town of Bury was first formed into a parliamentary borough, at the request of a small body of Radicals, Mr. Grundy was induced to offer himself as a candidate in opposition to Mr. Walker. The result of that contest was that Mr. Walker received 306 votes and Mr. Grundy 153. Afterwards, Mr. Walker became more liberal as a politician and gave such satisfaction by his votes in Parliament, that Mr. Grundy was amongst his warmest supporters, and it was probably owing to the amalgamation that Mr. Walker triumphantly carried the election in 1841 by a majority of 97 votes. In the election of 1832 a piece of plate was presented to Mr. Grundy by the people of Bury. He usually wore a blue dress coat, with bright brass buttons, yellow waistcoat, drab breeches, and top boots. He died at the age of 75 years, and was interred at Bank-street chapel.

JOHN AND ROBERT KAY.

In the year 1738, John Kay (a relation of the celebrated Dr. Fletcher), a native of Bury, introduced the means of throwing the shuttle by means of the picking-stick, instead of the hand, and hence called the fly-shuttle. In consequence of the fury of the populace, he was compelled to remove to Colchester. By his invention a weaver was enabled to perform twice the usual quantity of work, and to weave cloth of any width. In 1760, Robert Kay, son of the above John Kay, invented the drop-box, by which a weaver could at ease use any one of three shuttles, and thereby produce a fabric of three colours with nearly the same expedition as he could weave a common calico. The invention of setting cards by machinery also belongs to another of this ingenious family.

THE RIOT OF 1826.

The year 1826 was one of utter ruin to many, and entire stagnation of business to all, bands of rioters or discontented workpeople moved about the country, entering mills and places of manufacture wherever they could force an entrance, and breaking all the machinery they could lay hands upon. The large cotton and other factories that now stand around Bury were then unbuilt, but those that were in existence were threatened, and in order to avert the danger watch was ordered by the magistrates to be kept in every direction from which it might be expected the mob would advance. The upper part of Mr. Edmund Grundy's house in the Wylde commanded a view of the country beyond the bridge, in which way it was apprehended a body of insurgents would approach the town

In order to repel them effectually, and be a sufficient protection for the property, a military detachment was sent to Bury, and stationed, under arms, in the Market-place, ready to move at the first intimation in whatever direction their services were required. Ned Kenyon took his place as sentinel on the roof of Mr. Grundy's house, and the first periods of his watch passed away without the looked-for signal to the armed and vigilant soldiers below that the expected foe was visible, although since early morning it was believed each minute that the summons for a quick departure would be given, as it was known the previous evening that the rioters had threatened to be in Bury before long. However, the hour of noon came, and Ned was hungry, and thought it the most natural thing possible that he should go down to Mr. Grundy's hospitable kitchen to get his dinner, which he did, not thinking the proceeding of sufficient importance to be communicated to the gentlemen and officers below who might be interested in the fact that their stationed .sentinel was absent from his post. Ned proceeded quietly with his refreshment, not averse to gossip with the wondering servants, who questioned him as to the result of his lofty observations. But hark! what signifies this tumult in the Wylde, deepening into an uproar that disturbs even Ned Kenyon in the quiet kitchen? "Rioters! rioters!" "The mob! the mob!" and rushing up Bolton-street came eager flying messengers craving hurriedly for that help and defence already too long delayed at the time when most urgently required. An old woollen mill in Woodhill-lane was the object of attack; and even by the time the first intimation of danger could have reached the soldiers was already completely in the hands of the enemy. Now there was hurrying to the point of vantage on the roof to take cognizance of the dreaded approach; and from hence it was visible that, besides the mill, now completely invested, Brandle-some-lane was swarming with crowds of desperate and violent men, still pressing onwards to aid in the scene of destruction. The military arrived in the neighbourhood of the building with the utmost speed to make a stand against advancing numbers, and pressing forward through the opposing crowd, were greeted with hoarse shouts of derision and cries of triumph as the wrecked and gutted building came into view. This piece of destruction might at least have been prevented had Ned Kenyon not considered his comfortable and leisurely dinner of as much.importance as the duty he had been appointed to perform.

PARLIAMENTARY ELECTIONS.

1832.—THE FIRST ELECTION.

Bury returns only one representative to Parliament, and was one of the towns enfranchised by the Reform Act of 1832. The first election took place on the 12th of December of that year, when the candidates were Mr. Richard Walker and Mr. E. Grundy, both Liberals. The following is a report of the proceedings in connection with this election, copied from the *Manchester Guardian* of December 15th, 1832 :—

"Tuesday last being the day appointed (by Samuel Holker Haslam, Esq., the returning officer for this borough) for the nomination of the candidates, in the course of the morning a very great number of the Tottingtonians, as they are called, in other words, members of the Tottington political union, and also of the Heywood political union of the working classes, came into the town bearing a variety of blue flags (Mr. Grundy's colour) and placards inscribed "Exclusive dealing." These, joined by Mr. Grundy's partisans, paraded the town with bands, escorted Mr. Grundy to the hustings, and drew up in the Square an hour before the appointed time for business, monopolising all the space immediately in front of the hustings, to the exclusion of the friends and voters of Mr. Walker, the other candidate.

" Mr. Grundy took his station to the left of the returning officer, and was surrounded by his friends, four of whom, Mr. Matthew Fletcher, Mr. John Greenhow, Mr. John Kay, and Mr. Thomas Bird, wore a blue paper round their hats, on which were the words, ' One of the conspirators.' Mr. Grundy wore a blue hat, with a similar bill upon it, and to this he frequently directed the attention of the mob in front, by taking it off, holding it out to them with one hand, and pointing to it with the other, exclaiming at the same time, ' One of John Edward Taylor's conspirators, gentlemen.' Amongst the flags of his supporters we observed some with the following inscriptions, 'Heywood National Political Union of the Working Classes,' ' Tottington Political Union,' ' One volunteer is worth two pressed men,' ' Grundy, the friend of the rising generation,' ' The people, the source of all power,' ' An equitable adjustments and no corn laws,' &c. There were several besoms with blue bills round them, inscribed, ' Come forward to the poll.' We must not omit to mention that several printed placards were borne on poles, having the inscription, ' The inhabitants of Tottington are determined to follow up the system of exclusive dealing till they have obtained their constitutional rights.'

" About half-past nine, the procession of Mr. Walker's friends approached the hustings, and Mr. Grundy immediately called out to the mob, ' Stand firm, my lads.' This they did, to the exclusion of the pink party from the front of the hustings, and as often during the proceedings as a few of the latter were seen to have elbowed their way to that part of the Square opposite their candidate, on a signal given a rush was made by the unionists, and the pinks were borne completely out of the Square. On the pink banners were the inscriptions, ' The rights and liberties of the industrial classes;' ' The abolition of all useless places and unmerited pensions;' ' Liberty will eventually triumph over tyranny and injustice;' ' A man of integrity is the people's best safeguard;' ' He's a friend to the workman, a friend to the poor, a friend to Reform; what would you more?' ' Peace in the land and plenty to the poor,' &c. On the friends of Mr. Walker taking their station on the hustings, Mr. Matthew Fletcher proposed to the mob to give three groans for Mr. Samuel Woodcock, junior. These were given accordingly. About ten o'clock, Samuel Holker Haslam, Esq., the returning officer, accompanied by William Grant, Esq., one of the magistrates of the county, took his seat on the centre of the hustings; the sheriff's precept and the act for more effectually preventing bribery and corruption in the election of Members of Parliament were then read by the magistrates' clerk. Mr. Grant next administered the oath to the returning officer, and he was duly sworn to return such person as should to the best of his judgment appear to have the majority of legal votes. Mr. Haslam then requested of all present to aid him in maintaining peace and order, and said he should consider it a personal favour to himself if they would accord a fair and impartial hearing to every gentleman who should address them. Having asked if any gentleman present had a candidate to propose as a representative for the borough, Edmund Grundy, Esq., banker, proposed Mr. Richard Walker, in a speech to which we regret our inability, owing to the demands upon our space, to give insertion. He animadverted with great force on the system of exclusive dealing, which he said was nothing more or less than bribery; and it put him in mind of a man he had heard of who was said to be so much the friend of liberty that he would let no one have any but himself.—Mr. Edmund Grundy (candidate): I say you are a liar, sir.—Edmund Grundy, Esq.: I did not allude to you; but to a person living at Bolton.—Mr. E. Grundy: Oh, then, I beg your pardon; I understood you did, sir.— Edmund Grundy, Esq., concluded by observing that to a member of Parliament there were four indispensable requisites—a good heart, a well-informed mind, a sound judgment, and an even temper; and he knew no one in which these qualities were more united and prominent than in his friend, a fellow-townsman, Mr. Walker. (Cheers.)—Mr. William Rathbone Greg then came forward, and immediately Mr. Grundy's party on the hustings directed a man to advance opposite to Mr. Greg, bearing a placard with the words, 'Indictment for conspiracy; Mr. W. R. Greg, prosecutor.' Mr. Greg smiled at this, bowed to the crowd, who saluted him with deafening groans, and seconded the nomination of Mr. Walker in an excellent speech, which, however, could only be heard by those on or near to the hustings.—Mr. Greenhow then nominated Mr. Grundy, in an oration in which he defended exclusive dealing, on the ground that it was an agreement amongst the Radicals to trade with one another, and was in force among many religious *sexes* and denominations.—Mr. Fletcher having several times waved his hand to the crowd, which was understood by Mr. Walker's party on the hustings as a signal for the mob to rush towards the pinks and sweep them out of the Square, several gentlemen addressed him, and warned him to desist, or he would merit exclusion from the hustings, for, being a non-elector, he had no right there.—Mr. Newbold, ironfounder, seconded the nomination.—No other candidate having been nominated, Mr. Walker proceeded to address the assemblage, which at this time must have exceeded 8,000 in number. He stated that he had been waited upon by two or three hundred of the electors, a decisive majority of them, and but for their requisition he should not have presumed to come forward to solicit their suffrages. If elected, he would uphold the constitution in King, Lords, and Commons; he would extend the principles of Reform in all its ramifications, to the removal of abuses both in Church and State, to the curtailment of the expenditure, and to the better adaptation of taxation. He should belong to the party of neither Whig, Tory, nor Radical, but vote for those measures which he considered best calculated to promote the interests of the people. His feelings were in favour of the present administration, because he thought them honest men; but he would always support good measures and oppose bad ones, by whomsoever introduced. (A Voice: Will you support a motion for inquiry into the Manchester massacre?) No; not that I don't regret the proceedings of that day, but that I can see no good that would result from an inquiry. Mr. Walker concluded by saying that if elected he would serve his fellow-townsmen freely, honestly, and independently.—Mr. Grundy (the candidate) then spoke for about an hour and a quarter, in a very violent strain, directing a torrent of the coarsest abuse we ever remember to have heard by any man in a respectable station, against the gentleman who he supposed had written various election squibs against him, and whose conduct he said was brutal, savage, ruffianly, and hellish, and the curse of God would rest upon it. He was particularly wroth against his relatives, Mr. R. T. Grundy, and Messrs. S. Woodcock, senior and junior. He then proceeded to dilate upon what he would do if returned to Parliament. He would have the malt, hop, and soap taxes abolished; and respecting the amount of those he read a statement, his authority for which, he said, was the *Manchester and Salford Advertiser*, of November 3, 1832. After going through his intended political doings, *à la Cobbett*, he returned to his abuse of his relatives; of Mr. John Edward Taylor, than whom, he said, there was not a more despicable apostate under the sun, and there was nothing so detestable in his (Mr. Grundy's) sight as an apostate and a renegade. He would say to Mr. Samuel Woodcock, jun., as was said to Cain, that he would set a mark upon him that he might be known as a rogue and a vagabond. (' Shame.') He would stigmatise him as a disgrace to mankind while his arm remained on his body, and he would will it to his children to warn him of it afterwards. (Hisses.) Mr. Grundy concluded by saying that if elected he would endeavour to fulfil his duty to the best of his ability, and according to those *Christian principles* which he had imbibed from his youth upwards.

" The returning officer then took the show of hands, first for Mr. Walker, and then for Mr. Grundy. The majority in favour of the latter was very great, there being, we understand, hardly any electors present except those on the hustings, and many perhaps of the majority of those who raised their hands for Mr. Grundy not being even inhabitants of the town. Mr. Haslam having declared the show of hands to be in favour of Mr. Grundy, a poll was demanded on behalf of Mr. Walker by E. Grundy, Esq. Mr. Walker then moved a vote of thanks to the returning officer, which was seconded by Mr. Grundy, the candidate, and passed by acclamation. The proceedings were then adjourned to the following morning, when the poll commenced.

" At nine o'clock on Wednesday morning the polling commenced. The inhabitants of the neighbouring townships, particularly of Radcliffe and Tottington, crowded the streets. By half-past two in the afternoon the numbers were :—

For Mr. Walker................................... 306
For Mr. Grundy 153

Leaving a majority of 153 for the former candidate, the number of voters in the borough being 529. Under these circumstances the blues gave up the contest, and the numbers having been declared, Mr. Walker was declared to be duly elected. The Square was at this time filled

with people, both the candidates were present, but Mr. Walker was
advised not to address the crowd, as several stones had been thrown,
one of which struck a young gentleman of the name of Calrow, and
knocked out some of his front teeth. Mr. Grundy did speak, as did Mr.
Fletcher, who attributed their failure to 'bribery.' The noise and
uproar was very great, but the proceedings having terminated, the
people dispersed without committing any serious damage. Since then,
however, several gardens belonging to the pink party have been broken
into and wantonly destroyed.

" On Thursday morning, Mr. Walker's workpeople went down in a
body, but peaceably, and without banners or music, to that gentleman's
house, to congratulate him on his success. Some of the blue party
afterwards sent to Tottington and other neighbouring places for their
' unrepresented ' friends. A large concourse of people, with music and
flags, paraded the town, and broke the windows of almost every house
in the principal streets which was inhabited by a pink. The riots were
solely occasioned by the improper conduct of the blues. The leaders of
that party paraded the streets with blue placards in their hats, and blue
ribbons and favours, as though for the purpose of exciting the people.
Mr. Grundy also made his appearance, with his blue hat and the
inscription above noticed. With the exception of the one noticed, we
have not heard of any personal injuries being inflicted."

THE ELECTION OF 1835.

On Thursday, January 8, 1835, Mr. Walker was put in nomination a
second time, and there being no other candidate, was returned without
opposition. Mr. Thomas Norris was the returning officer. Mr. Walker
was nominated by Mr. Edmund Grundy, banker, and was seconded by
Mr. John Greg, cotton spinner. Mr. Walker addressed the meeting at
some length. A number of his workmen paraded the town on the
following day with music and pink flags, conducting themselves in a
peaceable manner.

THE ELECTION OF 1837.

At this election the candidates were Mr. Richard Walker, Liberal, the
late member for the borough; Mr. Sergeant Spankie, Conservative, the
ex-member for Finsbury; and Mr. James Paul Cobbett, Liberal, of
London. The committees of Mr. Walker and Mr. Sergeant Spankie
determined that they would not carry to the hustings either flags or
party colours of any description, and this resolution they fully carried
into effect; but it was not so with Mr. Cobbett's party, who proceeded

to the hustings, the crowd being composed for the most part of non-electors, who were preceded by a band of music, and green and white flags and banners. Two men also walked in this procession, bearing each a pole with a piece of bread and cheese affixed thereon. Underneath was pasted a piece of paper, upon which were the words, " This is an Englishman's dinner under the new Poor-law Act." Upon Mr. Cobbett's compartment of the hustings a flag was displayed which bore the words, " No bastile!" The nomination took place on the 25th July. The usual proceedings having been gone through after the arrival of the candidates at the hustings, the returning officer, Edmund Grundy, Esq., banker, of Bury, called upon the electors to nominate their respective candidates, and expressed a hope that the election would be conducted with peace and good order, and that the best man might win.

Mr. Richard Harrison proposed Richard Walker, Esq., as a fit and proper person to represent the borough in Parliament; and during the greater part of his address the Cobbettites continued a system of bawling and hooting, which prevented the greater part of his address from being heard. Mr. Cobbett, however, interfered; partial silence was procured, and Mr. Harrison pointed with confidence to Mr. Walker's votes in Parliament as an earnest that he would not neglect the interests of the constituency.

Mr. S. Woodcock seconded the nomination.

Mr. James Hutchinson proposed Sergeant Spankie as a fit and proper person to serve the borough in Parliament; and if excellence of private character, and good management of his private affairs, was any guarantee for the efficient and faithful discharge of a man's duties, then he would say that the learned Sergeant was fully qualified to represent the borough.

Mr. Edmund Hardman, of Chamber Hall, seconded the nomination of the learned gentleman, who, he said, was a staunch supporter of the institutions of the country. He would not consent that any person should coerce the Queen, or " wallop" the House of Lords.

Mr. Fletcher, surgeon, proposed Mr. James Paul Cobbett; and he spoke for upwards of an hour in support of the claims of the candidate, and in opposition to Mr. Walker. Whilst he gave the latter gentleman credit for the highest excellence of private character, he grounded his opposition to him from the fact that Mr. Walker was opposed to the total repeal of the Poor-law Amendment Bill. He charged Mr. Walker with having pledged himself to household suffrage, and with not having redeemed his pledge by voting for a motion to that effect in the House of Commons. (Mr. Walker here distinctly denied having made any such pledge.) He much regretted that Mr. Walker had allowed himself to be made a cat's-paw by Mr. Joseph Hume and his party in Parliament.

Mr. Edward Potts seconded the nomination.

Mr. Walker then came forward, and with some difficulty obtained a hearing. He fully admitted the right of Mr. Fletcher, or any other gentleman, to scrutinise his conduct. He only claimed fair play, which every Englishman ought to have. There were two honourable gentlemen opposed to him, and all he asked was that they would give their support to the best man. If the electors considered that he had any claim upon their confidence, and that he was a proper person to represent their interests in Parliament, he should be happy to receive at their hands a renewal of their confidence. If, on the contrary, the electors thought that either of his honourable opponents were more worthy of their confidence, he would willingly shake hands with them, and they should have his best wishes and services to promote the·interests of the town. But he had received a very bad character that morning from the seconder of the learned Sergeant, and the proposer of Mr. Cobbett. In the first place, the seconder of Sergeant Spankie considered him (Mr. Walker) as the destroyer of the Church; whilst, on the other hand, Mr. Fletcher seemed to think he was too much of a preserver of that institution, and was, at best, only an amphibious reformer. He declared that he was not a destroyer of the Church; he fully intended to show himself a reformer of its abuses, but he did not deserve the character which Mr. Hardman and Mr. Fletcher had given him. With respect to Mr. Hardman, he would undertake to place his character in comparison with that of Mr. Hardman's, and leave it to the people of Bury to say which of the two was the best supporter of the Church. He begged that gentlemen, when they spoke about him, would only talk of his public and not his private character; and he would say that such attacks as he had been that day subjected to, did not come well from a neighbour, and one whom he had always looked upon as a friend. Mr. Walker then referred to several measures which had been brought before Parliament, and replied at some length to Mr. Fletcher's observations upon his votes on the Poor-law Amendment question.

Mr. Fletcher and others then asked Mr. Walker a long list of questions. respecting the new Poor-law, all of which he answered.

Mr. Sergeant Spankie then addressed the crowd. He said he did not come forward upon grounds of personal hostility to Mr. Walker, for whose private character he entertained the highest respect, but whose public opinions and principles he held to be highly mischievous. He would apply the revenues of the Church in promoting the proper business of religion, and in giving each man his proper share in the emoluments which were forthcoming for the support of religion. He would not support the abuses in the Church and State. No man was less interested in those abuses than he was, for he had never received a single favour from Government. He was created a king's sergeant-at-law three years before he went to Parliament, and he would state with confidence that there was not a more independent member of the House of Commons than he had been; and he defied any member of Parliament to say that during the time in which he was in Parliament he had ever asked a single favour. They might call him a Tory or they might call him a Whig, but he was not a Tory in the sense in which it was accepted. He was a Whig until the granting of the Catholic emancipation. He was a Whig in conscience, and would give the utmost freedom of conscience, but he disapproved of the passing of the Catholic Emancipation Bill. He concluded by thanking the electors for the patience with which they had listened to him.

Mr. Cobbett addressed the electors in a speech which lasted two hours and a-half in its delivery. After referring at some length to the Poor-law Amendment Act, and to universal suffrage, he said that he would not repeal the Corn Laws unless the repeal was accompanied by an equitable adjustment of the National Debt. He protested against the Liberals meddling with the property of the Church; and with respect to the honesty of Whigs and Tories, he remembered a portion of Scripture wherein Christ was mentioned as being crucified between two thieves, and when he looked upon his right hand and upon his left, he almost fancied himself as undergoing the dreadful operation of crucifixion. He loudly declaimed against the sham Radicals, as he called a number of Reformers, after which he spoke for about an hour in condemnation of the Poor-law Amendment Act.

Upon a show of hands being taken, there were about 150 hands held up for Mr. Walker, besides those of a number of that gentleman's supporters upon the hustings; for Sergeant Spankie there were three hands held up, in addition to those of his friends upon the hustings; but there was a large forest of hands held up for Mr. Cobbett. Mr. Cobbett having been declared as having the show of hands in his favour, a poll was demanded on behalf of Mr. Walker and Sergeant Spankie, and it announced that the poll would be open the next day.

Mr. Grundy having exhorted the people to good order, the crowd dispersed.

After the nomination, crowds of Mr. Cobbett's friends picqueted the streets during the night, in order to prevent voters from being fetched up by Mr. Walker's canvassers; and if a pink were seen, he were lucky to get into any place of shelter. The " greens," who had been greatly excited by the harangues of Mr. Matthew Fletcher, personally ill-treated such of Mr. Walker's friends as fell into their hands. Their conduct was cowardly and dastardly in the extreme, inasmuch as they did not in any instance make any attack but when they had a very powerful number in their favour. Several gentlemen who were going quietly through the streets were attacked and beaten very severely.

Mr. Walker's canvassers were very active, early on Wednesday morning, in getting their voters to the polling booths, so that when the returning officer and his deputies opened their courts electors in abundance were ready to be polled. The voting began at eight o'clock, and at nine the result was placed beyond a doubt, and from ten o'clock until four o'clock scarcely a vote was given. The numbers at the close of the poll were:—

Walker 251
Cobbett..................................... 96
Spankie..................................... 87

About noon, when it was beyond doubt that Mr. Walker would be at the head of the poll with a large majority, the mob, which had come prepared with shillelaghs and clubs of a very formidable description, became exceedingly violent. They forced open two of the doors of the houses where polling booths were erected, and committed the most abominable acts of depredation and destruction. They broke open the King's Arms Inn, and got to the bar which they completely gutted. The Riot Act was read, and the military sent for. The soldiers arrived just in time to prevent the sacking of Mr. Walker's house, the mob being on their way to that place when their progress was arrested by the military. It is due to Mr. Cobbett to state that he exerted himself to the utmost in attempting to quiet the disturbance, and it was owing to his influence that more damage was not done. Many of Mr. Walker's voters had their windows broken. The damage done amounted to about £150.

On Thursday morning the returning officer declared the numbers at the close of the poll. Neither Mr. Walker nor Mr. Sergeant Spankie were present. Mr. Cobbett addressed the electors. He left the town on Thursday night, first telling his friends that he would never come to Bury again without previously ascertaining who invited him—that he would never again come at the invitation of those who had invited him upon that occasion, and that he was convinced that any opposition to Mr. Walker would be useless.

THE ELECTION OF 1841.

The candidates at this election were Mr. Richard Walker, Liberal, and Mr. Henry Hardman, Conservative. The nomination took place on Wednesday, the 20th June. There was not the slightest attempt made at disturbance by the supporters of either party, and the proceedings of the day were conducted in the most peaceable manner.

Mr. Richard Ashton, of Longfield, proposed Mr. Richard Walker as a fit and proper person to represent the borough. He said that the principles which Mr. Walker had always maintained entitled him to their warmest support, and he could not help from remarking that the election of the Conservative candidate (Mr. Hardman) would bring discredit upon the borough, which had been enfranchised by the party whom that gentleman opposed, and whose friends would have withheld from the electors of Bury the political privileges they were enjoying. The speaker then complained that Mr. Hardman had not furnished the constituency with a fair indication of his political opinions ; he had left the electors entirely in the dark ; and, if returned to the House of Commons, would have to consult Sir Robert Peel before he avowed any decided course. Although he respected the private character of Mr. Hardman, and although he was born in the same place which gave birth to that eminent statesman, Sir Robert Peel, he trusted that the town of Bury would not send a member to support a Government which that honourable baronet might form, but that they would again return their tried representative, Mr. Walker.

Mr. Richard Hamer, of Bury, seconded the nomination, and expressed a conviction that the interests of the borough, as well as the welfare of the country, would be best secured by the measures which Her Majesty's Government had submitted to Parliament.

Mr. James Openshaw, of Fern Grove, then nominated Mr. Henry Hardman to represent the borough in Parliament. He said it was a duty incumbent on the electors of Bury to send to Parliament such a member as would protect the institutions of the country, and oppose to the utmost the inroads which the existing administration were making upon it. He felt every confidence in stating that the result of the canvass left no doubt as to the return of Mr. Hardman.

Mr. James Hutchinson seconded the nomination.

Mr. Walker, the late member, in coming forward to address the electors was loudly applauded. The hon. gentleman commenced by expressing his gratification that the contest was being conducted in good humour and good spirit on both sides. It was not a personal conflict between himself and Mr. Hardman, with whom he was on most intimate terms; it was a contest between principles, and it was for the electors to determine to whom they would give the preference. His opinions on all the great national questions then agitating the country were so well known that he need not repeat them on that occasion. He considered that he would best serve the interests of his constituents when he gave his earnest support to the Government then in power, as being the most liberal administration that had ever ruled the country. He believed that the ebbing and flowing of trade would be best avoided by the introduction in the system of Government of those free-trade principles which would allow the exchange of commodities between foreign countries to be regular and constant. After referring to various measures, he said that if they did him the honour, for the fourth time, to send him to Parliament, he would serve them faithfully, and do all in his power to alleviate their distresses, to find employment for them, and to remove from their abodes wretchedness, discontent, and want.

Mr. Henry Hardman was then heard throughout a lengthy address with great patience. He alluded to the Corn Laws, to the Police Force, and the Poor Laws.

A show of hands was taken, and it was declared in favour of Mr. Hardman. A poll was demanded on behalf of Mr. Walker. A vote of thanks having been given to the returning officer, the candidates, with their friends, retired to their committee rooms, where they addressed the electors. The poll, which took place on Thursday morning, resulted in the return of Mr. Walker, the returns being:—

For Mr. Walker	325
For Mr. Hardman	228
Majority for Mr. Walker	97

THE ELECTION OF 1847.

This election passed off in Bury without a contest, Mr. Richard Walker, the previous representative, being returned without any opposition. The nomination took place in Union-square, on Friday, the 30th of July. The proceedings commenced at ten o'clock by Mr. James Hutchinson, the returning officer, reading the precept and the other legal official documents. At the conclusion of this formal business, Mr. Richard Ashton nominated Mr. Richard Walker as a fit and proper person again to represent the borough. He remarked that they all knew Mr. Walker. For the previous fifteen years he had been their representative, and in five successive parliaments had he faithfully and honourably discharged the trust reposed in him. They might accept the proof of the past as a guarantee and pledge of what the future would be ; and it was a pleasing and gratifying evidence of the satisfaction which Mr. Walker's past conduct had given to the electors generally that no competitor appeared to contest the borough with him, but that he was allowed to walk over the course quietly. (Laughter.) Whether the absence of opposition might be partly attributable to the triumph of free-trade principles or no he could not say, but he believed it was far more owing to the estimable character and private worth of their late representative.—Mr. Abraham Wood seconded the nomination.—The returning officer having inquired if any other candidate was to be proposed, and received no reply, he declared Mr. Walker duly elected. Mr. Walker then presented himself, and said : Brother electors and fellow-townsmen,—The honour which you have conferred upon me by electing me as your representative in the next ensuing Parliament, is the greatest you could possibly confer upon any citizen ; and feeling it to be such, I will endeavour always to discharge my duties in such a way as to reflect no discredit upon your choice, whilst it may gain some honour for myself. For the last fifteen years your interests have been confided to my keeping, and I have endeavoured during that period to discharge my duties towards you honourably and truly, without preference to any class and any interests, but solely for the public weal and for the comfort and happiness of all Her Majesty's subjects. I shall continue to be actuated by the same motives, having no other object in view but to promote the prosperity of this great country. When I first appeared before the electors of Bury it was after the Reform Bill had opened up the representation of the empire. I then came forward as the advocate of liberal opinions, and the experience which I have since obtained has served but to confirm me in those opinions, and to convince me that they were, and are, the right ones to profess and advance. Many laws have since been passed which squared with those opinions, and it is satisfactory to reflect that I was at least one of the pioneers which made the way for the great changes which have taken place. But of all these changes, the greatest and most important and the most satisfactory was that which was carried out through the late Parliament. After its long and arduous struggle free-trade has at length gained its greatest victory. We have now the privilege of dealing with all the nations of the world. We can receive the food which they have in abundance, and we can give them in return the manufactures of this country. The consequence will be increased employment and the opportunity of receiving satisfactory remuneration for labour, for I believe we shall find the best stimulus given to trade and manufactures by that great measure. Immortal credit is due to Sir Robert Peel for having carried that measure through Parliament, for having contributed so largely to the comfort and happiness of every labouring man in the community. During the fifteen years that I have served you in Parliament I have always advocated the principles of civil and religious liberty, thinking, as I do, that perfect civil and religious liberty is the right of every Englishman. Thanks to the triumph of those principles. We may now, whatever be our principles, whatever be our opinions, meet as friends, as neighbours, and as Christians ought to meet. One question which occupied the attention of Parliament during the past session is, I regret to say, exciting considerable difference of opinion amongst Englishmen. Upon that subject, gentlemen, I will say nothing at present but this, that I wish to see all classes of Christians treated alike, and that I hope and trust to see such measures introduced in the next session of Parliament as will prove satisfactory to every class of Her Majesty's subjects. I have long been a friend of education; the State punishes crime; it goes to vast expense in providing means of punishment; I therefore think it is the duty of the State to teach the people, to instruct them in the duties which they owe to God and man; and as the State has the power and the means to punish, I hope it will use the means and the power at its command to enlighten and instruct, so that crime may be prevented, and the business, as well as the expenses, of our criminal courts reduced; for the more people are instructed the more honest citizens will they become. As to political parties, or their present condition, I can say little, because party feeling, I rejoice to think, is nearly extinct. There is now very little difference between the sentiments of the leaders of the parties as to the principles upon which this country should be governed. Sir Robert Peel and Lord John Russell seem to me to be working together for the benefit and the general good of the people of England. Lord John Russell, who is now at the head of the Government, came into power when he was in a large minority in the House of Commons, and he could not have remained in office one single month if Sir Robert Peel had not supported him. How the present elections may terminate I am sure I know not, but I think the result will be a majority in favour of the present administration. Gentlemen, I cannot conclude without sympathising with you upon the great privations which our people have been subjected to in consequence of the failure of the crops, not only in this country but throughout all Europe, and of the failure not only of the corn but of the cotton crops to a great extent, by which the amount of employment has been greatly

N

reduced, for in these districts a famine in cotton would be almost as disastrous, and nearly as fatal, as a famine in corn. I hope and trust that the calamity is now passed away. We have a prospect, with God's blessing, of an abundant harvest and cheap bread, and with that we may expect increased trade and extensive employment, for we always find cheap food and good trade go together. Once again, gentlemen, I thank you for the honour you have done me in electing me your representative. It may probably be the last time I shall appear before you. (Cries of " No, no," " God forbid," and " We hope not.") I shall, however, whilst able, discharge my trust towards rich and poor with such fidelity as to be enabled, when the time arrives at which that trust shall be ended, to say that I have done my duty.—Votes of thanks were then accorded to the returning officer, and the proceedings terminated.

CHAPTER XI.

The General Elections of 1852, 1857, 1859, 1865, and 1868—The Census Returns of Bury and District since 1801—Population of the Borough—Population of the Townships—District of Local Boards—Ecclesiastical Districts.

THE ELECTION OF 1852.

There were two candidates for the honour of representing Bury at this election, namely, the Right Hon. F. Peel (L.-C.), and Viscount Duncan (L.). For some time before the election both the candidates were busy addressing meetings in various parts of the town, and there was every appearance of the contest being a severe one. The nomination took place in Union-square, on the 8th of July, before Mr. William Openshaw, as returning officer. The following gentlemen, amongst others, were upon the hustings:—Captain Peel; Messrs. John Robinson Kay, James Harrison, John Walker, William Hutchinson, Richard Hacking, Richard Walker, jun., Thomas Openshaw, Henry Hardman, George Wike, Joshua Knowles, John Grundy, Thomas Wrigley, T. L. Openshaw, James Wrigley, Mark Philips, R. N. Philips, Edmund Grundy, &c. There were 170 police officers brought into the town in addition to the usual force connected with the division. In the Square and in the principal streets there was a profuse display of pink scarfs, and flags bearing the inscription, "Lord Duncan for the people," and many of his lordship's friends sported pink rosettes. On the other side there was no show of flags or favours of any kind, at least, it there was, it was of little or no consequence. At the time appointed for the commencement of the proceedings some three or four thousand persons had assembled in the Square, and that number was subsequently very nearly doubled. On the arrival of the candidates the precept was read over, and the other formalities gone through by the returning officer.— Mr. John Grundy, of Outwood Lodge, proposed Viscount Duncan to represent the borough in Parliament. After referring to the conduct and character of Lord Duncan, he called upon the electors not to allow the borough to be handed over, bound hand and foot, to the care of a young gentleman whose opinions were so little known that when he first made his appearance amongst them his own chairman declared that he did not know what Mr. Peel's opinions were.—Mr. Jonathan Openshaw, of Bank House, seconded the nomination. He said he was quite sure that a great many of the supporters of Mr. Peel would be very glad to see Lord Duncan elected.—Mr. Richard Ashton proposed Mr. Peel. He expressed his conviction that Mr. Peel had the strongest claims on the support of the electors of Bury. Lord Duncan's address, he said, was out the first, but Mr. Peel had a requisition sent to him, signed by 418 voters, before Lord Duncan's address was issued.— Mr. Ormerod Walker seconded the nomination.—There being no other candidate to propose, Viscount Duncan rose to address the meeting. He said that his honourable opponent had described him as a bad Bath bun. He regretted that he should have made use of such an expression, but if he were to banter personal observations with him he felt that he should only be wasting his time and those of his hearers; and that if his hon. opponent waited until the next day, he would probably find that instead of being a bad Bath bun he was a Bury simnel. The noble lord then referred to several measures, and at the close of his remarks the Hon. F. Peel addressed the assembly in a lengthy manner.—The Rev. W. R. Thorburn also addressed the meeting; and on a show of hands being taken there was at least three or four to one in favour of Lord Duncan. A poll was demanded on behalf of Mr. Peel, and the proceedings terminated with a vote of thanks to the returning officer.— The polling took place the next day, the following being the result of the poll at the close:—

Right Hon. F. Peel 472
Viscount Duncan 410
                                                    ———
              Majority for Mr. Peel......... 62

When the poll had closed Mr. Peel, with Mr. Ashton (his chairman), endeavoured to address the people in front of the Derby Hotel and took his place on a carriage for that purpose. The people were unwilling to listen to his address, and he subsequently spoke from one of the windows of the hotel. The police had to interfere to preserve order. He briefly thanked the crowd for the honour they had conferred upon him. A meeting of the friends of Lord Duncan took place in the Albion Assembly Room. He said that though he was a beaten candidate he was not an unpopular one. He came to Bury to fight a battle for the independence of the borough, and he had fought it as well as he could. He thanked his friends for the support they had given him, and although they had been overborne by the power which had been brought against them, yet he should be glad if those two great measures for which he had contended, —namely, the Ballot and the extension of the suffrage—should pass. If they could not find a more wealthy candidate to come before them again, he would rather experience a defeat in Bury than obtain a victory in some other places. He believed that he had polled a larger number of votes than had ever been polled during any previous contest. Mr. John Grundy (Outwood Lodge), Mr. John Grundy (Summerseat), Mr. R. N. Philips, and other gentlemen afterwards spoke.

THE ELECTION OF 1857.

At this election, which was caused through a difficulty with the Chinese, the candidates were the Right Hon. F. Peel, a Liberal Conservative, and Mr. R. N. Philips, the late high sheriff of the county, Liberal. Mr. R. Ashton was chairman of Mr. Peel's committee, and Mr. T. Wrigley the chairman of Mr. Philips' committee. The nomination took place in Union-square, on the 27th March. Mr. Ashton proposed Mr. Peel, and he was seconded by Mr. O. O. Walker. Mr. T. Wrigley proposed, and Mr. Jonathan Openshaw seconded the nomination of Mr. Philips. The show of hands was declared in favour of Mr. Philips. At the polling the next day, Mr. Peel took the lead in the forenoon, but in the afternoon Mr. Philips headed his opponent, and at the close of the poll was 35 votes in advance. Mr Philips afterwards addressed the electors at the hustings, as did also Mr. Grundy, of Summerseat, and Mr. T. Wrigley. The official declaration of the poll was made on the following Monday by Mr. Hutchinson, the returning officer. For the purposes of the election the town was divided into five districts, and the following figures will show the number of votes recorded for each candidate in the respective districts :—

	Peel.	Philips.
No. 1.—St. Paul's School, Bell-lane	87	... 97
,, 2.—National School, Stanley-streeet..............	97	... 155
,, 3.—Trinity School, Mosses	98	... 148
,, 4.—Irwell School, Bolton-street	129	... 110
,, 5.—Elton School, Croston Brow	119	... 55
	530	565

The return of Mr. Philips at this election was petitioned against, the petitioners alleging that "an organised system of bribery and intimidation was resorted to, which was utterly destructive of the freedom of election." The commission of inquiry, which commenced their sitting on the 3rd of July, 1857, were Mr. Hull (chairman), the Hon. C.

Howard, Mr. Beamish, Mr. W. F. Knatchbull, and Col. T. Herbert. The counsel for the petitioners were Mr. E. James, Q.C.; Mr. Phinn, Q.C.; and Mr. Clark. Mr. Monk and Mr. Tindall Atkinson appeared for the sitting member. After a sitting of six days, the chairman announced that the commission had come to the following resolutions :— " That Robert Needham Philips, Esq., was duly elected a burgess to serve in the present parliament for the borough of Bury. That it has been proved by uniform evidence before the committee, that the late election for the borough of Bury was conducted with unusual sobriety and order ; and although, in the course of it, some practices of an illegal complexion were resorted to on behalf of the sitting member, there is no evidence to induce the company to believe that such practices were authorised by him."

THE ELECTION OF 1859.

Early in April, 1859, it became noised abroad that Lord Derby, being defeated in Parliament, intended to appeal to the country, in order to vindicate the conduct of himself and his government. On the 22nd of that month Parliament was prorogued until the 5th of May, and in the Royal Speech which was delivered by commission, it was stated that the appeal to the people had been rendered necessary by the difficulties experienced in carrying on the public business of the country, as indicated by the fact that within little more than a year, two successive administrations had failed to retain the confidence of the House of Commons.

It would appear, from the eagerness with which the electioneering campaign was entered into in Bury that the embers of the fire of 1857 had scarcely died out. Indeed, on the 4th of April, before Lord Derby had announced in the House of Lords the intention of the Government to dissolve Parliament, a meeting of those persons favourable to the candidature of the Right Honourable F. Peel, for the representation of the borough of Bury, was held at the Derby Hotel. When intelligence was received that a general election was at hand, after some discussion, it was resolved that a requisition should be got up with a view to test the feeling of the electors, and the probabilities of Mr. Peel's success. So largely was the requisition signed, and so warm was the feeling in favour of Mr. Peel, that on Wednesday evening, the 6th of April, Mr. R. E. Ashton was deputed to wait on Mr. Peel and lay the state of parties before him. This was done. Mr. Peel arrived in Bury the following afternoon, and addressed a large assembly of the inhabitants from a platform in front of the Derby Hotel, explaining his views on the reform bill of the Government, and expressing his determination to fight the battle of the representation vigorously and fairly. In the meantime Mr. Philips and his supporters had not been idle. A placard appeared on the walls on Tuesday morning, the 7th inst., in which Mr. Philips offered himself for re-election, and on the same evening he addressed a number of the electors and non-electors in the Albion Assembly Room, when Mr. John Grundy, of the Dales, presided. In the meantime the addresses of the candidates appeared on the walls.

After this a paper warfare was entered into, and meetings of the supporters of each candidate were continued. On the 25th, however, Mr. Philips retired from the contest, the resignation being publicly announced by an address which he issued, of which the following is a copy :—

To the Electors of the Borough of Bury.

Gentlemen,—When I again consented to become a candidate for the representation of the borough of Bury in Parliament, I believed that I was obeying the call of a public duty, and although I expected to be opposed resolutely, I certainly could not have anticipated that any means, however unscrupulous, would be resorted to by my opponents to prevent my re-election.

This morning I find on the walls of the town an anonymous placard, with which my name is being busily associated, and that personal charges are made against me of a character which no man, living or dead, has hitherto ever dared to associate with my name—a circumstance which convinces me that even my private life and domestic happiness are not secure from the attacks and insinuations of my opponents. I will not continue a contest with parties so unscrupulous, and I have, therefore, determined to WITHDRAW MY NAME AS A CANDIDATE for your suffrages.

I rejoice to say that in retiring from this contest I carry with me the sincere good wishes of a large majority of the inhabitants of the town ; and I believe that, if I had remained a candidate for your suffrages, I should have been returned at the head of the poll. I have, however, nothing to gain by occupying a seat in Parliament; and as I now find that, in addition to the sacrifice of time and injury to business which such a position involves, I am to be made the object of attacks in private life, I am determined not to have public honour at such a price.

I return my warmest thanks to those gentlemen who have supported me up to this time, and I withdraw from this contest in the firm belief that the principles of sound reform and good government are safe in their hands.—I remain, gentlemen, your faithful servant,   R. N. PHILIPS.
The Park, April 25th, 1859.

There was considerable surprise at the result of the contest, and it was thought, and indeed announced, that Mr. Peel would walk over. On Wednesday, the 27th of April, Mr. Thomas Barnes, of Farnworth, who had sat in the House of Commons from 1852 to 1857 for Bolton, but who had been rejected in the latter year, and at the present election, arrived in Bury about four o'clock, and addressed a public meeting in Union Square the same evening. Shortly afterwards Mr. Barnes issued an address to the electors, and the contest then commenced between the supporters of Mr. Peel and Mr. Barnes.

The nomination took place on Friday, the 29th, Mr. William Hutchinson being the returning officer. Mr. O. O. Walker, of Chesham, proposed, and Mr. Richard Hacking seconded, the nomination of Mr. Peel. Mr. Thomas Wrigley next proposed Mr. Barnes as a fit and proper person to represent the borough, and the motion was seconded by Mr. Scholes Walker. When the candidates had addressed the crowd, a show of hands was taken, which was declared to be in favour of Mr. Peel. A poll was demanded on behalf of Mr. Barnes, and at eight o'clock the next morning the real work of the contest was begun in earnest. The declaration was made at the hustings at a quarter before five o'clock, as follows :—

> For Mr. Peel 633
> For Mr. Barnes 477
>
> Majority for Mr. Peel......... 156

After the declaration, a riotous scene ensued. Stones and brickbats were hurled in almost all directions, and it was not until Mr. Superintendent Milne and his men had interfered, that anything like order was restored. Mr. Peel, Mr. O. O. Walker, and Mr. Richard Walker, subsequently addressed the electors.

THE ELECTION OF 1865.

On Thursday, July 6, 1865, Parliament was dissolved by Royal Commission, and on the following day the proclamation authorising the election of a burgess to serve in Parliament was read in front of the Derby Hotel, in Union-square, and at Whitehead Bridge, by Mr. W. Openshaw, returning officer, and Mr. W. H. Norris, his clerk. The nomination was fixed to take place on the Tuesday following, and the election on the 12th July.

The candidates who sought the honour of representing the borough in St. Stephen's were Mr. R. N. Philips (L.) and the Hon. F. Peel (L.-C.). The register contained the names of 1,313 electors. Meetings in the open air in various parts of the town were quickly got up, and vigorous addresses were delivered. The hustings for the nomination were erected in Union-square, and the proceedings in connection with this now formal part of a general election were commenced at nine amid heavy rain. It was estimated that about 20,000 persons were present.

The proceedings commenced with the reading of the writ authorising the election, after which William Openshaw, Esq., took the oath required by law, stipulating that he was prepared to conduct the proceedings in a fair and equitable manner, and that he had no bribe from any party. Addressing the crowd, Mr. Openshaw asked for a fair and impartial hearing for every gentleman who might address them, and he trusted that every elector would assist him in maintaining the peace of the borough.

Lieutenant-Colonel Hutchinson then came forward to nominate the Right Hon. F. Peel. He said that when Mr. Peel came before them some thirteen or fourteen years before he was a comparative stranger to them. He was known only as a man of great promise, and bearing the name of Peel—a name which was more worthy of honour than any ever known to Bury, but it was not so as regarded Mr. Peel being unknown to them then. Mr. Peel came before them, known unto them as one having sat as their representative during two Parliaments, and he had earned the right to sit as their representative again. He was known to them as a man of the strictest integrity and honour. He (the speaker) regretted that the town had been placed in the turmoil of a contested election. There was one fact of a very peculiar nature about that election, and that was, that there was only one candidate. Until the previous day they were not aware who the opposing party had for their candidate. (Confusion.) Although they had seen Mr. Philips's name put before them, until Mr. Philips came forward they did not believe he had serious intentions of contesting the borough. At that moment Mr. Philips was not a candidate. (Great confusion.) He supposed that in a few minutes Mr. Grundy would be addressing them on behalf of Mr. Philips, which he had a perfect right to do, but Mr. Grundy doing that would not make Mr. Philips a candidate, but only Mr. Grundy's nominee. (Disapprobation.) The way in which Mr. Philips had been brought out as a candidate had not been respectful to the electors of Bury. (Groans.) Mr. Philips had shown by every means which he could that he did not want to go to Parliament. He might have been returned for Manchester without opposition had he pleased, and if he desired to go to Parliament, why did not he take his seat for Manchester, and not create a turmoil at Bury? Mr. Philips had placed himself in a false position by allowing himself to be nominated by the party who were at that time supporting him. He had allowed himself to be nominated by them simply in order that the party might be kept together. If by any unforeseen mischance Mr. Philips should be returned for the borough, what could they expect him to do? Why, that he would take his seat, and that as soon as he could accept the Chiltern Hundreds, or otherwise place them in the position of an unrepresented borough. The old proverb said that they might take the horse to the water, but they could not make him drink ; and they might send Mr. Philips to Parliament, but they could not make him work. Mr. Hutchinson concluded by moving the Right Hon. F. Peel as a fit and proper person to represent the borough in Parliament. (Cheers and groans.)

Mr. Henry Oram seconded the nomination. The uproar was so great that for some time Mr. Oram was unable to proceed with his remarks. Pointing to Mr. Peel, Mr. Oram said he was there, but where was Mr. Philips ? (Cheers, and counter demonstrations.) Were they prepared to drop the substance in order to secure the shadow ? Why had they all that turmoil ? Was it for principle ? No, it could not be. Mr. Philips was the chairman for Mr. Gladstone for South Lancashire, and wanted to get him returned, and yet he was opposing Mr. Peel, a member of the same department in the government as Mr. Gladstone. Mr. Philips, had he chosen, might have been returned for Manchester without a contest, for Mr. Abel Heywood had repeatedly stated that he would retire in Mr. Philips's favour. He (Mr. Oram) could not interpret Mr. Philips's conduct in the matter as anything but a desire to gratify his personal ambition. (Confusion.) He concluded by calling upon all to support Mr. Peel.

Mr. Thomas Grundy commenced to address the throng by telling them that those who lived in glass-houses ought not to throw stones. Mr. Oram had thought proper to tell them that Mr. Philips was the nominee of the Grundy family, but he forgot to tell them that Mr. Peel was the nominee of the Tories. (Great cheering.) Was it not a remarkable circumstance to see Mr. Hutchinson, a member of a family who had always shown themselves downright Tories, supporting Mr. Peel, a member of Lord Palmerston's government, while only the previous day he was in front of the Derby Hotel supporting the three Conservative candidates for South Lancashire. (Loud cheers.) Mr. Philips was not ashamed of the Grundy family, and of those of Union-street too ; and he (Mr. Grundy) had much pleasure in proposing Robert Needham Philips, Esq., as a fit and proper person to represent the borough of Bury in Parliament. (Immense cheering, followed by groans from the Peelites.) He had not heard all that had been said on the other side of the hustings, but he understood that they had been complaining of the manner in which Mr. Philips had been brought forward. It had been said that he (Mr. Grundy) had been chiefly instrumental in bringing Mr. Philips forward in the contest, and if it were so, he looked upon it as one of the best actions of his life. The state of the canvass, as well as the condition of the register, had fully justified them in the course they had pursued. Why had not he (Mr. Grundy) as much right to bring forward a candidate as Harry Oram ? (Loud laughter and cheers.) The Grundys had done something for Bury, but he (Mr. Grundy) had never heard of the Orams doing so. They did not need Mr. Philips being there, for they were able to return him without him being present, and he had no doubt that his next duty would be to bring Mr. Philips before them to thank them for returning him as a member for Parliament. He proposed R. N. Philips, Esq., as a fit and proper person to represent them in Parliament.

Mr. T. L. Openshaw seconded the nomination of Mr. Philips. He said that if they returned Mr. Philips to Parliament he would go unshackled by any official ties. Mr. Peel's supporters would have them believe that there was no difference between the candidates. To his (Mr. Openshaw's) mind the question of the ballot and of the abolition of church rates were essential points of difference. To both of them Mr. Philips was pledged, but Mr. Peel had voted against them, and would vote against them again. The question of the ballot was one to which the majority of the electors were favourable, and he believed that there was not any constituency which required it more than the borough of Bury. With respect to church rates, he would have all religions to support themselves. He would treat Churchman, Dissenter, and Catholic alike, for, although a Churchman himself, he felt ashamed when he found the Church taxing others who were conscientiously opposed. Mr. Peel had twitted Mr. Philips with supporting Mr. Gladstone's candidature, because he happened to be a member of the same Government; but in that Government Mr. Peel had only held a subordinate position, and so long as he held that office he was obliged to vote as the Government directed him. Mr. Gladstone was brought forward for South Lancashire by the great Liberal party residing therein, but Mr. Peel was brought forward mainly by the Tories of Bury. His proposer and seconder were Tories, and he dared to say that nine-tenths of Mr. Peel's supporters would vote for the Tories in the county election. Mr. Openshaw concluded by asking them to rid themselves from the dominion of the Tories in the borough.

The Right Hon. F. Peel, on presenting himself was received with a storm of mingled cheers and groans, which for some time prevented him from proceding with his address. While it was going on, Mr. Grundy stood forward and appealed to the friends of Mr. Philips that as Mr. Peel was unwell they would be as quiet and cause him as little inconvenience as possible. Mr. Peel said that in consequence of his condition he should ask them to allow him to address them with his hat on. He then proceeded to say that that was the fourth general election at which he had been nominated as a fit and proper person to represent them in Parliament. (Loud cheers and groans.) Each time the opposite party had nominated candidates to oppose him. Who had they been ? They had been respectively Lord Duncan, Mr. Barnes, and Mr. Philips. (Uproar.) With regard to Lord Duncan, after being defeated at Bury he was returned for another constituency, and accepted office in the very Government of which, at that time, he (Mr. Peel) was a member. Then, as regards Mr. Barnes, the Government of which he (Mr. Peel) was a member had received that gentleman's support, and would undoubtedly have received the support of Mr. Philips had he been in the House of Commons. He was far from saying that there was no difference between Mr. Barnes, Mr. Philips, and himself. If Mr. Philips got a majority at the poll, he would but reluctantly take his seat. If Mr. Philips was so indifferent to becoming their member, why did they seek to thrust a greatness upon him,—why did they press him against his will into their service ? They had learned from a placard which had been published that Mr. Philips was not a candidate. (Great uproar.) After stating his views upon various subjects, he asked his friends to continue the splendid efforts which they had been making on his behalf until the following night, when he would again have the honour of knowing that he was their representative in Parliament. (Cheers, groans, and hisses.)

The Returning Officer then took a show of hands, and declared the same to be in favour of Mr. Philips.

Mr. Henry Oram came up to the returning officer, and said that he protested against the decision, because a great many of those who had held up their hands for Mr. Philips were women.

Lieut.-Colonel Hutchinson having demanded a poll on behalf of Mr. Peel, the returning officer announced that the election would take place the next day, commencing at eight o'clock in the morning, and closing at four in the afternoon.

On the motion of Mr. Peel, a vote of thanks was given to the returning officer, after which Mr. William Gregson offered a few remarks to the assembly.

Upon coming down from the hustings Mr. Gregson was seized by several non-electors, and having been elevated shoulder-high, he was carried in triumph through the streets, amid loud cheering, to the door of Mr. Philips's central committee room.

After the above proceedings, a large crowd assembled in front of the Albion Hotel. Mr. T. Wrigley addressed the people from one of the windows, remarking that although he had not been able to take much part in the proceedings of that morning, he had the pleasure of knowing that he employed a large number of those who had attended, and helped to swell the popular vote. It was a matter of great pleasure to him that the popular vote had resulted in a triumphant majority for Mr. Philips, and it showed that if the people of Bury, as a man, were allowed to express their opinions fairly, it would not be a matter of discussion as to who should be a member for the borough. He would not say a word desiring to create ill-blood, but would say that what they wanted as member for Bury, was not one who rode behind the coach, but one who was prepared to go in advance of public opinion. He believed Mr. Philips to be a respectable man, but they did not want a man as their member who was willing to be the cat's-paw of the Government—to be at the beck of whoever might be at the head of the Government. They wanted a man who had courage to stand up for the people, and declare what were their desires. That election would not be won by shouting. It would not be won by crowding the streets, for their policy from the first had been to use every possible means to preserve the peace. He sympathised with those who were not in a position to vote as freely as himself, but, nevertheless, hoped that on the following day they would find Mr. Philips at the head of the poll.

Mr. T. Grundy and Mr. John Grundy next spoke, after which three cheers were given for Mr. Philips, and one for Mr. John Grundy.

The town presented an excited appearance during the whole of the following day. From an early hour in the morning crowds of men patrolled the streets, rows every now and then occurred, and the services of the police were repeatedly brought into requisition. Immediately after the close of the poll, vast numbers of persons began to make their way towards Union-square, it having been announced that the returning officer would make the official declaration at a quarter before five o'clock. By that time both sides of the hustings was crowded, and the space in front was thronged by a concourse as large, if not larger, than that present at the nomination. Exactly at the time announced the returning officer, assisted by his clerk (Mr. Norris, solicitor), began to add up the returns from the different polling booths, the result of which was as follows :—

District. Polling Places.	Philips.		Peel.
No. 1.—St. Paul's School	107	...	102
,, 2.—National School	158	...	110
,, 3.—Trinity School	153	...	117
,, 4.—Irwell School	114	...	152
,, 5.—Elton School	63	...	91
Total	595		572

The returning officer having declared Mr. Philips elected by a majority of 23, Mr. James Park (Mr. Philips and his friends not having arrived) proposed, and Mr. Edwin G. Wrigley seconded, a vote of thanks to Mr. Openshaw, for his impartial conduct as returning officer. Mr. Openshaw acknowledged the compliment. After this a long interval occurred in the proceedings. In the absence of Mr. Philips, Mr. James Park, Mr. Richard Ward, and Mr. Job Rothwell signed the indenture of his election, and the books were closed and sealed, as required by law, by the returning officer. Mr. J. Scholes Walker and Mr. D. Thomas afterwards addressed the crowd, and the Rev. J. Shaw (United Methodist Free Church) was proceeding with some remarks when considerable excitement was created by the announcement of the arrival of Mr. Philips, which was immediately followed by men rushing into the Square by the Union-street entrance. Upon Mr. Philips approaching to the hustings, the most enthusiastic demonstrations were made by the people; hands were clapped, hats, umbrellas, and handkerchiefs were waved, and the most vociferous cheering indulged in. After Mr. Philips had thanked the electors, the crowd were addressed briefly by Mr. Thomas Grundy, Mr. Thomas Wrigley, Mr. Smithells, and Mr. G. L. Ashworth. The proceedings concluded with hearty cheers for Mr. and Mrs. Philips.

THE ELECTION OF 1868.

In the early part of 1866 the Russell Government, pledged to Reform, brought in a bill to extend the franchise, the basis of which gave no very great extension of the franchise. Mr. Gladstone, who introduced the bill, was defeated by the Conservative party and the Adullamites on the question of ratal *versus* rental, and the consequence was the accession of the Conservatives to power whilst in a minority of 70. Mr. Disraeli, in the following year, undertook to introduce a Reform Bill, and did so in the first instance by bringing in a series of resolutions, which were almost as soon withdrawn. Following these was introduced what was afterwards termed "The Ten Minutes' Bill," the principal feature of which was the £6 borough franchise; but this was suddenly withdrawn, and the Government reverted to its "original, policy," and introduced a bill professing to give household suffrage. It met with much opposition, and several alterations were made in it. In the early part of 1868 Mr. Gladstone introduced his resolutions on the Irish Church question in opposition to Mr. Disraeli's proposal of levelling up, and this was made the main question on which the decision of the new electoral body was to be taken.

On the 28th of August, at a meeting held in the Town Hall, the Conservatives adopted Lord Chelsea, the son of the Earl of Cadogan, as their candidate, his lordship having accepted the offer previously made to him. Immediately after this meeting Mr. Philips's address was issued, offering himself for re-election. Lord Chelsea issued his address on the 2nd of September, and on the 7th of the same month delivered his first address in the Drill Hall, where he was adopted as a " fit and proper person to represent the borough." The explanation of his political views may thus be summed up—he was dead against the Ballot ; the Reform Bill was a final measure ; he would not vote for the Permissive Bill ; he was opposed to the disestablishment and disendowment of the Irish Church, but was willing to adopt the recommendation of the commissioners appointed to inquire into the condition of that church ; and he would protect the funds of trades' unions for benevolent purposes. On the following Monday, Mr. Philips addressed a meeting at the Drill Hall, and was there also adopted as a candidate. He expressed himself in favour of Mr. Gladstone's resolutions, of the Ballot, of amending the Reform Bill on several points, and of national economy. After this the candidates addressed the electors almost nightly in various parts of the town and suburbs.

On Monday, the 16th November, the nomination took place in Union Square. The weather was very favourable, and a larger number of persons assembled than on any previous occasion. Mr. Park officiated as returning officer, and Mr. Crossland as his clerk. Mr. T. L. Openshaw proposed, and Mr. J. S. Walker seconded the nomination of Mr. Philips. Lord Chelsea was proposed by Lieutenant-Colonel Hutchinson, and seconded by Mr. H. Oram. Both candidates subsequently addressed the crowd. On a show of hands being taken, the returning officer declared it to be in favour of Mr. Philips, and a poll was demanded for Lord Chelsea by his proposer. About three o'clock the same afternoon a row took place in Paradise-street. Some children were shouting in front of the Conservative committee-room, and a number of men came out of the Britannia Inn to drive the children away. A body of Irishmen organised themselves, and drove the men who had come out of the Britannia Inn into Stanley-street, where they were dispersed by the police. Several heads were broken, and some formidable sticks and other weapons were taken from the combatants. The polling took place on Tuesday, and on Wednesday morning, at the hustings, in front of several thousands of persons, Mr. Park declared the result to be:—

Robert Needham Philips	2830
Lord Chelsea	2264
Majority for Mr. Philips	566

The declaration was then signed by Mr. Park, Mr. John Grundy, Mr, R. Ward, Mr. W. Hodgson, Mr. Joseph Sykes, Mr. Thomas Hyslop. Mr. Robert Hall, Mr. John Heap, and Mr. John Downham.

The following is the result of the polling in the various districts in which the borough was divided:—

No.	District.	Philips.	Chelsea.
1.—Walmersley-road, Limefield, &c.	....	200 ...	240
2.—Freetown, Barnbank, &c.	....	289 ...	140
3.—Bell-lane, Huntley Brook, &c.	....	245 ...	162
4.—Stanley-street, Rock-street, Paradise-street, &c.		267 ...	152
5.—Union-square, Clerke-street to Walker-terrace		211 ...	196
6.—Rochdale-road, Pimhole, &c.	....	225 ...	186
7.—Garden-street, Princess-street, part Mosses ...		247 ...	163
8.—Mosses, other part	....	305 ...	133
9.—Fleet-street, Market-street, Bolton-street, &c..		196 ...	204
10.—Silver-street, Manchester-road, &c.	············	190 ...	177
11.—Bolton-road, Daisyfield, Hinds, &c.	....	172 ...	186
12.—Elton-fold, Cockey Moor-road, &c.	....	105 ...	102
13.—Crostons, Elton-road, Woodhill, &c.	....	178 ...	223

THE CENSUS RETURNS OF BURY AND DISTRICT.

PARISH OF BURY.	1801.	1811.	1821.	1831.	1841.	1851.	1861.	1871.
Township of Bury	7072	8762	10583	15086	2071·)	25484	30399	32607
Elton	2080	2540	2897	4054	·702	6778	8171	9827
Heap	4283	5148	6552	10429	14856	16048	17351	16977
Walmersley-cum-Shuttleworth	2166	2619	3290	3456	4880	4802	5324	5346
Tottington-lower-end	4314	5917	7333	9280	9929	10691	11764	12519
Tottington-higher-end	1246	1556	1728	2572	3446	2958	3726	3595
Cowpe Lench, New-hall-hey, and Hall Carr	676	786	1224	1519	1716	2154	2855	3638
Musbury	463	589	728	1231	1386	1228	997	1130
Total of the Parish of Bury	22300	27917	34335	47627	61625	70143	80587	85647

POPULATION OF THE BOROUGH.

	1861.	1871.
Bury parliamentary borough	37563	41517
Bury Improvement Act		38592

POPULATION OF THE TOWNSHIPS.

	1861.	1871.
Ainsworth township	1803	1854
Ashworth ,,	233	174
Birtle-cum-Bamford	2350	2403
Bury township	30397	32607
Elton ,,	8172	9827
Heap ,,	17353	16770
Hopwood ,,	2281	3655
Pilkington ,,	12303	11943
Pilsworth ,,	343	386
Radcliffe parish	8838	11445
Tottington-lower-end township	11764	12519
Walmersley-cum-Shuttleworth	5298	5346
	101135	108929

DISTRICTS OF LOCAL BOARDS.

	1871.
Heywood Local Board	19564
Radcliffe ,,	11445
Whitefield ,,	9069
Ramsbottom ,,	4205

ECCLESIASTICAL DISTRICTS.

	1871.
Bury Parish Church	7495
St. John's, Bury	5878
St. Paul's, Bury	8716
Holy Trinity, Bury	6327
St. Thomas's, Bury	3565
All Saints', Elton	9431
Christ Church, Walmersley	3175
St. John's, Shuttleworth	2984
Tottington Chapelry (St. Ann's)	5525
Holcombe Chapelry	3089
St. Paul's, Ramsbottom	4205
Ainsworth Chapelry	1854
Ashworth Chapelry	174
Bircle	2614
Birch Chapelry	4143
St. Luke's, Heywood	9270
St. James's, Heywood	7605
Unsworth Chapelry	1512
Ringley Chapelry	1362
All Saints', Stand	4820
St. John's, Stand-lane	3966
Radcliffe Parish Church	5428
St. Thomas's, Radcliffe	6017

CHAPTER XII.

Gentry of Bury and Neighbourhood in 1664—Hat Manufacture—The Monumental Tablets in the Old Parish Church—Elton: Early History—All Saints' Church, Elton—A Prolific Family—St. Stephen's Schools, Elton— Primitive Methodism in Elton—The Brandlesholme Bull—Ancient Disputes as to Tenants' Rights— Tottington: Early History—St. John's Free Church, Tottington—The Wesleyans of Tottington—Ramsbottom: Early History—Manufactures, &c.—The Grant Family—Chatterton Fight—Henry Pendlebury—Joseph Porritt, Esq.—St. Andrew's Church—St. Andrew's Presbyterian Church: outline of its History— Nuttall Hall—The Grant's Arms.

GENTRY OF BURY AND NEIGHBOURHOOD IN 1664.

In the " Chetham Miscellanies," vol. 1, is published " A Fragment illustrative of Sir William Dugdale's Visitation of Lancashire" in 1664, by virtue of a commission given under the great seal of England on the " second day of February in ye seventeenth year of ye raigne of our Most Gracious Sovereign, Lord Charles ye Second, by ye grace of God, of England, ffrance, and Ireland Kinge, Defender of ye Faith," &c. The document authorises divers persons residing within the hundred of Salford to make their respective appearances before Sir William Dugdale at the sign of the King's Head, in Salford, for the purpose of registering their descent, and justifying their titles of esquires and gentlemen, as well as their right to such coats of arms and crests as they usually showed forth and bore. Amongst the names of the " gentlemen and esquires" from this district appear the following :—

Birkle .... { Thomas Holt, of Grislehurst, Esq.
                    { Mr. Richard Smethurst.

Heywood.........Robert Heywood, Esq.

Heap .... { Mr. Roger Holt.
                { Mr. William Langley.

Prestwich...... { Mr. James Willson.
                { Thomas Holland, Esq.
                { Mr. Kenion.

Radcliffe.........Edward Radcliffe.

*Roddmall ......Captain John Allen.

Tottington ... { Mr. Booth, of Booth.
                   { Mr. Thomas Nuttall.

---

* Or Roddinell. The place here intended is Redvales, near Bury.

HAT MANUFACTURE.

As the manufacture of hats is carried on to some extent in Bury and the neighbourhood, the following extracts from the " Chetham Miscellanies," vol. II., may not be uninteresting to the trade and the public generally :—" About the year 1780 round hats first became fashionable, and some ten years later cocked hats disappeared from common use. Up to this period the chief manufacture was coarse stuff hats, composed of a mixture of common wool and fur, the nap being laid on at the plank; afterwards an improvement was introduced under the name of cordy hats. These consisted of an English wool body with a covering of cod wool or camel's hair worked on, and, before ruffing was discovered, carded up with a small card. In 1805 plated hats began to supersede cordy hats. These were formed from a felt body, into which were worked hairs, seal, coney, or beaver's wool, or other furs, and then carded out as before. About this time the price of pate-wool fur (fur from the head of the rabbit) was 15s. per pound. During the time that stuff hats were in vogue, beaver ranged from 120s. to 200s. per pound. Silver beaver, or ' silver ewens,' for drab hats was even as high as 210s. per pound. The weight of a stuff hat, when finished, fifty years ago was ten ounces ; in 1842 they were made to weigh only four ounces and a-half. At the former period an English wool body weighed six ounces and three-quarters to seven ounces, now they vary from three to three and a-half ounces. After the wool had been washed and carded, the body maker commenced operations, and for bowing, basining, boiling, and planking, he received, in 1805, 8s. per dozen. A new method of raising the nap by the process called ruffing was discovered about the year 1800, and five years subsequent to this discovery the workman was paid 16s. per dozen, and could complete two dozen per week under the old system of gluing after ruffing, and three dozen per week, when, previous to ruffing, the hats were rendered waterproof by chemical agency. Waterproofing came up about 1805 ; it was accounted a grand discovery, although it did not arrive at perfection until fifteen years afterwards ; each manufacturer had his own peculiar proof. The next operation, that of dyeing, was always under the control of the master. In 1841, body makers could earn from 25s. to 30s. per week ; ruffers about the same ; and finishers from 30s. to £3. Formerly females, chiefly the daughters of those who had large families, were employed, some at body making, others at ruffing, and it was not at all unusual to see two or three sisters hatting together. In these prosperous times the rent of a cottage, to which usually a small garden as well as a hat shop was attached, was about £9 per annum in Denton.   In 1805 large quantities of drab bonnets for females began to be manufactured from the finest wool, in order to render them light of wear.   At this period the price for ruffing them varied, according to size, from 7s. to 12s. per dozen—the operative could then earn 30s. weekly at this employment. The bonnet branch was very brisk, especially in the winter season, from 1818 to 1840, at which period no less than one hundred dozen were manufactured each week by Messrs. Peacock alone.   The felt hat trade reached its greatest prosperity about the year 1840, when not less than two thousand dozen were manufactured weekly in Denton and Haughton. Many of the London houses had their establishments in these hamlets, some of them receiving the bodies from Denton, and dyeing and finishing them in the Metropolis.   But as customers would not purchase any other than a 'London hat,' or at least one sold under that designation, so each Denton firm, in order to accommodate itself to the popular prejudice, had its fictitious London names for insertion on the crown lining, just as silk hats now claim Parisian origin.   One old Denton firm inscribed their manufacture ' Stephen and Co., Regent-street,' and latterly ' Willis and Co., Bond-street,' names which, it is needless to say, represented but imaginary firms.   About this time the silk hat was brought prominently into notice, but its introduction at first excited no alarm amongst the felt hat makers, who, in blind security, could not foresee the revolution in public taste about to happen, but treated the discovery with contempt. Silently, however, it advanced in the favour of the people ; and, as if to add to the discomfiture of the artisans of the old school, dissensions multiplied between the employers and their servants, in which the latter, elated by a long season of prosperity, miscalculated their power, and entered into combinations which hastened their ruin.   It was in 1841 that, in order to resist alleged abatements made by an *Oldham* house, lots were taken, and the result was a strike against a *Manchester* firm, then actually paying the highest rates in the trade.   This turnout commenced in Oldham January 23, 1841, with the finishers, who were afterwards joined by the body makers and the ruffers ; but about the middle of May following they were obliged to resume work on the previous conditions. Before this time silk hats had competed with stuff ones to little purpose, but the masters, as a body, determined to resist the strike by every possible means ; orders unexecuted by the one class of workmen were transferred to the other, and even some of the masters now commenced in the silk line.   It was afterwards admitted by all parties that this strike had caused silk hats to become general at least ten years sooner than they would otherwise have done.''

Presbyterian Church, Bury, Lancashire.

THE MONUMENTAL TABLETS IN THE OLD PARISH CHURCH.

At the time the old parish church was pulled down, a little over two years ago, the monumental tablets, erected in various parts of the sacred edifice, were carefully taken down, and removed in safe custody to another part of the town. There is no doubt but that all of them will be put up again when the church, now in course of erection, is ready to receive them. The following inscriptions are upon the tablets, some of which are very large, chiefly of white marble, and elaborately worked :—

Sacred
to the Memory of Matilda,
youngest daughter of RICHARD KAY, Esquire,
of Limefield, in this parish ; and the
beloved wife of Major-General
Sir THOMAS HARTE FRANKS, K.C.B.,
Born July 13, 1809,
Died November 19, 1857.

Having followed her husband's fortunes through his military career in India, from 1842 to 1856, this heroic woman, conscious of approaching death, nevertheless urged him to obey the summons of duty, and leave her in England for the war against the revolted army of Hindostan, cheered him to the last by her letters, but was not spared to welcome his return.

In grateful remembrance of her noble and tender constancy, this record is inscribed by her bereaved husband :

Beneath this Tablet
Are deposited the remains of
ROBERT NUTTALL, ESQUIRE,
of this town,
Who Died 2nd February, 1776,
æt. 47 years ;
and of MARY, his Wife,
Niece of the Rev. ROGER KAY,
Founder of the Grammar School here,
and Prebend of Sarum.
She died at Woodhill, 6th July, 1802,
aged 72 years ;
Also JOHN NUTTALL, ESQUIRE,
their son,
Who died at Overleigh Hall,
in the county of Chester,
27th December, 1813,
æt. 44 years ;
AND ELIZABETH, HIS WIFE,
daughter of Jonathan Haworth, Esq.,
of Horcroft, in this county,
who died 7th of April, 1799,
æt. 25 years.

In memory of
RICHARD CALROW, ESQUIRE,
who died May 28th, 1850,
aged 35 years.
This tablet is erected by his workpeople as a mark of grateful attachment to an
honourable, generous, and considerate master.
" The memory of the just is blessed."

In memory of
JOHN SHEARSON,
Born 24th January, 1832,
Died 18th May, 1838;
and also of
EDWARD SHEARSON,
Born 20th July, 1835,
Died 21st November, 1851.

To the memory of
their most Affectionate Father,
WILLIAM BAMFORD, OF BAMFORD, ESQUIRE,
this monument was erected
by his much afflicted daughters,
ANN AND MARGARET,
in Testimony
of their pious regard and tender affection
to the man;
his sweetness of manners and goodness of heart
endear'd him to all that knew him;
he was a kind husband,
an indulgent parent,
an easy master,
a cheerful companion,
a sincere and generous friend
to all.
He was a good man;
herein exercising himself
to have always a conscience void of offence
toward God and toward man.
After a bad state of health,
of many years continuance,
which he bore
with all the patience and resignation of a Christian,
he departed this life.

Sacred to the memory of
LIEUTENANTS ROBERT AND GEORGE HOOD, R.N.,
sons of the Rev. Richard Hood, LL.D., of this town,
the former of whom, while engaged in the
Overland Arctic Expedition,
under the command of Captain Franklin, R.N.,
after having with unshaken fortitude endured
unparalleled dangers and privations,
and by his skill in science,
essentially contributed to the utility of the enterprise,
was assassinated by an Iroquois, October 20th, 1821,

and thus terminated, at the early age of four-and-twenty,
a short but brilliant career,
distinguished by varied talent and steady determination,
which were rapidly opening the path to the
highest honours of his profession.

The latter, under Captain Owen, R.N.,
employed also in the cause of science
on the eastern coast of Africa,
perished by a fever, February 26th, 1823, being also
24 years of age.
If his services were less distinguished,
or his fate attracted less of public sympathy
than that of his lamented brother,
he required a more prominent station
for the display of his uncommon talents
and acquirements.
As a tribute of sincere respect
for the merits of their fellow-townsmen,
this monument was erected
by some of the inhabitants of Bury.

Here rest in Christ
the mortal remains of
THE REV. GEOFFREY HORNBY, LL.B.,
Rector of this Parish,
during 31 years an affectionate pastor
of an attached flock;
he was the third son of
the Rev. Geoffrey Hornby,
Rector of Winwick,
and to the Honble. LUCY, his wife,
thinking most humbly of himself and charitable
to his friends,
he exemplified in his life
" the wisdom that is from above," which " is first pure, then peaceable, gentle, and
easy to be entreated, full of mercy and good fruits."
On the 4th of March, A.D. 1850,
in the 70th year of his age,
after a painful illness, borne with
Christian constancy,
he gladly fell asleep in Christ.
This tablet is erected to his memory
by his sorrowing wife.

Sacred to the memory of
THE HONBLE. GEORGIANA HORNBY,
the loved and beloved wife of
THE REV. GEOFFREY HORNBY,
Rector of this Parish,
whom she survived six years.
She died at Leamington,
July 23rd, 1856,
Aged 68.
This tablet is erected by her sorrowing
children.
" Blessed are the dead who die in the Lord, even so saith the Spirit, for they rest
from their labours."

To the memory of
STANLEY BYNG HORNBY,
Lieutenant in the Royal Artillery,
second son of
the Rev. Geoffrey and Georgiana Hornby.
He was born November 15, 1814,
and died, Bahamas,
November 21, 1843.

To the memory of
FREDERICK JOHN HORNBY, LIEUT. R.N.,
fourth son of
the Rev. Geoffrey and Georgiana Hornby.
He was born July 1, 1819,
and sailed in May, 1843, in H.M.S. Terror,
with the Arctic expedition,
under Rear-Admiral Sir John Franklin,
Never, alas! to return.
" Not our will, but Thine, oh God, be done."

ELTON.

The township of Elton, which is in the parish of Bury, extends in a south-easterly line in the town. It is a populous township, and constitutes part of the borough. The manufacture of cotton is carried on here to a considerable extent, as well as bleaching, dyeing, ironfounding, paper-making, &c. Brandlesholme Hall, the ancient seat of the Greenhalghes, is in this township. The older portions are of the time of Henry VII. It was built of the usual ornamental style of stone, brick, and wood. By marriage with Alice, daughter and heiress of Henry de Brandlesome, to Henry, son and heir of John Greenhalghe, in the time of Richard II., the Brandlesholme estates passed into the Greenhalghe family. The last heir male of the family was Henry Greenhalgh, Esq., who died about the middle of the last century. In Elton the Bury Co-operative Provision Society have large branch stores, situated in the main thoroughfare, which have a rather imposing external appearance. For some time back the building of cottages has gone on somewhat rapidly in this portion of the town, the erection of several large mills and workshops in the locality having no doubt contributed to the influx of the population.

Elton Church, Bury, Lancashire.

ALL SAINTS' CHURCH, ELTON.

By a Deed Poll, dated June 1st, 1843, the Right Hon. Edward, Earl of Derby, conveyed to the Rev. Geoffrey Hornby, Rector of Bury, upon trust for ecclesiastical purposes, a portion of a field in the township of Elton, called "Goose Hill Bank," and also the building then standing on a part of the land so conveyed, this building being, in fact, the present church erected before the conveyance of the site. Its erection had been in progress for about two years before this date. It is built in the Norman style of architecture, and the interior is beautifully decorated. The ceiling is of a cream colour, formed into quatrefoils of excellent design. The whole is treated in dark grey, relieved with red, which forms a tasteful contrast to the dark beams by which the ceiling is divided. The intersecting bay across the nave to the transept is ornamented with a broad border, in brighter colours than the rest of the ceiling. From the angles of this bay there are diagonal beams, at the intersection of which there is a ventilator, ornamented with an appropriate design, and relieved with bright red. The frieze is a trefoil leaf, in rich brown, upon a light grey ground. An excellent effect is produced round the double windows by the introduction of a broad margin in light stone colour, outlined with vermilion and black lines, and bearing an ornament in dark colour. Over the windows is a semi-circular ribbon-scroll, bearing Scriptural texts in purple letter, underneath which is a spandril, with bright yellow ground and purple ornament. The ornamentation (which varies slightly in the transept windows) is well conceived, very chaste, and sparkling in design and colour. The dado is painted a warm chocolate colour, with circular ornament in green, outlined with black. The centres of the ornament are alternately a cross, and the monograms I.H.S. and I.H.C. The dado is topped by a border, with dog-tooth ornament (in black, on a light ground), underneath which is a rich blue band, outlined with black. The cost of the church, about £2,500, was defrayed entirely by subscriptions, at the head of which was a gift from Lord Derby of 500 guineas, in addition to the value of the site. The architect furnishing the plans was Mr. J. Harper, of York, who died before the building was completed. The masonry was executed by Mr. Hopkinson, of Bury, and Mr. Birtwistle executed the rest of the work. The church was first used for Divine service on Sunday, April 30, 1843. The consecration by the Bishop of Chester, Dr. Sumner, who was afterwards Archbishop of Canterbury, took place on St. Peter's Day, June 29, in the same year. At that time the present diocese of Manchester had not been formed, and Bury was in the diocese of Chester. On the occasion of this visit to the town the Bishop of Chester consecrated two churches on one day—All Saints', Elton, and St. George's, Unsworth. The burial ground attached to All Saints' Church was also consecrated, the Bishop and clergy walking through it.

An order of Her Majesty in Council, dated December 13th, 1843, assigned Chapelry districts to the Chapels of Saint Anne, Tottington, and of All Saints', Elton. Up to this time Elton had not been a separate ecclesiastical district, but was a part of the parish of Bury. The district now formed includes all that portion of the township of Elton, which lies west of the River Irwell.

1847. National Schools in connection with Elton Church were built on land adjoining the graveyard, the site being given by Lord Derby. The schools for boys and girls were commenced on September 4th, 1847; that for infants on January 7th, 1861.

1849. The church was beautified at a cost of £40, raised by subscription.

1853. In March of this year stained glass was placed in the chancel window by the Rev. T. Potter, as a memorial of his wife.

1856. The bell originally placed in the tower was replaced by one from Stand Church at a cost of £55, raised by subscription.

1858. The Rev. T. Potter, the first incumbent, died on September 12th. The Rev. Edward Westerman, M.A., of Queen's College, Cambridge, was appointed his successor by the Rector of Bury, duly licensed by the Bishop of Manchester on October 5th, and instituted on November 28th.

1859. In February of this year a stone wall was built, and gate pillars and iron gates placed at the entrance to the churchyard. August 20th, the first confirmation held in All Saints' Church, the number of candidates being 127.

1861. In the spring of this year alterations were made in the church. It was re-seated with uniform pews, stalls were provided for the choir, the organ was removed from the west gallery (which was re-arranged for Sunday scholars,) into the south transept; the entrances at the two transepts were built up, and a porch and vestibule made at the west end; gas pipes were laid, and a new font provided. The whole cost was £536. The church was re-opened on May 12th.

1862. A memorial window of stained glass placed in the north transept by the Hutchinsons, of Radcliffe. On Advent Sunday, November 30, the Sunday evening service was commenced.

1864. August 29th : Possession was taken of a new parsonage-house, built on a site given by Lord Derby, and adjoining the Tottington-road.

The cost of it was upwards of £1,500. In December a stained glass window was placed on the north side of the church, in memory of Mr. and Mrs. Oram, of Bury.

1865. September : A stained glass window placed on the south side, in memory of Mrs. Geldard.

1868. Alterations were made at the east end of the church. A reredos was placed against the east walls ; the floor and a portion of the walls of the chancel were tiled ; a credence table was put up ; a "constructive choir" was formed by a stone parclose ; a stone pulpit was erected ; a new prayer-desk and seats for singing men and boys were provided. The cost of the whole work was £300.

1869. The south vestry was pulled down and replaced by a larger one, at a cost of £123. The walls and ceiling were cleaned and decorated, at a cost of over £200.

1870. January 2nd : The weekly offertory and celebration of the Holy Communion was begun. February 18th : A legacy of £600 was received, under the will of Mr. T. Openshaw, the interest of which was to be applied for the benefit of deserving poor people in the parish of Elton.

A PROLIFIC FAMILY.

A local celebrity, named Betty Hardman, aged 82, died at Hinds, Elton, on the 4th February, 1858, leaving only a brother surviving out of a family of twenty children. She was the mother of thirteen children ; she lived in the same neighbourhood 62 years, and never had a funeral out of her house with the exception of her husband, James Hardman, bleacher. Her husband came to that neighbourhood 82 years before her death, with his father, Richard Hardman, from Radcliffe, to Barlow's, to bleach for Messrs. Peel and Yates. Betty Hardman's mother and three children had 84 children amongst them, two had 22 each, and two 20 each.

ST. STEPHEN'S SCHOOLS.

On Thursday, the 28th July, 1870, new schools were opened in connection with St. Stephen's, with a special religious service conducted by the Rev. E. Westerman, and afterwards a tea party. They are situate in Belbeck-street, which connects Bolton-road with Cockey Moor-lane. The site was given by the Earl of Derby, and was well selected, being high and on a good gravel foundation. The style of architecture is that of pointed gothic of about the 14th century. The building is placed 12 feet back from the line of the street, so as to afford a good approach ; it is about 108 feet on the front, and built with two wings, the extreme width from back to front being 72 feet. The wings form respectively the boys' and infants' schools, with girls' school in the centre. At the back of the building two spacious play-grounds, bounded by a substantial wall, are provided for the use of the girls and boys. The cost of the erection, with the boundary wall, was about £2,200, which amount was raised by voluntary subscription, assisted by a grant from the Committee of Council on Education. The building was designed, and the work carried out, under the superintendence of Mr. James Farrer, architect.

PRIMITIVE METHODISM.

For a long time the Primitive Methodists residing in Elton had no place of worship in their locality, and in consequence of this, up to a few years ago, not a few of that body were in the habit of attending the chapel in Walmersley-road, which was more than a mile and a half distant from their residences. In order to meet this want the present chapel and schools in Wellington-road, off Bolton-road, was commenced in the year 1868, the four memorial stones being laid on the 6th of July, by Mrs. Driffield, Mrs. Wild (Heywood), Mrs. T. Eastham (Littlewood Cross), and Mrs. D. Eastham (Walmersley). It is a plain, substantial building, in the Italian style of architecture, both chapel and school being under one roof. The entire cost of the building was about £600, and was erected under the personal superintendence of the Rev. J. Mould, the superintendent minister of the district, who during his ministerial career has had considerable experience both in designing and superintending the building of places of worship.

THE BRANDLESHOLME BULL.

During ten or twelve years of the closing quarter of the eighteenth century one great terror to people on this country side of Bury was the Brandlesholme Bull, whose domain comprised that extensive, unenclosed piece of land known as Brandlesholme Moor. A woman was gored to death by him whilst crossing the moor; several other deaths were laid to his charge; he broke the limbs of men and boys at his pleasure, and generally conducted himself in a most unwarrantable manner. Numbers of unwary ones suffered almost an equivalent to death in the terror and exhaustion of his unchecked pursuit, sometimes for a long distance, unrestrained by a fence or other impediment, and yet no word was ever suggested as to limiting his freedom. He knew his power and maintained it. His bovine majesty roamed over so large an extent of territory that the wayfarer, in passing over the moor, often knew not in which direction to anticipate his approach. Much of the land now richly cultivated then lay fallow and unenclosed, as if of small value; the science of husbandry was scarcely inaugurated, and but a small portion was required for actual use. Long after he was dead, the exploits of the dreaded Brandlesholme Bull occupied considerable space in many a countryman's memory or narration.

ANCIENT DISPUTES AS TO TENANTS' RIGHTS.

From the "Chetham Miscellanies" it appears that the land in Cockey Moor has given rise in bygone days to several litigations, for we find that at one time the tenants of one lord in one township had common right upon land with the tenants of another lord in an adjoining township. It seems from a document found in the Muniment Room at Middleton, which bears no date, but the writing is clearly that of the early part of the reign of Henry VIII. (about 1514 or 1515), that one of these litigations took place at that time. The tenants of Middleton and Radcliffe had been accustomed, time out of mind, to have common promiscuously in both lordships' lands, being contiguous and open to each other ; but the property of the soil of Cockey Moor seems to have been, perhaps, altogether in the lord of Middleton. The verdict of the Attorney General and jurors, who were all magistrates and influential men in the county, and closely connected by family ties with both the disputants, has not been recorded ; but as there are no evidences as to the litigation in the court of the Duchy of Lancaster, and as the township of Ainsworth continued to be parcel of the manor of Middleton and passed with .a co-heiress of the last Sir Ralph Assheton to an ancestor of the Earl of Wilton, it may be fairly assumed that the decision was in favour of Mr. Assheton. The litigation, however, respecting Cockey Moor did not terminate with the "Examynatyons" which were made at that time, as, in the 3rd Edward VI. (1549), Richard Assheton prosecuted in the Duchy Court Robert Aynsworth and others for trespassing on grounds called "Cokkamore" in Aynsworth in Middleton. The various feuds and disputed claims respecting the commons, with the riots, assaults, and rescues which arose out of them, were, during the first half of the sixteenth century, a fruitful source of emolument for the lawyers, and of anxiety to the litigants, as the Duchy Records abundantly evince. Richard Assheton, involved in this dispute, was an eminent man, and his name is still fragrant in his native village. He distinguished himself by his bravery and valour at Flodden, and by his piety and munificence in rebuilding the Church of Middleton. He added considerably to his paternal estate, retained the royal favour and his country's gratitude, avoided the pilgrimage of grace, embraced the reformed faith, and dying in a good old age (2 Edward VI.) escaped the persecutions of the next reign.

TOTTINGTON.

TOTTINGTON was formerly in the successive possession of the Houses of Lincoln and Lancaster, and was the seat of the superior court, to which the manors of Bury, Middleton, Chadderton, and Alkrington, owed suit and service. After serving as a portion of the reward given to General Monk, Duke of Albemarle, for the services he rendered in restoring the House of Stuart to the throne of England, the manor is now enjoyed by the Duke of Buccleugh, in whom is vested the Albemarle possessions. The manor, or as it is sometimes designated the honour or forest of Tottington stretches five miles on the banks of the Irwell, from Elton to the opening into the parish of Whalley, and is three miles in breadth, from Shuttleworth to Edgeworth in the parish of Bolton. Sir Thomas Pilkington had possessions in Tottington and Shuttleworth, before the dissolution of the monasteries, but they passed with his other forfeited estates to the Stanleys. At the time the property of Monk Bretton was awarded, Holcombe was granted, by letters patent under the seal of Henry VIII., to John Braddyll, of Whalley, gentleman, by the description of " all those lands, etc., lying in Holcame, otherwise called Holcome and Tottington, Co. Lancaster, to the late priory of Monk Bretton, Co. York, recently belonging. The manor was divided in the 17th century for parochial and police purposes into two townships called Tottington-Higher-End and Tottington-Lower-End.

ST. JOHN'S FREE CHURCH.

St. John's Free Church of England, in Sandy-lane, was opened and consecrated for religious service by the Rev. the Bishop of the Free Church of England on the 10th of April, 1868. It is a substantial structure of stone, tooled and pitch-faced. In front is a portico supported by four stone columns, above which is a bell turret. The outside measurement is 64 feet long, 39 feet wide, and 25 feet in height to the square of the roof. The building inside presents a neat appearance. The pews are made of pitch-pine, flange-backed, and varnished. In the north end is a gallery, in which is placed a splendid organ, and seating for about 100 persons. Altogether the church will accommodate about 400 persons, and 150 seats are free and unappropriated. In the north-east end of the building is a large three-light diaphime window, on which are figures of the Apostles and other Scripture illustrations. The materials for this window were given by Messrs. Hugh Roberts and Sons. Immediately underneath is the communion, to the right of which stands the pulpit, on a pedestal about two feet high, and on the left is the reading desk. In the centre of these is the communion table, over which is the Scripture text—"Do this in remembrance of me." The plans of the building were prepared by a Building Committee, consisting of various gentlemen connected with the church. The church is lighted by three large sunlights, suspended from the ceiling, and the roof is of open timber work. The entire cost of the building was £1,250, in addition to which £150 was laid out on the organ. In the afternoon of the same day the Bishop consecrated the burial ground attached to the church, and in the evening a tea meeting was held. After tea Mr. Hugh Roberts was presented with a handsome and valuable timepiece by the teachers and scholars of the Sunday School, as an expression of gratitude for the services he had rendered for a period of fifteen years, seven years of which he had provided a room free of expense.

THE WESLEYANS.

As the old Sunday School used by the Wesleyans, and which was established on the 17th of February, 1822, was found too small, the foundation-stone of new Wesleyan day and Sunday schools was laid on the 16th of May, 1868, by James Barlow, Esq., who was at that time Mayor of Bolton. They are after the Italian style of architecture, and are situated immediately behind the chapel, in what is called "Club Row Meadow." The building is rectangular in shape, 40ft. 6in. long, by 42ft. wide, inside measurement. The exterior is of stone, and has a substantial appearance. The architect was Mr. E. Simpkin, of Bury. The schools comprise two storeys, the bottom room being divided into class-rooms, and one large room for infants. The upper storey is thrown open into one room as a general meeting room for the scholars and for public meetings, &c. The premises cost £1,800.

RAMSBOTTOM.

This is a large and populous village in the chapelry of Holcombe, township of Tottington-Lower-End, and parish of Bury. It is 11½ miles north of Manchester, and 3½ miles north of Bury.

Ramsbottom has many claims upon the attention of the tourist. The beauty of the surrounding scenery, with its varied glories of hill, dale, wood, and water, put to shame many places of greater note, and attract the attention of the landscape painter in every direction. The village itself is picturesque ; it is pretty regularly built ; has some striking public buildings ; can boast of a good water supply ; is not ill provided with gas ; and presents a marked contrast to its appearance when the manufacture, printing, and dyeing of cotton goods, stimulated by the introduction of machinery, was in the hey-day of its prosperity; when fortunes were made rapidly, when profits were high, and " hands " had to be imported to meet the growing demand. Looking back at the latter part of the last century, we find that Ramsbottom contained only some half dozen cottages of small pretensions ; but now the spirit of change came over every thing. Originally it formed a part of the ancient forest of Rossendale, extending from Pendle Hill to Prestwich, with the river Irwell winding its course circuitously through the forest or royal hunting ground, and often has the solitude been broken, and the genii of the woods been roused from his lair by a blast from the royal bugle of " time-honoured Lancaster," John o' Gaunt—a great contrast to the prosaic utilitarian spirit which characterises the year of grace, 1873. At the period indicated, Rossendale was just emerging from the silence and solitude of the wasted forest land, to the more civilised condition of farming or agriculture, with a sprinkling of the trades in embryo, that were so soon to revolutionise the whole district ; for what was then a wild, partially wooded valley, is now become one vast emporium of manufactures and commerce, nay, there is a possibility of the valley, in point of population and wealth, exceeding some of the famed cities of Europe, yet at the time to which reference has been made there was little to indicate such a future. It needs little stretch of the imagination to realise the position of the village at that day to bring back the good old times, as they are called, when the hours of labour were almost unlimited, when men left their looms or other employment to follow the hounds, when every stride a person took he was obliged to look out for the roots or stumps of trees in the common roads of that day, and when trout and other fish were plentiful in the Irwell. It was said that at this time the sides of the hill on either hand were densely wooded, and sloped towards the river. The sylvan nature of the scene has excited the muse of more than one poetic mind. The Rev. Richard Smetham, formerly a preacher here, wrote a poem called "Natal Love," illustrative of the place, town, and manners. He commences with the following lines :—

> Shall e'er I cease to love my native soil?

And then, speaking of his return after years of absence, he says—

> "Beneath yon tree begirt with kindly seats,
> Whose ample shade o'erhangs the highway side,
> I see a smiling group of damsels fair,
> With flail, and sticks, and wheels, and cotton cards,
> All busy as the bee in summer sun,
> Whose sonnet sweet beguiles the hours away.
> The limber lads upon the green I see,
> With rosy cheek at eventide. Playful
> As kids or lambs, till youthful pith is spent,
> And drowsy night her sable mantle spreads ;
> Now putting on a graver face, they all
> In circlets stand, and fearful stories tell
> Of pale or bloody ghosts that oft are seen ;
> When each alarmed, betakes himself to flight
> With nimble speed; and every shaking leaf,
> Or rustling breeze, becomes a spectre ;
> Nor is he safe till close to mother's lap."

The Grant family now come upon the scene with which they were to be identified so closely, so nobly, and so well. Their story is familiar in the mouth of the people as household words. Everybody can tell of the family being ruined by a pitiless Morayshire flood. How houseless and forlorn they sought and wooed fortune in a more Southern clime. How they came to England—to Lancashire—to Ramsbottom. How, in the midst of their direst distress, the sunlight of prosperity dawned upon them.

> "This truth of old was sorrow's friend,
> Times at the worst will soonest mend.

Then we have that touching picture of the family at the close of day. Tired, weary, and travelworn, they rest and partake of their last remaining morsel of bread and cheese on a little knoll or eminence above Walmersley Road. While here the whole family seem to have been struck with the beauty of the surrounding scenery, for a wish simultaneously escaped the lips of the party that the valley below might become theirs. How far this wish was fulfilled it is useless to say. For other particulars in reference to this family, the reader will find

P

narrated in another portion of this work. The different stages of
their success have been celebrated in song and story, and some of the
songs are still in existence in which they were popularised at that
time. The Peels gave up by degrees their connection with printing and
dyeing. The ruined farmer was now a flourishing tradesman, and he
took what was then a logwood grinding, dyeing, and printing place,
situate at Ramsbottom, on the Old Ground, as the place where the old
dry houses stood is still called, notwithstanding that the site is being fast
filled with buildings. The cotton mill at Nuttall, a village about a mile
off, was purchased after a number of years, and there commenced their
fabulous rate of money making—buying the cotton in the raw state ;
selling it printed, dyed, and finished, or bartering with foreign merchants ;
thus securing to themselves all the profits of these well-paying trades.
There was also at Stubbins, a less village about half a mile off, a printworks kept by the Sandifords, a local family of some standing. The
gates at the bottom of the road leading to the hall at Stubbins are still
called Sandiford Gates.

Rather later, that is, at the commencement of the present century,
the Messrs. Ashton arrived here. They came originally from
Middleton, near Manchester, where they, no doubt, used the more
ancient orthography (Assheton), as used by the author of the
" Lancashire Witches." From Middleton, also, came several skilled
hands in the cotton manufacture, some of whom located—to use a
Yankee phrase—and their children and grandchildren are fulfilling at
the present time the same positions occupied by the first immigrants.
Of course the improvements in machinery suggest that this is hardly
true to the letter, but it is quite so in spirit. They introduced a
number of apprentices from the metropolis, some of whom are still
living. The Messrs. Grants had a number from Hull, some of whom
are still with them, having served several apprenticeships under that
firm exclusively,—a rare occurrence now-a-days, when people are bent
on removing every time there is a temptation, particularly if it be a
money one. The foregoing formed the staff of pioneer employers,
capitalists, and workpeople.

The opinions and actions of the people next require attention. What
the causes of these acts are, are not always made plain ; some are
attributed to external agency, others are fruits of a man's inner life, the
result of education, force of circumstances, &c. Such are the political,
moral, or religious movements that work up ever and anon in
Ramsbottom and elsewhere. One of these movements, namely, the
Radical and Chartist, took a deep hold of Ramsbottom. This was an

importation from Middleton, one of the head-quarters of the ultra Radicals, the residence of Sam Bamford, the late Radical historian and poet. Some of the inhabitants attended the monster meeting in Manchester, which led to the well-known Peterloo massacre, and were wounded there. More than one carried the marks with them for life ; one man died here in 1862 who received a flesh wound in the arm. In 1826 occurred Chatterton fight, and an account of it may be interesting to the reader. The following is the most concise version extant, at least among the residents, communicated by parties on the spot, and within a mile of it at the time. The chief cause of complaint was against the power-looms, founded and fostered in ignorance by the old hand-loom weavers. A mob, the greater part of whom were from Rossendale, resolved, in their meetings, to destroy all the power-looms in the country. The Messrs. Ashton had a small body of soldiers—green jackets, or sharp-shooters—to check the advance of the mob whenever they might show themselves, billeted in the mill. One day, word being sent that the mob was on the march, the soldiers were ordered off to meet them. They were remarkably patient, for after the reading of the Riot Act by William Grant, Esq., the officer did not give the word to fire till some of the soldiers were wounded with the stones thrown by the men and women who formed the mob. The women here, as elsewhere, took part in the mad attempt to beat the soldiers. Some were killed, and others seriously injured, before the mob dispersed. An anecdote is told to the present day of a certain farmer and his better half, who, being in the field at the time of the fight, when they heard the report of the shots he gave her the advice in local dialect, "Lie thee deawn flat." There being a small hill between them and the battle, she inquired, "Con bullets cum throo't greawnd?" In later times there was a partial repetition of this description of mob law, called plug drawing. A lawless rabble of beardless lads, who, in their march of mischief, drew the plugs of the different mills that happened to be working, caused the operatives to lose a month's work, and few, if any of them, were willing to allow the plugs to be drawn; in fact, at the Messrs. Ashton's mill one woman had to be kept from speaking to the crowd; she protested in no measured terms against opening the gates to the villainous rabble who composed the mob, and the gatekeeper would not open them till the manager gave the word. He was one of the men who came with the Ashtons from Middleton, and in 1826 acted as purveyor to the soldiers billeted in the mill at Chatterton fight. The people were subsequently agitated by the Chartist, Dr. Macdowell, who harangued the inhabitants on the glorious charter of the people, the six points of which would make them the freest nation under heaven. After this came the Feargus O'Connor scheme, and found its supporters and victims. The fever amongst the chartists rose to such a height at one time that they moulded bullets *ad libitum*. They were, however, never used. Some are buried, it is said, at Rosebank, Stubbins Lane, and perhaps other places as well.

During this time a few other persons had entered upon a profitable course of business of one kind or another; perhaps the most prominent among these was the firm of Grieg, Watson, and Grieg, the principal of which, Thomas Grieg, Esq., the author of several political pamphlets, bought an estate among the Grampians worth £40,000, some years since, to which he retired. The firm is now Watson and Stark. Another case is the Porritt Brothers. The Congregationalists formerly held their services in a room in this mill.

The use which the river Irwell is of to the inhabitants of this valley can hardly be conceived. It is in use at almost every turn of the road in one way or another, either turning water wheels or carrying away the refuse of the different dyeing, bleaching, and printing works, or fulfilling some other part of the multifarious uses to which water can be put.

The railway gave a new impetus to trade, and materially aided to develop the resources of the place by placing Manchester within forty minutes' ride, and excellent communication on every side. Several new houses are in course of erection, and a number of others are just finished. They were much needed, as indeed houses are likely to be for some time to come, notwithstanding the much-assisted emigration. Here, as in all centres of population, exists the greatest latitude of opinion in regard to religious worship. There are Churches of England, Churches of Rome, and Churches of Scotland ; Wesleyan, Free Churches, and Primitive Methodists ; the different dissenting bodies, Swedenborgians, and Unitarians, though these last have no chapel they have made several attempts to get a stand in the village. This neighbourhood is rendered famous to some, on account of the nonconformity of Henry Pendlebury, at Holcombe, in 1662. [See under head of Holcombe.] The library in connection with the Wesleyan Sabbath School contains a volume of his sermons, with his biography prefixed—a very interesting part of the book. It is there stated that he was buried at the Bury Old Church. After his secession or ejection, it is said he lived and preached in Walmersley Road. A house is still shown, called Bass House, as the place where his congregation worshipped, and where some say he resided. After his death Dundee Chapel was built. This probably served till a part of the congregation built a new chapel in Bury, and the other in

Walmersley Road, called Park Chapel. The next variety was the Wesleyans, who had a name and a place here more than sixty years since, though they built no chapel or preaching place till 1825, but occupied a room lent by the Grants, called the Old Dry House. At one time they had a very flourishing congregation, but one of their members did them much harm. When the Messrs. Grant had been some time in the country, and wishing for their primitive religion, they procured the Dundee Chapel, and introduced the Established Church of Scotland. The Swedenborgians were next. The Established Church formerly used the Athenæum for public worship. They have now a handsome structure, well attended, in a good situation, called St. Paul's.

One of the most successful woollen manufacturers in Ramsbottom at that time was the late Joseph Porritt, Esq., who died on the 14th June, 1868. He was the eldest of a family that has long been connected with Ramsbottom and the immediate district. When a young man he commenced business in Bury, and afterwards removed his business to a mill at Dearden Clough, some thirty-five years ago. Some time after that he and his brothers became partners in the Stubbins Vale Mills, which they built, and they continued to carry on the business of woollen manufacturers until about 1858, when Mr. Porritt withdrew from the concern and commenced business operations at Spring Wood Mill, which he continued to work until his death, in conjunction with his sons, under the style of Joseph Porritt and Sons. He built Sunny Bank Mill, at Helmshore. By his workpeople he was much esteemed, and he always took considerable interest in the political questions of the day. In politics he was a Liberal, and frequently officiated as chairman at Reform meetings in Ramsbottom. As a member of the Local Board of Health, he took great interest in the improvement and good management of the district. For the last thirty years of his life he held the office of Deacon at Park Independent Chapel, of which place of worship he was a zealous and liberal supporter. In the Sunday school he took an active part, and for a long period he officiated as superintendent. His remains were interred in the ground adjoining Park Chapel, being followed to the grave by the members of the Local Board of Health, the deceased's workpeople, and a large concourse of persons.

St. Andrew's is the title of a new church situated very pleasantly on a grassy eminence. The immediate occasion for the building of St. Andrew's Church is thus explained. A Nonconformist congregation at Ramsbottom had for generations worshipped in a small building called Dundee Chapel, which had been built for the celebrated Puritan divine, Henry Pendlebury, who was ejected from the Establishment, and his living at Holcombe as one of the "two thousand" ministers who were cast out of the Church and from their homes and old associations by the Act of Uniformity more than 200 years ago, and when the Grant Brothers worshipped in the old chapel along with their aged mother, one Peter Ramsay was the minister—a man so given to plain speaking about the shortcomings of his flock that only those accustomed to Puritan denunciations of the ancient sort could go through the ordeal without taking his pointed admonitions as a personal affront.   Peter had managed to offend the old lady, Mrs. Grant.   It must have been serious, for when "her lads" returned home from the Manchester warehouse she unburdened her grievance to them.   The sons "nursed their wrath to keep it warm" until it could be let off with full effect next Sabbath.   Peter the Puritan Apostle was delivering his text from the pulpit—"First Epistle of Peter and"—but there he was rudely stopped.   One of the brothers said "Nay, I think it's the last epistle of Peter here;" and at a gesture the unfortunate Peter was roughly hauled out of his preaching box and hustled into the chapel yard by a number of rough youths who appeared to understand what they were about.   The little congregation followed Peter into the yard, and there he preached to them a stirring sermon. He, however, took his "epistles" elsewhere, and migrated to a chapel at Holcombe Brook.   Dundee Chapel was then shut up for some time, there being no minister, and possibly also a division in the flock.   The Rev. Andrew MacLean, then a young Scotchman favourably known as a good theologian and antiquarian scholar, received a call to the pastorate of Dundee Chapel in the names of 143 members of the congregation. He came, and the little flock increased in numbers so fast that the old chapel could no longer hold them, and then it was that Mr. William Grant stepped in with his timely project of a memorial church to be dedicated to St. Andrew, and for the Presbyterian form of worship. Neither the founder nor the congregation seemed to have troubled themselves about legal instruments, and no arrangement as to ownership or private rights was made or mentioned.   It was always understood that the new church was built "for Dr. MacLean," in the sense in which churches usually are built "for" ministers.   The minister and congregation entered into possession of "their" new chapel as a matter of course, and Mr. Grant then had the old building converted into a school, for which purpose it has continued to be used.   The same benevolent giver secured £100 to the pastor towards his stipend so long as he should remain the minister, the actual payment being £200, with the seat rents in addition.   No charity collections were ever made in that church, the late Mr. William Grant insisting upon paying all the benevolences that were required, and, in fact, defraying all incidental expenses.   His successor continued the same system.   The founder of the church remained an elder in connection with it up to his decease.   At the beginning of June, 1869, Dr. MacLean received from William Grant, Esq., a month's notice to quit the pastorate of the church, which had extended over a period of 39 years.   The doctor was in his seventieth year, and had become so infirm that he could not do duty in the pulpit without fainting.   He kept his notice to himself until his "days of grace" were nearly run out, when he received a second communication to the effect that his "employment of pastor" of the church claimed by William Grant, Esq., would be terminated in three months from the date of the notice, and his "stipend of £200 per annum in respect of the said employment would cease to become payable or be paid."   Mr. Grant was not then a member of the Presbyterian congregation, but attended the Episcopalian Church at Ramsbottom.   The matter in dispute between Mr. Grant and the congregation was taken in hand by the Lancashire Presbytery, and a deputation from that body had an interview with the congregation in the church shortly afterwards.   The deputation urged the necessity of raising funds for the support of their aged minister and for an assistant, and the meeting was unanimous in its determination to support their pastor in his position and to maintain their rights.

After this, Mr. William Grant issued a circular to the members of the congregation of St. Andrew's, of which the following is a copy :—" St. Andrew's Church, Ramsbottom, was built in 1832, and was intended (as the founder, by the inscription inserted in the foundation stone, declared) to be held in connection with the Established Church of Scotland.   St. Andrew's has hitherto remained in the hands of my predecessors and myself, and is now (as I am advised by Sir Roundell Palmer and other eminent counsel) my absolute private property, subject to no charitable trust.   Although I have for some time past been dissatisfied with the existing state of things—considering the incessant change of preachers, and continual uncertainty as to who would conduct the services, prejudicial to the best interests of the people, still I have been disinclined to take active steps to terminate it.   When, however, Dr. MacLean intimated to me his ill-health, and the ' great expense ' of finding ' supplies,' I was led to suppose that he would be glad to be relieved of his charge ; hence my intimation to him that I would be ready (as I still am) to grant him a retiring pension of £200 per annum.   I may cause the church to be placed in connection with the Established Church of Scotland—if agreeable to that body—in which case the services would have to be conducted strictly in accordance with her form of worship. With regard to Dundee Chapel, which I believe to be held in trust, I shall be ready to convey such interest as I may have in it to trustees, to be approved by the Charity Commissioners, to be held upon such trusts as the commissioners may declare to be subsisting with regard to it. I do not desire anything except what belongs to me, but what is my own I mean to dispose of as I think proper. I have a high regard for those who attend the present services, and have always endeavoured to evince this feeling, and I trust that the steps which I intend to take will meet with the approbation of many of them—I will hope all; but should there be, as very possibly there may be, some dissentients, I can but ask them that they will give me credit for doing what I conscientiously believe to be right.—I remain, yours truly,   WILLIAM GRANT."

Shortly after this, and before the matters in dispute were settled, Dr. MacLean died, that event taking place on the 22nd October, 1869. At the present time the service of the Church of England is observed every Sunday in St. Andrew's Church, and there is a very fair attendance in the morning and in the afternoon.

In 1866, the church was cleaned and renovated at the expense of William Grant, Esq., the late representative of the Grant family, and was re-opened at the end of that year. The decorations are the work of Messrs. Crowther, of Manchester. The ceiling is divided into thirty panels, and supported by spandrils, is painted with a neutral tint, and the mullions dividing the panels are decorated with coloured ornamentation of a Gothic character. The spandrils supporting the ceiling, and containing escutcheons, with the armorial bearings of the Grant family, and national arms of Scotland, are highly ornamented in gold and colours. The walls are painted a warm stone colour, and the spleys of the windows are decorated to harmonise with the mullions and spandrils. The organ was built by Messrs. Gledhill and Wild, of Rochdale. The reading desk and communion table are of oak, and were supplied by Messrs. Sidebotham, Banks, and Co., of Manchester. The most prominent feature is the stained glass windows. On the walls are several marble tablets to the memory of the different members of the Grant family. Among the rest is one which contains the following inscription:—

" William Grant, Esq., Spring Side, the Founder of this Church. Born at Elchies, in Morayshire, Scotland, on the 15th day of April, 1769; Died at Spring Side, on the 28th of July, 1842. Distinguished by vigour of understanding, spotless integrity of human character, and true benevolence of heart, he lived a benefactor to his species, and died universally lamented."

Ramsbottom has sent out its full quota of emigrants—soldiers, sailors, adventurers, political lecturers, ministers, and missionaries.   The author of "Natal Love," before quoted, says of the inhabitants:—

> Some, well I know, to Afric's burning suns
> Have gone, no more to see their native soil;
> Others, alas! high raised on baseless hope,
> Themselves transplanted to the western world,
> To seek for fickle, faithless fortune there;
> And some have perished in their country's cause,
> A few perchance on fortune's lap high fed have grown to greatness.

Both at home and abroad he might have said truthfully.   On the hills on the eastern and western side of the village there are towers erected, which are conspicuous for many miles round.

ST. ANDREW'S PRESBYTERIAN CHURCH.

After the Presbyterians were ejected, by the order of the late Mr. William Grant, from St. Andrew's Church, they continued to meet in Old Dundee School, the use of which was allowed them by the deceased gentleman.   Although probably discouraged, it would appear that the congregation were not disheartened, for they gave a call to the Rev. J. Kerr Craig, a Scotch minister, and determined to erect for themselves a new church.   Accordingly, in September of 1872, the corner-stone of a new and handsome church was laid, by Mr. Thomas Matheson, of Liverpool, in the immediate neighbourhood of the church from which the congregation had been ejected.   On the occasion of the laying of this corner-stone the Rev. J. Kerr Craig read the following history of the church; and, although some of the facts stated are contained in another page of this work, there are a few other details given, which will not render it out of place to repeat the whole:—

"*Outline of the History of St. Andrew's English Presbyterian Church, Ramsbottom.*"

" The origin of this congregation may be dated from 1662, when the Act of Uniformity was put into force.   The Rev. Henry Pendlebury, M.A., was minister of the chapelry of Holcombe at the time, but he left the Established Church and ministered to an affectionate congregation in Bass Lane until his death, which took place on the 18th of June, 1695.   He was aged 70 years, the 45th of his ministry.   His successor was the Rev. Edward Rothwell, a person of some property, who gave the congregation a piece of ground not many yards below Holcombe township, and on this plot a chapel was built and a burial ground laid out in 1712.   The chapel came to be known as ' Dundee ' Chapel, for what reason it is hard to say.   The chapel was opened as a place of worship

on Tuesday, August 5th, 1712. The preachers on this occasion were
the Rev. Mr. Rothwell and Rev. Mr. Gilliburn. From entries in a
memorandum book, which still exists, it is clear that Mr. Rothwell was
a Presbyterian. The chapel was not long opened when it was found
necessary to erect another in Bury (at that time five miles distant by
road), seeing that many of the congregation belonged to that town.
The Bury chapel was opened in 1719, and continued to be used as their
place of worship until the erection of the present handsome Unitarian
Chapel, which was built a few years ago. A young man of the name
of Braddock, trained for the ministry by Mr. Rothwell, became his
assistant, and the two supplied Dundee and Bury chapels alternately.
Both congregations were considered one during Mr. Rothwell's life.
After Mr. Rothwell's death, it appears that Mr. Braddock confined his
services to Bury, and Dundee had only occasional supply. By-and-by
the people of Dundee wished to have a minister of their own. It seems
there followed a succession of twelve or fourteen English Presbyterian
ministers at Dundee Chapel till the beginning of the present century.
The people were so poor that they could not afford to support a minister.
The greater number of these were orthodox, but a few were suspected
to be Arians. This is borne out by a funeral sermon preached in
Dundee Chapel by Mr. Brown, in the year 1824. He says: ' Sometimes
the gospel was faithfully preached, and a concern for religion aroused
in the hearts of many. At other times the cause of God seemed to
languish and "Ichabod" to be written on our walls, while doctrines
contrary to those which gladdened the hearts of the departed were
promulgated from this pulpit.' Mr. Rothwell's ministry extended over
a period [of more than thirty years; it commenced about 1699, and
ended about 1736. Mr. Braddock's began in 1720, and ended in 1770.
The Rev. Mr. Main was the next to undertake the spiritual oversight
of the congregation, and after a very brief stay he was succeeded by
the Rev. Mr. Holmes. Towards the close of the 18th century he
received an invitation to be minister of the Independent Chapel at Park,
in Walmersley. He was translated, and an effort was made to appropriate the Dundee property to the benefit of the Park, but a lawsuit
prevented this, and saved the ancient place from being altogether
extinguished. About the beginning of the present century 'Dundee
Chapel' was supplied with students from Manchester, one of whom, the
Rev. Peter Ramsay, became the minister, and was there when the
Messrs. Grant first arrived on our eastern hills and beheld the rich
valley of the Irwell. It is said that they sat on the hillside and wished
for what they afterwards attained. We draw a veil over the remainder

of Mr. Ramsay's history in Ramsbottom, and merely add that he after-
wards became minister of a congregation at Haslingden. He was in
Ramsbottom only two or three years. The next minister was Mr.
Thomas Nelson, of Auchtergavan parish, Scotland, who arrived about
1813, and remained about three years. Mr. Nelson was not ordained.
Through the influence of Dr. Jack, of Manchester, the following preachers
were sent down by the Associate Synod of Scotland, during 1817:—
Rev. Andrew Scott, of Cambusnethan; Mr. John Robb, Rev. William
Proudfoot; Messrs. William Nicholl, William Fraser, and George Brown.
Mr. Brown arrived in the month of June, 1818. On the 27th of August
he was ordained. The Rev. George Lawson, of Bolton, preached, and
the Rev. Dr. Jack, of Manchester, gave an account of the Presbytery's
proceedings in reference to the ordination; he also received the confession
of Mr. Brown's faith, and offered up the ordination prayer. The Rev.
Dr. Stewart, of Liverpool, concluded with a charge to the minister and
a short address to the people. On the 17th of January, 1819, Messrs.
Abram Hamer and William Grant were ordained as elders in connection
with the congregation. In 1820 Mr. Brown found it necessary for his
own sake and the welfare of the congregation to resign his chapel. We
prefer to abstain from entering into the details bearing upon this
unhappy occurrence. Mr. Brown was pastor of the congregation for
eleven years. He was afterwards settled in Brampton. He is now
dead (1872). After the removal of Mr. Brown in 1829 the congregation
invited Mr. Andrew MacLean to become their pastor. He accepted the
' call' and was formally ordained. The ' call' was signed by W. Grant,
John Grant, L. Grant, John Grant, and 136 other persons. After
Mr. MacLean's settlement it was found necessary to have a larger place
of worship than Dundee Chapel, and W. Grant, Esq., of Springside,
erected the sacred edifice which stands on an elevation a few hundred
yards to the north of the new building. Mr. (afterwards Dr.) MacLean
continued to minister to the congregation for nearly forty years. In
1869 a correspondence took place between W. Grant, Esq. (nephew of
the founder of St. Andrew's Church), and Dr. MacLean, which resulted
in the church being closed on September 29th, 1869, by Mr. Grant's
orders. It continued closed until 1871, when it was opened in connection with the Anglican Church. The closing of the church was no
doubt a severe trial to the aged pastor, who was at that time confined
to a sick bed. For a period of nearly forty years he had ministered to
the congregation. In the early years of his ministry he was always
ready to take an active part in every good work which required his
services. But the bell which for so many years had summoned his

people to worship had not long ceased to toll when the veteran preacher received the summons of death. On the 22nd October, 1869, the appointed hour arrived when he should cross death's gloomy river. He died in his 72nd year, and in accordance with his own request he was buried in Dundee Chapel graveyard, the resting-place of many staunch supporters of the Presbyterian cause."

After the laying of the corner-stone the work of erection of the sacred edifice was rapidly pushed forward, and it was opened for divine service on Thursday, October 23rd, 1873, the sermons on the occasion being preached by the Rev. Dr. Fraser, of London. The following is a description of the new building, which was erected from designs prepared by Messrs. Blackwell and Booth, architects, of Bury and Manchester :—
The church is pleasantly situated, and forms a most picturesque object, as seen from the East Lancashire Railway in approaching Ramsbottom from Bury. The original designs of the architects have been carried out in their integrity, even to the extent of constructing and finishing the gallery at one end of the church, for which " preparation " only was originally provided in the contract. The only portion not absolutely completed is the spire, but now that the other portions of the work are out of hand it is expected that a very short time will suffice to place the top stone on that. There is accommodation in the church for 700 worshippers, 500 on the ground floor and 200 in the gallery. The internal dimensions are—91 feet long and 42 feet wide, and the height from floor to ridge is 47 feet. The roof is open, and is in one span without any intermediate pillars for its support, thus leaving the whole body of the church clear from any obstruction, except two light iron pillars under the gallery. The seats are all open benches without doors. All the roof timber and also all the benches and other woodwork are of pitch pine, very lightly stained and varnished. There are two entrance porches on opposite sides of the chapel, in the second bay from the front, and between each of these and the chapel there is a vestibule and swing doors at both ends as a security against cold draughts. One of these porches is carried up on a tower and spire to a height of about 120 feet. The sessions room is at the rear of the church, and there is also a vestry with lavatory, etc., and a separate entrance and lobby thereto. The organ chapel is on the side opposite to the vestry, and is open on two sides to the church. The whole of the building is constructed of Fletcher Bank and Holcombe stone, which, as is well known, is of the most durable character.

NUTTALL HALL.

Nuttall Hall (at one time called Nuthall Hall) was formerly the seat of Richard de Notogh, born before 41 Edward III. (1368), and living

20 Richard II. (1397), and 10 Henry IV. (1408); it[*] descended to Richard de Notogh living 9 Henry VII. (1493-4). After many intermediate descents, the estate passed from this family, probably by marriage, to Miles Lonsdale, of Field House, Esq., about 1698, and was conveyed by his descendant and representative Ann, only child of Henry Lonsdale, Esq., about 1790, in marriage to the Rev. Richard Farmby, of Farmby, LL.B., by whom it was sold to Mr. Grant.

THE GRANTS' ARMS.

The Grants' Arms Inn, in the centre of the village, is chiefly remarkable from being at one time the residence of the whole family, and the Market Place formed their garden and orchard, extending to the present road. On every side new residences are springing up, and few sites, better or healthier, could be had in the county.

CHAPTER XIII.

Early History of Holcombe—Mr. Henry Pendlebury—Early History of Radcliffe—
Radcliffe Charities—Radcliffe Tower—Fair Ellen of Radcliffe—Radcliffe Shag—
Rev. Samuel Compston—William Cockerill and Family—The Lancaster
Family—Radcliffe Parish Church—Rectors of Radcliffe from 1583—St.
Thomas's Church, Radcliffe—St. John's Church, Radcliffe—Richard Wroe,
D.D.—Christ Church, Walmersley—The late John Robinson Kay—The late
Christopher Roberts.

HOLCOMBE.

———◆———

Holcombe, or Holcombe Brook, is a chapelry in the township of
Tottington Lower End, three-quarters of a mile south of Ramsbottom.
For the most part the inhabitants are occupied in the manufacturing
establishments in the neighbourhood.　Some years ago the chapel which
stood here was taken down, and a handsome church built by subscription,
and a grant from the Church Building Society, upon its site.　In 1852 was
erected upon the summit of Holcombe Moor a handsome square tower,
built of stone, to the memory of the late Sir Robert Peel, from the
summit of which an extensive view of the surrounding country can be
obtained on a fine, clear day.　In the summer time the moor is much
frequented by holiday pleasure seekers, the majority of whom ascend
the monument, and have their appetites sharpened by the strong healthy
breezes which the summit always affords.　Holcombe Moor is interesting
on account not only of the picturesque and charming view which it
commands of the surrounding landscape scenery, but of its historical
associations.　How many of the inhabitants of that district are cognisant
of the fact that they are day by day treading upon ground that has been
impressed with the footprints of predecessors who have participated in
the conflicts, characterised perchance by bloodthirstiness, of ages which
have fled into the past ?　The site of the castle at which prisoners were
tried, condemned, and sometimes gibbeted, is unknown perhaps save to
a few ; but the record of these facts will inseparably connect Holcombe
with the " stirring times " of " ancient days."　We find that in 1662,

Holcombe Hill & Sir Robt. Peels monument, Bury.

Mr. Henry Pendlebury, who preached in a chapel near the castle, was with others ejected from his living. He, however, appears to have had a circle of friends who built him another chapel, in which he ministered to their spiritual necessities between 22 and 23 years, when he "finished his course." This chapel was then taken possession of by the Lord of the Manor (the Duke of Buccleuch), and it was converted into a court-house, the jurisdiction of which included Bury and extended as far as Middleton. About 80 years ago, the Lord of the Manor gave his sanction to the court-house being used as a Church of England school-room. At length the scholars became so numerous that the place was found to be too strait, and a new school-house, towards which the present Duke of Buccleuch handsomely contributed, was erected. The building committee of the new school disposed of the old court-house and school to Mr. Ellis Howarth, of Dundee. According to old manuscripts, Mr. Henry Pendlebury, already alluded to, "preached his first sermon at Ashworth-Chappel in 1648, and continued there for some time as probationer. He was set apart to the ministry at Turton-Chappell, near Bolton, together with Mr. James Livvesey, after they had been examined and had disputed and performed their preparatory exercises before the second classes in Lancashire, who met ordinarily at Bury. The day of their ordination was October 3, 1650. Mr. John Tilsley was moderator, and gave the charge with much eloquence and faithfulness. Mr. Bath, of Rochdale; Mr. Furness, of Bury; Mr. Pyke, of Ratcliff; and Mr. Scolweld, of Heywood (i.e., Schofield of that town, surely is meant) being assistants, all laying on their hands. He made his confession solemnly and accurately, and made the usual promises with much reverence and humility. He afterwards preached some time at Horridge Chapel ; and thence, in 1651, remov'd to Holcomb, where he diligently apply'd himself to his studies, preaching, discipline, and administering all ordinances, till he was ejected in 1662. He still continu'd in the exercise of his ministry, and was instrumental for the good of many. He dy'd of a languishing disease, June 18, 1695, Ætat. 70, with these words in his mouth, ' Father, come, and take me to thyself.' He had read over most of the ancient Fathers, and had fully study'd the controversies betwixt Protestants and Papists, as appears by his writings. He wrote a treatise concerning Transubstantiation, which was carry'd by a friend of his privately to Archbishop Tillotson, who caused it to be printed, he so much approved it. He hath written a treatise on the sacrifice of the mass. He preached many excellent sermons on Christ's Transfiguration, many copies of which are abroad. But 'tis the desire of some that the author's original might be penned and printed. Since his death, a treatise of his hath been printed, on II. Cor., iv., 18, called 'Invisible Realities, the real Christian's great concernment,' etc., where may be seen a further account of this good man's life.' "

RADCLIFFE.

EARLY HISTORY.

Radcliffe is a town and parish in the southern division of Lancaster and in the Bury union, seven miles N.N.W. of Manchester and 2½ miles S.S.W. of Bury. The parish is ecclesiastically in the archdeaconry and deanery of Manchester. The word "Radcliffe" is Saxon, and is derived from a cliff of red rock on the south side of the Irwell, below the confluence of the Roch, and opposite to the village of Red, or Radcliffe. At one time the name was Rade-clive. The French language was, however, much introduced at the time of the Norman conquest, and the appellation de Rugemont was often given to this village, and in the early periods of English history used as a surname of several members of the Radcliffe family. This cliff, after having more than a thousand years ago given a name to the village, is still in existence. Blackburn-street, the principal street which runs through the town, is a portion of the Roman vicinal road from Manchester to Ribchester. There are only four places in the Salford hundred mentioned in the Domesday Book, and Radcliffe is one of the four. In this book it is stated that Edward the Confessor held Radcliffe for a manor with hides of land, one belonging to Salford. It was the only immediate property of the king in the hundred; over the rest of the hundred of Salford he was only lord-paramount. This place, along with other lands between the Mersey and the Ribble, remained in the hands of the Crown till it was granted, in the reign of Stephen, to Ranulph de Gernous, Earl of Chester, subject to the feudatory claim of Roger de Mareshey, which he relinquished in favour of Ranulph de Blundeville. Between de Blundeville and de

Mareshey a contract was entered into respecting the claim, of the date
of 15 Henry III. (1231), but the pedigree of the family assumes a de
Radecliffe anterior to the reign of Henry II., and the name of Henry de
Radecliffe appears among the witnesses to the charter of Robert de
Lathom, on the foundation of Burscough Priory, in the reign of
Richard I.

In 6 Edward I. (1278), William de Radecliffe was deputy to Theobald
Walter, high sheriff of the county of Lancaster ; but it appears that
before this time Simon Radecliffe, supposed to be the uncle of William,
demised lands in this place for a term of years to Henry de Oswaldtwisel.
The connection of William de Radeclive with Theobald Walter, who as
lord of Amounderness possessed Routhclive, now Rawcliffe, has led to
the supposition that the manor of Radcliffe was formerly a portion of the
barony of Kendal ; but this, on investigation, is found to be erroneous.
The parish of Radcliffe, in Salford hundred, doubtless gave name to the
family of Radcliffe, before that place was in the possession of the Earls
of Chester.   In the record of fees held in the reigns of John and Henry
III., as exhibited in the *Testa de Nevill*, William de Radeclive occurs in
the *Inquisicio Comitatus Lancaster*, fol. 401-405, where he is said to hold
by 6s. a carucate of land of the fee of Ranulf Fitz-Roger's heir, a ward
in the custody of Eustace Fitz-Moreton, for the King, besides twelve
bovates of land in Edgworth.   In 30 Henry III. (1246), Adam de
Radeclive petitioned against Roger de Oswaldtwisel for the lands
demised in Radeclive, for a term of years, by his grandfather, of whom
he was the heir.   In 4 Edward I. (1276), Richard de Radclyve had a
writ of novel disseisin, and held lands, etc., in Tottington, of the fee of
Roger de Montebegon ; this Richard accompanied the King in his wars
in Scotland, and obtained from him a charter for free warren in his
manors of Radcliffe and Querndone, dated from Strevelin 32 Edward I.
(1304).   Sir John Radclyve, of Ordsal, a younger son of this Sir Richard,
accompanied Edward III. in his wars in France, and introduced the
honour of knighthood into the family in 1347.   The Radcliffes enjoyed
the privilege of free warren and free chase in the territories of the duchy,
and held at various times the offices of seneschal and minister of the
forests of Bowland and Blackburnshire ; and the stewardship of Rossendale also devolved upon them.   The chiefs of the family, as well as
several collateral branches, filled the station of high sheriff in the county
in successive reigns ; a rank which, in the early period of our history,
was equal to that of lord-lieutenant.   Ralph de Radclyffe, the son of
Richard, dying without issue before 5 Edward III. (1331), bequeathed
his manors of Radcliffe, etc., to his uncle, William de Radclyffe, of

Radcliffe Tower, called the great William, lord of Edgeworth and
Oswaldtwisel, who became seised of Culcheth in 20 Edward I. (1292), in
right of his wife Margaret, one of the daughters and co-heiresses of
Gilbert de Culcheth.

James Radclyffe, of Radclif Tower, had letters patent, dated at
Pontefract Castle, 15th August, 4 Henry IV. (1403), conveying a
licence to enclose his manor-house of Radclif, held in chief of the Kings
as of the Duchy of Lancaster, with walls of stone ·and mortar, and
likewise to rebuild within the same walls a certain Hall, with two
towers, and to kernel and embattle the walls, hall, and towers, and to
hold the same as a fortalice to himself and his heirs for ever. These
letters patent were couched in the following words :—" The King, etc.,
greeting. Know ye, that of our especial grace we have granted and
licensed, for us and our heirs, as much as in us is, to our beloved
esquire, James de Radcliffe, that he his manor-house of Radcliffe
(which is held of us as of the Honor of Lancaster, *in capite*, as it is said)
with walls of stone and lime (*i.e.*, mortar) to enclose anew, and within
these walls a certain hall, with two towers, of stone and lime, in like
manner to make anew ; and those walls, hall, and towers, so made, to
kernel and embattle [" *Kernellare et battelare*"] . And the manor-house
so enclosed, with the hall and towers aforesaid so kernelled and
embattled, for a certain fortalice he may hold to him and his heirs for
ever, without any accusation or impediment of us or our heirs, or our
officers, or those of our said heirs whatsoever. In testimony whereof
we have caused these letters to be made patent. Witness the King, at
the Castle of Pontefract, on the 15th day of August [1403], by the
King himself." Richard Radclyffe, in the fourth descent from this
James, in 15 Henry VII. (1499-1500), settled his estates upon his
brothers, John and Roger, and their male issue, with remainder over to
Robert, son of John, Baron Fitzwalter, and his heirs ; with the
remainder to Thomas Radcliffe, lord of the manor of Framesden, in
the county of Suffolk. The Radcliffes, Barons Fitzwalter, descended
from Sir John, the second son of James above-mentioned ; and the
Framesden branch from Henry Radcliffe, the eighth son; John Radcliffe
died without legitimate male issue ; his brother, Roger Radcliffe, left
another John, who died a minor in 1518 ; and Robert, son of John,
Baron Fitzwalter, his cousin and next heir, succeeded to the manor of
Radcliffe at the age of 30. In 1529 Robert was created Earl of
Sussex ; and in 1538 he presented Robert Assheton, acolyte, to the
church of Radcliffe. The grandson of Robert, Thomas, the third Earl
of Sussex, lord president of the north, sold Radcliffe to Andrew Barton,

of Smithells Hall, and died in 1583. This Earl was succeeded by his brother Henry, whose son Robert, the fifth Earl, survived all his legitimate issue, and conferred the manors of Attleborough, Henham, and Debden upon his natural daughter Jane, then married to Sir Alexander Radcliffe, of Ordsal, son of Sir Alexander, who was one of the knights created by Queen Elizabeth on the destruction of the Spanish Armada. The manor of Radcliffe remained in the family of Barton till it was conveyed in marriage by Grace, daughter and heiress of Sir Thomas Barton, about 1632, to Henry Ballasye, M.P., eldest son of Thomas, Viscount Fauconberg, and was sold by the first Earl, about 1722, to James Whalley, of Sparthe, Esq., and Christopher Baron, of Oswaldtwisle, gentleman, in equal moieties. Both moieties seem to have been purchased by Thomas, Earl of Wilton, for, in 1809, the whole belonged to the Earl, the manor being then described as co-extensive with the parish, and the Earl entitled to all the soil and royalties in the commons of the manor.

Sir Thomas Barton, Knight, held the Manor of Radcliffe 12 Charles (1636). Thomas Barton, of Smithells, Esq., had an only daughter and heiress, Grace, married to Henry Ballasye, son and heir of Thomas, Viscount Fauconberg, whose son Thomas, the second viscount, married Mary, the daughter. of Oliver Cromwell, Lord Protector, in 1657. About the year 1722, Thomas, first Earl Fauconberg, of the new creation, sold the manor of Radcliffe, in two equal moieties, to James Whalley, of Sparthe, and Christopher Baron, of Oswaldtwisle, for £3,700. In the early part of the present century one moiety (or probably the whole manor) was sold by Sir James Whalley Smythe Gardiner to Lord Grey de Wilton, for upwards of £16,000.

The affairs of the town are conducted by a Local Board of Health, which was established in May, 1866.

The manufactures carried on at Radcliffe are bleaching, paper making, spinning, calico printing, ironfounding and machine making, and nankeen, fustian, and check weaving. The canal which passes through one end of the town offers the advantage of navigation between Bolton and the city of Manchester. The East Lancashire section of the Lancashire and Yorkshire Railway have a station and a goods warehouse here, and thus direct communication is obtained to Manchester on the one side and the various towns of East Lancashire on the other. There are extensive collieries here, which afford employment for a considerable number of persons, besides being a local advantage to the manufactories in and around the town.

In the year 1831 the inhabitants of Radcliffe and Pilkington made an effort to obtain the elective franchise, and for that purpose to become attached to the borough of Bury. In this attempt they were unsuccessful, but though Radcliffe appears geographically in more immediate connection with Bury than some other parts of the borough, it was judged advisable by the commissioners to adhere to the boundary formed by the Irwell on the south, though the same rule was not observed to the west.

The charities of Radcliffe are few and to a small amount. The Rev. Dr. Wroe bequeathed, in 1718, £10 to the poor of Radcliffe ; and the Rev. William Lawson, in 1757, bequeathed the same amount; these two sums were laid out, it is presumed, towards the improvement of the estate purchased with Guest's charity, as the sum of 20s., part of the rent set apart, is annually given in money to poor persons attending Divine service on Christmas Day, as the produce of Dr. Wroe's and Mr. Lawson's gifts. There is also a bequest of £5 by William Yates.

From the registers it appears that in 1655, in this parish, as in other parishes in the Salford hundred, Edward Hopwood, Esq., the magistrate, published the banns of marriage.

The parish registers commence in 1559, in which year there were 10 baptisms, 9 marriages, and 27 burials ; in 1560, 17 baptisms, 8 marriages, and 4 burials ; while in 1831 there were 144 baptisms, 29 marriages, and 91 burials ; in 1832, 161 baptisms, 32 marriages, and 93 burials.

RADCLIFFE TOWER.

Radcliffe Tower, which is now in ruins, was anciently, says Mr. Baines, one of the most considerable manorial residences in the county of Lancaster. Of the antiquity of this tower there is no precise information, but it appears that Richard Radcliffe, High Sheriff of the county in 32 Edward III. (1358), was of Radcliffe Tower, as was also his predecessor, William de Radcline, one of the Knights of the Grand Inquest, 13 John (1211-12). In 4 Henry IV. (1403), this mansion was rebuilt and embattled. The tower was built with stone strongly grouted, with a door communicating with the house. On the top tower, beneath the castellated rampart, at a depth of about four feet, was a covering of lead, which has long since disappeared. Over the great entrance-door of the tower, from each of the three storeys, was a funnel, resembling an ancient chimney, with which these manorial fortresses are furnished, in order that the domestic garrison might resist the entrance of an enemy by pouring upon him boiling pitch, or casting down offensive missiles. Generally these strongholds of the border counties were enclosed by a moat, but there are no remaining traces of such external protection at

Radcliffe Tower, and it is probable that none existed. So late as 1818, Dr. Whitaker says of this place:—

The old hall (adjoining the tower) is 42 feet 2 inches in length, and in one part 26 feet and in another 28 feet in width. The two massive principals, which support the roof, are the most curious specimens of carved woodwork I have ever seen. The broadest piece of timber is 2 feet 7 inches by 10 inches. A wall-plate on the outside of one beam, from end to end, measures 2 feet by 10 inches. The walls are finished at the squares with a moulded cornice of oak. The pillar at the right has neither capital nor moulding, and appears to have been inserted at a later period, when the hall underwent a repair. On the left side of the wall are the remains of a very curious window-frame of oak, wrought in Gothic tracery, but square at the top. Near the top of the hall, on the right, are the remains of a doorway, opening into what was once a staircase, and leading to a large chamber above the kitchen, the approach to which was by a door of massy oak, pointed at the top.

Mr. Thomas Barritt, who died in 1820, sketched in one of his manuscript memorandum-books the remains of the tower and hall, as they stood in his time. The hall buildings seem to have then formed two sides of a quadrangle, the tower standing at the corner or commencement of a third side. Its ruins were then as high as the roof of the hall; and both show dilapidation and modern repairs. In 1833, the hall was used as a hay-loft and cow-shed. Nothing visible remains of the moulded cornice of oak, the massy principals, ornamented pillars, the painted doorway, or the curious oak window-frame mentioned by the learned doctor. The principal part of the edifice, which stands within a few yards of the church, near a cluster of cottages, is a neglected ruin, and the remains of what may be properly called the tower partake of the general dilapidation. All the fabric except the tower is of brick, enclosed in squares of wood; and the large chamber above the kitchen, originally 18ft. by 18ft. 2in., has been converted into two rooms, to render it more suitable to the accommodation of its present inmates. The west and south sides of the quadrangle still remaining are supported by substantial buttresses; but where these supports are wanting, the walls have fallen; and part of the materials from the east and north sides of the building, as well as of the tower, have been used in the erection of a neighbouring corn mill. Since 1835 the tower has been almost entirely demolished. Mr. Samuel Bamford thus treats of the old hall and tower in 1844, in his " Walks in South Lancashire ":—

This interesting relic of old English domestic architecture was taken down many years ago, to make room for a row of cottages for the workpeople of Messrs. R. Bealey and Sons, bleachers. It is understood that the Earl of Wilton, to whom the place belonged, sold the materials to the firm, and let the land to them. . . This venerable pile was highly interesting to all who loved to gaze on the relics of other days; and it was probably calculated to convey a more correct idea of the rude but strongly-built habitations of our forefathers, than any other object to which the curious in this neighbourhood had access. . . . The materials were chiefly beams and planks of solid black oak, which, together with the simplicity of the construction and the rudeness of the workmanship, testified to the great age of the edifice. The square tower, or fortified part of the ancient residence, still remains, but tottering with decay. The vaulted roof of the lower room almost hangs by a single stone, and unless it be protected from further wanton outrage, it must soon share the fate of the hall, and leave only its name in the remembrance of things that have been.

Mr. Baines says :—" Amongst the common people a story is currently believed that the kitchen of Radcliffe Tower was the scene of a cruel tragedy, perpetrated by a menial on the daughter of the lord, to gratify the malice and cupidity of a stepmother ; and a red stain on the floor marks, it is said, the place where the victim placed her bloody hand while her murderer perpetrated the atrocity. Although there is nothing in the family history to support this counterpart to the footmark of the martyr George Marsh, at Smithells Hall, and although, for sixty years back at least, there has been no such relic to be found in Radcliffe Tower as the blood-stained flag, the tradition is not on that account the less firmly believed ; and the story of " Fair Ellen of Radcliffe " (in Pepys' black-letter collection, under the title of " Lady Isabella's Tragedy ; or, The Stepmother's Cruelty,") inserted in Dr. Percy's *Reliques of Ancient English Poetry*, has embodied and perpetuated this local romance. The following is a copy of the ballad entitled " The Lady Isabella's Tragedy :"—

There was a lord of worthy fame,
  And a hunting he would ride,
Attended by a noble traine
  Of gentrye by his side.

And while he did in chase remaine,
  To see both sport and playe,
His ladye went, as she did feigne,
  Unto the church to praye.

This lord he had a daughter deare,
  Whose beauty shone so bright,
She was beloved both far and neare
  Of many a lord and knight.

Fair Ellen was this damsel call'd,
  A creature faire was she;
She was her father's only joye,
  As you shall after see.

Therefore her cruel stepmother
  Did envye her so much,
That daye by daye she sought her life,
  Her malice it was such.

She bargain'd with the master cook,
  To take her life awaye:
And taking of her daughter's book,
  She thus to her did saye:—

Go home, sweet daughter, I thee praye,
  Go hasten presentlie;
And tell unto the master-cook
  These wordes that I tell thee:

And bid him dresse to dinner streight
    That fair and milk-white doe,
That in the parke doth shine so bright,
    There's none so faire to showe.

This ladye, fearing of no harme,
    Obey'd her mother's will;
And presentlye she hasted home,
    Her pleasure to fulfil.

She streight into the kitchen went
    Her message for to tell;
And there she spied the master-cook,
    Who did with malice swell.

Nowe, master-cook, it must be soe,
    Do that which I tell thee:
You needes must dresse the milk-white doe
    Which you do know full well.

Then streight his cruell bloodye hands
    He on the ladye layd,
Who quivering and shaking stands
    While thus to her he sayd:—

Thou art the doe that I must dresse,
    See here, behold my knife;
For it is pointed, presently
    To ridd thee of thy life.

O then, cried out the scullion boye,
    As loud as loud might bee,
O save her life, good master-cook,
    And make your pyes of mee!

For pityes sake do not destroye
    My ladye with your knife;
You know shee is her father's joye,
    For Christe's sake, save her life.

I will not save her life, he sayd,
    Nor make my pyes of thee;
Yet, if thou dost this deed bewraye,
    Thy butcher I will bee.

Now when this lord he did come home
    For to sit down and eat,
He called for his daughter deare
    To come and carve his meat.

Now sit you downe, his ladye say'd,
    O sit you down to meat;
Into some nunnery she is gone,
    Your daughter deare forget.

Then solemnlye he made a vowe
    Before the companie,
That he would neither eat nor drinke
    Until he did her see.

O then bespoke the scullion-boye,
    With a loud voice so hye—
If now you will your daughter see,
    My lord, cut up that pye:

Wherein her flesh is minced small,
　　And parched with the fire;
All caused by her stepmother,
　　Who did her death desire.

And cursed bee the master-cook,
　　O cursed may he bee!
I proffered him my own heart's blood,
　　From death to set her free.

Then all in blacke this lord did mourne,
　　And for his daughter's sake
He judged her cruell stepmother
　　To be burnt at a stake.

Likewise he judged the master-cook
　　In boiling lead to stand;
And made the simple scullion boye
　　The heire of all his land.

RADCLIFFE " SHAG."

Radcliffe was formerly noted for its "shag," which was in appearance a large bear-like dog; and, after the canal was made, many a drunken loon, with footing far from steady, returning late at night along its banks, was sure to meet with this horrible "shag," which, after a tremendous struggle, always finished by throwing its opponent in the water. At least such was the account given, when in the middle of the night, a wight, dripping wet, would arouse his wife to let him in. And the simple neighbours often believed the tale, though some, more acute, would be so sceptical as to assert that the ale barrel had much more potency in the matter than the much aspersed "shag."

REV. SAMUEL COMPSTON.

The Rev. Samuel Compston died at Radcliffe on the 1st of July, 1870. For seven years, up to 1838, he was resident in Bury, during which time he was one of a few zealous men who preached in the neighbouring villages, and who originated the Castlecroft Congregational Church. On leaving Bury he repaired to Radcliffe, where he remained for twelve years, during a part of which time he laboured as a home missionary, and officiated as secretary to the Radcliffe and Pilkington Total Abstinence Society. Bradford was his next sphere of evangelical labours, in the capacity of an agent of the town mission. After five years' faithful discharge of his duties he became pastor of the Independent Church at Settle, where he laboured for twelve years. On retiring from the pastorate, chiefly on account of declining health, he returned to Radcliffe. He, however, continued to preach and lecture in various parts of the country. In Bury and Radcliffe, as well as in Yorkshire, he was well known from the fact of his identifying himself with every public movement in the religious, political, and temperance world, and was much respected by all who knew him. The Rev. W. Roseman preached his funeral sermons, on the Sundays immediately following the funeral, at Radcliffe, Bury, and Settle.

WILLIAM COCKERILL AND FAMILY.

Among the men who have risen from Radcliffe to places of eminence and position through their own untiring exertions must be mentioned the name of William Cockerill, who became an eminent ironfounder at Liege, in the Netherlands, or Belgium. He was the first maker of power-looms at Haslingden, and subsequently removed to Radcliffe, where he became a working blacksmith. Here, after having attained middle life and surrounded himself with a family, he became dissatisfied with the prospect for himself and his children, and resolved to seek abroad for that opening in business which he could not find at home. Accordingly, in 1796, he proceeded with some other workmen to St. Petersburg, encouraged to take this step by the Empress Catharine. The accession of Paul ruined his prospects in Russia, and for fear of detention he made his escape to Sweden; from thence he proceeded to the Netherlands, there, unpatronised, to seek fortune with his own head and hands. The settlement in the province of Liege of William Cockerill, whose far-seeing and comprehensive mechanical genius wrought an entire change in the heretofore sluggish industries of the country, is perhaps the most important event that has yet taken place in the social history of Belgium. Not only did this new and fitting field for his labours and inventions possess abundant supplies of coal, iron, and other elements of manufactures, but people were animated with a keen anxiety to bring all these hitherto dormant resources into active service. Of the Liegeois in particular, who have been for centuries a busy people, it might justly be said that, at that time, they required nothing in order to compete with the English but a knowledge of those mighty mechanical agents which had already been developed in Lancashire and other parts of England. In such circumstances the arrival of William Cockerill was the most auspicious event for the prosperity of the country that could have happened. When seeking for employment he first made offers to some extensive woollen manufacturers of Verviers, a town within the province of Liege, to construct for them machines of his own invention for the carding and spinning of wool, and for other purposes connected with the production of cloth fabrics. His propositions were accepted, and William Cockerill forthwith came over to England, removed his family from their country home in Radcliffe, and settled with them permanently in Belgium, scarcely foreseeing that his children and their descendants were to be the inheritors of a wealth and magnificence rivalling that of princes.

And now begins the story of his son, James Cockerill. The youth, a boy 12 years of age, at a period before the family was summoned from England, left his mother, and through difficulties which were then very great, set out to join his father on the continent; and, although so young, his services became so important to his father, that at the age of 15 he returned to England in order to purchase machinery, the pattern of which his father desired to obtain. His arrival at Hull, in the month of September, 1802, during a critical period, joined to the extremely unsettled political affairs of Europe, rendered him at once an object of suspicion as an emissary from France, or an agent to obtain information for Napoleon's officials detrimental to the British Government. He was arrested in Hull almost immediately upon landing, and from thence imprisoned in York Castle, under circumstances that rendered a long detention probable. However, after this had continued for some time, his youthfulness, good behaviour, and total absence of any criminality, so excited the compassion of one of the keepers of the prison, that he helped the boy to disguise, and successfully connived at his escape. Whilst a prisoner, James had formed acquaintance with a company of sailors from Hamburg, likewise incarcerated on suspicion, and from these men he heard the suggestion of plausible plans by which he might, when once free, elude observation of any marked degree, and eventually rejoin his father. On regaining liberty, he walked by the least frequented roads from York to the coast, where he had expected to meet a vessel, but found that such as would have favoured him were prohibited. He had given up all hopes of being able to execute his father's commission, and could not communicate by writing. Almost in despair, he turned again inland, and, suffering from want and destitution, hiding by day and walking only in the darkness of night, often in uncertainty as to the direction in which he was travelling, as he, an escaped prisoner, feared to make inquiry lest he should be re-arrested, he at length reached the neighbourhood of Haslingden, the first place where he could feel assured of safety, concealment, and protection. Footsore, hungry, weary, consequent upon his last hard days of travel and isolation, he did not venture into the town until the "edge of dark," trusting in his endeavours to trace out the dwellings of men whom he knew he could trust as the faithful and assured friends of his father's earlier years; but, on turning into the main thoroughfare, near a little wayside inn, what was his consternation on approaching sufficiently near, in the fast waning light, to read, in large letters, on a bill conspicuously posted, a full description of himself, and a certain reward offered for his apprehension as a State prisoner broken out from the Castle at York. This appalling menace crushed at once the boyish courage that had hitherto sustained him. He had been ignorant of this great publicity, from the avoidance of towns or villages in his route, and from not daring to make open inquiry as to what he desired to know; whilst this, his last day of journeying, had been passed in a thicket on the solitary hills in the vicinity of Haslingden. At last he met with kind friends who supplied him with clothing and other necessaries, and when thoroughly recovered from famine and fatigue, he proceeded to Accrington, still in secret, for fear of detention, remaining undiscovered for seven months with relatives of his father and mother. But the short armistice of 1803 having by this time been proclaimed, the brave boy was enabled to return in safety to his anxious and expectant family, leaving England by a small trading boat from Shields. In the year 1813, William Cockerill, the ex-blacksmith of Radcliffe, retired from business with a large fortune, leaving to his two sons, James and John, the entire management, responsibility, and profit of his various immense establishments. A few years afterwards James also retired from more active pursuits, leading until his death a life of elegant leisure corresponding to the princely society in which he moved. His death took place at a comparatively early period, and it may be that the imprisonment and privations undergone during the dangerous first visit to his native land might be the means of hastening his decease. John Cockerill, who was now left alone to sustain the enterprises established and in progress, was said to possess the most enlarged mind of them all, and in him seemed to culminate the greatness and prosperity of the society. He erected, in 1815, the first manufactory for steam engines, on a large scale, which had yet been seen in Belgium. His machines were soon distributed through the whole continent of Europe, and he was the recipient of special favours and marks of distinction and appreciation from the several great rulers of the period, Napoleon the First having, at an earlier time, visited the workshops of the firm, and had a long gratifying interview with Mr. Cockerill, the remembrance of which the Emperor afterwards sustained by the conferring of several distinguished honours and privileges. Between the years 1821 and 1823 John Cockerill organised a still more extensive establishment, in the erection of ironworks of vast size at the village of Seraing on the Maese, distant a few miles from the city of Liege; and besides himself conducting the new gigantic enterprise, he still kept in action the extensive foundries originally possessed by his father in Liege, holding large shares in mining and colliery establishments, and possessing great cotton-spinning factories, as well as linen manufactories, where these stuffs were finished in all forms, including many varieties of texture in weaving. He was also proprietor of a paper manufactory; and it was at his instigation that the printworks near Liege was established, numbering amongst its partners himself, the Prince of Orange, Leopold King of Belgium, and some others. It proceeded under this direction or patronage only a few years, being broken up at the revolution in 1830. All of these establishments, with their diversity of purpose and operation, John Cockerill, in a measure, superintended in person; but at the same time it was especially remarked of him that he invariably took care to have the best of servants and overseers, sparing no expense in bringing such persons from all countries of Europe to his various works. Regarding the printing business, Mr. Cockerill selected many of the best workmen from several parts of Lancashire for his purposes, constituting his cousin, Mr. William Yates, of Radcliffe, and New Mills, Derbyshire, as his manager in chief of the works. The last great public undertaking of his life was to come forward, unassisted and unrivalled, to offer himself as the contracting party with the French Government for the construction of the railroad between Paris and Brussels, at that time a most stupendous enterprise to be undertaken by one individual. This remarkable man did not seem to be stimulated in his great career of industrial enterprise merely by the desire of personal emolument or aggrandisement, but to regard himself and his acts as one who has a high and extensive mission to execute, namely, of providing the world with machines to expedite the spreading of wealth and comfort amongst its inhabitants, and to aid and strengthen manual labour in all its multitudinous forms. On all private occasions the use of his wealth was most liberal and generous. His household establishments were maintained with the greatest splendour; and when travelling he was preceded by couriers as a prince. It was said he could travel over the continent of Europe, stopping only at houses or palaces belonging to himself. He died in the year 1840, at Warsaw, on his way to St. Petersburg, at an intimation from the Emperor of Russia that his services and personal attendance were in immediate request in that capital. No undertaking seemed too vast for his achievement, and popular faith and acclamation waited upon all the industries which himself or his father originated. Many years after his decease the peasantry of the provinces and towns where his works were situated obstinately refused to credit the authenticity of his death, believing that the jealousy of Russia at their own prosperity was the sole cause of his disappearance; and that he languished long in a foreign dungeon, to reappear some day, and come amongst them with his former power and splendour; the memory of the Lancashire, Radcliffe-born boy being to the inferior classes of his adopted country as a remembrance of one endowed almost above the natural power of man, and whose beneficent action had awakened their country from sterility and torpor to activity and wealth, and a community of industrial interests with all sister kingdoms of the Continent.

THE LANCASTER FAMILY.

The first complete lead tube was made in Radcliffe by Mr. John Lancaster, at his works, which are up to this day known by the name of the Pipe Mill. He was by trade a plumber and glazier, and was born in 1818, in Stand-lane, Pilkington. Previously all the pipes were made out of long strips of sheet lead, the edges of which were brought together and soldered. He died at the residence of his son, in Union-square, Bury. One of his sons was the inventor of the great Lancaster gun that was sent to the siege of Sebastopol; another of his sons is at present member of Parliament for Wigan. The Lancasters had formerly an estate in Birtle, and there they commenced to manufacture checks; they also sunk a coal shaft at Oakenrod, near Rochdale. On leaving Oakenrod, they endeavoured to form a pit at Patricroft, in the parish of Eccles, and in the township of Worsley, upon the estate of Sir Humphrey de Trafford. Sir Humphrey only gave them permission to sink one shaft, and when they proved that there was coal under the red sandstone, which was then opposed to the theory laid down by geologists, Sir Humphrey refused to allow them to sink another shaft for the ventilation of the pit. Messrs. Lancaster and Sons then became somewhat embarrassed, and Mr. James King, cotton spinner and manufacturer, Rochdale, came to their aid, offering them the use of £300,000, if they required it. They then left Patricroft, and removed to Ince, and opened other works, which they called New Patricroft. Here their industry and indomitable perseverance were highly successful, and in course of time the present John Lancaster, Esq., M.P., left the concern, having realised a handsome fortune. The Earl of Crauford and Balcarres afterwards joined the concern, which is now perhaps the most successful in the county, and is known by the name of the Wigan Coal and Iron Company. The hon. member for Wigan (Mr. Lancaster) was born in Stand-lane, and for a long time followed his father's business as a plumber and glazier. The following incidents in connection with the history of this remarkable family may perhaps not be deemed uninteresting: In June, 1845, there was a very heavy storm of hail, and many thousands of feet of glass were broken by the hail in the conservatories at Heaton Park. Mr. John Lancaster was sent for by Earl Wilton to repair the great damage which was done. Mr. William Lancaster, one of the sons, superintended the works while they were in progress, and at dinner-hour one day he said to Earl Wilton's butler, "I understand your master is fond of music." The butler replied that he was, and that they had a music saloon, which contained all kinds of musical instruments. In particular, the room contained a bass violin which was given to Earl Wilton by his father (the Marquis of Westminster). It was made at Cremorne, by an Italian, for George the Fourth, when he was Prince Regent. When the violin was brought to England by the Italian he heard something about George the Fourth that he did not like, and he refused to part with the instrument until he received £500, which was the sum he required for it. The Marquis of Westminster, however, bought the instrument, and gave it to Earl Wilton, as stated. After the colloquy above referred to between William Lancaster and the butler, William got hold of one of the fiddles in the music saloon, and commenced to play upon it. The Earl of Wilton, hearing the music, came to him, and said, "You can fiddle a bit." After playing for a short time longer, William Lancaster remarked that he must go and look after the glazing of the windows. The Earl of Wilton observed, "Never mind the windows, nor the glass either, for your wages are going on so long as you stop here." He then went on playing for about five hours, when the Earl said to him, "You don't know the value of that fiddle you have been playing upon; it is worth £50, but I have one here (reaching hold of another) that was made for George the Fourth, which is worth £500." The Earl then gave William Lancaster a violin, which he said was worth £50. He took it to Mr. Sudlow, organist of the Cathedral, Manchester, and he pronounced it to be worth £500. After William Lancaster's death, which took place about eight years ago, at Broughton, the violin, considered not to be worth above 50s., was taken to Manchester, where it was advertised for sale, and ultimately realised the handsome sum of £450.

RADCLIFFE PARISH CHURCH.

This church, which is dedicated to St. Mary, is of considerable antiquity, with a low, square tower, about the age, supposed by Dr. Whitaker, of Henry IV., and coeval with the building of Radcliffe Tower. The most ancient part of the building is in the Norman style of architecture. An ancient manuscript, yet in a state of preservation, carries the age of the structure to the year 1282. Its antiquity is, however, doubtful, as there is no mention of it in Pope Nicholas's ecclesiastical valuation made in 1291. Two arches on each side divide the nave from the side aisles, the arches being supported by plain massive columns, bound by a simple fillet. Carved squares of oak, with tracery at the intersections, sustain the roof. From an incised date it appears that the tower was rebuilt in 1665. There are also the arms of Beswicke, of Manchester, and the words "Carolus Beswicke, rector," still remaining upon it. There was no clock in the steeple until the year 1785, when the late Sir Ralph Ashton bequeathed forty guineas towards the expense of furnishing the town with a public clock, and the requisite additional sum was supplied by subscription. The south transept, or, as it is commonly called, the "Sun Chapel," is a chantry chapel, which, from its style of architecture, appears to have been founded about the middle of the fifteenth century, at which time it was not unusual to throw out chantries in the form of transepts. In 1846 a north transept was added, the south porch removed, and through the tower a west doorway opened. At the same time all the seats in the nave and transepts were renewed of substantial old oak. The east, south, and north windows of the chancel were filled with richly-stained glass; the first being an obituary window in memory of Thomas Hutchinson, Esq., and the others being presented by a lady. The chancel walls were faced with terra-cotta, disposed in figured quarries, and a reredos of good design added. These improvements were effected under the superintendence of the Rev. Nathaniel Milne, the rector, at a cost of nearly £1,000, towards which he was a liberal contributor. The following dates and initials were revealed, beautifully inlaid in coloured wood, on removing sundry layers of paint from the pulpit and desk :— On the first panel of the pulpit "1606," with a mullet beneath, the armorial cognisance of the Ashtons ; on the second panel, a boar's head erased, their crest, with the initials "S. R. A." (Sir Richard Ashton) ; on the third is the Ashton mullet, and the letters "L. S., P., R. W.," probably denoting Leonard Shaw and Robert Walkden, who were rectors during the alterations made early in the seventeenth century ; on the fourth panel, the initials "I. I.," with a mullet between them ; and on the fifth, the letters "T. H., I. M.," probably the initials of the churchwardens. The reading desk appears to have been the gift of Charles Beswicke, M.A., the rector, from the initials " R., C. B.," and the date " 1665," still remaining. As a border round the upper part of the desk, is the following text, in old English letters :— " All my words that I shall speak unto thee, receive into thine heart, and hear with thine ears.—Ezekiel, iii. chap., 10 verse." In 1817 the chancel and vestry were rebuilt, the former at the cost of the Earl of Wilton, the patron of the advowson, and the latter out of the parochial rates; probably the east side of the church, which is also modern, was built at the cost of the parish. To the north, in one window, are the arms of Radcliffe, and, in the same window, the head of a queen crowned with an ancient coronet; another window, with the same aspect, is enriched with oak leaves and acorns, surmounted with the head of a king wearing his diadem, the portrait of which resembles that of Edward III., but not in the slightest degree that of Henry VI., though it is true that the Radcliffes were zealous Lancastrians. The window to the east bears the representation of a boar's head in a shield, placed there no doubt since the connection of the Ashtons with the manor and church of Radcliffe; and in a window to the west is a painting of St. John the Evangelist, in a white vest and a blue robe, his cap, palm, hair, and glory all of a bright yellow, with an almost obliterated background. These early works of art are being rapidly effaced by time; and the monument of James de Redcliffe, the founder of the tower, and his lady, formerly the attraction of the chancel, has now disappeared. Before the monument disappeared, says Mr. Baines, the country people, from a superstitious veneration, were accustomed to break from it small fragments, which they kept in their houses, or wore about their persons as amulets. The late venerable self-taught antiquary, Barritt, of Manchester, in his unpublished MSS., has described and sketched this monument, on which he remarks:—"In the chancel of Radcliffe church is an elaborate stone, greatly decayed; on it are the traces of a knight in armour and his lady. At the upper part of the stone are two escutcheons—on one the arms of Radcliffe, the other defaced. The Latin legend is in old black character, but almost mouldered away, not a word to be made out, except the remains of ' Jacobi Radcliff' (the supposed owner of Radcliffe), which words, to all appearance, must shortly perish. No date was to be found."

The living of Radcliffe church is a rectory. It does not appear that at any time since the Reformation the advowson has been in any of the Radcliffe family. From the Bartons to the Ashtons of Middleton it passed by purchase. It was conveyed in 1769, by Eleanor, younger daughter and co-heiress of Sir Ralph Ashton, Bart., to Sir Thomas Egerton, Bart., created Baron Grey de Wilton, Viscount Grey and Wilton, in 1801, and in the present Earl of Wilton it is now vested.

The registers begin in 1558, although it is believed that registers have been kept in the church since 1200. It is known that some time between these two dates a fire broke out in the church, and it is generally posed that the earliest registers were then destroyed. Within the last three or four years great alterations and improvements have been made in the sacred edifice, a considerable portion of the expense having been defrayed by Mrs. Starkie, mother of the present esteemed rector. A new chancel has been built, the old pews taken out and supplanted by neat open benches, a portion of the church has been re-roofed, and the general appearance, especially of the interior, much improved.

LIST OF RECTORS OF RADCLIFFE FROM 1583.

(Principally from the Register of the Ecclesiastical Court.)

Institution.	Rectors.	Patrons.	Cause of Vacancy.
Feb. 4, 1583	Leonard Shawe		
May 24, 1624	Robert Walkden	Robert Holt, John Green-acres, and Robert Wood, for this turn, patrons.	Death of Leonard Shawe.
	Robert Osbaldeston ..		
Feb. 3, 1637	Peter Shawe	Sir Ralph Ashton	Death of Robert Osbaldeston.
	Thomas Pyke		Ejected 1662.
	Charles Beswicke		Died 1697.
June 8, 1698	Charles Pinckney	Sir Ralph Ashton	Death of Charles Beswicke.
Jan. 23, 1699	Roger Dale............	Sir Ralph Ashton	Deposition of Chas. Pinckney.
Oct. 5, 1716	Edward King..........	Sir Ralph Ashton	Death of Roger Dale.
Mar. 18, 1719	Henry Lester	Sir Ralph Ashton	Death of Edward King.
July 14, 1724	William Lowston......	Sir Ralph Ashton	Death of Henry Lester.
April 6, 1757	Richard Ashton	Sir Ralph Ashton	Death of William Lowston.
Oct. 15, 1757	Richard Wroe	Sir Ralph Ashton	Resignation of Rich. Ashton.
Oct. 1, 1784	Thomas Foxley	Ths. Lord Grey de Wilton	Death of Thos. Foxley.
1838	N. Milne, M.A.	Earl of Wilton...........	Resignation of N. Milne.
1867	H. A. Starkie..........		

ST. THOMAS'S CHURCH.

This church was consecrated by the Lord Bishop of Manchester, on the 8th of October, 1864. It was erected on the site of the old district church, which was built at the expense of the late Marchioness of West-minster, mother to the present Earl of Wilton, and was consecrated in 1819. The old church was of a very substantial character, but too small to accommodate the increasing population, and was of a style of archi-tecture that did not well admit of enlargement. It would only accom-modate 513. It was therefore found necessary to take it down altogether, and in 1862 a faculty was obtained for that purpose, the congregation in the meantime worshipping in the Market Hall, to which the seats and the greater part of the furniture of the old church was removed. The foundation stone was laid on the 21st of July, 1862. The building is calculated to accommodate 1,200 people, of which 512—the entire accommodation in the galleries—are free sittings; and the plan consists of nave, 84 feet by 24 feet; north and south aisles, each 15 feet wide; chancel, 35ft. 6in. long and 19 feet wide, a western tower 17 feet square inside, a chapel at the east end of the north aisle for Lord Wilton, and

R.

a vestry 13ft. by 10ft. 9in. at the east end of the south aisle. The
staircases to the galleries are at the west end of the church, on either
side of the tower, with entrances distinct from those to the body of the
church. The structure is designed in the perpendicular style of architecture, and externally the aisles are divided into six bays, with a three-
light window in each, with traceried heads; the clerestory, with a similar
number of bays, having two-light windows also with traceried heads.
The western window in the tower as well as the eastern window in the
chancel have five lights each, representing incidents in the life of our
Saviour, the incredulity of St. Thomas, &c., and add much to the beauty
of the structure. These, as well as the rest of the stained glass, have
been produced by Messrs. Edmondson. The aisles, as also the clerestory,
are surmounted by a bold and handsome battlement; and the north and
south sides of the chancel, as well as the eastern gable, are ornamented
with a pierced parapet of graceful design, divided by crocketted pinnacles,
which form the terminations of the buttresses. The external walling of
the church is constructed of parpoints, with Hollington stone dressings.
The tower is 120 feet high to the top of the pinnacles, and externally
is 25 feet square. It is divided into three stages above the entrance,
respectively for the organ, the clocks, and belfry stage above. The clock
dials are centred in ornamental tracery, and the belfry windows are of
three lights each, there being two on each side of the tower, the whole
surmounted by a battlement, which is crowned by lofty crocketted
pinnacles. The whole of the timber is pitch pine, stained and varnished.
The building is from the designs of Mr. W. Walker, St. Ann-street,
Manchester. The contractor for the stone and brick work was Mr. A.
Pilling, of Bolton; the rest of the works being carried out by Messrs.
Allen, Howarth, and Co., of Radcliffe. The heating apparatus was supplied by Messrs. Bland, of Bury; and the altar railing, which is of
elegant design, was executed by Mr. Dovey, Manchester. A beautiful
memorial window, by Messrs. Edmundson, of Manchester, has been
placed in the eastern end of the church. It was given by the
Astbury family, and is in memory of John Meir Astbury, of Stand
Lodge, who died November 1, 1845. The pulpit, which is of pitch pine,
is of octagonal form, supported upon an elaborately-moulded pedestal,
and cost £50, raised in subscriptions.

ST. JOHN'S CHURCH.

This church, which is situated in Stand-lane, was consecrated on the
19th February, 1866. It is a substantial building, erected entirely of
stone, and is in the modern style of architecture. The four chancel

windows are of stained glass, and represent incidents in the birth, adoration, crucifixion, last supper, resurrection, and ascension of Christ. The whole of these chancel windows, and the carved eagle lectern, are the gift of the Rev. W. D. Carter. In the north transept is another stained window, which was purchased by the subscriptions of the Sunday-school children, and bears the appropriate representation of Christ blessing little children. The whole cost of the church was about £4,000. The site of the church and the endowment was given by Lord Derby, who was also a liberal subscriber to the building fund.

PRIMITIVE METHODIST CHAPEL.

The Primitive Methodist Chapel and School in Railway-street were opened on the 17th October, 1867. Previously they (the Primitive Methodists of Radcliffe) taught and preached in a small room in Sugar-lane. The entire cost of the new erection was about £750. The buildings were designed and erected under the immediate superintendence of the Rev. J. Mould, the circuit minister.

RICHARD WROE, D.D.

At the Hams, in the parish of Radcliffe, was born, on the 21st of August, 1641, Richard Wroe, D.D., Warden of the Collegiate Church of Christ in Manchester, and Prebendary of Chester. He was the son of Mr. Richard Wroe, a yeoman, and received his education in the Free Grammar School of Manchester. In June, 1658, he was entered a student of Jesus College, Cambridge, where, in 1661, he took his degree of Bachelor of Arts. On the 6th of May, 1669, he was incorporated in the same degree in the University of Oxford, and shortly after appointed Chaplain to Dr. Pearson, Bishop of Chester. In that year, on a visit of the Grand Duke of Tuscany to the University of Oxford, he was appointed to keep a public philosophy act for his Highness's entertainment, and acquitted himself with much applause. On the 11th June, 1672, he received his degree of Bachelor of Divinity, and was made a Fellow of the Collegiate Church of Manchester, on petition, on the 9th of March, 1675. On the 15th of March, 1678, he was collated Prebendary of the 5th stall of Chester Cathedral, and was inducted to the Vicarage of Bowdon, in the county of Chester. In the year 1683, on the resignation of Dr. Stratford, he petitioned the King for the Wardenship of the College of Manchester, and, having been formerly made Prebendary of Chester, and Chaplain to the Bishop, who by the statutes of the college is appointed visitor, received a strong recommendation in two letters from that prelate to Dr. Pearson, the Archbishop of Canterbury. On the 1st of May, 1684, he was inducted to the Wardenship of Manchester, and created Doctor of Divinity in 1686. He died at Manchester, 1st January, 1717-18, and was buried in the vault below the choir in the Collegiate church there. He was an admirable scholar, a sound divine, and a most elegant preacher. By the clergy he was styled the Chrysostom of Lancashire, and among the common people he had usually the appellation of Silver-tongued Wroe.

WALMERSLEY AND SUMMERSEAT.

Walmersley is a township and ecclesiastical parish in the parish of Bury. It is situated on the east bank of the Irwell, and is two and a half miles north of Bury. Some of the land is under cultivation, but the inhabitants are for the most part employed in the works in the district and also at Bury. Christ Church is a neat stone structure, erected in 1838, and consists of chancel, nave, and a low square tower, which contains a clock. It has a gallery to the west which contains an organ. There are 677 sittings. The registers date from 1838. The living is a vicarage of the annual value of £120, with residence : it is in the gift of trustees, and at present held by the Rev. Charles Wyatt Smith, M.A., of Trinity College, Oxford. In the township are the remains of a beacon tower, probably erected in the reign of Elizabeth, under the influence of the threatened invasion from the Spanish Armada, when a rate was imposed on the inhabitants of Lancashire for keeping these watch towers and flaming messengers of danger in proper order.

THE LATE JOHN ROBINSON KAY.

This gentleman, who died at his residence, Walmersley House, on the 25th March, 1872, was a native of Burnley, in which town he was born on the 20th of July, 1805. In 1834, he married the daughter of Richard Hamer, Esq., of Bury Bridge. His father, in 1829, removed to Brooksbottom, where, assisted by his son, he laid the foundation of a business which has been uninterruptedly carried on. Round his extensive works at Brooksbottom and Longholme there soon gathered a thriving and happy colony of workpeople. Besides occupying an important position as a merchant and a manufacturer, Mr. Kay was a director of the Lancashire and Yorkshire Railway Company, of the Manchester and County Bank, and of the Thames and Mersey Insurance Company. He was a prominent and influential member of the old Wesleyan Methodis

Society; but though he was a devoted and consistent member of that body, he was free from anything narrow or sectarian. Upon the subject of education he took a warm interest, and chiefly through his instrumentality the schools at Summerseat were erected, while his last public act in connection with this topic was the laying of the foundation-stone of the College Chapel, at Westminster, in the erection of which he took a deep interest, and towards which he was the largest contributor. In politics he might be described as a moderate Liberal. He took an active part in promoting the passing of that beneficent act of legislation, namely, the bill for shortening the hours of labour of women and children in factories. On the 22nd of February, 1849, he was placed in the commission of the peace, and was for many years an active magistrate of this division. His remains were interred in a vault at the Wesleyan Chapel, Summerseat, on the 30th of March, 1872.

Summerseat, with Brooksbottom, adjoins the township of Walmersley. It contains three mills, a handsome Gothic stone structure, used by the Wesleyans, and a school.

THE LATE CHRISTOPHER ROBERTS.

Christopher Roberts, of Summerseat, was an able machinist and mathematician, to whose suggestions, for the first twenty years of the establishment of the printworks and cotton factories, the firm of Peel and Yates was indebted for many of the most valuable and economical improvements in the construction of machinery, or the adaptation of well known modes to still greater uses. Long afterwards, when the infirmities of age had stolen upon him, his opinion carried authority, and, if visiting the Ground, he would be an honoured guest at Chamber Hall. Christopher Roberts, the contemporary of Watt, Arkwright, Kay, and Cartwright, had in his power the means of originating a fortune along with those whom he advised ; but, in his disposition calm and philosophical, he kept aloof from the pursuit of wealth, and died, as he had lived, blameless, a man of little worldly ambition, uniting in his character literary and scientific attainments of no ordinary nature with goodness, purity, and simplicity; and what at that time was considered as widely marking him out from other men was the early adherence he gave to the religious doctrines then newly promulgated by Emanuel Swedenborg. So impressed was he by their truth, that so long as his strength permitted he walked each Sunday from Summerseat to Manchester—a distance of fourteen miles—returning the same day, to hear the Rev. John Clowes, Rector of St. John's, Manchester, preach in public the same impressive opinions that had so deeply interested himself.　It may also not be forgotten that, during the closing thirty years of the past century, much obloquy and even bodily ill-treatment was often incurred by those bold enough to give in their adherence to the Swedish seer; old Christopher's ponderous Latin and other books being often spoken of by his country neighbours as "unked"—that is, uncouth, strange.　His residence was the Old Hall, Summerseat.

CHAPTER XIV.

Early History of Prestwich—The Prestwich Poor-law Union—The Charities of Prestwich—Prestwich Schools—The Parish Church of Prestwich—Extracts from the Accounts of St. Mary's Church, Prestwich—The Tablets in Prestwich Parish Church—Mrs. Julia Younge—Rectors of Prestwich—Kirkhams—An Unwelcome Tithe—The Death of Mr. Huskisson—Handsome Presents—Rhodes—Great Heaton—Little Heaton—Prestwich Parish in 1778—Whitefield and Stand, Unsworth—The Dragon of Unsworth.

PRESTWICH.

PRESTWICH is situated almost half way on the highroad between Bury and Manchester. The origin of the knightly family of Prestwich, says Mr. Baines, is lost in remote antiquity, their ancient tenure justifying the opinion that they were seated at Prestwich before the Norman Conquest. A Robert de Prestwich died in or before the 7th John (1206). He was succeeded by his son, Adam de Prestwich, who was probably father to a second and grandfather to a third Adam, whose widow, Alicia, was living in 1325. The second Adam de Prestwich probably married a heiress of the family of Pendlebury, and thus the manor of Wickleswick, in the parish of Eccles, came to the Prestwich family. About 1320, by default of male issue, the Prestwich estates passed in the female line, in marriage, to a branch of the Langleys in Langley, now first settled at Agecroft. A collateral branch of the Prestwich family held the manor of Hulme from 1434 to 1600, when the estate there (mortgaged in 1654) was transferred by Act of Parliament to the Mosleys of Ancoats. In April, 1664, the last male representative of this branch, Thomas Prestwich, Esq., was created a baronet, which title expired with him; at least the baronetcy was declared to be extinct in 1689. Among the inquisitions in the early part of the reign of Elizabeth, there is an imperfect document, without date, taken on the death of Sir Robert Langley, which occurred on the 3rd of September, 1531, and in which Sir Robert is found to have died seised of the manor of Prestwich, the manor of Pendlebury, the manor of Agecroft, together with lands and messuages and other property in Alterington, Tetlowe, Oldham, Crompton, and Manchester. The family continued to reside at Agecroft till the death of Sir Robert Langley, without male issue, when his extensive estates underwent partition amongst his four daughters, one of whom, Anne, marrying William Dauntesey, Esq., of West Lavington, Wilts., conveyed Agecroft into the family. The eldest daughter of Sir Robert Langley married for her second husband, Alexander Reddish, Esq., of Reddish. The issue of this marriage consisted wholly of daughters; one of whom, Sarah, married Clement, the fifth son of Sir Edward Coke, Knight, the celebrated lawyer, and the manor continued in possession of the Cokes of Norfolk till the time of the late Mr. Coke, who, wishing to increase his landed property in Norfolk, sold his possessions in Lancashire, and, amongst his other estates, the manors of Prestwich and Pendlebury, to Peter Drinkwater, Esq.

The parish of Prestwich is about fifteen miles in length and about four in breadth. It is in the hundred of Salford, and in the archdeaconry and rural deanery of Manchester. Much of the land is in pasture, although within the past few years several shops, as well as handsome villa residences, have been erected. The parish includes the townships of Prestwich, Great Heaton, Little Heaton, Tonge-with-Alkrington, Oldham Chapelry, and Pilkington, which includes the hamlets of Whitefield, Outwood, and Unsworth—the hamlet of Whitefield being identical with the new parish of Stand.

The Heaton estates, which are situated in this parish, acquired by the marriage with Margaret, daughter and co-heiress of Sir Robert Langley, passed into the Egerton family, as by a subsequent match did part of those of the Ashtons of Middleton. Heaton House, a seat of the Earl of Wilton, is a handsome modern structure of stone, erected by Wyatt, with columns of the Ionic order, and a circular projection in the centre, surmounted by a spacious dome. This handsome mansion is situated in a verdant and well-wooded park, five miles in circumference, and having an area of 700 statute acres, at the entrance to which is an elegant Doric lodge. At some distance from the house, on a bold eminence, stands a circular temple, commanding extensive views in the four adjoining counties of Cheshire, Derbyshire, Staffordshire, and Yorkshire.

The earliest provision for the aged poor in Prestwich was by paying out of the poor-rates for their board and lodging in the houses of cottagers. In 1716, a plot of land and some cottages at Raineshow were bought for a poor-house; and these cottages were thus used till 1819, when a new workhouse, to accommodate 120 persons, was built on this site. The Prestwich Poor-law Union includes twelve townships, viz., Blackley, Bradford, Beswick, Cheetham, Crumpsall, Failsworth, Harpurhey, Great and Little Heaton, Moston, Newton, and Prestwich. The townships comprising the Prestwich Union were joined to Manchester for poor-law purposes in 1841, and termed the Manchester Union, an arrangement which remained in force until 1850, when the Poor-law Board dissolved the Union, and formed the Prestwich Union, leaving Manchester a single township. In the same year the Guardians of the Union agreed with the Overseers of Prestwich to hire their workhouse at a yearly rental of £70, which workhouse had been unoccupied for a considerable time, the Guardians agreeing to make such alterations as seemed necessary. But the continued increase in the Union up to this time rendered the accommodation inadequate. The Guardians, therefore, early in the month of June, 1865, resolved to build a new workhouse, and finally decided to erect a new building at Crumpsall. The ceremony of laying the corner-stone of it was performed on the 24th of May, 1868, by John Taylor, Esq., who was the Chairman of the Board. The architect was Mr. Worthington, and the contractor Mr. Neill, of Manchester. The site, which is over 20 acres, cost £4,300. The contract was let for £21,773; the foundations cost £3,220; furnishing, purchasing of site, £12,730.

The charities in the parish of Prestwich, as exhibited in the sixteenth report of the commissioners appointed by Parliament for inquiring concerning the charities, are:—Sir Thomas Grey Egerton's charity of £10 a year to the poor of the parish; Elizabeth Bent's charity, lost from neglect; Sir Holland Egerton's charity, the interest of £20 expended in bread for the poor; the Earl of Wilton's charity, the interest of £1,000, distributed in clothing to the poor; Baguley's charity, of the amount of seven guineas per annum, distributed to the poor, principally in clothing; Stand School charity, being a bequest of Henry Siddal, tailor, of Whitefield, of a messuage, with four acres and a half of land, in Whitefield, in the township of Pilkington, towards the endowment of a grammar school; Ringley School, endowed by Nathan Walworth with a messuage and 120 acres of land; James Lancashire's bequest of the sum of £50 to Unsworth School; in 1847, a sum of £212 (the residue of benefactions and donations) was invested in the North-Western Railway consolidation stock, bearing interest at 10 per cent per annum, the interest to be applied for the use of the poor of the parish of Prestwich for ever. In 1848, Mr. Lewis Nóvelli, a resident, left by will to trustees £1,000 to be invested, and the interest to be distributed twice a year by the rector and churchwardens in money, food, or clothing amongst the poor, aged, or sickly inhabitants, attendants of some Protestant church, and not in receipt of parochial relief.

The earliest school in Prestwich was one in Rooden-lane, existing more than 80 years ago. In one room children of both sexes and all ages received instruction, while in an upper room girls were taught needlework; the master lived on the premises; and there was an enclosed playground. To this school Sir Thomas Egerton gave £5 yearly, on condition that eight poor children were taught gratis. About 1811 this building was pulled down, and the school removed to the site known as Lady Wilton's school, on which was then erected the present building for the village school and its teacher. In 1816 a meeting of the inhabitants led to a subscription, which, aided by a grant of £100 from the National Society, amounted to nearly £1,000, and the present school premises were erected that year on a portion of the glebe, chargeable with £5 yearly rent to the rector. The scholars were transferred thither in May, 1817. It had but one room, capable of containing 250 children, under a master; a mistress teaching the girls sewing on Saturdays. In 1817 a partition wall separated boys from girls, the latter having then a regular mistress. The Countess of Wilton's school for girls was maintained, and the girls clothed, at her ladyship's sole expense. Since her death, memorial schools have been built by subscription, bearing her name. In 1840 an infants' school was established by public subscription, but has since been maintained by the Earl. It is in a substantially-built room, capable of holding 200 children.

ST. MARY'S PARISH CHURCH.

The Rev. John Booker, B.A., late curate of Prestwich, has written a somewhat lengthy and interesting history of this ancient edifice. In it Mr. Booker says that this church was included in the return which Pope Nicholas IV. caused to be made in 1288 of a survey of all ecclesiastical benefices in England. The value of the living was then estimated at £18 13s. 4d. per annum, of which sum one-tenth, or £1 17s. 4d., was assigned to King Edward I. In the year 1535, another general valuation was made of Church property in obedience to a royal mandate issued by Henry VIII. The result of that inquiry showed the annual value of the living of Prestwich to be at that time £46 4s. 9½d. It was about the year 1450, as is supposed, that the present structure was built, or nearly a century before the commencement of the Reformation. This latter event necessarily led to a change in the form of worship heretofore prevailing in Prestwich, and to the abolition of a chantry (or chapel endowed for the maintenance of a priest, whose duty it was to daily perform mass for the souls of the founders and such other persons as were specified in the Deed of Endowment) which was established within the church. Queen Mary, in the first year of her reign, restored this abolished chantry, along with twenty-eight others connected with parish churches in Lancashire. At this period of the Church history Prestwich was associated with the name of John Bradford, the martyr, who, in those times of peril, did not shrink from denouncing there, as elsewhere, the attempt to bring England again under Popish subjection. John Bradford was born at Manchester ; qualified in 1548, at Cambridge, for the reception of holy orders ; and was burnt at the stake at Smithfield, June 20, 1555. On the 13th of August, 1557, Prestwich Church was the scene of probably the first ordination that had ever taken place within its walls. The candidates were two in number. One was Mr. John Angier, jun. (son of the celebrated minister of that name at Denton), whose call was to Ringley ; and the other, Mr. William Coulbourn, whose destination was Ellinbrook. The accounts of the churchwardens and overseers of the church commence about the year 1645, and are continued uninterruptedly to the present time. Some of the items in the early accounts are rather amusing, as, for instance, there are the following :—

		s.	d.
1647	Paid maimed soldiers	2	4
—	Paid to little Besse	0	4
1648	Paid to Dennis wife and a lame wench	9	6
1649	Paid to Robert Hunts for a chist (coffin)	4	10
1653	Paid charges about a child left in the lane of our town ...	7	8
1655*	Received of the wife of George Hulton for swearing and other misdemeanour	16	8
1656	Received by Thomas Heawood for the poor of both Heatons at the funeral of my Ladie Stanley	3	9

* Note.—In 1650, an Act was passed entitled " An Act for the better preventinge and suppresienge of the detestable sin of prophane swearing and cursing." The fine to go either wholly or in part to the poor of the parish. The following are some of the provisions of this Act:—1. A record of all convictions to be kept by the Justice of the Peace, and the names of the offenders so convicted to be published quarterly. 2. The penalty attached to be a graduated one, so as not to press too heavily upon the poor man, it is presumed, who might be disposed to indulge. For the first offence: A lord, 30s.; a baronet or knight, 20s.; an esquire, 10s.; a gentleman, 6s. 8d.; all inferior persons, 3s. 4d. For the second offence, double the aforesaid. For the tenth offence, " he or she shall be adjudged a common swearer, or curser, and be bound with sureties for the good behaviour during three years." In default of payment of the fine, the offender to be set in the stocks for three or six hours, according to the frequency or infrequency of previous convictions.

		s.	d.
1656	Paid to ringer November 5th	4	0
—	Paid for a new communion table	12	0
—	Allowed for candles to ring (curfew bell) eight of the clock	3	6
1657	Paid to Robert Ward for killing 130 rooks and crows......	3	4
—	Paid to Daniel Schofield for one fox...........................	1	0
—	Paid to James Barlow for one hedgehog	0	2
—	Paid to short Mary	0	2
— *	Paid to George Milln's son for mossing the church.........	6	8
1658	Paid for an act for the observation of the Sabbath Day ...	0	6
1660	Paid Als Haslame for relief and to the beadle in Manchester when she was in the dungeon	3	4
—	Paid Henry Dolfin's wife for keeping two children of Thomas Johnson's..	20	0
—	Paid for a suit of clothes for the lad...........................	6	0
—	Paid Thomas Heape for drawing the King's arms	40	0
—	Paid ringers on King's (Charles II.) birthday	2	0
1661	Paid two atturnies fees	6	8
—	Paid for 1,100 nails for slater and messenger twice to Manchester...	7	10
—	Paid to Thomas Unsworth for three days' work............	3	0
1662	Paid for a sirplis..	70	0
—	Paid for a linen tablecloth......................................	11	0
—	Paid for making and setting on the fringe	12	0
—	Paid to Ralph Smethurst for writing the Creed, the Lord's Prayer, liming and painting windows	12	0
1663	Paid for a pair of clogs for Allin's child	0	3
—	Paid for a pair of shoes for Richard Allin....................	2	0
—	Paid for swine's grease and salad oil (for the bells)	1	5
1664	Paid for the pulpit cloth and Book of Common Prayer ...	172	0

---

* Rushbearing, a custom yet observed in some parts of Lancashire, was only discontinued about thirty-three years ago in Prestwich. This item of expenditure is of yearly occurrence in the churchwardens' accounts, and is sometimes entered as money paid for "dressinge the church," or "dressinge the church and steeple." It was the ancient practice to decorate the church with garlands, in anticipation of the Wakes Sunday (the Sunday immediately succeeding St. Bartholomew's Day), and to provide a cart upon which had been erected a solid cone or pyramid of rushes adorned with watches, plate, ribbons, and flowers—contributions lent with the utmost willingness on such occasions. On the summit of the pyramid was seated a man decorated with ribbons, &c., and to the cart were yoked twenty or more men similarly habited, who acted also as morris dancers. After the cart had traversed the village, attended by a band of music, and had received its tribute of admiration, it was removed to the churchyard, where it was dismantled, and the rushes strewed on the church floor (a not unnecessary precaution against the dampness of a stone floor then without anything to protect the feet), there to remain until replaced by the next year's succession.

		s.	d.
1665	Paid for the great arke* in Manchester	41	8
—	Paid for fetching the arke to the church	3	0
—	Paid to Richard Haddocke for bands and locks	51	8
—	Paid for seven yards of bease to line the arke	8	8
—	Paid to John Boardman for lineinge the arke	5	10
—	Paid for brasse neales for the arke	2	0
—	Paid for a midwife to Ann Hilton	1	0
1666	Paid to Mr. Weate for weighing a boule (bowl)	0	6
—	Paid to another goldsmith for weighing it	0	4
—	Spent when we went to Manchester to weigh the boule	2	0
1667	Paid charges in going ten several times out of the town upon needful business concerning the town's affairs	5	0
1669	Paid for a warrant for Robert Unsworth and James Rothwell, who denied to view the poor and make the poor book, which afterwards was ordered to a trial at law	2	0
1670	Paid for providing a godfather for a child	1	0
1671	Paid for a cart load of coals	2	8
1672	Paid Dr. Lake (rector) to get the boule changed at York	46	9
—	Paid for a warrant and presentinge of Ege Croft bridge at the quarter sessions	2	6
1673	Paid for ringing at bringing in of Christmas	3	6
1674	Paid for physic for Mary Ogden	0	11
1675	Paid for diet drink and two bottles of ointment for a lame lad, which was laid on the town by an order from the justices	7	9
1678	Paid to Sarah Grant for her pains about the burial of Jacob's children, and for bringing two certificates about the burial in woollen.†		
—	Received from Mr. Foefield for a fine for burying his wife in linen	50	0
1683	Paid to James Jones by justice order who was bitten with a mad dog	16	6

* The Parish Chest, in which the registers of baptisms, marriages, and burials are deposited. It is of oak, firmly put together, and rendered additionally secure by strong iron bands. It has three locks, as prescribed by the Act passed in the first year of Queen Elizabeth. The glories of its green "bease lineinge" are now somewhat faded, but its "brasse neales" are resplendent as ever, untarnished by the lapse of nearly two centuries.

† At this period an Act was in force which provided that at every interment a certificate should be produced, certifying that the winding sheet of the deceased person was composed of woollen material and not of linen, the object of the enactment being "to encourage the woollen manufactures of these kingdoms, and to lessen the importation of linen from beyond the seas." Any infringement of this Act subjected the offending party to a fine of £5, half of which fine was assigned to the poor of the parish.

		s.	d.
1683	Paid to a cripple brought in a barrow	0	3
1684	Paid to ringers at coronation day (James II.)	3	6
1691	[Dec. 17. The Church broken into, and, amongst other things, the pulpit cushion stolen, the offertory money also, from May to December, amounting to £1 4s. 9d., taken away.]		
1692	Paid for going to the assizes about Robert Blackley concerning the breaking of the Church	40	0
1702	Paid for order for changing names in Common Prayer Book (death of William III.)	0	8
1705	Paid for ringing for the news of our victory in Germany (Blenheim)	2	0
1709	Paid to the ringers for victory (Malplaquet)	7	0
1713	Paid for ringing for the news of peace (Treaty of Utrecht)	2	0
1715	Paid for ringing at the landing of King George	3	0
1716	Paid to the ringers for the news from Preston (Defeat of the Pretender)	2	0
1721	Paid to Abraham's Ruddal's order his charges for re-casting the four old bells into five, and adding a sixth new one of his own metal ....£125 1s. 5d.		
—	Paid for carrying the old bells to Salop, and bringing the new bells back ....£16 8s. 6d.		
—	Paid Joseph Wrigley for taking down the old bells and hanging the new ....£38 8s.		
—	Paid for bell ropes, weighing 31lbs., at 6d. per lb.	15	6
—	Paid to a mason his day's wages for viewing the church	1	0
—	March 6, paid when the new bells were first rung	10	0
1728	[A hearse, now first used in Prestwich, bought at a cost of £13 16s. 4d.]		
1730	Paid Milles mare for 60 days' work	60	6
—	Paid for ringing when Unsworth chapel was consecrated	5	0
1732	Paid for a new hood for Rev. Dr. Goodwin	56	6
—	Church pewed at a cost of £74.		
1736	July 18, parishioners resolved to buy a new pulpit cloth and cushion, and to give the old pulpit cloth and cushion to Unsworth chapel for ever ; and also that 13s. a year be given to George Grimshaw, of Roodenlane, for the time being and a new coat (not exceeding 20s.) every other year, for his trouble and pains in wakening sleepers in the church, whipping out dogs, keeping children quiet and orderly, and keeping the pulpit and church walls clean.		
—	Paid for a new pulpit cushion and hangings ......£15 9s.		

		s.	d.
1736	Paid for a new coat for George Grimshaw and a new bobber	20	0
1737	Paid for new Bible (the Church Bible now in use) 120		0
1740	Paid for ringing for the news of taking Porto Bello	2	6
1741	Paid for ringing for the taking of Carthagena (sum not stated).		
1743	Paid for ringing for the victory at Dettingen	2	6
—	Paid for penance form, and mending the wainscot	0	10
1745	Paid for ringing twice for the victory over the Scotch rebels	18	0
1746	Paid for taking off and laying on again the higher roof of the church ....£22 3s.		
1747	Paid for books and orders about infected cattle	12	0
1752	Paid George Grimshaw for making a grave..................	0	2
1759	Paid to the ringers when French ships were taken.........	6	0
—	Paid to the ringers when Quebec was taken	6	0
—	Paid to the ringers when Thurot was defeated	3	0
1761	In this year Sir John Prestwich, of London (claiming to represent the old local family of that name), announced his intention of giving an organ to the church, an offer which led to much dissension among the parishioners, some of whom, regarding the contemplated gift as an innovation on the simplicity of the form of worship heretofore prevailing, would decline it, whilst others as eagerly pressed its acceptance. The matter was referred to the bishop by the lovers of primitive simplicity. Pending the decision it was decided to erect a gallery for the reception of the organ, which, however, never arrived, Sir John having probably withdrawn his offer on finding opinions so much divided.		
—	Tenor bell re-cast by Tyler and Ruddall, of Shrewsbury, the total expenses for the same being £58 19s. 6d.		
1762	Paid for ringing for the taking of Havannah	9	0
—	Paid for spurring book (banns book)	0	8
1763	Meeting at the Osteridge (Ostrich) about building Reignsough [work] house. I spent 2s.		
1764	Paid the expense of taking and wedding Thomas Barlow to Esther Ryle ....£2 11s. 6d.		
1770	Paid for a weathercock, spindle, &c............£19 3s. 9d.		
1777	Paid ringers on taking of Philadelphia......................	21	0
—	Paid for 7800 bricks	93	6
1782	Tower of the church restored at an expense of £18 to the parish, exclusive of Sir Thomas Egerton's contribution.		

s. d.

1791   June 30. Faculty granted to twelve parishioners for erecting a gallery on the north side of the church, 28ft. front by 15ft. at east and 12ft. at west end; to raise the roof of the north aisle, &c.; to sell and dispose of the seats to parishioners resorting to Divine service; an account of the sale to be sent to the court, the parish allowing £10 for the roof.

1797   Paid ringers for ringing for Admiral Duncan's victory...... 5 0

1798   Feb. 14. Resolved at a vestry meeting that the churchyard be forthwith drained, which was accordingly done at an expense of £17 5s. 8d.

1800   March 14. Faculty granted to the Rev. James Lyon and others who had erected (the preceding year) a south-west gallery, 16ft. by 12ft., to let and sell the seats to parishioners for defraying the expenses, the overplus to go in aid of the church rate.

1801   Aug. 14. Faculty granted by Bishop Majendie to Rev. James Lyon to remove the pulpit from south-west end of chancel to the centre and near the east end of chancel. The six additional pews thus secured to be confirmed to the Rev. James Lyon and his successors to set and let to parishioners.

1802   Ringers' wages advanced from £6 to £9 per annum and their duty defined.

1803   The vestry being in a ruinous condition, a new one was erected at a cost of £182 3s. 6d.

1806   Jan. Agreement between Rev. James Lyon, rector, and John Lever, of Alkrington, Esq., for the payment of £1 1s. per annum for allowing the rafters of the gallery above the Lever chapel to rest on the chancel walls.

—   New communion rails..............................£11 6s. 6d.

—   Ringers' wages advanced to £12 per annum.

1810   Church broken into and pillaged.

1811   Oct. 20. At a vestry meeting it was resolved that there shall be a new eight days clock for the church, and that there shall be dial plates or faces on the east, north, and south sides of the steeple. The total cost of the same was £175 10s.

1813   Paid ringers for good news of downfall of Buonaparte... ....£1 10s.

1814   New gates to churchyard provided at a cost of £71 5s. 3d.

1818   Paid ringers at Queen Charlotte's burial for minute bell ....£2 7s.

1820   Paid for black drapery for pulpit, reading desk, etc., on the death of George III........................£11 1s. 8d.

1822   The church again burglariously entered.

1824   April 14. A vestry meeting held to take into consideration the propriety of purchasing and for the extension
of the churchyard. The proposition was unanimously
entertained, and the following year steps were taken to
carry it into effect. A plot of land at the west end of
the church, in extent 3,895 square yards, was purchased
at a cost of £450. The expense of enclosing the entire
graveyard with the present substantial fence amounted
to £415 7s. 5d.; the iron palisades surmounting the
wall, £181 16s. 11d. To meet this and other incidental
expenses it was agreed to borrow the sum of £1,230, to
be repaid from the rates in annual instalments extending
over 20 years, interest meanwhile to be allowed after
the rate of 5 per cent. This debt was extinguished in
1845. At this meeting it was further resolved that a
convenient and commodious approach should be made
to the church, and " that the rector and churchwardens
be requested to close the gates of the churchyard so as
to prevent carriages driving into it, as soon as a proper
approach is made; the land being provided by the
parish, and consequently for the sole purpose of burying
the dead." The church was consecrated in 1827.

1825-6 Subscription entered into for purchasing an organ,
amounting to £1,100. The organ was erected at an
expense of £800; the residue of the subscriptions, with
additions, forming a fund for the future endowment of
an organist.

1837   Rectory-house rebuilt. The cost was defrayed by loan
(under Gilbert's Act) from Queen Anne's bounty, with
additions from private sources, making a total expenditure of not less than £5,000. The amount derived
from Queen Anne's bounty was £2,485, to be repaid
in 30 years.*

1848   Mr. Louis Novelli, an inhabitant of Prestwich, bequeathed
to trustees, for the use of the rectors of Prestwich in
perpetuity, an oil painting, a copy of Raphael's

---

* The old Rectory-house, known, from its situation, as " The Deyne," stood about
midway between the present structure and the entrance gate from the Rectory-lane.
It was interesting from its high antiquity, being built in the post and petrel style,
which ceased in the reign of Henry VIII. or Queen Elizabeth. On its removal
traces were discovered of its having once extended considerably beyond its later
limits. As originally designed it was in the form of a square, or a figure bearing
resemblance to the letter H, cloisters being carried round the several sides of the
edifice. Walker, in his " Sufferings of the Clergy," during the time of the Civil
wars, speaking of the forcible ejection of Mr. Allen from the living of Prestwich,
says:—" They," *i.e.*, the rebels, " pulled down for him ten or fourteen bays of
building." It is probable the damage then sustained was not fully repaired, and
that the house was never restored to its original dimensions.

"Madonna del Seggiola," to be transmitted in succession from rector to rector, and to be preserved in the rectory house.

1849   Oct. 20. Miss Sarah Eleanor Johnson, by codicil to her will, "gives and bequeathes to the Rector of Prestwich for the time being the sum of £50, and to the incumbent of All Saints' Church, Stand, for the time being, the like sum of £50, free of legacy duty, to be laid out in some suitable decoration of the said churches, either in painted window, new font, lectern, or other article to be selected on true Catholic ecclesiastical principles."

1850   The altar-cloth, bearing date 1702, replaced by a handsome crimson velvet covering for the table, the present of Mrs. Drinkwater, of Irwell House.

—   Sept. 15. A special ordination held in Prestwich Church by the Lord Bishop of Manchester, at which priest's orders were conferred upon the Rev. Francis Owston, B.A., of Cath. Hall, Cambridge, who was about to proceed to the Cape.

1851   A general ordination held in Prestwich Church by the Lord Bishop of Manchester.

The earliest patrons of the church on record were the family of Prestwich, resident here as early as the reign of Henry III. In this family the patronage continued until about the year 1320, when the estates of the Prestwich family, together with the advowsons of the church, passed by marriage to the Langleys of Agecroft. In this family it remained until the year 1651, when, upon the death of Sir Robert Langley, of Agecroft Hall, without male issue, his estates were divided amongst his four daughters, the third of whom, Katherine, having married one of the family of Assheton, of Chadderton, received for her share, besides other property, the advowson of Prestwich. With the Asshetons it continued until the year 1710. In that year the Rev. William Assheton, the last male representative of his family, sold it to the Hon. Thomas Watson Wentworth (the purchase money being £1,000 in hand, and £100 per annum for ten years), of Wentworth Woodhouse, in the county of York. In the year 1744, Thomas, Earl of Malton, the only son of Mr. Wentworth, sold the advowson to the Rev. John Griffith, D.D., who became rector here in 1752. In the year 1755, Dr. Griffith sold the advowson to Mr. James Collins, of Knaresborough, who again transferred it, by sale, in the year 1758, to the Rev. Levett Harris. Mr. Harris sold the advowson in 1781 to Mr. Matthew Lyon, of Warrington, whose son, instituted rector on the death of Mr. Harris in 1783, resold it in 1815 to Robert, first Marquis of Westminster. The patronage is now vested in Thomas, Earl of Wilton, second son of the late Marquis of Westminster.

The church, dedicated to St. Mary, is a venerable structure, built of red sandstone of Lancashire, which, being of a soft and friable nature, has in some places become much decayed with the lapse of years. Situated on an eminence overlooking the well-wooded valley of the Irwell, and embosomed in fine old beech trees of about a century's growth, the effect of its noble proportions is greatly heightened. It consists of a nave, chancel, and two side aisles terminating in chapels, a tower, and south porch. The style is that of the Florid or Perpendicular, the latest of the pure Gothic styles, which prevailed between the years 1460 and 1540. The chapels are of a later period, and partake more or less of the debased character. Of the date of these it is not easy to speak with any degree of accuracy, although it cannot fall much short of the date assigned to the main structure of the church itself. The Rev. Canon Raines, in his notes to Bishop Gastrell's *Notitia Cestriensis*, speaks of the existence of the chapels as early as 1561, when, on the death of Sir Robert Langley, they passed in marriage with the daughters and co-heiresses of Sir Robert; the one now known as the Wilton Chapel (with the advowson of the church) to James Assheton, Esq., of Chadderton, and the other, since designated the Lever Chapel, to James Legh, Esq., who had settled at Alkrington; which latter, on the sale of the estate about 1630, was conveyed to John Lever, Esq., and by his descendant, Darning Rasbotham, Esq., was sold in 1844 to Messrs. Lees, of Clark's Field, Oldham. The chapels, therefore, it will be seen, lay claim to a considerable antiquity. The tower of the church is 19 feet square, and supported by buttresses; the body of it is of four heights or storeys, with an embattled parapet, and surmounted by a vane. The first or basement storey constitutes the principal entrance to the church; the second storey is where the ringers assemble. Above this is a small chamber, from which a narrow passage leads to the roof of the church. The upper, or fourth storey, contains the bells, which are six in number. The height of the tower, from the base to the top of the parapet, is 86 feet. Originally it was surmounted by pinnacles springing from the angles and also from the centre of each parapet; but during some repairs (probably in 1782) these were taken down, and have not since been replaced. The interior of the church contains a few monuments, but none of them are of very great interest. In a vault in the chancel, adjoining the grave of the Rev. Isaac Allen, are deposited the remains of the Rev. James Lyon, a late rector. His monument is affixed to a pillar in the chancel to the left of the pulpit, and was originally designed to commemorate the fiftieth anniversary of his incumbency. It is of white marble, executed by Sievier, at a cost of £250. The lower division contains a number of elaborately-chiselled figures represented as communicants in the act of receiving the Holy Sacrament or Lord's Supper. Above is a bust of Mr. Lyon. The inscription runs thus :—

On the twenty-second day of March
MDCCCXXXIII
The Reverend JAMES LYON MA
Of Brazenose College Oxford
Completed the FIFTIETH YEAR of his resident Incumbency as Rector of this Parish
In commemoration of which event
and in testimony of the affectionate regard and attachment of his Parishioners
THIS TABLET
Erected by Public Subscription is placed here to record their estimation of
a character Distinguished alike for simplicity of manners, integrity
of principle, and the peaceful and consciensious discharge
of his duties as a CHRISTIAN PASTOR.

A stone on the floor of the church, near the reading desk, marks the grave of a former curate of the parish :—

Here are interred the remains of the Rev. JACOB SCHOLES, M.A., the beloved Curate of Prestwich above 61 years. He was buried here June 12, 1754, in the 85th year of his age.

Entering the church by the south-west door, immediately to the right, and at the foot of the stairs leading to the gallery, is the grave of Thomas Henshaw, the benevolent founder of the Blind Asylum in Manchester and the Blue Coat School in Oldham, in which latter town he resided, carrying on the business of a hat manufacturer. By his will, bearing date November 14, 1807, he bequeathed £20,000 for the endowment of a Blue School in Oldham, and the same amount for the endowment of a Blind Asylum in Manchester. By a codicil to the will, dated January 9, 1808, he bequeathed £20,000 more to the Blue Coat School. In 1828, when the sums left to these charities had accumulated to £100,000, steps were first taken to carry into effect the provisions of the will. He was interred March 4, 1810, in the grave of the Taylors, of Crumpsall, his relatives.

The Wilton Chapel, situated on the north side of the chancel, is the burial place of the family of the Earl of Wilton, and contains several memorials. The most conspicuous of these is a monument surmounted by the family arms sculptured in white marble, and bearing the following inscription :—

Sacred to the memory of
The Earl and Countess of Wilton.

In a Vault beneath in this Chapel are deposited the remains of Thomas, Earl of Wilton, Viscount and Baron Grey de Wilton, and Baronet. He died on the 23rd of September, 1814, in the 65th year of his age. Prior to his elevation to the Peerage, as Sir Thomas Egerton, Baronet, he was representative of the County of Lancaster in three successive Parliaments; and being distinguished by the peculiar regard and esteem of his Sovereign, George the Third, was in the year 1784 freely and unsolicitedly raised to the Peerage by the title of Baron Grey de Wilton, being the title of a maternal ancestor in the reign of James the First; and in the year 1801 was created Viscount Grey de Wilton and Earl of Wilton. The deceased Earl was eminently correct in his observance of every religious and social duty, zealously attached to his king and country, peculiarly attentive to the calls of charity, and ready to do every good work. On different occasions, during times of disturbance and danger, he quitted the enjoyment of his peaceful habits and domestic quiet for the troubles and anxieties of a military life, both in England and Ireland, as Colonel of a regiment of Royal Lancashire Volunteers, whose services were no less useful and important to the country than honourable to himself and to those under his command.

In the same Vault are deposited the remains of the Relict of the deceased Earl, Eleanor, Countess of Wilton, daughter and co-heiress of Sir Ralph Assheton, of Middleton, Baronet. She died on the 3rd of February, 1816, in the 67th year of her age, not less distinguished than her departed Lord by her strict attention to every religious and moral duty, and actuated by the same principle of doing good.

Deceased children of the Earl and Countess of Wilton.

Frances Egerton, born in 1774, died an infant.

Thomas Grey Egerton, born in 1777, died an infant.

Both deposited in the vault beneath.

Also Louisa Egerton, born in 1772, died an infant.

Thomas Grey Egerton, born December 21, 1780, died Dec. 21, 1793.

Frances Mary Egerton, born Sept. 4, 1788, died Oct. 4, 1796.

These three deposited in Grosvenor Chapel, London.

The Lady Amelia, only daughter of the Earl and Countess Grosvenor, who died at Heaton House, on the 27th of March, 1814, in the 12th year of her age, is likewise deposited in this vault.

This monument was erected by the daughter and only surviving issue of the deceased Earl and Countess, the Countess Grosvenor; a tribute of affection for her family, and of respect for the memory of her beloved parents.

Another tablet on the east side is thus inscribed :—

Near this place are deposited the remains
of Sir Thomas Grey Egerton, Bart.,
who departed this life at his seat at Heaton
in this parish, July 8, 1756, in the 35th year of his age.
He was a person of unblemished Honour and Integrity
and served the Publick in several capacities
with Fidelity and Reputation.
In the year 1747 he was chosen one of the Representatives
of the Borough of Newton in this County,
and at the end of that Parliament was importuned
to accept the same Trust again,
But, preferring the satisfaction of a private station,
declined it and retired to his country seat,
where he made great improvements, and lived
Usefully, Hospitably, and Charitably
amongst his neighbours.
To the needy and distressed he was a constant Friend,
relieving them liberally whilst he lived
and perpetuating his bounty by considerable Appointments
at his Death.
He was happy in his Fortune, his Family, and his Friends,
and blest with such a share of Health as might flatter him
with the Prospect of a long enjoyment of these Blessings ;
But alas ! (so precarious and uncertain is human Happiness)
he was but off in the midst of these pleasing circumstances,

and at an age which is best suited to the enjoyment of them;
He dyed however totally resigned to the Divine Will,
with God, with man, and with himself at Peace.
He took to wife Katharine one of the daughters of the Revd.
John Copley, late Fellow of the Collegiate Ch. of Manchester,
and Rector of Thornhill, in Yorkshire, and by her
had two sons, one of which only survived him.
His mournful Widow erected this monument
as a sincere Testimony of her Affection
and Regard to his memory.
Underneath also lie the remains of Dame Katharine Egerton,
Relict of Sir Thomas Grey Egerton, Bart. and mother of the present
Lord Grey de Wilton. Died May 24, 1791, aged 70 years.

The Lever Chapel is situated on the south side of the chancel, and contains many memorials of the Levers of Alkrington.

The church also contains, among others, memorials of the family of Milne, of Prestwich-wood.

The most ancient memorial in the churchyard is a rudely-sculptured stone, bearing the date 1641. At the south-east corner of the church, beneath the shade of a spreading tree, are deposited the remains of Julia, wife of Charles Mayne Young, the celebrated comedian. The deceased lady accompanied her husband in 1806 on a professional tour through the provinces, and spent a few days in Manchester. She visited Prestwich, and was much charmed with the picturesque beauty of the churchyard, marking one particular spot as, to her mind, more beautiful than the rest. Short as was their stay she lived not to quit Manchester, and her remains are now deposited in the quiet of the grave which she had so lately indicated. In the yard there is also a monument to the memory of the late John Brooks, Esq., of Manchester. It is of beautiful design, and made of granite and white marble. It cost about £3,000.

RECTORS OF PRESTWICH.

RALPH LANGLEY.—He was the first rector of whom any information has been obtained. He was the second son of Sir Robert Langley, of Agecroft, whose family, as before stated, were patrons of the living of Prestwich for many years, and are said to have erected the present church. Was rector of the parish as early as 1428, to which he had been advanced by the patronage of his father. In 1454 he leased all the tithes, oblations, and emoluments (except the glebe land and the free rents) belonging to the Parochial Chapel of Oldham to Sir Henry Pendlebury, Priest of the chantry of Middleton, for the term of three years, at an annual rent of 43 marks (£28. 13s. 4d.). In 1465 he was elected warden of the College of Manchester, then lately established. In 1481 he exchanged the wardenship of

Manchester for the Prebendal stall of Finsbury in the Cathedral Church of St. Paul's. He died in 1490, and was buried at Prestwich.

THOMAS LANGLEY.—Rector in 1507, and still rector in 1515, but no further information respecting him is extant.

SIR WILLIAM LANGLEY.—Rector in 1535, and still rector in 1561. Further information with regard to him, like his predecessor, unobtainable. He died probably in 1569, for it appears, from the Book of Presentations in the Diocesan Court at Chester, that in that year his heir was presented to the living. The prefix, " Sir," was a common term of courtesy formerly applied to priests.

SIR WILLIAM LANGLEY.—Nominated July 8, 1569, on the presentation of James Assheton, of Chadderton; resigned 1611; buried at Prestwich in 1613. This is the earliest presentation to the living contained in the Diocesan records at Chester.

JOHN LANGLEY, M.A.—Nominated May 10, 1611; died rector 1632; buried at Prestwich.

ISAAC ALLEN succeeded Mr. Langley immediately. He lived in times of great confusion and insecurity, arising from the politico-religious changes which then agitated the land—the overthrow of the monarchy and the establishment of a Commonwealth—and his attachment to the Episcopacy and his love of order drew down upon him the disapprobation of those who held opposite opinions, and who then formed the dominant party. At the commencement of the civil wars, Presbyterian opinions were rapidly gaining an ascendancy, and Prestwich did not escape the notice of the self-constituted authorities who now assumed the office and exercised the functions of the deposed bench of bishops. For some time Mr. Allen kept possession of his church with the concurrence of a large majority of his parishioners, disputing the competency of the tribunal which summoned him to Manchester to make restitution. In 1644, the Presbyterian cause having become supreme in authority, and the times being such as to sanction the use of almost any means, however arbitrary and unjust, for the attainment of a desired end, the forcible ejectment of Mr. Allen was obtained; the Rectory-house was assailed, and a portion of it demolished; and the Rector himself seized upon and removed to Manchester, where he suffered a term of imprisonment. After his discharge, an attempt was made by his friends to secure his appointment to the parochial chapelry of Oldham, but the effort was unsuccessful. Having, therefore, no resources, he betook himself to Ripponden, in Yorkshire, where he supported himself as best he could in the exercise of his ministry, which appears, from the testimony of Mr. Oliver Heywood, not to have been unsuccessful. He speaks of him at this time as " old Mr. Allen, who had been parson of Prestwich, a solid, substantial preacher, who had been turned out in the war-time for not taking the covenant. He found shelter there ; they loved him well." Meanwhile, the vacated living of Prestwich was filled by several incumbents in rapid succession. A Mr. Langley, a Mr. Porter, and a Mr. Brierley seem to have obtained a temporary settlement here until, in the year 1646, it was conferred upon

TOBY FURNESS. He was a thorough Presbyterian, and met with little sympathy from his congregation, in which the Episcopalians greatly outnumbered their opponents. He was seldom absent from the Classis in Manchester, to which Prestwich belonged. In September, 1648, notice was given in the Parish Church at Prestwich that Mr. Furness having a call to Burie, desireth dismission from the Classis from Manchester. No adverse opinion being expressed, his wish was acceded to; " the Classis granted him dismission from Prestwich, with a desire that God would bless him in his removal." Strenuous efforts were put forth to recall Mr. Furness, but they were in vain, and towards the close of July, 1650, steps were taken to provide a successor. A public fast was held in Prestwich at the request of the inhabitants. The Rev. Richard Hollinworth preached, the Rev. John Angier and the Rev. William Walker prayed; after which they proceeded to confer with the inhabitants, but with no result. In the month of August the attempt was renewed. The same clergy were again deputed to confer with the parishioners ; their entreaty seems to have prevailed, and Mr. John Lake was installed preacher of God's Word at Prestwich. Scarcely had he accepted the charge than he found himself at variance with his patrons, and he removed to the Parochial Chapel of Oldham. Again a public fast was decreed for Prestwich (March 12, 1651), " on the ground of the great and crying sinns of the tymes, the heavy judgments of God upon us, and hanginge over our heads, and the generell sensilesness of people under both sin and judgment." In 1652, however,

NATHANIEL RATHBAND was nominated to the oversight of the parish. The sturdy opposition of the parishioners to Presbyterian rule was in no way relaxed, and in 1656 or 1657 he resigned. The Presbyterian Assembly then suffered itself to be drawn into a written controversy with the Episcopalians ; terms of agreement between the contending parties were drawn up ; Mr. Allen was recalled from his banishment, probably in 1658, and was reinstated in the living, which he continued to hold until his death, which took place in 1660. He was buried in the chancel of the church.

EDWARD KENYON.—Instituted to the Rectory by Edward Assheton, Esq., in 1660. Died 1668.

JOHN LAKE.—Instituted in 1668 ; resigned 1684.

WILLIAM ASSHETON, B.D.—Became Rector in 1685, on the presentation of his father, James Assheton, Esq., of Chadderton. In 1718 he contributed the sum of £200 to Shaw chapel, in the parish of Prestwich, to meet a grant of £200 from the Governors of Queen Anne's bounty. In the following year he gave £200 to Ringley chapel, also in the parish of Prestwich, to meet a grant of equal amount from the Governors of Queen Anne's bounty. In 1725 he united with the Rev. James Banks, Rector of Bury, in a benefaction of £200 to meet a grant of a like amount from the Governors of Queen Anne's bounty, for the augmentation of the perpetual curacy of Holcomb, in the parish of Bury. He died Feb. 25, 1731, aged 82 years, and was buried in his own chapel in Prestwich Church.

RICHARD GOODWIN, D.D.—Presented to the living on Mr. Assheton's death, by the Hon. Thomas Wentworth, and was rector until 1752. In 1732 he gave £200 to Shaw Chapel, to meet a like grant from the Governors of Queen Anne's bounty.

JOHN GRIFFITH, D.D.—In 1744 he purchased the advowson of Prestwich, being then rector of Eckington, in the county of Derby, and was inducted Nov. 11, 1752. He retained these livings till his death in 1763.

LEVETT HARRIS, M.A.—In 1756 he became curate of Prestwich, where he remained for two years. In 1758 he purchased the advowson of Prestwich, and was instituted to it in December, 1763. He died December, 1782.

JAMES LYON, M.A.—Ordained in 1781 to the curacy of Prestwich ; instituted to the living on the presentation of his father, March 22, 1783. In 1833, having completed the fiftieth year of his incumbency, the event was celebrated by a jubilee. He died Aug. 13, 1836, aged 79, and is buried in the chancel of the church.

THOMAS BLACKBURNE, M.A.—Presented in 1836 to the living by the Earl of Wilton, receiving also at the same time the appointment of Domestic Chaplain to his patron. He died August 5, 1847.

JOHN RUSHTON, D.D.—In 1825 he was ordained to the curacy of

Langton, in the parish of Blackburn; 1825, appointed incumbent of Newchurch in Pendle ; 1843, the archdeaconry of Manchester was conferred upon him ; 1849, created honorary canon of Manchester.

KIRKHAMS.

A portion of Prestwich is called " Kirkhams." It takes its name from a person named Kirkham, and his house, which still bears the designation of " Kirkham's house," was erected by him in 1733. He was church-warden for Prestwich in 1752, and died in 1768. He was interred within the church, near the font.

AN UNWELCOME TITHE.

When the Rev. Thomas Blackburn, M.A., was rector of Prestwich, a rather amusing incident took place at a christening in the church. The father of the child was Mr. William Chapman, of Pendlebury, and after the worthy rector had performed the ceremony he was asked by Chapman if he did not accept tithes, or a tenth part of a man's possession. The rector replied that he did. " Then," said Chapman, " this is my tenth child—a tenth part of my possessions—take it as a tithe." It is almost needless to say that such a tithe was not accepted, but Chapman's wit saved the christening dues, the clergyman declining to take them.

THE DEATH OF MR. HUSKISSON.—HANDSOME PRESENTS.

The particulars of the lamentable accident which resulted in the death of Mr. William Huskisson, at the opening of the railway between Manchester and Liverpool, in 1830, are too well known to call for repetition here, but one or two incidents which took place after Mr. Huskisson's death, and which are connected with that event, are unknown to many. After the accident, Mr. Huskisson was conveyed to the residence of the Rev. Thomas Blackburn, who was the vicar of Eccles, and here it was that Mr. Huskisson breathed his last. In consideration of the care, kindness, and attention manifested by Mrs. Blackburn towards Mr. Huskisson, Mrs. Huskisson presented to that lady a Bible printed throughout in gold. If possible, a still more valuable present awaited Mr. Blackburn ; for, in a great measure owing to his kindness to Mr. Huskisson, he was presented by Thomas, Earl of Wilton, in September, 1836, with the living of Prestwich Church. As Vicar of Eccles the Rev. T. Blackburn had been in receipt of about £500, but by the presentation made to him by the Earl of Wilton he came into possession of no less than an income of £2,400. The Earl of Wilton was present at the Rev. T. Blackburn's residence when Mr. Huskisson died.

RHODES.

The late Mr. Thomas Barritt, the antiquary, gives the following account of Rhodes:—" In Prestwich parish is a place called The Rhodes, where there is an old hall nearly surrounded with a moat. This appears to have been long ago the seat of some old family of note, but of what name I cannot learn. There is, however, a tradition in that neighbourhood that the first Earl of Derby had lands given him in Lancashire by his stepson, Henry VII., that belonged to gentry in this county; particularly in Broughton, Pilkington, Prestwich, Bury, and Chetham. The owners of these estates, not taking the part of Henry, were by him outlawed, and were driven from their homes by the Earl of Derby. Amongst them was Sir John Chetham, of Chetham, whose seat was at what is now called Peel, a little beyond Scotland Bridge, Manchester. His house was razed. . . . This land is now owned by the present Earl of Derby (1780), who likewise owns one-half of Rhodes estate, and one-half of the old hall; which is now divided into two dwellings. On a chimneypiece in one of the old parlours is observed the letters ' H. P.,' which recalled to memory that this house was once the residence of the Prestwich family of Prestwich, one of which family founded Prestwich Church. All or great part of this estate was sold by the sequestrators in the time of the civil war in the reign of Charles I., and one-half was bought by a Mr. Fox, whose family hath lived there till very lately. But after the Restoration, Charles, Earl of Derby, son of that Earl who was beheaded at Bolton, laid claim to the share that Mr. Fox had bought, who was determined to keep his purchase. The Earl, on finding this, had recourse to the following stratagem: It was pretended that two oxen had been stolen from Knowsley; but they were privily conveyed one night into the shippon of Mr. Fox, who was seized on as the thief, and threatened with being sent to prison. Mr. Fox, knowing his innocence, and that the charge was a juggle, was willing to go to prison; but the persons sent by the Earl, and instructed how to proceed, finding this, offered him the Earl's pardon on condition that he would deliver up the land, which Mr. Fox still refused, and persisted in going to prison. But when he had got a little from home, his wife and children followed, and persuaded him to hearken to the terms proposed by the Earl's servants, who then offered him his release upon these terms: That the Earl should receive again the estate, and Mr. Fox still continue thereon and become the Earl's tenant, and, paying rent for the same, continue, he and his heirs, tenants for ever; which place they now enjoy."

GREAT HEATON.

Nearly the whole of this township, which was formerly called Heaton Reddich, belongs to the Earl of Wilton, and it contains Heaton House, already mentioned. About half of the land of the township is enclosed within the park wall. In 1851 the township had in it neither church, chapel, school, public-house, beerhouse, nor provision shop. Here there has been a gradual decrease of the population owing to the throwing of small farms into one, and to the declension of hand-loom weaving, which used to be carried on to a considerable extent. A legacy of £10 was left by John Wolstenholme to the poor of this township, the interest of which is yearly given in linen cloth to poor persons not receiving weekly or constant parish relief. The "Heaton Charity" consists of the interest of £20 to be expended in bread, left by Sir Holland Egerton in 1730; the interest of £200 left by Sir Thomas Grey Egerton, in 1756; and the interest of £1,000 left by the late Earl of Wilton in 1814. This charity is yearly dispensed at Heaton House at Christmas time.

LITTLE HEATON.

In this township, which was formerly known as Heaton Fallowfield, stood the Old Hall of the Heaton branch of the Hollands, a half timbered house long since removed. About half the land in this township belongs to the Earl of Wilton, whose maternal grandfather, the first Earl, increased the estate by about 100 acres. In 1848, and for twelve years previously, there was no school here, or in Great Heaton, as before mentioned, though the population in that year was about 1,000. In May, 1848, a school was begun in a cottage-room; and in 1850 a commodious school-house, capable of containing 130 children, was erected at the sole cost of the late Countess of Wilton, and the school transferred thither in the month of June of that year. An evening school for adults was also opened, and a Sunday school, in connection with St. Margaret's Church, is well attended.

From an account of the state of the parish delivered by the rector to the Bishop of Chester at his visitation nearly one hundred years ago, namely, in 1778, we learn that the parish then contained 13 hamlets, about 3,500 houses, and that its chief resident families were those of James Starkey, Esq., of Polefield; Sir Thomas Egerton, Bart., of

Heaton ; Sir Watts Horton, Bart., of Chadderton ; Ashton Lever, Esq., of Alkrington ; Robert Radcliffe, Esq., of Foxdenton ; and Joseph Pickford, Esq., of Royton. There were about 200 families of Presbyterians in the parish, 150 Methodists, three or four Quakers, a Dissenting meeting-house at Stand (now Unitarian), and a Methodist Chapel in Oldham. There were then seven Episcopal chapels in the parish, and at Stand there was a Dissenting grammar school, endowed by Mr. Siddall, of Whitefield, with two old cottages and about two acres of land, worth then about £7 yearly. This charity was left only to encourage a grammar schoolmaster to reside, consequently no scholars were taught free. In 1778, Mr. John Pope, minister of the Gospel, was the master. Amongst the most important local families must be first named the Hollands of Heaton, ancestors of the Earl of Wilton, a family which long occupied the Old Hall at Little Heaton ; another branch residing at Rhodes, and another at Clifton. The family claim descent from Sir Stephen, son of Sir Stephen, son of Sir Otho Holland, lord of Skevington, co. Lincoln, *temp.* Edward the Confessor ; the places called Holland, both in Lincolnshire and Lancashire, being ancient possessions of this family. In the reign of John the line divided, and in the elder branch a succession of knights continued till the reign of Henry VII. The Sir Robert Holland who was secretary to the Earl of Lancaster, whom the people slew for his treachery in October, 1328, was of the second line, and his fifth son, Sir William Holland, was the progenitor of the Hollands of Denton, from whom branched the Hollands of Clifton, and those of Sutton, near Prescot, and those of Rhodes. The Hollands of Heaton are supposed to derive descent from Alan, a sixth son of the above Sir Robert, but it is probable that they are of the Denton branch. The most distinguished member of this branch of the family was Colonel Richard Holland, the Parliamentary governor of Manchester in the civil war, in which, in the siege of Manchester, the storm of Preston, and the siege of Lathom House, he took a prominent part. The Heaton estates remained in the family of Holland till 1684, when, by failure of male issue, the property passed to the Egertons, on the marriage of Sir John Egerton (third baronet) with Elizabeth, sister and sole heiress of Edward Holland, Esq., of Heaton and Denton. The Prestwiches of Prestwich and the Langleys of Agecroft have already been alluded to. The Levers of Alkrington claim their descent from Levingus de Leaver (near Bolton), living about the time of the Norman Conquest. The Alkrington estates, in the parish of Prestwich, came into the possession of the Lever family about 1630, by purchase from the Legh family, and from that time Alkrington formed their residence till the extinction of the Lever family about 1840. The Tonges of Tonge, in this parish, derive their descent from Thomas de Tonge, son of Alice de Wolveley, herself the heiress of the family of Prestwich.

WHITEFIELD—STAND.

The hamlet of Whitefield or Stand is situated about three miles from Bury, and contains a considerable number of cottages, shops, and better class dwellings. Its sanitary and other matters are arranged by a Local Board of Health.

At Stand is the Old Hall of the Pilkingtons, forming the Stand in the park, from whence the place derives its name. According to tradition, the hall was originally a storey higher than at present, with a flat roof, for the purpose of viewing the hunting below.

Upon a rising piece of ground stands All Saints' Church, which can be seen for several miles, owing to the commanding position it occupies. The first stone of the erection was laid by the Earl of Wilton, on the 3rd of August, 1822, and the building was consecrated by Dr. Blomfield, then Bishop of Chester, Sept. 8, 1826. The style of architecture is gothic, of the fourteenth century. The church contains a nave and side aisles, with spacious galleries round three of its sides; and at the west end of the nave is an open arcade, with noble arched entrances, from which a lofty tower, enriched with turrets and pinnacles, rises to the height of 186 feet from the ground. The entire accommodation of the interior consists of 1,836 sittings, 978 of which are free or open seats for the use of the poor. The entire cost of the building was £14,987 4s. The Earl of Derby gave the site of the church, and he also gave the land for the parsonage-house, which is a neat structure near to the church, erected at the sole expense of James Ramsbotham, Esq., of Stand, who liberally annexed it to the church for ever.

The late Rev. Richard Slate, of Preston, was formerly pastor of Stand Independent Church, and in 1810 he founded a school there in connection with the place of worship. In the time of his successor, the Rev. James Deakin, the rooms were enlarged. In the early part of 1866, as the school premises were not large enough to meet the requirements, a movement was made for the erection of new schools. On the 23rd of June of that year the corner-stone of the schools was laid by Thomas Barnes, Esq., who was then member for Bolton. The erection of the minister's house was also commenced at the same time, adjacent to the school. The whole buildings, which cost about £1,500, were erected from designs prepared by Mr. Maxwell, of Bury.

UNSWORTH.

The hamlet of Unsworth is situated about three and a half miles from Bury. The principal place of worship is St. George's Church, of which the Rev. B. Crompton is the minister. It was rebuilt in 1843. In 1846, a chapel was erected by the Wesleyan Methodists; and in the same year a National School was established.

Some of the families resident in Unsworth have long been noted for their longevity. In one week in November, 1857, three persons were interred in the churchyard here, whose united ages amounted to 240 years. They were the remains of John Bradbury, aged 78; James Whitworth, 84; and Thomas Holt, 78. The ages also of the late schoolmaster, clerk, sexton, and leading singer are very remarkable. The following is extracted from their respective tombstones:—James Greaves, schoolmaster, of Unsworth, aged 87 years; Sarah Greaves, his wife, 90 years; Ann Greaves, his sister, 87 years; Benjamin Greaves, his son, 81 years; Ann Greaves, his daughter, 83 years; James Greaves, late clerk of Unsworth Church, 83 years; John Fletcher, singer, of Unsworth Church, 86 years.—(John Fenton, sexton, cut the above in his 86th year.) The following two verses are on the gravestone of John Fletcher:—

> Full seventy years that's past and gone
> I was a singer here;
> But now I have my place resigned,
> It plainly doth appear.
>
> My motive thus for singing here
> Was only that of love;
> And now I am no more with you,
> I hope to sing above.

On the 20th June, 1873, the remains of Prudence Walker, of Gravel Mill, Unsworth, were interred in the graveyard attached to the Parish Church, Prestwich. She was the wife of James Walker, farmer, and was in the 79th year of her age. Prudence Walker was one of an old Unsworth family, whose names and ages are as follows :—Betty, eldest sister, still living, aged 92 years ; Nanny (sister), aged 83 years, mother of the late Thomas Wroe. The last mentioned family have long been known on account of the musical talents which they possessed. The other members of the deceased's family were Betty, now dead, aged 85, and Mary, aged 76, and Joseph, aged 73. Very few persons can boast of belonging to a family noted for such longevity, living or dead, as could the deceased, whose remains now repose over those of her mother, who departed this life at the age of 88 years. The deceased enjoyed good health up to within about two years before her death, when she accidentally fell down the bedroom stairs, by which her system received such a shock that all medical skill to prolong her life was in vain. She was born and lived during the whole of her life under a thatched roof, was never in a railway train, and never saw the sea.

In a recent edition of "Lancashire Legends," by the late John Harland, F.S.A., and T. T. Wilkinson, F.R.A.S., &c., the following account is given of the Dragon of Unsworth:—" Traditions respecting the ravages formerly made by the so-called dragons occur in many counties. Yorkshire has claimed the legend of the Dragon of Wantley, and Lambton Worm has rendered the county of Durham famous. One of the most noted dragon stories of Lancashire has its locality assigned to Unsworth, a small village or hamlet about three miles from Bury. The principal mansion in this village is occupied by a lineal descendant of the ancient family of Unsworth, who probably derived their name from the homestead they have so long occupied. The house contains little worthy of notice; but it has long been famous for containing an ancient carved oak table and panel connected with a legend attaching to the family. It is said that Thomas Unsworth was the owner of this property when the district was devastated by an enormous dragon, which was not content with its ordinary fare, but proceeded to swallow up the women and children. The scales of this dragon were so hard and firmly set, that bullet shots by the guns of those days took no effect upon the monster; and the owner of Unsworth, finding this the case, loaded his gun with his dagger, and mortally wounded the dragon under the throat, as it was raising its head to rush at its assailant. The table is said to have been constructed after this event, and was partly carved by the dagger which had destroyed the reptile. The carvings on the table and panel are somewhat curious. One is a representation of St. George and the Dragon, another contains rude figures of the Eagle and Child, a third the Lion and Unicorn, and a fourth of the Dragon of Unsworth. The crest of the family consists of a man in black armour holding a battle-axe in one hand; and tradition states that this is a portrait of Thomas Unsworth, in the dress he wore at the time of the conflict. What may have given rise to the legend it is quite impossible to determine; but an estate was once granted to a member of this family for some important military service, and this may have had something to do with its origin. There are several carvings of the dragon in the possession of the family. One of these resembles a long serpent, with the head and wings of a sphinx; another represents the monster as a serpent in folds, with stings at the ends of tongue and tail. The initials C. V., under the head of one of the figures, serve to indicate that the carvings have been executed for one of the owners of the mansion."

CHAPTER XV.

Early History of Heywood—Peter Heywood and the Gunpowder Plot—Heywood Hall—The Progress of Manufactories in Heap—Railway and Canal Traffic—The Mechanics' Institution—The Places of Worship in Heywood—The Heywood Magistracy—The Rise and Progress of Congregationalism in Heywood—Early History of Bamford—Peacock Hall—Bury Improvement Commissioners since 1846.

HEYWOOD.

HEYWOOD is in the township of Heap, in the parish and manor of Bury, from which it is distant about three miles. Heap is bounded on the north by Birtle-cum-Bamford, on the south by Pilsworth and Hopwood, and partly by Unsworth, on the west by Bury, and on the east by Bamford, Castleton, and Hopwood. In the earliest known mention of Heap the place is termed "Hep," which is supposed to imply a tract of country overgrown with hawthorn berries. The name might arise from the unevenness of the surface, "Heep" (Saxon) indicating a mass of irregularities. This part of the country, in the remote times of the Britons and Romans, consisted almost wholly of deep thickets and heathy fields. The first settled inhabitants were, for the most part, the Saxons; they cleared the ground of its excess of native timber, and commenced an extensive cultivation of the soil. Heap was doubtless inhabited by at least one Saxon family, whose descendants, it is probable, quietly conformed to Norman rule. In that era, or perhaps earlier, the place was annexed to the lordship and church of Bury. The local family of Hep, or Heap, has been extinct a considerable time. No important events occurred to the early possessors of Heap for several centuries; the district progressed slowly in the amount of its population and the extent of its cultivated land, yet there was not even a group of houses, for the homesteads were far apart from each other, generally erected in sheltered spots, by the sides of the woods and on the banks of rivulets; then it was that a large portion of this part of the county abounded in scenes of rural beauty, from the intermixtnre of groves and lawns, in a state of almost native wildness.

There were in the township, in the fifteenth century, several closes, or heys, of land around a wood, not far from the centre; hence originated the name of Heywood. A few houses were shortly afterwards erected, and they received the designation of Heywood. For many generations a family bearing the name flourished here; but they were never of much note in county genealogy, though more than one were active in public affairs. The name of Robert de Heywoode occurs in the year 1492; and in the reign of Elizabeth, Edmund Heywood, Esq., was required by an order, dated 1574, to furnish a coate of plate, a long bowe, sheffe of arrows, steel cap, and bill, for the military musters. James Heywood, gent., was living before 1604.

It may not generally be known, even in Lancashire, that one of the main contributors to the discovery of the conspirators implicated in the gunpowder treason was Peter Heywood. Yet this was so; for Heywood is the birthplace and was the country residence of the zealous Lancashire magistrate, Peter Heywood, of whom an account is given in Lord Clarendon's History of the Great Rebellion. He was a native and resident of Heywood Hall, which was erected during the sixteenth century. It is said that he apprehended Guido Faux coming forth from the vault of the House of Parliament on the eve of the gunpowder treason, November 5, 1605. He probably accompanied Sir Thomas Kneuett, in his search of the cellars under the Parliament House. Mr. Heywood narrowly escaped assassination at a subsequent period, by the hand of a frantic Dominican friar, for urging " poor Catholics" to take the oath of allegiance and supremacy. The renowned historian, Stove, thus writes :—" In the late built church of St. Ann's, Aldersgate-street, London, is one flat stone in the chancel laid over Peter Heiwood, that deceased Nov. 2, 1701, youngest son of Peter Heiwood, one of the Councellours of Jamaica, by Grace, daughter of Sir John Muddeford, Knight and Bart., great grandson of Peter Heiwood, of Heiwood, in the County Palatine of Lancaster, who apprehended Guy Fawkes with his dark lanthorn, and for his jealous prosecution of Papists, as Justice of the Peace, was stabbed in Westminster Hall, by John James, Dominican Friar, Ann. Dom. 1640.

> ' Reader ! if not a Papist bred,
> Upon such ashes lightly tread.' "

The ivy-covered old Heywood Hall was the seat of the Heywoods, and now goes to preserve the memory of one of the most ancient families in the parish.

A Peter Heywood, of Heywood (supposed to be the son of Peter Heywood, the magistrate), was one of the gentlemen of the county who

compounded for the recovery of their estates, which had been sequestered
in 1643-5 for supporting the Royal cause. He re-obtained his property
for the sum of £351.

In the visitation of 1664 are traced two lines of the Heywoods, those
of Heywood and Walton. From the latter was descended Samuel
Heywood, Esq., a Welsh judge, uncle of Sir Benjamin Heywood, Bart.,
of Claremont, near Manchester.

The property of this ancient family, principally consisting of Heywood
Hall and adjoining lands, is said to have been purchased by Mr. John
Starkey, of The Orchard, in Rochdale, in the latter part of the seventeenth or the beginning of the eighteenth century. Mr. Starkey was
living in 1719. His descendant, John Starkey, Esq., married Mary,
daughter of Joseph Gregge, Esq., of Fell Foot, near Cartmel. In 1791,
Mr. Starkey served the office of high sheriff of the county. From this
family branched the Starkies, of Redvales, near Bury.

Heywood became a village of agricultural labourers' cottages during
the sixteenth century ; and as intercourse gradually increased between
the towns of Bury and Rochdale, the local importance of the spot was
seen, and accordingly rendered available for the convenience and
advantage of an augmenting population. The place formed a group of
rural dwellings at a time when the cotton manufacture began to prevail;
and the apparatus then in use to carry on this now extraordinary business
was about as rude and simple as the cotters' habitations of the olden time
were, compared to those of the present day.

The first cotton factory erected in Heap was Makin mill, on the banks
of the Roch, north of Heywood, built about 1780, by the opulent firm of
Peel, Yates, and Co., of Bury. The first spinning mill commenced at
Heywood was at Wrigley Brook. At that time Heywood was a village
of about 2,000 inhabitants. The cotton spinning and weaving trades
materially augmented during the first fifteen years of the present
century, and consequently mills and dwellings increased every year. In
1817 there were in Heap ten cotton mills, in 1824 seventeen, in 1828
twenty, and in 1833 twenty-seven. The number of steam engines
engaged in the cotton trade in 1833 was thirty-four, the aggregate of the
horse-power of which amounted to 905, exclusive of one engine used in
machine making, one in paper making and four in collieries, and of three
woollen mills, where the machinery was moved by water. In 1834-5,
a return of Robert Rickards, Esq., factory inspector, set down the number
of cotton mills in Heap at 31, the steam engines as equal to 801, and
water wheels to 160 horses' power, and the total number of persons
employed 4,467. The number of mills newly built or enlarged during

1835-6 was three, the power of whose engines was equal to that of 94 horses. The number of cotton manufacturing concerns in 1838 was about 37, and the number of cotton mills in Heap in 1839 was about 34, and of steam engines 42 ; of the latter there were 38 in the village of Heywood and the vicinity, whose power was equal to that of 1,038 horses. The number of carding engines was 377, power looms 4,167, spindles 236,124, and the number of hands directly employed 5,190. The hours of work at that time were twelve hours per day, and nine on Saturday.

The Lancashire and Yorkshire Railway Company have a station here, and direct communication is thus obtained to Manchester, all parts of Yorkshire, as well as to Bolton, Liverpool, and the north. In 1840 what was then called the Manchester and Leeds Railway passed within a mile and a half of Heywood, over the Heywood Branch Canal. Near the termination of that water a railway station was formed for the accommodation of passengers to and from Heywood, to Manchester, Rochdale, &c. The trains commenced stopping at Bluepits for Heywood passengers on the 15th September, 1839 ; but there was no conveyance thence to Heywood until the 3rd of October following, when a packet boat was established, and conveyed passengers on the canal to and from the railway station and Heywood several times a day.

In 1835 a number of the principal inhabitants endeavoured to procure a general lighting of the streets, but owing to some factious opposition the proposal failed. The streets and the town generally are now lighted with gas supplied by the Heywood Gas Light Company, who were incorporated by an Act of Parliament which received the royal assent April 11, 1826 ; the company's works are at Hooley Bridge, and were established in 1827.

On the 7th of May, 1840, a public meeting of the inhabitants was held at the Queen Anne Inn, Mr. Thomas Grundy, solicitor, in the chair, when it was resolved to establish an institution for the mental and moral improvement of the working classes. Strenuous efforts were made to carry out the object of the resolution, and the result was that a Mechanics' Institution was erected. It is situated in a central part, and contains a large room for public meetings, a reading-room, and other rooms for recreation and the diffusion of knowledge.

One of the most ancient places of abode is Heap Fold. It was once the residence of a local family named De Heap.

Formerly the local government of the place was entrusted to the constables nominated by the ratepayers, and appointed at the court of the manor of Bury. An efficient deputy-constable was employed for some time at a salary of £90 per annum. Such was the extent of crime at one time that in 1835 it was considered necessary to hold petty sessions, and accordingly the magistrates of the district commenced to hold the sessions at the Queen Anne Inn, on the 22nd of July in that year. They were held every alternate Friday, and the magistrates usually in attendance were John Fenton, Esq., M.P., R. Walker, Esq., M.P., William Chadwick, George Ashworth, and H. Kelsall, Esqrs. The sessions are now held on alternate Wednesdays in the new and commodious Court-house adjoining the police station.

The following is a complete list of the places of worship, &c., in Heywood, with the dates of their erection, as near as can be ascertained:—

St. Luke's Church, date unknown, but prior to 1611
Wesleyan Methodist Chapel, built 1805, enlarged 1828
St. Luke's National Sunday School, built 1815, enlarged 1835
New Jerusalem Temple, built 1828, enlarged 1838
Baptist Chapel, built 1834
Independent Chapel, opened 1836
Wesleyan Methodist School, built 1845, opened 1846
Wesleyan Methodist Association Chapel, opened 1836
Wesleyan Association Sunday School, Heady-hill, opened 1837
St. James's Church, opened Jan. 1, and consecrated Sept. 28... 1838
St. James's Sunday School, built 1837
St. James's Sunday School, Heady-hill, built 1841, opened... 1842
Primitive Methodist Chapel, opened Dec. 25 1835
Bamford Chapel, built 1800, enlarged 1841
Methodist New Connexion Chapel, opened 1844

St. Luke's Sunday School, designated the National School, is a commodious edifice, erected in 1815 by subscription, and enlarged in 1835. It was intended for the daily education of 500 boys on the national plan, but has become a Sunday School for the instruction of children in the principles of the Established Church.

St. James's National and Sunday School is a large and substantial structure, erected in 1838, principally by means of the proceeds derived from a bazaar, or sale of articles of fancy work, held for the purpose in St. Luke's National School in 1837. This exhibition and mart of ornamental productions was highly creditable to the ladies and gentlemen of Heywood and the vicinity, and gave a favourable indication of their public spirit when duly tested in projects of general usefulness. The receipts of the bazaar amounted to £1,500, which, with £400 granted by the Lords of the Treasury, and National Society for Building and Enlarging Schools, and other contributions, formed the school building fund. The school was opened Jan. 1, 1839.

For upwards of 220 years there was only one episcopal chapel within Heap, that of St. Luke's, or Heywood Old Chapel, but on the 1st of January, 1838, St. James's Church was opened. St. Luke's Chapel appears to have been founded early in the seventeenth century, for some years ago the inscription —" F. H. 1611 "—was found upon some wood near the south side of the altar. The initials are those of Francis Holt, Esq., of the family of Holt, of Gristlehurst. In an inquisition taken at Manchester, June 19, 1650, by the Parliamentary Commissioners for inquiry into ecclesiastical livings, it is recommended that Heywood chapel be made a parish church. The Rev. George Thomson was minister here during the civil wars, and the period of the Commonwealth, when Presbyterianism was the ascendant faith. On the restoration of episcopacy, in 1662, Mr. Thomson was incumbent, but as he declined to conform to that change he was ejected from the curacy on St. Bartholomew's Day, August 24, 1662. The edifice seems to have been improved in the reign of James the Second. A dial on the east side of the exterior bears the date 1686, and the initials of Robert Heywood, Esq., of Heywood, who was Governor of the Isle of Man, 1678. About the middle of the last century the building was altered, and in 1805 it was considerably enlarged. The living, a perpetual curacy, was augmented by the Governors of Queen Anne's bounty by a grant of £200 from George the First, and £200 given by William Bamford and Mr. John Starkey in 1719. The registers of baptisms commence in 1747, and of burials in 1765. In the interior is a tablet commemorative of " John Starkey, of Heywood, Esq., who died March 11, 1780, aged 64," also of " Esther, his wife, died November 4, 1784, aged 64." On the south side of the altar is an elegant monument, thus inscribed:—

Sacred to the
memory of
Elizabeth, the beloved wife
for fifty years
of James Starkey, of Heywood, Esquire.
She died at their residence,
Fell Foot, Winandermere,
August 28, 1835,
universally regretted,
aged 67.

A third mural slab is in memory of " Alexander Hill, of Heap, Gent., who died August 9, 1776, aged 62; Martha, his wife, who died Nov. 5,

1796, aged 92; Alexander Hill, jun., Esq., who died July 17, 1826, aged 76; and Mary, his wife, who died Oct. 14, 1794, aged 38."

ST. JAMES'S CHAPEL.

The first stone of this chapel was laid on the 2nd July, 1836, by R. Orford, Esq., and was first opened for divine worship on New Year's Day, 1838. The cost of erection, amounting to about £3,000, was principally defrayed by subscriptions, and partly by a grant from the Diocesan Society.

THE RISE AND PROGRESS OF CONGREGATIONALISM.

The rise of Congregationalism in Heywood dates from the year 1798, when at the instance and with the assistance of Mr. Robert Kay, of Brookshaw, near Bury, father of Sir J. P. Kay-Shuttleworth, the Rev. J. Winder, of Bury, commenced preaching there. Afterwards, the Rev. Mr. Parsons, the minister of Bamford Chapel, prosecuted similar efforts, and so also did his successor, the Rev. Mr. Grey. There was, however, no manifest progress sufficient to lead to the engagement of any stated room for divine worship for upwards of 20 years after Mr. Winder's first efforts. But a mile or so to the northward, sweetly shaded by pines and poplars, stood Bamford Chapel, all this time with a zealous church and a flourishing Sunday-school. Of this school Sir James Kay-Shuttleworth, by the way, was for a time the supporter, and there by his own confession did he conceive many of those incitements to ponder the great question of popular education which in later times have borne so much fruit. In April, 1821, Mrs. Fenton, of Bamford Hall, authorised the Rev. Thomas Jackson, of Bamford, to open a preaching room at Heywood at her expense, in which he preached on the Sunday evenings. In 1832, the small chapel in Oak-street was taken upon a rental, the Rev. John Ely being chiefly instrumental in bringing about that result. On the 10th of October, 1823, it was opened. On the 24th July, 1824, a church was formed, consisting of three members, the Rev. John Ely and Thomas Jackson attending on the occasion, commending the church to the care of the Divine Head, and offering the members fitting counsel. The school buildings are 66 feet by 33 feet, and comprise infant and other class-rooms in the basement, and also a small lecture-room. Above these there is a large room stretching the whole length of the building, capable of holding 600 persons. In the chapel there is accommodation for about 835 persons, and in the schoolrooms for 600. The contract, exclusive of lighting, heating, and furniture, but including fencing, was let for £4,537. To this must be added for lighting, heating, and furniture, cost of site, charges of lawyers, and clerk of works, about £1,200 ; total, £5,737.

The ceremony of laying the memorial stone of the Congregational Chapel and Schools in York-street took place on the 10th of April, 1868. They are erected in the Gothic style of architecture, with red brick and stone facings, the architect being Mr. W. F. Paulton, of Reading, and the contractor Mr. F. Dawson, of Bury. The dimensions of the chapel are 66 feet by 42 feet, with a transept 20 feet by 11 feet in the clear, with side and end galleries. There are vestries for the minister and deacons at the back of the chapel. In 1834 the county union voted a grant of £50 to Heywood to aid the church in getting suitable supplies. On Good Friday, 1835, the foundation stone of a new chapel was laid by John Fenton, Esq., M.P., of Crumble Hall. During the pastorates of the Revs. W. Orgar, which was five and a half years, and John Harrison, thirteen and a half years, with an interregnum of two years, the chapel and schools became well filled ; and in the latter part of 1867 an enlargement of the building was effected, during the pastorate of the Rev. E. Davies. This enlargement, however, consisted only in the addition of some classrooms, extra area and light in large schools, an organ gallery, and a vestry. During the pastorate of the Rev. J. R. Thomson, M.A., the remaining cost of this enlargement was defrayed, but even while that cost was being met, there grew a strong conviction that entirely new and larger premises were becoming necessary. The cotton famine and panic followed (during Mr. Jones's pastorate), but in the midst of it the talk of new buildings was continually heard. This talk resulted in the appointment of a committee to consider and report as to the desirableness of a new chapel, or school, or both. The two leading recommendations of the committee adopted by the church were to the effect (1) " that the claim of our denominational principles for a wider recognition and representation in Heywood, the inadequacy of the school buildings fitly to accommodate even the numbers at present in attendance, the incapacity of the chapel to afford from time to time the sittings required, and, above all, the duty of the church to extend her influences and agencies for the further evangelisation of the town,— alike point to the desirableness of a new chapel and schoolrooms of larger capacity and improved design ; (2) that it is desirable to keep in view, and at the proper time to secure a central situation for the proposed erections, such as will fairly accommodate the several districts in which the present members of the church and congregation reside."

A plot of land was offered to the church in May, 1864, but the committee not obtaining such conditions of lease as their solicitors considered essential, the negotiations lapsed. A more successful negotiation for a plot of land in York-street was then begun. Immediately upon the settlement of the Rev. John Yonge as pastor of the church, the building in York-street was begun.

ST. LUKE'S CHURCH.

The foundation stone of this church, which stands upon the site of an old chapel, was laid on the 31st of May, 1860, by the Rev. William Hornby, M.A., of Heywood, and vicar of St. Michael's-on-Wyre.

It is designed in the most beautiful character of ecclesiastical architecture, which flourished during the period of Edward III,, and built in a solid and substantial manner, with Yorkshire parpoint and Staffordshire ashlar stone externally, and Bath stone ashlar work internally. The roofs are open, of pitch pine, springing from a lofty clerestory, with the lights carried on slender shafts of coloured stone. The east window is of seven lights, of noble proportions. The west window is also very large, and of six lights. The clustered columns in the chancel, with the shaft of the chancel arch, as well as the shafts of corbel supporting the roofs, are of local-coloured stones, mixed with marbles and sepetine. The seats are of pitch pine, varnished, suitable to the church, and with raised stalls of richer character in the chancel. The chancel is paved with Minton's tiles ; the other passages are flagged. The edifice comprises a parallelogram of 131 feet by 67 feet, divided into a chancel 42 feet by 22 feet ; a nave of 80 feet by 24 feet wide, and aisles 16 feet 6 inches wide, extending the whole length of the nave and chancel, excepting where meeting the vestry with the heating-chamber under, on the south side of the chancel. On the north side, next to York-street, and approached by a wide flight of steps, is a detached tower 23 feet square, exclusive of the buttresses, and a spire of the total height of 188 feet, forming the principal entrance into the church ; whilst on the south side, next Church-street, is a porch forming an entrance from this side.

A recess in the foundation stone was enclosed by a plate bearing the following inscription :—

The first stone of this Church, to be built to the glory of God, and dedicated to St. Luke the Evangelist, was placed here by the Rev. William Hornby, M.A., of Heywood, and vicar of St. Michael's-on-Wyre, on the thirty-first day of May, being Thursday in Whitsun-week, in the year of our Lord MDCCCLX., and the twenty-third year of the reign of Her Majesty Queen Victoria. Julius Shadwell, incumbent; John James Mellor, churchwarden; John Turner, sidesman ; John Clarke, architect.

After the stone had been laid, Albert Royds, Esq., Deputy Provincial Grand Master of East Lancashire, laid the corner-stone masonically, as appears from the subjoined inscription, which was placed under it :—

Gloria in Excelsis Deo.

The corner stone of this Church, to be dedicated to the worship of the Almighty, according to the rites of the Established Church of Great Britain and Ireland, to be called St. Luke's Church, raised by public subscription, erected upon the site of the old chapel in Heywood, was masonically laid by Albert Hudson Royds, Esq., R.W. Deputy Provincial Grand Master of East Lancashire, assisted by the provincial grand officers and brethren of the Napthali Lodge, 333, Heywood, on Thursday, May 31st, A.L. 5860, A.D. 1860, in the 23rd year of the reign of Her Majesty Queen Victoria. Stephen Blair, Esq., P.G.M., E.L.; S. G. Taylor, W.M.; James Greenhalgh, S.W.; George Ashworth, J.W. No. 333.

BAMFORD.

The Rev. Canon Raines, in his *Notitia Cestriensis*, says:—" The estate of Bamford was granted to Thomas de Bamford by Sir Adam de Burg, *temp.* Henry III., for his homage and service, and two marks (28s. 8d.) and a yearly rent of 18d. at the feast of St. Oswald the King (Aug. 5); and the same Sir Adam afterwards granted all his lands in Bamford to Alexander de Bamford for a pecuniary consideration and a yearly rent of 40d. payable at St. Oswald's Day. The estate descended lineally to William Bamford, Esq., who died in 1757, leaving by his wife Margaret (daughter of Edward Davenport, of Stockport, Esq.) three daughters and co-heiresses; and all of them dying without issue, it was devised by Ann, the eldest, in 1779, to William Bamford, of Tarlton Bridge, a remote kinsman, afterwards Sheriff of Lancashire, who married, in 1786, Anna, daughter of Thomas Blackburne, of Hale, Esq.; but dying in 1806 without male issue it passed with a distant female relative in marriage to Robert Hesketh, of Upton, Co. Chester, Esq., who assumed the surname of Bamford in 1806, and was grandfather of Lloyd Hesketh Bamford-Hesketh, of Gwyrch Castle, Co. Denbigh, Esq. Bamford was purchased by Mr. Joseph Fenton, whose son, James Fenton, Esq., in 1841, took down the hall, which had been rebuilt in the time of Queen Anne, and erected near the former house a large and handsome modern house."

PEACOCK HALL.

Situated midway between Gigg and Heap Bridge is Peacock Hall. It occupies an eminence overlooking the valley of the Roche, and a considerable expanse of country around Bury. It has for many years

been a place of resort for young persons, especially during the lifetime
of its former occupant, an old dame who took great delight in furnishing
tea and other refreshments, and in discoursing on such topics as were
interesting to her customers. The old woman died many years ago, and
the house afterwards became the residence of John Kay, believed to be
her brother. He was interred on the 7th July, 1869, in the burial
ground attached to Unsworth Church, having attained the age of 84
years. The coffin in which he was interred he ordered to be made for
him twenty years before his death, and he kept it in his dwelling during
the whole of that period. It is stated by his friends that being of a
careful turn, and apprehensive that a carpenter in Heywood who owed
him a small sum would never pay him, he got him to take his measure,
and make for him what, in this locality, is sometimes called his
"last suit." Two months before his death the old man caused the
coffin to be neatly upholstered under his own superintendence ; and it is
impossible to conjecture what strange thoughts must at times have
occupied the mind of a man who for twenty years, day and night, in
seasons of sorrow and sadness, and in a lonely dwelling, had about him
so dismal a reminder of his own mortality.

BURY IMPROVEMENT COMMISSIONERS SINCE 1846.

The following is a list, so far as can be ascertained, of the Bury
Improvement Commissioners since the passing of the Bury Improvement
Act in 1846 :—

1846.

Thomas Openshaw.
Thomas Oram.
Edmund Hardman.
John Lomax.
Oliver Ormerod Openshaw.
Matthew Fletcher.
John Hoyle, the elder.
John Openshaw.
Jonathan Openshaw.
Micah Barlow.
John Haslam.
Richard Walker, jun.
Thomas Greenhalgh, jun.
Lawrence Park.

Lawrence Rogers Openshaw.
Christopher Clemishaw.
Thomas Horrocks.
William Barrett.
Matthew Peel.
William Bowman.
James Parks.
Henry Bridge.
John Rothwell.
Robert Taylor.
John Mitchell.
William Bridge.
John Clemishaw.

1847.

Richard Walker, jun.
John Openshaw.
Matthew Peel.
Lawrence Park.
Robert Battersby, jun.
James Openshaw.
William Bowman.
Robert Taylor.
Joseph Pilkington.
James Parks.
Thomas Greenhalgh, jun.
Thomas Openshaw.
Jonathan Openshaw.
John Mitchell.

John Hoyle, the elder.
Thomas Horrocks.
John Rothwell.
John Clemishaw.
Henry Bridge.
Lawrence Rogers Openshaw.
Christopher Clemishaw.
Matthew Fletcher.
William Barrett.
Edmund Hardman.
Oliver Ormerod Openshaw.
John Openshaw.
John Lomax.

1848.

James Parks.
Oliver Ormerod Openshaw.
William Barrett.
John Clemishaw.
Thomas Horrocks.
Christopher Clemishaw.
William Harper.
Jonathan Openshaw.
James Hoyle.
Thomas Openshaw.
Thomas Oram.
Edmund Hardman.
John Lomax.
Matthew Fletcher.

John Hoyle, the elder.
John Openshaw.
Richard Walker, jun.
Matthew Peel.
Lawrence Park.
Robert Battersby, jun.
William Bowman.
Robert Taylor.
John Pilkington.
Thomas Greenhalgh, jun.
John Mitchell
John Rothwell
Henry Bridge

1849.

John Mitchell.
Matthew Fletcher.
John Pickering.
James Kay.
James Clarkson Kay.
James Barrett.
Daniel Smith.
George Howarth.
Thomas Openshaw.
William Harper.

Thomas Horrocks.
Jonathan Openshaw.
Christopher Clemishaw,
Lawrence Park.
Robert Taylor.
John Openshaw.
James Hoyle.
Robert Battersby, jun.
William Bowman.
John Pilkington.

James Parks.
James Openshaw.
Matthew Peel.
Richard Walker, jun.

Thomas Greenhalgh, jun.
John Rothwell.
Henry Bridge.

1850.

Richard Walker, jun.
Matthew Peel.
James Parks.
Lawrence Park.
John Holt.
Joseph Clemishaw.
Edward Potts.
Robert Wood.
Robert Hall.
William Harper.
Christopher Clemishaw.
George Howarth.
James Clarkson Kay.
Thomas Horrocks.

James Kay.
Daniel Smith.
Matthew Fletcher.
John Mitchell.
John Pickering.
Jonathan Openshaw.
James Barrett.
Jonathan Openshaw.
James Hoyle.
James Park.
Robert Taylor.
James Pilkington.
Robert Battersby, jun.

1851.

John Openshaw.
Thomas Horrocks.
James Openshaw.
Peter Oswald Polding.
James Livesey.
James Whitehead.
William Harper.
Thomas Openshaw.
James Parks.
Matthew Peel.
John Mitchell.
John Pickering.

Robert Wood.
John Holt.
George Howarth.
Robert Hall.
James Clarkson Kay.
Richard Walker, jun.
James Park.
Daniel Smith.
James Kay.
James Barrett.
Joseph Clemishaw.
Lawrence Park.

1852.

Christopher Clemishaw.
John Alcock.
John Mitchell.
James Kay.
Samuel Grundy.
Thomas Grundy.
John Hoyle.

James Whitehead.
Joseph Clemishaw.
James Openshaw.
John Mitchell.
William Harper.
James Parks.
James Barrett.

James Barrett.
Thomas Price.
John Openshaw.
Matthew Peel.
Robert Wood.

Thomas Horrocks.
Robert Hall.
James Park.
John Holt.
James Livesey.

1853.

James Park.
Thomas Aitken.
Robert Hall.
John Holt.
Robert Wood.
Matthew Peel.
John Hutchinson.
John Young, jun.
Richard Haworth.
Thomas Horrocks.
James Barrett.

John Mitchell.
James Kay.
Christopher Clemishaw.
John Openshaw.
James Whitehead.
William Harper.
James Livesey.
Thomas Grundy.
John Hoyle.
James Openshaw.
James Parks.

1854.

Thomas Roberts.
James Openshaw.
Thomas Horrocks.
William Wanklyn, jun.
Thomas Price, jun.
Henry Peel.
William Harper.
John Unwin.
John Parkinson.
Thomas Grundy.
James Kay.
William Harper.
Matthew Peel.

John Young.
Robert Hall.
Richard Haworth.
John Holt.
James Park.
John Mitchell.
Christopher Clemishaw.
John Hutchinson.
John Hoyle.
James Barrett.
Robert Wood.
Thomas Aitken.

1855.

James Barrett.
Christopher Clemishaw.
James Kay.
John Mitchell.
George Openshaw.
William Davenport.
Edward Bate.

William Wanklyn.
John Holt.
John Young.
John Unwin.
Richard Haworth.
James Park.
Henry Peel.

Thomas Grundy.
John Scholes Walker.
John Hutchinson.
Thomas Roberts.
John Parkinson.

William Harper.
Thomas Price.
Robert Wood.
Matthew Peel.
Thomas Horrocks.

1856.

Richard Walker.
William Grundy.
James Park.
Matthew Peel.
Joseph Webb.
James Hoyle.
Randal H. Alcock.
John Holt.
Robert Wood.
William Wanklyn.
William Davenport.
John Mitchell.
John Parkinson.

William Harper.
Thomas Grundy.
George Openshaw.
Henry Peel.
Thomas Horrocks.
James Kay.
James Barrett.
Christopher Clemishaw.
John Unwin.
James Openshaw.
William Davenport.
John Scholes Walker.

1857.

Richard Kenyon.
Thomas Roberts.
William Wanklyn.
Matthew Fletcher.
William Price.
James Openshaw.
Joseph Newbold.
John Parkinson.
John Unwin.
Matthew Peel.
James Kay.
Robert Wood.
George Openshaw.
James Park.

James Barrett.
John Mitchell.
John Holt.
William Davenport.
Christopher Clemishaw.
George Openshaw.
R. H. Alcock.
Richard Walker.
William Harper.
John Scholes Walker.
Joseph Webb.
Thomas Grundy.
James Hoyle.

1858.

James Kay.
Christopher Clemishaw.
John Mitchell.
George Openshaw.

Joseph Webb.
James Park.
John Parkinson.
Richard Kenyon.

John Scholes Walker.
Henry Oram.
Robert Hall.
Jacob Kershaw, jun.
Samuel Rothwell.
Richard Walker.
William Wanklyn.
Joseph Newbold.
John Holt.
John Unwin.

Christopher Clemishaw.
Robert Wood.
W. H. Price.
Henry Oram.
John Mitchell.
Matthew Fletcher.
Matthew Peel.
Thomas Roberts.
James Hoyle.

1859.

Matthew Peel.
James Park.
John Holt.
Robert Wood.
Joseph Webb.
Richard Howarth.
John Hoyle.
Samuel Smith.
Samuel Openshaw.
William Wanklyn.
John Parkinson.
Joseph Newbold.

James Kay.
Thomas Roberts.
George Openshaw.
Robert Hall.
Matthew Fletcher.
William Price.
Jacob Kershaw.
John Mitchell.
Samuel Rothwell.
Christopher Clemishaw.
James Park.

1860.

Joseph Newbold.
Thomas Openshaw.
Thomas Roberts.
Richard Hacking.
Joseph Webb.
Thomas Mitchell.
George Openshaw.
John Parkinson.
John Melling Wike.
John Hamer.
Edward Barlow.
Thomas Lloyd Price.
Thomas Fletcher.

George Openshaw.
James Park.
Richard Ward.
Thomas Grundy.
Thomas Holt.
James Kay.
Matthew Peel.
Robert Hall.
John Parkinson.
Samuel Openshaw.
John Hoyle.
Robert Wood.

1861.

Richard Ward.
Henry Peel.
John Pickering.

Thomas Openshaw.
John Hoyle.
Joseph Webb.

Samuel Renshaw.
James Kay.
Thomas Holt.
John Barrett.
Robert Hall.
George Booth.
Richard Hacking.
Samuel Smith.
John Hamer.
John M. Wike.

Joseph Newbold.
John Parkinson.
Matthew Peel.
Robert Wood.
Samuel Openshaw.
Thomas Price.
Edward Barlow.
Thomas Mitchell.
Thomas Fletcher.

1862.

Thomas Roberts.
John Scholes Walker.
Matthew Peel.
Edward Barlow.
Thomas Fletcher.
George Openshaw.
James Park.
John Holt.
Samuel Smith.
Thomas Openshaw.
Robert Hall.
Thomas Holt.
Richard Ward.

James Parker.
Joseph Newbold.
John Parkinson.
John M. Wike.
Samuel Renshaw.
James Parks.
John Pickering.
Robert Wood.
George Booth.
Thomas Fletcher.
Henry Peel.
John Barrett.

1863.

Thomas Openshaw.
John Parkinson.
Thomas Grundy.
John Hamer.
John Nuttall.
Joseph Webb.
Robert Wood.
Joseph Newbold.
John Horrocks.
John Scholes Walker.
Thomas Fletcher.
Samuel Renshaw.
Robert Hall.

John Holt.
James Park.
Henry Peel.
Thomas Holt.
Richard Ward.
George Booth.
Thomas Grundy.
Samuel Smith.
John Barrett.
Thomas Roberts.
John Pickering.
Robert Hall.

1864.

Thomas Holt.
Thomas Lomax Openshaw.

John Holt.
James Park.

Robert Hall.
Henry Peel.
George Booth.
Richard Ward.
Thomas Mitchell.
Samuel Cook.
James Hill.
John Scholes Walker.
Matthew Peel.
John Parkinson.
John Nuttall.

Thomas Grundy.
John Horrocks.
Edward Barlow.
Samuel Smith.
Robert Wood.
Joseph Webb.
George Openshaw.
Thomas Openshaw.
Thomas Fletcher.
Thomas Roberts.

1865.

James Park.
Samuel Smith.
Thomas Roberts.
Richard Walker.
Matthew Peel.
John Holt.
James Parks.
Edward Barlow.
Thomas Fletcher.
James Park.
Robert Wood.
Samuel Cook.
Thomas Mitchell.

Thomas Openshaw.
Henry Peel.
George Booth.
Thomas Lomax Openshaw.
John Horrocks.
Thomas Grundy.
John Nuttall.
John Hamer.
Joseph Webb.
Robert Hall.
John Parkinson.
Richard Ward.

1866.

Thomas Grundy.
Joseph Webb.
John Nuttall.
Robert Wood.
Samuel Renshaw.
Thomas Openshaw.
Robert Crossland.
Joseph Newbold.
Abel Ashworth.
Richard Ward.
Thomas Holt.
Richard Walker.
Thomas Mitchell.

Henry Peel.
Robert Hall.
James Parks.
Matthew Peel.
Thomas Lomax Openshaw.
Samuel Cook.
John Holt.
Thomas Fletcher.
George Booth.
Edward Barlow.
Thomas Roberts.
Samuel Smith.

1867.

William Fairbrother.
Thomas Holt.
Samuel Cook.
Robert Hall.
John Wormald.
Adam Ashworth.
Henry Peel.
Robert Peers.
John Parkinson.
Samuel Smith.
Abel Ashworth.
John Nuttall.
Thomas Roberts.

Joseph Newbold.
Matthew Peel.
Richard Walker.
Robert Crossland.
Thomas Openshaw.
Joseph Webb.
Thomas Fletcher.
Robert Wood.
Edward Barlow.
James Parks.
Samuel Renshaw.
John Holt.

1868.

Richard Walker.
James Park.
Thomas Roberts.
Edmund Herbert Grundy.
John Bolton.
Robert Kay.
Richard Ward.
Joseph Sykes.
William Kenyon.
Robert Wood.
Henry Peel.
Samuel Renshaw.
John Nuttall.

Robert Hall.
Abel Ashworth.
Adam Ashworth.
John Parkinson.
Robert Crossland.
Joseph Newbold.
Robert Peers.
Thomas Holt.
William Fairbrother.
Joseph Webb.
John Wormald.
Samuel Cook.

1869.

Thomas Openshaw.
Joseph Webb.
Matthew Peel.
James Alfred Openshaw.
Samuel Renshaw.
Robert Wood.
Charles Walker.
Thomas Barlow.
Edward Barlow.
E. Herbert Grundy.

Thomas Roberts.
Joseph Sykes.
John Wormald.
William Fairbrother.
John Parkinson.
Adam Ashworth.
John Bolton.
Richard Walker.
Samuel Cook.
Robert Hall.

Robert Kay.
Robert Peers.
Henry Peel.

James Park.
Thomas Holt.

1870.

Randal Hibbert Alcock.
Robert Hall.
William Fairbrother.
Samuel Cook.
John Duckworth.
Robert Peers.
Adam Ashworth.
John Wormald.
Robert Crossland.
Robert Wood.
Samuel Renshaw.
Robert Crossland.

Joseph Sykes.
John Bolton.
James A. Openshaw.
Matthew Peel.
Thomas Openshaw.
James Park.
Edward Barlow.
Thomas Barlow.
Joseph Webb.
Thomas Roberts.
Charles Walker.
Richard Walker.

1871.

Lawrence Booth.
John Bolton.
John Parkinson.
James Unsworth.
John Hoyle.
William Richard Crompton.
James Maxwell.
James Park.
Joseph Sykes.
Robert Peers.
Thomas Barlow.
John Duckworth.
Edward Barlow.

Samuel Renshaw.
Robert Crossland.
Samuel Cook.
William Fairbrother.
Randal H. Alcock.
Adam Ashworth.
James Alfred Openshaw.
Charles Walker.
Thomas Openshaw.
John Parkinson.
Matthew Peel.
Joseph Webb.

1872.

Thomas Blunt.
Thomas Ormerod.
Thomas Clifford Davies.
Thomas Openshaw.
Joseph Webb.
Thomas Barlow.
John Wormald.
Abel Ashworth.

W. R. Crompton.
James Maxwell.
R. H. Alcock.
John Parkinson.
Joseph Sykes.
John Bolton.
Lawrence Booth.
Robert Crossland.

Matthew Peel.
John Hoyle.
James Unsworth.
Robert Peers.
Adam Ashworth.

John Duckworth.
Robert Hall.
James Park.
William Fairbrother.

1873.

Church Ward.

John Bolton, St. Mary's-gate.
George Clough, South View, Wilson-street.
John Wormald, Bank-street.

Thomas Ormerod, Union-street.
Joseph Burrow, Agincourt Villa.
Robert Peers, Bolton-street.

Redvales Ward.

James Maxwell, The Ferns.
James Unsworth, Goshen.
Thomas Barlow, Bankfield.
Thomas Clifford Davies, Rhiwlas.

Thomas Parker, Tenterden-street.
Walker Wm. Ormerod, Summerfield.

East Ward.

John Parkinson, Spring-street.
John Hoyle, Bent Cottage.
Thomas Openshaw, Brick House.
Benjamin Barritt, 1, Ingham-st.

Robert Hall, The Derbys, Manchester-road.
William Fairbrother, Georgiana-street.

Moorside Ward.

Joseph Sykes, Boulevards.
James Park, Fernhill.
Abel Ashworth, 283, Holly Bank, Rochdale-road.

Thomas Blunt, Alfred-street.
Robert Crossland, Mayfield.
John Wardleworth, Water-street.

Elton Ward.

Lawrence Booth, Highfield.
James Edward Worsley, Wood-street.
Matthew Peel, Tithebarn-street.

Joseph Webb, Crostons-road.
Christopher Hardman, Bolton-road, Elton.
Richard Olive, Woolfold.

EX-CHAIRMEN OF COMMISSIONERS.

Richard Walker 1846-7	Richard Hacking......... 1860-1
,, ... 1847-8	,, ... 1861-2
,, ... 1848-9	,, ... 1862-3
,, ... 1849-50	J. S. Walker 1863-4
,, ... 1850-1	,, ... 1864-5
,, ... 1851-2	James Park 1865-6
John Openshaw 1852-3	,, ... 1866-7
,, ... 1853-4	,, ... 1867-8
John Hutchinson 1854-5	,, ... 1868-9
,, ... 1855-6	Richard Walker 1869-70
Richard Walker 1856-7	,, ... 1870-1
,, ... 1857-8	Robert Hall 1871-2
William Wanklyn 1858-9	Samuel Cook 1872-3
,, ... 1859-60	William Fairbrother ... 1873-4

CHAPTER XVI.

Chronological History of Bury and Neighbourhood—The House of Stanley,

CHRONOLOGICAL HISTORY.

1086.

Bury Parish Church known to be in existence in this year,

1485.

October 30.—First Earl of Derby created.

1507.

October 21.—Richard Smyth instituted Rector of Bury.

1540.

Parish registers were first made all over England.

1557.

February 4.—Richard Johnes instituted Rector of Bury.

1568.

August 18.—Walter Keny instituted Rector of Bury.

1575.

Bury parish registers commence about this date.

1608.

July 6.—Hugh Whatmough instituted Rector of Bury.

1623.

August 23.—George Murray instituted Rector of Bury.

1648.

August 28.—Tobias Furness instituted Rector of Bury.

1651.

October 15.—Seventh Earl of Derby beheaded at Bolton.

1660.

February 26.—John Greenhalgh instituted Rector of Bury.

1668.

Thomas Greenhalgh, Esq., of Brandlesholme, High Sheriff.

1670.

February 26.—Thomas Gipps instituted Rector of Bury.

1678.

January 12.—Darkness at noon in England.

1681.

February 28.—Mr. John Warburton, F.R.S. and F.S.A., Somerset Herald, born.

1695.

June 18.—Rev. H. Pendlebury died.

1704.

July 16.—John Kay born; invented fly shuttle, 1733.

1712.

March 5.—James Bancks instituted Rector of Bury.

1726.

Thomas Hopwood, Esq., of Hopwood, High Sheriff, passed through Bury on the way to Lancaster assizes.
May 6.—Bury Grammar School founded.

1730.

March 1.—Rev. Roger Kay died.
November 9.—Unsworth Old Chapel consecrated.

1737.

James Lancashire bequeathed £50 to Unsworth Chapel, Heywood Chapel, and Walmersley.

1743.

July 19.—John Stanley instituted Rector of Bury.

1748.

August 2.—Bury National School founded.

1749.

James Starkey bequeathed £30 for the use of Heywood School.

1752.

May 27.—First organ erected in Bury Parish Church.

1759.

May 11.—Mr. J. Warburton, herald, of Bury, died.

1765.

January 18.—Mr. Thomas Norris born.

1769.

July 3.—Sir Richard Arkwright's first throstle patented.

1770.

Cloth printing commenced in Bury.
June 8.—St. John's Church, Bury, consecrated.

1773.

Messrs. Peel and Yates commenced cotton manufacture.
August 6.—Bury Parish Church closed for repairs.

1774.

August 21.—A committee appointed to repair or rebuild the Bury
Parish Church.

1775.

Improved system of carding introduced by Messrs. Peel and Yates.

1776.

February 2.—A commission was appointed to rebuild the Bury Parish
Church (leaving the tower and spire standing).

1777.

May 14.—Mr. John Grundy died at Seedfield.
September 14.—Shocks of earthquake felt in Bury.

1778.

February 6.—Sir William Henry Clarke, Bart., instituted Rector of Bury.

1780.

November 5.—The new Parish Church at Bury opened.
December 12.—Mr. John Hall, of Holly Mount, died.

1783.

June 10.—Robert Peel married Miss Yates at Bury.
June 28.—Mr. Booth, surgeon, Tottington, died.

1784.

April 9.—Smith killed his child, but was prevented from drowning himself at Bury bridge.

July 4.—First stone of Union-square, Bury, laid by Mr. Robert Howarth.

1785.

January 13.—London *Times* newspaper established.

October 13.—A new clock ordered for Bury Parish Church.

September 23.—Floods at Bury.

1787.

June 26.—William Yates died.

July 4.—Bury Theatre, Moss-lane, fell ; 6 persons killed and 60 injured.

1788.

February 5.—Sir Robert Peel born at Chamber Hall.

April 23.—J. Wesley preached at Bury.

1789.

First printing press made in Bury by Mr. Robert Collinge.

The Right Hon. William Yates Peel born at Chamber Hall.

1791.

March 3.—John Wesley died, aged 88.

June 30.—Manchester, Bolton, and Bury Canal Company formed.

1792.

An organ erected in St. John's Church, Bury.

1793.

February 3.—£5 notes first issued.

April 29.—New Road Chapel, Bury, opened.

August 3.—Sir Richard Arkwright died.

1796.

September 24.—First coal boat run on Bury and Bolton Canal.

1797.

Messrs. Peel and Yates contributed £10,000 to the Government.

1798.

June 22.—Park Independent Chapel opened.

October 18.—Lady Clerke presented colours to Bury Loyal Volunteers.

1800.

The Pillory last used in Bury.

November 20.--Sir Robert Peel, first baronet, created.

1801.

November 28.—John Lomax, Esq., born.

1802.

Lady Peel attended the Guild at Preston.

1804.

July 20.—Sir J. P. Kay-Shuttleworth born.

1807.

November 19.—Bethel Chapel, Bury, opened.

1812.

December 28.—Meeting in Bury for raising funds for the distressed in Russia.

1813.

July 18.—W. Yates died.

1814.

March 23.—Resolution passed to enlarge yard and widen Fleet-street.

1815.

February 15.—Thomas Yates died.

1816.

June.—The Right Hon. William Yates Peel called to the bar at Lincoln's Inn.

1817.

The Right Hon. William Yates Peel returned as member for Bassing.

January 6.—Wesleyan Chapel, Bury, opened.

March 10.—Blanket meeting, Manchester.

1818.

The Right Hon. William Yates Peel returned as member for Tamworth.

Gas first made in Bury by Mr. Ben. Bassett.

February 16.—Old Market Cross taken down.

July 30.—Packet sunk in Bury Canal.

September 23.—Geoffrey Hornby instituted Rector of Bury.

1819.

June 17.—The Right Hon. William Yates Peel married to Lady Jane Eliza Moore.

August 16.—Peterloo meeting.

1820.

December 21.—Dr. Cunliffe died.

1821.

Mr. Ellis Cunliffe, surgeon, died.

1822.

March 30.—Bury Savings Bank established.

August 3.—Stand Church stone laid by Lord Derby.

1824.

Sir William Peel, K.C.B., born.

1825.

September 30.—Cass and wife murdered at Birtle.

1826.

April 23 to 26.—Power-loom riots; six persons shot; estimated damage, £20,000.

September 8.—All Saints' Church, Stand, consecrated.

1827.

June 26.—Samuel Crompton died; invented mule, 1775-9.

1828.

April 18.—Bury Gas Company established.

June 29.—Balloon ascent from Gasworks.

1829.

March 6.—Bury Dispensary founded.

May 30.—Shuttle gathering and riot at Rochdale.

1830.

February 14.—Butcher-lane old mill burnt down.

May 3.—First Sir Robert Peel died.

July 23.—Beerhouses first opened.

September 15.—Liverpool and Manchester Railway opened; Huskisson killed.

1831.

The Right Hon. William Yates Peel returned as member for the University of Cambridge.

February 21.—Rev. Robert Hall died.

August 17.—"Rothsay Castle" wrecked.

1832.

Bury Branch Manchester and Liverpool District Bank opened.

May 7 to 12.—"Skipper's" feat of walking 60 miles a day.

August 25.—First appearance of cholera in Bury.

November 3.—Fire at Walker's foundry.

December 12.—First General Election for Bury—Mr. Walker (L.), 306; Mr. E. Grundy (L.), 153.

1833.

August 29.—Ten Hours Act passed.

1834.

The Rev. H. C. Boutflower appointed to the incumbency of St. John's Church, Bury.

June 15.—St. Andrew's Church, Ramsbottom, opened.

July 10.—Lady Shore Colliery inundated.

July 11.—B. Crompton, Bury, died.

August 7.—Jacquard died; invented the loom in 1790.

August 14.—Bury Market Act passed.

November 26.—Sir Robert Peel summoned by His Majesty to form a Government.

December 10.—Sir Robert Peel, Premier first time.

1835.

The Right Hon. William Yates Peel returned for Tamworth.

January 6.—General Election at Bury—Mr. Walker returned without opposition.

March 31.—J. Barlow murdered his wife ; executed August 12, 1835.

April 29.—Edmund Yates died.

1836.

A Mechanics' Institution commenced in Silver-street, Bury.

January 5.—Resolution passed to light Bury streets with gas.

February 28.—Bamford Wesleyan Chapel opened.

May 13.—Bury Banking Company formed.

June 24.—First stone of Hardy's Gate bridge laid.

July 2.—St. James's, Heywood, corner stone laid.

October 8.—Baptist Chapel, Freetown, opened.

1837.

June 18.—First sermons in Brunswick Old Chapel.
July 26.—General Election at Bury : Votes recorded—for Mr. Walker, 251; Mr. J. P. Cobbett (L.), 96 ; Mr. R. Spankie (C.), 87.

1838.

April 20.—Walmersley Church opened.
May 7.—Old Grey Mare Inn, Bury, taken down.
June 11.—Bury and Radcliffe Waterworks Company established.
October 2.—Corner-stone of St. Paul's Church, Bury, laid by Lord Stanley.
October 20.—First steamer from Liverpool to New York.
December 13.—Rev. T. Foxley, Radcliffe, died.

1839.

January 7.—The Old Church spire was damaged by a hurricane.
August 12.—Chartist rising in Lancashire.
December 24.—Bury Market opened.

1840.

January 10.—Penny postage commenced.
February 14.—Bury police first in uniform.
April 1.—Last election of a select vestry in Bury.
April 29.—Rural police introduced.
October 11.—First fair at Tottington.
October 30.—Mrs. Thomas Yates died.

1841.

Bury Market opened.
January 11.—John Grundy, Esq., appointed magistrate.
July 1.—General Election at Bury—Mr. Walker, 325; Mr. H. Hardman, (C.), 288.
May 26.—St. Paul's Church, Bury, opened.

1842.

January 14.—First petty sessions in Commercial Buildings, Bury.
February 28.—Mr. William Grant died ; H. Hardman, Esq., appointed magistrate.
June 17.—Fire at Battersby's factory.
June 29.—St. John's Church, Bury, consecrated.
August 9 to 12.—Plug-drawing riots at Bury.

1843.

January 20.—Sir Robert Peel's secretary shot.

March 15.—Meeting of Anti-Corn Law League at Bury.

April 18.—Last change ringing in Old Church tower, Bury.

April 30.—All Saints' Church, Elton, first used for divine service.

June 29.—All Saints' Church, Elton, consecrated.

August 1.—First interment at All Saints', Elton.

September 4.—Mr. S. Woodcock, Bury, died,

October 7.—Fire at Bolton-street Mill, Bury.

October 25.—Corner-stone of new tower of Bury Parish Church laid by Thomas Norris, Esq., F.R.S.

1844.

Bury Mechanics' Institution removed to the Wylde.

Rev. B. Crompton appointed to St. George's Church, Unsworth.

June.—Rev. R. Fletcher appointed to St. Thomas's Church, Radcliffe.

July 7.—Mr. John Grundy, Silver-street, died.

August 5.—East Lancashire railway works began.

1845.

January 2.—Strike at Vulcan Works, Bury.

March 25 and 26.—The new Tower of Bury Parish Church was opened by change ringing.

April 29.—Wellington Barracks opened.

October 1.—Rev. H. P. Hughes appointed to Shuttleworth Church.

1846.

June 27.—Sir William Peel, K.C.B., promoted to the rank of Commander.

July 1.—Birtle Church consecrated.

July 25.—Free-trade rejoicings in Bury.

July 27.—Bury Improvement Bill passed.

September 9.—Bury Congregational Chapel opened.

September 26.—East Lancashire Railway opened.

December 17.—Heywood Constitutional Association commenced.

1847.

March 25.—Bury County Court commenced.

April 20.—R. N. Philips, Esq., M.P., appointed magistrate.

April 21.—New County Court opened in Commercial Buildings, Bury.

July 23.—Wesleyan Chapel, Summerseat, opened.

July 30.—General Election at Bury—Mr. Walker's return unopposed.

September 17.—Unsworth Wesleyan Chapel opened.

1848.

The Rev. John Walker appointed to St. John's Church, Bury.

January 26.—Radcliffe Congregational Chapel opened.

February 28.—W. Fenton, Esq., Meadowcroft, appointed magistrate.

March 1.—Fire at Bolholt Printworks ; damage, £2,500.

May 10.—Wesleyan Chapel, Woolfold, opened.

June 11.—Shuttleworth Church opened.

November 20.—Liverpool and Bury Railway opened.

1849.

February 22.—J. R. Kay, Esq., Walmersley House, appointed magistrate.

June 5.—Rev. S. G. F. Perry appointed to Tottington Church.

November 13.—Rev. G. Nightingale appointed to Holcombe Church.

1850.

Rev. T. Wilson appointed to Birtle Church.

February 2.—Derby Hotel, Bury, opened.

March 4.—Rev. Geoffrey Hornby died.

March 28.—Rev. E. J. G. Hornby instituted Rector of Bury.

May 2.—Bury Post-office removed to Broad-street.

July 2.—Sir R. Peel died.

September 20.—Court-room, Bury Town Hall, opened.

October 3.—Corner-stone of Bury Athenæum laid by Lord Stanley.

October 4.—Bury Agricultural Society inaugurated.

1851.

St. John's Church, Bury, licensed for the solemnisation of marriages.

April 18.—Wesleyan Chapel, Heywood, opened.

May 8.—Decided to light Heywood with gas.

October 10.—Queen visited Manchester.

December 26.—Bury Athenæum Hall opened—"Messiah" performed.

1852.

Mr. Thomas Norris died at Howick House.

Peel Monument inaugurated at Bury, and one upon Holcombe Moor.

January 26.—Fire at Ringley-road Colliery.

February 14.—Accident at Knowsley-street Station; two killed.

February 18.—Mine flooded at Birtle; seven persons drowned.

February 21.—Turn-out of cotton operatives at Radcliffe.

February 22.—Lord Derby first time Premier.

July 11.—General Election at Bury—Mr. F. Peel (L.-C.), 472; Viscount Duncan (L.), 410.

August 4.—Boiler explosion at Pittfield Mills, Birtle.
August 9.—"Steeple Jack" fixed vane on Bury Parish Church.
September 9.—Peel Tower, Holcombe, inaugurated.
October 13.—John Just died.
October 22.—Bank-street Chapel, Bury, opened.
November 18.—Wellington's funeral, public mourning in Bury.
December 5.—Lower Croft reservoir burst.

1853.

January 3.—Joseph Fenton, Esq., Bamford Hall, appointed magistrate.
February 18.—Baptist Chapel, Knowsley-street, opened.
March 29.—Manchester created a city.
May 24.—Rev. W. A. Conway appointed to St. James's Church, Heap.
November 23.—Bury Athenæum opened.

1854.

January 1 to 5.—Snowstorm, railway stopped.
January 9.—Thomas Wrigley, Esq., Timberhurst, appointed magistrate.
February 18.—Font erected in Bury Parish Church, to memory of Rev.
G. Hornby.

1855.

February.—R. Walker, M.P., died.
March 12.—Daniel Grant died.
May 6.—Mr. J. Grant died.
July 31.—Bury Parish Churchyard closed for interments.
September 17.—Bury illuminated in honour of the fall of Sebastopol.
October 10.—Organ opened at Bethel Chapel, Bury.
November 10.—First transaction of the Bury Co-operative Society.
December 4.—Mr. E. Grundy, Wylde, Bury, died.

1856.

February 25.—Richard Bealey, Esq., Radcliffe, appointed magistrate.
May 4.—Stand Church bells first rung.
July 23.—Hon. Mrs. Hornby died.
August 8.—Storm in Irwell valley; one man killed by lightning.
August 20.—Boiler explosion at Hampson Mills.
December 31.—Explosion at Ringley Fold Colliery; one life lost.

1857.

January 11.—Mrs. Kay, Stanley-place, Bury, died.
January 21.—Bury Union Workhouse opened.
February 19.—Ratepayers decided to buy Bury Gasworks.

April 19.—Mr. R. Ashton died.

March 28.—General Election at Bury—Mr. R. N. Philips (L.), 565; Mr. Peel (L.-C.), 530.

May 5.—Mr. E. Grundy, Park Hills, died.

May 31.—Dedication Service of Unitarian Cemetery, Bury.

July 9.—Bury election petition against the return of Mr. R. N. Philips refused.

August 1.—Mr. Charles Openshaw died, aged 78.

August 12.—Right Hon. F. Peel married.

December 30.—New organ opened in Brunswick Chapel, Bury.

November 7.—Wesleyan School, Pits-o'-th'-Moor, opened.

1858.

January 1.—Gasworks taken by Bury Improvement Commissioners.

January 19.—Rev. E. J. Smith appointed to St. John's Church, Bury.

March 27.—Fire at East Lancashire Goods Warehouse, Brooksbottoms.

April 27.—Sir W. Peel, K.C.B., died.

April 30.—Boiler explosion at Bottoms Hall Mill, Tottington.

May 17.—Fire at Hartley's Mill, Heywood.

June 1.—Right Hon. W. Yates Peel died.

July 26.—Workhouse Cemetery consecrated.

August 25.—John Hutchinson, Esq., made magistrate.

September 18.—Rev. T. Potter, first incumbent of All Saints', Elton, died.

October 5.—Rev. E. Westerman appointed to All Saints' Church, Elton.

November 7.—Wesleyan School, Pits-o'-th'-Moor, opened.

1859.

April 30.—General Election at Bury: Right Hon. F. Peel (L. C.) 633, Mr. T. Barnes (L.) 477.

May 1.—Militia Barracks, Bury, opened.

June 13.—8th L.R.V. Corps formed.

July 4.—Jonathan Mellor, Esq., made magistrate.

August 3.—Bury election petition against the return of Mr. F. Peel refused.

August 13.—East Lancashire and Lancashire and Yorkshire Railways amalgamated.

August 20.—First confirmation in All Saints' Church, Elton.

September 26.—Hagside Colliery explosion.

October 27.—Dowager Lady Peel died.

November 21.—Bury Old Ragged School consecrated.

1860.

February 23.—Demonstration to Mr. F. Peel.

March 26.—Bury Church Union established.

April 13.—Boiler explosion at Two Brooks.

May 1.—Cotton train on fire at Pimhole.

May 17.—Kershaw's head cut off by train at Park's Siding, Bury.

May 31.—Corner-stone of St. Luke's, Heywood, laid.

June 1.—Corner-stone of Methodist Chapel, Heywood, laid.

July 2.—Heywood Rifle Corps formed.

September 4.—Helmshore railway accident; 10 killed, 50 injured.

September 13.—Christian Church, Bury, opened.

September 22.—Presentation of bugles to 8th L.R.V.

November 14.—Unitarian Chapel, Heywood, opened.

December 13.—New Jerusalem Chapel, Bury, opened.

March 26.—Death of Superintendent Sellers ; Bury Church Union established.

1861.

January 7.—Fire at Cockey Moor Colliery ; one death.

July 29.—Bury Grammar School enlarged.

August 14.—Fire at Bridge Hall Mills.

December 16.—James Hutchinson, Woodbank, died.

1862.

February 3.—Boiler explosion at Cockey Moor Colliery ; one death.

May 27.—Rev. J. Chell appointed to St. Paul's Church, Bury.

June 12.—Corner-stone of Brunswick Chapel laid ; Miss Yates died.

July 21.—St. Thomas's Church, Radcliffe, stone laid.

July 25.—Mr. R. Hacking died; public funeral on the 30th.

September 2.—John Lomax, Springfield, Bury, died.

September 10.—Bury relief fund commenced ; £3,565 subscribed.

October 18.—St. Luke's Church, Heywood, consecrated.

1863.

January 18.—Fire at Albion Hotel, Bury ; one man burnt to death.

February 25.—Ramsbottom ratepayers decided to adopt the Local Government Act.

March 6.—Presentation of a Bury Simnel to Her Majesty.

April 8.—O. O. Walker, Esq., Chesham, made magistrate.

May 28.—Bells of St. Luke's, Heywood, first rung.

June 4.—Rev. H. C. Boutflower died, aged 66.

July 10.—Hollins Young Men's Institute established.

August 3.—Joseph Fenton, jun., Esq., made magistrate.

1864.

April 15.—Eight horses burnt to death near Cheesden Bar.

April 27.—Ramsbottom Local Board formed.

May 2.—Bury Public Baths opened.

May 23.—Charles Cheetham, Esq., appointed magistrate.

June 24.—Roman coins, &c., found at Walmersley.

July 18.—Fire at Bolholt Printworks; five horses burnt.

October 8.—St. Thomas's Church, Radcliffe, consecrated.

November 6.—Holy Trinity Church, Bury, opened.

December 7.—Brunswick Chapel, Bury, opened.

1865.

February 14.—Rev. T. Ramsbotham appointed to St. Luke's Church, Heywood.

February 27.—John Fenton, Esq., Plumpton Hall, and Richard Kay, Esq., Heywood, appointed magistrates.

April 2.—Richard Cobden died.

April 14.—Corner-stone of Primitive Methodist Chapel, Bury, laid.

April 19.—Holy Trinity Church, Bury, consecrated.

April 25.—Rev. F. Wilson appointed to Holy Trinity Church, Bury.

July 12.—General Election at Bury—Mr. Philips (L.), 595; Right Hon. F. Peel (L.C.), 572.

July 30.—Mrs. F. Peel died suddenly.

August 22.—Congregational Chapel, Stubbins, stone laid.

August 25.—Foundations of Bury old Castle discovered.

September.—Bury Musical Society established.

1866.

January 14.—Fenian rising in Ireland.

February 15.—Primitive Methodist Chapel, Bury, opened.

February 19.—St. John's Church, Stand-lane, consecrated.

March 31.—Major Price died ; public funeral April 5.

April 18.—T. L. Openshaw, Esq., Heaton Grove, appointed magistrate.

May.—Radcliffe Local Board established.

May 28.—J. S. Walker, Esq., Limefield, appointed magistrate.

June 29.—St. Peter's District schools opened.

July 4.—Workmen's Exhibition at Trinity School, Bury.

August 8.—Hurricane ; damage at Walmersley.

August 25.—Burrows executed at Manchester ; murdered Brennan, May 21st.

October 3.—Bury Baptist Theological Institution founded.

October 23.—Mr. W. P. Woodcock, solicitor, Bury, died.

November 3.—Methodist Free Church, Heap Bridge, stone laid.
November 16.—Flood, the " Island " inundated.
November 28.—Gigg Mill burnt down.
December 10.—St. Thomas's Church, Bury, consecrated.
December 18.—Rev. T. Atherton appointed to St. Thomas' sChurch, Bury.

1867.

March 31.—Bury District Licensed Victuallers' Association established.
April 10.—J. J. Mellor, Esq., The Ferns, made magistrate.
May 23.—Bury Constitutional Association inaugurated.
October 21.—St. Thomas's Schools, Bury, opened.
November 5.—Rev. H. A. Starkie appointed to Radcliffe Parish Church.
November 16.—Mr. James Openshaw, Chesham, died.
December 5.—Fire at Ramsbottom railway station.
December 20.—Fire at East Lancashire railway goods station, Bury.

1868.

January 4.—Heywood Protestant Association inaugurated.
February 20.—Fire at Dawson's Hill Mill; one man burnt to death.
April 10.—Tottington Free Church consecrated. Mr. J. Parks, surgeon, died.
April 25.—Bury Market re-opened after roofing.
May 5.—Rev. C. W. Smith appointed to Walmersley Church.
May 13.—Murphy riot at Bury.
May 16—Corner-stone of Wesleyan Chapel, Tottington, laid.
July 6.—Stone laid of Primitive Methodist Chapel, Elton.
August 8.—Corner-stone laid of Church Schools at Hawkshaw-lane.
August 22.—Corner-stone of Armoury at Bury laid.
November 17.—General election at Bury: Mr. Philips (L.) 2,830; Viscount Chelsea (L.C.) 2,264.
November 26.—Election riot at Heywood.

1869.

January 6.—Jesse Leach, Esq., Heywood, appointed magistrate.
January 9.—Bury Co-operative Hall opened.
January 27.—Rawtenstall Conservative Association inaugurated.
February 25.—Bury and Elton Conservative Club inaugurated.
February 26.—Presentation to Lord Chelsea.
March 20.—Heywood Church Association formed.
March 29.—Accident at Hollingworth ; five persons drowned.
April 17.—Bury Church Sunday School Union formed.

May 9.—Smith's Mill, Heywood, burnt down.

May 10.—Mr. T. Openshaw, Primrose Hill, died.

May 21.—Bury Cemetery opened.

May 24.—Albert Fenton, Esq., appointed magistrate.

June 9.—Congregational Chapel, Heywood, opened.

July 15.—Fire at Albert Mill, Elton ; damages, £3,000.

July 17.—Radcliffe Hall Constitutional Association inaugurated.

September 13.—Broadfield Station opened.

September 18.—First burial at Bury Cemetery.

September 11.—Bury Cemetery consecrated. Bury Ragged School, stone laid.

September 26.—Mr. W. Grant took possession of St. Andrew's Church. Ramsbottom.

September 28.—Mr. Samuel Smith died.

October 18.—Edward Mucklow, Esq., Woodhill, and James Wrigley, Esq., Ash Meadow, appointed magistrates.

October 23.—Fourteenth Earl of Derby died ; Rev. A. Mc.Lean, of St. Andrew's, Ramsbottom, died.

October 25.—J. P. Ede, Esq., Woodbank, appointed magistrate.

November 17.—Heywood Reform Club inaugurated.

November 24.—Ramsbottom Constitutional Association inaugurated.

December 16.—St. John's School's opened.

1870.

March 16.—Mr. J. B. Edge, first coroner of this new district, elected.

March 24.—Bury Ragged School opened.

March 25.—Consecration of Bishop of Manchester.

April 12.—Rev. J. P. Yeo appointed to Edenfield Church.

April 21.—Heywood Conservative Club inaugurated.

April 20.—Mr. O. O. Walker died.

May 19.—Decided to restore Radcliffe Church.

May 28.—Boiler explosion and fire at Bury Ground ; Mr. G. Whitehead died, aged 65.

June 3.—Ramsbottom Liberal Club opened.

June 27.—Heywood petitioned for enfranchisement.

July 1.—Rev. S. Compston died at Radcliffe.

July 5.—Began to pull down the chancel of the Bury Parish Church of 1780.

July 9.—Storm and flood at Bacup ; damage, £100,000.

July 28.—St. Stephen's School, Elton, opened.

August 12.—Fire in Barlow-street, Bury.

September 8.—Mr. Thomas Grundy died, aged 64.

September 13.—Mr. John Hall, Mount Pleasant, died, aged 90.

September 28.—First stone laid of new chancel of Bury Parish Church.

1871.

January 24.—Rev. W. H. Corbould appointed to St. John's Church, Ramsbottom.

February 2.—J. P. Ede and Co.'s Mill burnt down ; five lives lost.

March 29.—Ratepayers appointed a committee to obtain subscriptions towards re-building Bury Parish Church, which was reported to be in an unsafe state.

April 22.—St. Thomas's Church, Radcliffe, re-opened, on completion of tower.

May 6.—Corner-stone of Methodist Free Church, Hopwood, laid.

May 13.—Fire at Canal Company's Warehouse, Heywood ; damages, £60,000.

June 17.—Sergeant-Major Butterworth accidentally shot at Broad Oak.

June 22.—Fire at Pendlebury's shop, Fleet-street.

July 5.—Bury Improvement Commissioners decided to apply for a charter of incorporation.

August 23.—Foundation-stone laid of St. Peter's Church, Bury.

August 24.—Mr. William Hutchinson died.

August 27.—Last service in Bury Parish Church of 1780.

September 3.—First church service in Bury Town Hall.

September 20.—Commenced to unroof Bury Parish Church.

September 28.—Tichborne trial commenced.

1872.

February 19.—Thomas Wrigley, Esq., took the oaths as High Sheriff.

March 6.—Thomas Wrigley, Esq., as High Sheriff, first met the Judges at Manchester ; great demonstration in Bury.

March 25.—Mr. J. Robinson Kay died.

April 1.—Working Men's Conservative Club, Elton, inaugurated.

April 15.—Bury New Market bought by the Commissioners.

May 18 to 25.—Bury Volunteers at Fleetwood.

June 28.—St. Peter's Church, Bury, consecrated.

July 25.—Bury Improvement Act extended.

September.—Corner-stone laid of St. Andrews' Presbyterian Church, Ramsbottom.

1873.

June 21.—Corner-stone of New Temperance Hall laid.

THE HOUSE OF STANLEY.

As the Derby family are at the present time and have been for so long connected with the town of Bury, a brief reference thereto will not be out of place.

The title of the Earl of Derby was created long before the titles of duke and marquis were known in this country. There were no dukes in England until the reign of Edward III., when that great warrior conferred that title on his sons, and on his cousin, the first Duke of Lancaster; and the title of marquis is somewhat less ancient in this country than that of duke. In very early times, even the sons of the king had no higher title than that of Earl, which had come down from our Danish and Saxon ancestors. The title of Earl of Derby was created in the twelfth century, and has been borne in succession by three families, namely, by De Ferrers, by the Lancaster branch of the house of Plantagenet, and by the house of Stanley. The title is in the highest sense historical. The first Earl of Derby, of the De Ferrers family, obtained his earldom for his distinguished services at the Battle of the Standard, fought near Northallerton, in Yorkshire, and in which a most formidable Scottish army, which had overrun the north of England, was defeated. The last member of the De Ferrers family who held this title forfeited his estates and his title by taking the side of the people in the barons' war, in the reign of Edward III., along with Simon de Montford and other distinguished members of the peerage. The title then passed into the house of Lancaster, and was borne as a separate title by the son of one of the Earls of Lancaster. It was also borne for a time by Henry of Bolingbroke, of the same family. The elder line of Stanleys of Knowsley becoming extinct, the peerage reverted to Sir Edward Stanley, Bart., descended from the youngest son of George Lord Strange, the son of Thomas, first Earl of Derby. This is the famous personage who, after trimming successfully between the rival houses of York and Lancaster, so as to stand in good credit with both by turns, finished up by deserting Richard III. during the Battle of Bosworth Field, and placing the crown on the head of his stepson, Henry Tudor. It was at least a profitable piece of perfidy. The gratitude of the new monarch heaped wealth upon the nobleman to whom he was indebted for his triumph. "Early in his reign," say the authors of the "Great Governing Families of England," "Henry VII. gave him almost all the estates forfeited in the north, and thus he acquired (after the battle of Stoke, 1487) the estates of Sir Thomas

Broughton, of Broughton; of Sir Francis Harrington, of Hornby; of
Francis Viscount Lovel; of Sir Thomas Pilkington, and what Sir Thomas
had in right of his lady, the heiress of Chetham.   From this Sir Thomas
came all the Stanley property in Salford Hundred."   The Earl had also
the estates of Pooton of Pooton, Bythom of Bythom, and Newby of
Kirkby, in Lancashire, " with at least twenty gentlemen's estates more."
Among their names occur those of Pilkington, Bury, Chetham, Cheetwood,
Halliwell, &c., all easily recognisable in this locality.   In this way the
vast fortunes of the Stanleys—vast before, but vaster now—were built
up, and as the battle of Bosworth Field had closed the Wars of the
Roses, the forfeited estates thus conferred were never resumed.   The
family continued to flourish during the reign of the Tudors.   In the
civil wars it was less fortunate, for it chose for once the losing side.
On this occasion, James, the seventh earl, distinguished himself by his
devoted attachment to the Royal cause.   Having been made prisoner
after the battle of Worcester, he was beheaded at Bolton, October 15,
1651.   It was his noble countess who became so famous for her gallant
defence of Lathom House, when it was besieged by 2,000 Parliamentarians.
The affair of Bosworth Field was not the first act of profitable treason
by which the Stanleys had made their way to power.   One of their
ancestors was with Richard II. at Conway Castle when Henry Bolingbroke was approaching with a numerous army to wrest the kingdom
from that feeble prince.   Sir John Stanley abandoned his sovereign,
joined the winning side, and was rewarded soon afterwards with the
sovereignty of the Isle of Man, becoming " the immediate landlord of
almost all the estates in the island."   This splendid gift remained in the
family till 1765, when, the prerogatives of royalty having considerably
diminished in the interval, what remained of them was sold to the
Crown for £70,000.   With one exception—namely, that of the Earldom
of Shrewsbury, which is held by a family closely connected with the
Stanleys—the Earldom of Derby is the oldest of the English earldoms
which now entitle peers of the United Kingdom of that rank to seats in
the House of Lords.

Several versions are given as to the origin of the peculiar crest worn by
the noble house of Derby.   One is that the head of the Lathom family,
wishing to get rid of an illegitimate child, caused it to be placed in an
eagle's nest.   The bird, however, instead of killing the infant, fed it—
an act which so moved the father that he removed the boy and brought
him up as his heir.   Another is that Sir Thomas Lathom, *temp*. Edward
III., having an only daughter, desired an heir.   He had, however, a
natural son by one Mary Oskatell.   This child he directed to be laid at

the foot of a tree where an eagle had built its nest, in which position he pretended that he had discovered it. His wife adopted the infant, and left the bulk of his property to his daughter, the wife of Sir John Stanley, whose descendants altered the Lathom crest from an eagle reguardant to what it now is.

Edward Geoffrey Stanley, fourteenth Earl of Derby, father of the present Earl, was born at Knowsley, on the 29th March, 1799, and died at Knowsley, on the 23rd October, 1869.

He was the eldest son of Edward Smith Stanley, thirteenth Earl, by Charlotte Margaret, second daughter of the Rev. Geoffrey Hornby. Educated first at Eton, and afterwards at Christ Church, Oxford, he gave evidence of the classical taste which in riper years exhibited itself in the translation of the Iliad, by gaining, when he had scarcely reached his 20th year, the Chancellor's Prize for Latin verse, the subject of his choice being "Syracuse." No sooner had he reached his majority than he became the representative of the little pocket borough of Stockbridge, which fell a victim to the Reform Bill of 1832. At this time his grandfather, still a hearty, hale old man, delighting in all the "sports" of the time, was yet alive; his father occupied a seat in the House of Commons as an adherent of the old Whig party; and young Stanley naturally ranged himself on the same side.

At the beginning of the present century the old Earl had a residence in Preston, and most generally spent some months of each year at the family mansion. Patten House was dismantled in 1835, being removed to make room for Derby-street. Here it was that Edward, Earl of Derby—the cock-fighting Earl—kept up, at his visits, a state and retinue that seemed, as far as possible in these modern days, to link his era with the courtly splendours and munificence of the past. He married, in the year 1797, upon the death of his first Countess, Elizabeth Farren, the admired and popular tragic actress; and the following year, his son, the future Earl, married his cousin, Margaret Charlotte Hornby, sister of Geoffrey Hornby, rector of Bury, the successor of Sir William Clerke. Geoffrey Hornby took up his residence at the Rectory upon Mr. Yates leaving it for Springside. The Earl of Derby made a noise in the world during his lifetime. The cockpits he established and patronised extended throughout Lancashire, and all his tenant farmers were required to bring up and maintain game cocks proportioned in number to the value of their holding. In an age of license he made himself conspicuous; he originated the races of the Derby and the Oaks.

For three years, however, the man who was hereafter to rank among the first of English orators remained a "silent member" of the House. The subject of his maiden speech, delivered the day after he attained his 24th birthday, was a Manchester Gas Bill, which he opposed. Six weeks later he made a bolder flight. The subject of discussion was the Irish Church, on which Mr. Joseph Hume had brought forward a motion. On this point, at least, the Earl was consistent from the beginning to the end of his political career. The Irish Church had always in him a staunch friend. He defended her in his youth; he seceded from the Whigs in middle age rather than consent to what appeared to him an interference with her privileges; and stood up sturdily on her behalf in his old age.

A year was now spent in foreign travel—chiefly in America—and then on the 31st of May, 1825, Mr. Stanley married the Hon. Emma Caroline Wilbraham, second daughter of Baron Skelmersdale, of Lathom House. Six children were the issue of this marriage, three of whom died in infancy, and three survived—namely, Edward Henry Smith (Lord) Stanley, now Earl Derby; Lady Emma Charlotte Stanley, married to Colonel the Hon. W. P. M. Chetwynd Talbot, brother of the Earl of Shrewsbury; and the Hon. Frederick Arthur Stanley, M.P., who married in 1864 Lady Constance, eldest daughter of the Earl of Clarendon.

In the year 1826 Mr. Stanley broke off his connection with Stockbridge, and became a representative for Preston, where his family possessed then, as it possesses now, the influence which wealth and old associations in this country especially gives. When Canning came to form his first and only Cabinet in 1827, Mr. Stanley was appointed Under Secretary for the Colonies. The circumstance of Mr. Stanley first taking office under a Tory Premier is explained by the fact that the Government was a coalition one, and the Whigs supported a minister with whom they agreed on most subjects then occupying public attention.

Then came the semi-military government of the Duke of Wellington, which for three years ruled the destinies of the country. A defeat on the question of the civil list brought the administration of the Duke to a close, and the Whigs, under the Premiership of Earl Grey, were once more called to office. The heir of Knowsley had by this time still further proved his value as a political adherent, and from the position of subordinate he was raised to the rank of a Cabinet Minister as the Chief Secretary for Ireland. At this stage of his career, the young nobleman met with an unexpected and, what was doubtless to him, a most galling mortification. His acceptance of office necessitated an appeal to his Preston constituents, and his unopposed re-election was naturally anticipated. The event, however, proved otherwise. A few months before, on the death of George IV., he had been opposed by Henry Hunt, who was then most signally defeated. Nothing daunted, however, Hunt now presented himself as a rival to the young patrician minister. Exceptional circumstances favoured his candidature. The Tories at this juncture regarded the Whigs with even more bitterness than the extreme Radicals, and the feeling exhibited itself at Preston in a coalition between the supporters of Hunt and the Tory party. Mr. Stanley's committee at first treated their rival with contempt, but they soon found reason to change their opinion. Those were the times when elections lasted many days, and scenes of the utmost disorder prevailed. Monster processions were got up every day in honour of Hunt, while at night flaming tar barrels shed their lurid glare in the streets. There was something done, too, besides all this noisy demonstration, and the return of each nights' poll showed an increasing majority on the part of the despised Radical over the aristocratic Whig. At length, after a seven days' poll, Mr. Stanley withdrew in disgust from the contest, the numbers being—for Hunt 3,730, for Mr. Stanley 3,392. Though rejected at Preston, Mr. Stanley had little difficulty in securing a seat. Sir Hussey Vivian resigned his seat for Windsor, and was succeeded by Mr. Stanley, who continued its representative until 1832. On the dissolution of Parliament, after the passing of the Reform Bill, Mr. Stanley was returned as a member for North Lancashire, which he continued to represent until he was called to the House of Peers, in 1844, under the title of Baron Stanley. At that time—to anticipate events a little—he had connected himself with the Conservative party, and was a member of the Government of Sir Robert Peel.

As a member of Earl Grey's administration Mr. Stanley threw himself strenuously into the struggle for Parliamentary Reform, and for two years his individual career can hardly be separated from that of his colleagues. He took a prominent and brilliant part in the debates, none surpassing him in his vehement denunciation of the rotten boroughs, and his advocacy of the right of the people to a full and fair representation in the House of Commons. It is reported of him that when the Reform Bill was first rejected by the House of Lords he leaped upon the table at Brooks's Club, and, denouncing the conduct of the peers, advised the nonpayment of taxes until their lordships gave way.

In March, 1833, Mr. Stanley was transferred from the post of Irish Secretary to that of Colonial Secretary, in succession to Lord Goderich, who had become Earl of Ripon, with the office of Lord Privy Seal. In his new capacity it was Mr. Stanley's good fortune to bring forward the great measure for the emancipation of the West Indian slaves—a measure which he recommended in language of the most stirring eloquence.

There was now a turning point in the career of the deceased nobleman. Hitherto he had appeared as a staunch adherent to the Whigs, and inclined to go with the most advanced of the party in the promotion of popular measures. The time had arrived when he was to take the first step in the direction which finally carried him completely into the opposite ranks. In May, 1834, Mr. Ward brought forward a motion in the House of Commons for the reduction of the Irish Church establishment, and recognising the right of the State to regulate the distribution of Church property in such a manner as Parliament might determine. The discussion of the question in the Cabinet revealed serious difference, and during the debate in the House of Commons on the subject, the news came that Mr. Stanley and Sir James Graham— the leaders of the minority in the Cabinet—had resigned. Their example was immediately followed by Lord Ripon and the Duke of Richmond, and so severely was the defection felt, that although for the time the Government was patched up, it never recovered the blow, and a month or two later fell from sheer weakness. Mr. Stanley was not content with merely seceding, but he attacked his colleagues in a most vehement manner, and in a speech which created great sensation at the time, accused the Government of being guilty of "thimblerig" practices.

On the downfall of the brief administration of Lord Melbourne, Sir Robert Peel was called to the head of affairs in December, 1834, on which occasion an offer of high office was made to Mr. Stanley, but declined, on the ground that the new premier had steadily opposed the whole policy of Lord Grey's Administration, while he (Mr. Stanley) was at issue with his former colleagues on only a single question—the Irish Church.

After a lapse of seven years Lord Stanley once more accepted office on the formation of Sir Robert Peel's second administration in September, 1841. The post assigned him was his old one of Colonial Secretary; and among his colleagues, though not a member of the Cabinet, was Mr. W. E. Gladstone, who became Vice-President of the Board of Trade and Master of the Mint. Without repeating the history of the struggle for the repeal of the Corn Laws, it may be stated that for the second time in his life, Lord Stanley—or rather Baron Stanley of Bickerstaff, as his title now was—found himself adrift in the political stream, his old colleagues imbued with new ideas and acting upon new principles, while he adhered to the traditions and policy of the past. Peel was deposed, and Lord Stanley accepted, though not without hesitation, the leadership of the Tories.

The administration was that which he formed in February, 1852. Twice previously, in 1845 and in 1851, he had been sent for by Her Majesty, but had on each occasion declined the responsibility of forming a government, avowedly because the only ministry he could reasonably hope to constitute at the moment must have depended for its existence upon the forbearance of political antagonists. At this third time of asking, though the noble lord's adherents in the House of Commons were in a minority, these feelings gave way to a belief that it was imperatively his duty to make the attempt, and he set about the formation of a government. After a premiership extending over a period of about ten months, Lord Derby placed his resignation in the hands of the Queen, and for six years remained out of office. Once during that interval, on the resignation of Lord Aberdeen's coalition ministry, in 1855, he received the Queen's commands to attempt to form a ministry, but resigned the task on finding Lord Palmerston declined his overtures for a coalition. When Lord Palmerston was defeated in February, 1858, on the second reading of the Conspiracy Bill, Lord Derby, in compliance with the emphatically-expressed wish of his sovereign, formed his second administration. This ministry was tempted to take up the subject of Parliamentary Reform, and what was styled at the time the "fancy franchise" bill was submitted to Parliament. The measure was received with derision by the Liberals, and ill-concealed dislike by the more stolid members of the Tory party, and the result was that on submitting the scheme to the crucial test of a division, ministers found themselves in a minority of 39 votes. Lord Derby resolved to appeal to the country against the decision of the House of Commons; but on the reassembling of Parliament a vote of want of confidence in the Ministry, moved by the Marquis of Hartington, was carried by a majority of 13, and Lord Derby resigned office on June 11, 1859.

On the 27th June, 1866, he again became premier, but a severe attack of gout in the winter of 1867 induced him early in the following year to resign, and on February 25, 1868, Mr. Disraeli succeeded him as chief of the Government. After that period the noble earl largely withdrew from public life, although when the Irish Church Bill of Mr. Gladstone was before the House of Lords he opposed it with nearly all his wonted vigour.

As an orator, Lord Derby took the very foremost rank among the public men of his time. Lord Aberdeen, who had listened to Fox and

Pitt, Burke and Sheridan, Granville and Grey, used to say that not one of them as a speaker was to be compared with Lord Derby, when Lord Derby was at his best. Indeed, abundance of testimony might be quoted in proof of his oratorical powers, especially in replying to an antagonist. The late Lord Lytton's reference to Lord Derby in his poem of " Timon " was peculiarly appropriate, both as to the noble earl's style of oratory and of his general characteristics as a politician :—

> One after one the lords of time advance ;
> Here Stanley meets—how Stanley scorns—the glance !
> The brilliant chief, irregularly great,
> Frank, haughty, rash—the Rupert of debate.

In the paths of literature, as well as politics, Lord Derby won no inconsiderable amount of fame. His translation from the " Iliad " when approaching his 70th year, to relieve the tedium of a sick bed, is not only a proof of his classical tastes, but is also one of the curiosities of literature. He is credited with the authorship of a work of a religious nature, " Conversations on the Parables," which appeared several years ago, and is to be found among the publications of the Society for the Diffusion of Useful Knowledge.

INDEX.

A.

	PAGE.
All Saints' Church, Elton	201
All Saints' Church, Stand	270
Ancient Mill, Bury Ground	56
Anglezark	53
Apprentice Children	61
Arkwright, Sir Richard	118
Armoury and Drill Hall	27
Assemblies, Bury	17
Ashton, Messrs.	210
Athenæum	127

B.

Baker, Mr.	49
Bamford, Early History	283
Bamford, Ann	16
Bank, the Savings	9
Baronetcy, Mr. Peel's, and Mr. Halliwell	77
Belmont	54
Bellmen, Bury	8
Bentley, Leah	100
Bevin, Dr.	42
Black Bull Inn, Blackburn	49
Bleaching	60
Block Pinners	65
Bobby Cabin	99
Booth, Betty	79
Bradshaw	54
Brandlesholme Bull	204
British Manufactures, Exportation of	69
Brooksmouth	55
Brown, Old Hector	44
Brunswick Chapel	159
Buckley, Mr. James	8
Buckley, Mr. Samuel	8
Buildings, Commercial	9
Buri, Adam de	2
Bury, Government of	1
Bury, Early History of	2
Bury, Ralph	3
Bury Lane	13
Bury and Bolton Canal	29
Bury, Appearance in Early Days	36

	PAGE.
Bury Bridge	40
Bury Hunt	45
Bury and her Patriots	45
Bury Ground, Mr. Peel's Survey of	56
Bury Ground, Appearance of in Early Days	59
Bury Ground, Profits on	77
Bury Improvement Commissioners	284
Burr's Mill	81
Butcher, an over-anxious	17
Butcher Lane	44

C.

Calico	51
Carding, Improved System	61
Carlilists	7
Castle, Bury	4, 35
Cemetery	132
Census Returns	192
Chamber Hall	32, 95
Chapels, the	158
Charities, the Public, of Bury	14
Chartists	7
Chatterton Fight	211
Cheshire Shore's Neezing Club	115
Christ Church, Walmersley	244
Chronological History	296
Clayton, Messrs.	55, 58
Clerke, Sir William	32, 106
Clerke, Speech of Lady	71
Clerke, James	106
Cockey Moor	54
Cockey Moor Lane	99
Cockerill, William	233
,, James	234
,, John	235
Coins, &c., Discovery of at Bury	4
Collinge, Mr. Robert	7
Compston, Rev. Samuel	232
Coaching Days	124
Co-operation	136
Congregationalism at Heywood	280
Conservatives	7
Constables, the Old Bury	48

PAGE.
Contribution, Handsome, to Go-
vernment 69, 85
Courthouse, the Old 44
Crompton, Mr. Benjamin 7
Crompton, Mr. William 8
Crooked Billet 41
Cross, the Old 43
Cunliffe, Dr. 42
Cunliffe, Mr. Ellis 110

D.

Darwen 53
Derby, Earl of 3, 49
Dispensary, the................55, 135
Doctor's Lane 57
Dorcas Society................. 103
Dragon of Unsworth 272
Dungeon, the 42
Duxbury, Thomas 61

E.

Earthquake 151
Early Cotton Manufacture in Bury 59
Early Patterns.................. 64
Elections, Parliamentary, 1832.... 165
,,   ,,   1835.... 169
,,   ,,   1837.... 169
,,   ,,   1841.... 174
,,   ,,   1847.... 175
,,   ,,   1852.... 179
,,   ,,   1857.... 181
,,   ,,   1859.... 182
,,   ,,   1865.... 184
,,   ,,   1868.... 190
Elton, Early History of 200
Entwistle, John 136

F.

Fair Ellen of Radcliffe 230
Female Attire 100 Years Ago 51
Female Designers 64
Field Days, Volunteer 72
Fight, a Cock 95
Fires at Bury Ground........... 58
First Partners, Bury Ground 59
Flemings, the 5
Fletcher, Samuel............... 40
Football Matches............... 41
Fox, Right Hon. Charles James .. 49

G.

Gas-making, Introduction in Bury 101
Gentry of Bury in 1664 194
Geological Excursion 129
Ginnel, the 41
Glebe Lands Leases 149
Gorton, Johnny 99

PAGE.
Grammar School 14, 122
Grant Family 140, 209
Grant, William 216
Grant's Arms, Ramsbottom 221
Greenhalgh, Thomas 136
Greenhalgh Family.............. 133
Greenough, Mr. 11
Grieg, Watson, and Grieg........ 212
Ground, the 58
Grove, Mr...................... 49
Grundy, Mr. Edmund........... 162

H.

Hall, Mr. John.................. 128
"Hamer" 44
Hare and Hounds 39
Hardman, Norris, and Hamer 80
Hartwood Green 53
Hat Manufacture............... 195
Haworth, Mr. Robert 10
Haworth, Mrs., and the Apprentice 67
Hayward, Mr. James 44
Heap, Progress of 276
Heaton House 248
Heaton, Great and Little 268
Henshall, Mr. 49
Heywood, Early History 274
Heywood, Peter 275
Heywood Mechanics' Institution.. 277
Heywood Churches and Chapels .. 278
Holcombe, Early History 222
Holker, Miss Judith 8
Holy Trinity Church 154
Hope and Anchor 39, 55, 56
Hopwood, Thomas 136
Horwich....................... 53
Howorth, Mr. Robert........... 7
Huskisson, Death of 266
Hutchinson Family............. 107
Hutchinson, Thomas and John .. 18

I.

Inn, Commercial 9
Inn, Eagle and Child 18
Inn, Hope and Anchor 39, 55, 56
Inn, Ship 39, 40, 48
Inn, Nancy Frigate 39
Inn, Hare and Hounds 30, 39
Inn, White Lion 39
Inn, Old Boar's Head 34
Inn, Old Grey Mare............. 44
Inn, Red Lion 49
Irwell House.................. 79
Ivin Tree Cottage 33

J.

Jacobins....................... 7
Jane, the Name 30
Jenny Roth'ell 32
Just, Mr. J. 9

K.   PAGE.

Kay, Rev. Roger 14
Kay, Ann 16
Kay, John 51
Kay, James 133
Kay, John and Robert 163
Kay, John Robinson 244
Kenyon, Ned.................... 164
Kirkhams 266

L.

Lacies, the De 2
Lancaster Family 237
Lancashire, James 16
Legacy, a Husband's 17
Liberals 7
Little John 11
Lomax, Squire 45
Lomax, William and John........ 119
Lomax, John 153
Long Jack o' Booth............. 67
Longevity in Unsworth 271

M.

Madam's Coach 57
Magistracy, the................ 6
Mangnall, Mr. 49
Manufactures of Bury, Early Men-
    tion of 5
Market, the 161
May, the 29th of 11
Maying Night 12
McMillan, Mr. Richard 121
Methodist Chapel, Openshaw Fold 160
Mill Brow 57
Miller's House, Bury Ground 56
Milne, Mr. A. 49
Mischief Night 12
Monument, Peel 7, 90
Monumental Tablets in Parish
    Church 197
Moss Lane Theatre, Fall of 18
Moulden Water 53
Muir, Mr. John................. 137
Murray, William 40
MacLean, Rev. Dr. 214

N.

Nancy Frigate Inn 39
National School 132
Norris, Mr. Thomas 125
Nuttall Family 119
Nuttall, Mr. Frank and Miss Yates 37
Nuttall, Mr. Frank, Character of.. 37
Nuttall, James 46
Nuttall Hall 220

O.   PAGE.

Old Boar's Head 44
Old Hare and Hounds............ 30
Old Grey Mare 44
Openshaw, Thomas 101
Openshaw, Charles 134
Openshaw, James 154
Opinion, a Wife's.............. 17
Otter Hunting 45
Owd Nip-cheese 12
Ox Roasting at Bury Old Cross .. 49

P.

Packet-boat, Upsetting of a 29
Paddle Wall....................34, 56
Painites 7
Parish Church 146
Parliamentary Troops in 1648 34
Parr, James 9
Partington, John 120
Parks, Dr. 42
Parties, Old Political, in Bury 7
Peacock Hall 283
Peel, Sir Robert, and the Plumber 101
Peel, Right Hon. F. 95
Peel, Sir William, K.C.B. 92
Peel, William Yates 91
Peel, Sir Robert 55
Peel Close, Blackburn........... 55
Peel, Mr., Conduct and Character 63, 66
Peel, Sir Robert, his Infancy 69
Peel, Speech of Lieut.-Colonel.... 71
Peel's Firm, Extension of 80
Peel's Family, Genealogy of...... 80
Peel's Firm, Benevolence of 81
Peel, Sir Robert, Address to Electors 82
Peel, the Second Lady 85
Peel, Sir Robert, Death of....... 86
Peel, Lady, and Preston Guild 87
Peel, Sir Robert, Mr. Smiles's Ac-
    count of 88
Peel, Sir Robert, Testimonies to
    Character of 89
Pedestrianism 31
Pedlers and Pack-horses 54
Pencillers 65
Pendlebury, Rev. H. 212, 223
Physic and Law 9
Pilkington, Roger 2
Pilkington, Sir Thomas 3
Pilkington, Richard and James .. 135
Pillory, the 43
Pimhole 101
Platt, Dr. 42
Porritt, Joseph, Esq. 213
Prestwich, Early History 247
Prestwich Union 249
Prestwich Charities............ 249
Prestwich Schools 250
Prestwich Parish Church 250
Prestwich Rectors 262
Primitive Methodism in Elton.... 204

PAGE.

Primitive Methodist Chapel, Radcliffe 243
Printing 7
Profits on Bury Ground.......... 64
Prolific Family 203

R.

Radcliffe Rectors 241
Radcliffe Parish Church.......... 238
Radcliffe Tower 228
Radcliffe Charities 228
Radcliffe—Early History 224
Radcliffe " Shag "...............60, 232
Ragged School 127
Ramsbottom—Early History 208
Rastrick, Mr. George 137
Rates of the Borough 4
Rectors of Bury 148
Red Lion Inn 49
Rejoicings for Victories 16
Republicans 7
Rhodes 267
Riley, Edmund.................. 9
Riot of 1826 163
Rivington 53
Road, the Roman................ 9
Roberts, Christopher 245
Robin Hood 11
Roll Call, Old Volunteer 74
Roman Relics, Discovery of 46
Roman Relics, Description of 47
Rothsay Castle, Wreck of 13
Rumpers 7
Rushbearing 252
Russia, Distress in 1812 10

S.

Shepherd, Robert 16
Ship Inn....................39, 40, 48
Shrievalty, the 136
Simnel Sunday—the Festivities .. 23
Simnel Sunday—Supposed Origin 24
Simnels, Receipt for Making...... 26
Skelton, Mr. 18
Slate, Rev. Richard.............. 270
Smetham, Rev. Richard.......... 209
Smith, Mr. Samuel 122
Smithy Lane.................... 54
Song, Volunteer 74
Spinning Jennies 30
Sports of the Early Inhabitants .. 10
Square, Union 10
St. John's Church, Radcliffe...... 242
St. Thomas's Church, Radcliffe .. 241
St. Andrew's Presbyterian Church,
  Ramsbottom 217
St. Andrew's Church, Ramsbottom 213
St. John's Free Church 206
St. Stephen's Schools 203
St. Mark's School 156
St. John's Church 151

PAGE.

St. John's Schools 152
St. Paul's Church............... 153
St. Thomas's Church 155
St. Peter's Church 156
Stanton, Mr..................... 32
Stanley, Rev. John 15
Stanley, the House of............ 313
Starkey, James.................. 16
Starkie, Le Gendre Pierce 45
Stott, Johnny 12
Sulley, Mr. Richard 137
Syphax and Nero............... 87

T.

Tablets in Prestwich Parish Church 260
Tamworth, Representation of 82
Tarry, Mr. William 13, 152
Temperance Hall 161
Tenants' Rights—Ancient Disputes 205
Tharcake and Parkin 109
Theatre, the Second at Bury 32
Thief with Horns and Tail 61
Thomas, Earl of Lancaster 2
Tootil, Joseph and James 44
Tottington—Early History 206
Traveller, a Young 52
Troop, Captain Starkie's 76
Tuggin at th' Nook 13

U.

Underground Passage, Discovery
  of an 97
Union Offices 136
Unsworth, Rev. Henry 99
Unwelcome Tithe 266

V.

Volunteers, Bury Loyal Association of 70

W.

Warburton, John................ 111
Walker Family.................. 118
Walker, Mr. Richard 8
Wall, Old Church 4
Walls, Foundation, Bury Castle .. 4
Warburton, Mr. Jacob 49
Wells Buckley 8
Wesley, Rev. John 32
Wesleyanism in Tottington 207
White Lion Inn 39
Whitehead Family 117
Winter Scene, Bury Ground...... 69
Witchcraft..................... 100
Wolfenden, Mr. 118
Wood, Dr. James 15
Works, Commencement of, Bury
  Ground 58
Wrigley Family, Old Residence of 96
Wrigley, Thomas................ 136

PAGE.
Wroe, Rev. Richard 243
Wylde, the..................... 40

Y.

Yates and Peel Family 49
Yates, Mr. Edmund 10, 45, 66

PAGE.
Yates, William..............16, 58, 66
Yates, Mrs. 51
Yates, Mr., and Horse Racing 77
Yates, Mr. Edmund—Illness and
  Marriage 78
Yates, Mr. William, and his Family 78
Yates, Captain, and Dinner Party 96
Yorkshire Johnny 38